How to Write Songs In Altered Guitar Tunings

Rikky Rooksby

For Roger Dalrymple – friend, musician, scholar – with sea glimpses from a terrace of air.

Songwriting for me is based mostly upon my belief that the guitar knows the song. If I listen to the guitar, put it into some weird tuning and begin to experiment, it plays me a melody. I say to the guitar, "Wow, that's beautiful, what's it about?" and the guitar replies, "How does it make you feel?" And I might say that it makes me think about this or that, and the guitar says, "Well, that's probably what it's about then." (DAVID WILCOX)

Sometimes the music dictates the tuning. Other times a tuning will create music. If you've just been on an airplane with a guitar and all the strings are tuned down [to avoid damage] *you get to your hotel room and check to see if it's all right. You've got jet lag and you want to go to sleep, but it's in some ridiculous tuning. You've no idea what it is and it's irresistible. That's fun as well.* (JOHN RENBOURN)

HOW TO WRITE SONGS IN ALTERED GUITAR TUNINGS

Rikky Rooksby

A BACKBEAT BOOK
First edition 2010
Published by Backbeat Books
An Imprint of Hal Leonard Corporation
7777 West Bluemound Road,
Milwaukee, WI 53213
www.backbeatbooks.com

Devised and produced for Backbeat Books by
Outline Press Ltd
2A Union Court, 20-22 Union Road,
London SW4 6JP, England
www.jawbonepress.com

ISBN: 978-0-87930-953-4

A catalogue record for this book is available from the British Library.

DESIGN: Paul Cooper Design
EDITOR: John Morrish

Origination and print by Regent Publishing Services Limited, China

10 11 12 13 14 5 4 3 2 1

CONTENTS

PREFACE

Think of songs such as Led Zeppelin's 'Kashmir', The Rolling Stones' 'Honky Tonk Women', Joni Mitchell's 'Big Yellow Taxi', Bad Company's 'Can't Get Enough', Stephen Stills's 'Love The One You're With', The Beatles' 'Dear Prudence', Coldplay's 'Yellow', Nick Drake's 'River Man', Bob Dylan's 'Mr Tambourine Man', Neil Young's 'Cinnamon Girl', or Crosby Stills Nash & Young's 'Suite: Judy Blue Eyes'. What do they have in common? All were composed and inspired by a guitar that was not in standard tuning.

Altered tunings are now an accepted method for creating great new guitar music. Up to the 60s they were largely the province of folk and blues guitarists, but the spread of musical influences from folk protest songs and electric blues into chart pop and counter-culture rock in that decade took them into the musical mainstream. By the end of the 60s, headliners such as Bob Dylan, The Who, The Rolling Stones, Joni Mitchell, and CSN&Y were writing and recording songs with them. And when Richie Havens walked out on stage at the Woodstock Festival, on August 15 1969, to face a quarter of a million people, he did so with a guitar in an altered tuning. Thereafter, altered tunings were used by acoustic and electric players alike in many popular music genres such as contemporary folk, college radio rock, indie, hard rock, grunge, New Age guitar and others.

There have been books about altered tunings, and editions of solo guitar music written with them. But this book takes a new approach. *How To Write Songs In Altered Guitar Tunings* focuses on how a songwriter can work with them. For the songwriter who composes with a guitar, altered tunings are a rich resource. If standard tuning fails to inspire when you want to write a song, the unexpected sounds and chords of an altered tuning will enchant your ear and bring the inspiration you seek.

In this book you'll find some 30 tunings, with guidance on what options each offers the songwriter and how a songwriter could use them. A journey of musical experiment starts with simple but surprisingly effective one-string alterations that ease you into the world of non-standard tunings. From there many avenues present themselves with open major and minor tunings and exotic hybrids. This book provides many tips on how to approach an altered tuning and how to invent your own.

How To Write Songs In Altered Guitar Tunings has a CD of audio examples so that you can hear what each tuning sounds like before you re-tune your guitar. These are chord progressions that could be part of a song. They are accompanied by chord boxes or standard notation / tablature. There is also a chord dictionary for immediate access to a selection of effective chord shapes in these tunings if you don't want to discover them yourself.

How To Write Songs In Altered Guitar Tunings will expand your sense of what the guitar can do, and perhaps lead to the songs you never thought you would or could write.

Rikky Rooksby

HOW TO USE THIS BOOK

How To Write Songs In Altered Guitar Tunings does not have to be read sequentially, so dip straight into any section that interests you. If you haven't read any of my other songwriting titles – such as *How To Write Songs On Guitar* and *The Songwriting Sourcebook* – it would be sensible to read **Section Two**'s basic overview of song structure and harmony so you can grasp the points made in the commentary on the 44 audio tracks.

The book has 12 sections. **Section One** explains what an altered tuning is, offers a brief history of guitar tunings, and describes their significance for songwriters. It deals with practicalities of tunings, some changes of tuning which don't quite qualify, and the difference between using them on acoustic guitar and using them on electric. **Section Two** is a crash-course in songwriting basics, such as how a song is written, what goes in it, verse and chorus structure, and harmony. This material is covered at greater length in my other books. **Section Three** is a gentle initiation into the art of the altered tuning via the single-string change. **Section Four** takes the principle one step further by looking at where changing two strings can lead you.

Section Five enters fully the world of altered tunings with six based on an open major chord, followed by information on how to tweak these into pleasing variations of a major chord in **Section Six**. **Section Seven** presents five open minor tunings, with **Section Eight** discussing open minor variants. In **Section Nine** the book gathers some other tunings, which are neither major nor minor. By now you may have some questions, so **Section Ten** is an FAQ on the subject of tunings. It can be fascinating to read the insights of famous songwriters who have used altered tunings to write songs; some of their observations are presented in **Section 11**.

The book is completed by **Section 12**, a chord dictionary that provides two dozen chord shapes for 30 altered tunings, representing an instant resource for song ideas. If you want to sidestep making chord shapes in a tuning, here is a selection laid out for you to start combining in sequences. More at-a-glance information is featured in the appendices, including a set of step-by-step 'transformations' showing how to get from standard tuning to an open tuning on each pitch.

The tunings in *How To Write Songs In Altered Guitar Tunings* are illustrated by a 44-track CD. Most of the audio tracks are strummed chord sequences; a few are intro or link passages. If the example has more precise playing than strumming it is written in conventional music notation and tablature. Each audio example includes one broader songwriting tip.

This book extends my multi-volume series on songwriting, which commenced publication in 2000. To find out more on chord sequences, melody, guitar chords and guitar tunings, and writing songs on keyboards (especially if you're a guitarist), get *How To Write Songs On Guitar* (2000), *The Songwriting Sourcebook* (2003), *Chord Master* (2004), *Melody* (2005), *How To Write Songs On Keyboards* (2005) and *Lyrics* (2006). If you write riff-based songs, *Riffs* (2002) is the most encyclopaedic study ever published about them. To learn more about the elements that make a magic recording, 100 songs from 1960 to the present go under the microscope in *Inside Classic Rock Tracks* (2001). Tips on how to record your songs more effectively can be found in *Arranging Songs* (2008). Information about these titles is at www.backbeatbooks.com and www.rikkyrooksby.com.

SECTION 1

ALTERED TUNINGS

OVERVIEW AND HISTORY

"If you're only working off what you know, then you can't grow. It's only through error that discovery is made, and in order to discover you have to set up some sort of situation with a random element, a strange attractor, using contemporary physics terms ... the twiddling of the notes is one way to keep the pilgrimage going. You're constantly pulling the rug out from under yourself, so you don't get a chance to settle into any kind of formula." (Joni Mitchell)

It is easy to take it as an immutable law that guitars are tuned EADGBE – 'standard' tuning – and that is all there is to say about guitar tunings. Thousands of great songs have been written by guitarists who composed in standard tuning.

As a tuning, EADGBE is an excellent musical compromise that does a number of things well. It provides readily playable chords for most keys and chord types. In some keys – notably C, G, D, and A, and their relative minors, A minor, E minor, B minor, and F♯ minor – enough of the basic chord shapes have open strings to produce a pleasingly resonant sound for little physical effort by the fretting hand. In addition, it is easier to put a key change into a song written in standard tuning. So for these reasons it might appear that the rule 'if it ain't broke, don't fix it' applies to EADGBE.

However, altered tunings are a formidable tool for any songwriter composing on the guitar. Going beyond the familiarity of standard tuning opens some exciting musical doors. When players write or talk about altered tunings it is notable how often they choose metaphors of colour and space, landscape, new territory. Songwriters can find much inspiration in altered tunings. This is chiefly because perhaps the majority of songwriters who compose on guitar do so by finding emotionally-charged chord changes. Altered tunings provide these by the bucket-load.

Guitar songwriters sometimes experience a feeling in standard tuning that chords are not inspiring them. What would be perfectly good sequences at other times can seem exhausted. A powerful remedy for this false impression is to change the tuning of the guitar. In essence, what an altered tuning can do for the guitarist songwriter is defamiliarise the fretboard. With the turn of a peg or two it removes – either partially or completely – the standard shapes and patterns which a songwriter can find through habit and which, at times, fail to inspire through being over-familiar. An altered tuning has the potential to make commonplace chord sequences exciting again because they sound different when voiced in new shapes. It can also offer a songwriter the chance to broaden the harmony of his or her songs through bringing in other chord types in effective shapes. Exotic chords often come in resonant open-string shapes in altered tunings. This is a strong incentive to extend your emotional response to a wider harmony. Even the simplicity of an open major tuning, where a single-finger barre creates a major chord, makes simple major changes sound new.

Guitar instrumentalists, who play solos in folk, blues and new age styles, have always gravitated to non-standard tunings to provide more open-string resonance and support than EADGBE gives finger-pickers. If the bass and some harmony come from open strings the fretting hand can move unhindered on the fretboard with the melody. But *How To Write Songs In Altered Guitar Tunings* is not about writing or playing instrumentals. You don't need to be a technically gifted player to reproduce the musical examples in this book. Exhibitions of guitar technique are irrelevant to most songwriting. In songs what matters is the melody, the lyric, and the supporting harmony. *How To Write Songs In Altered Guitar Tunings* is a book about songwriting, and finding chords for songs, in non-standard tunings.

Now you might say if I start writing songs in altered tunings I'll not be able to play them all live because there will be so many re-tunings, I'll forget the chord shapes for these tunings, and I'll need more guitars. This is true, up to a point, but there are ways round this. The amount of re-tuning between songs can be modified by clever sequencing of the songs. And a songwriter can use altered tunings not as a permanent destination for the song, but more as a territory to be raided for inspiration and ideas which can then, if desired, be returned to standard tuning, if that does not damage the ideas. I suspect the following is an experience common to many guitar-based songwriters who use non-standard tunings.

The scenario goes like this: a songwriter – we'll call him Bob – sits down to write a song. After an hour of strumming standard shapes in guitar-friendly keys like G, C, and D, nothing sparks his interest. One coffee break later, Bob fiddles with the tuning pegs and puts his guitar into an altered tuning. After a few minutes he finds an expressive and resonant two-chord change. He tries for other shapes in key with the first two. These fragments of music stimulate a mood that connects with some memories. A few words of lyric and melody come to mind; perhaps even a title. A creative momentum is established and the song takes shape. Later he records it with several guitar tracks. Guitar one is in the altered tuning. He works out the chords to over-dub a second guitar in standard tuning. By the end he finds that he has after all used several chord progressions that he played in standard tuning and rejected during the first uncreative hour. But he has a new song. What made the difference? The altered tuning.

The significance of altered tunings for a songwriter is as much about the generating of inspiration through timbre and defamiliarisation as it is about the altered tuning being a tangible property of the final song. The objection 'But you could have done that in standard tuning' can be countered with 'Yes, I could have but I *didn't* until the idea came to me. And it didn't appear until I re-tuned the guitar.'

A brief history of guitar tunings

How long have guitarists been using different tunings? Where did they come from?

It might seem that non-standard tunings are an invention of the last few decades, but some date back several centuries. They happened for several reasons, some of which were practical. When people learn guitar without a teacher or a tutor book, as many did, it is natural to tune the strings so they make a pleasing sound with as little fretting as possible. Altered tunings are also shaped by the style of music people want to play. There are traces of the altered tuning technique in the repertoire of other instruments. In classical music a solo violin may re-tune a string from its own standard tuning of GDAE (a technique known to violinists as 'scordatura'.) Orchestral double bass parts also occasionally featured re-tuning of the lowest string (E).

Looking back down the timeline of the guitar it becomes clear that the imagined authority of standard tuning was never engraved in stone. British fingerstyle guitarist John Renbourn, who has long explored the bye-ways of the guitar, once told me:

"I think this idea that there's only one tuning is an extremely limited view. The guitar actually had more tunings at one stage – open G and open D were common right the way through the 1800s. Then it whittled down to the one standard tuning. The others dropped by the way-side until they were taken up by folk players ... The guitar that was so popular as a parlour instrument eventually fell out of favour. The piano came in; socially, there was more kudos in owning a piano. The guitar went down on a social level, became more of a folk instrument. In America the open D and E tunings, which had come from Europe, went into blues and slide playing. No-one really knows where the open G tuning came from. As the guitar resurfaced [in the mid-20th century] as a more 'legitimate' instrument and found a platform in the concert hall, players like Tarrega set new levels of playing and transcribed other works. Standard tuning covered most bases in harmonic music. It's a sort of 'one size fits all' tuning, but not necessarily for the best advantage for lots of different types of music. As people studied the guitar, EADGBE was considered 'correct'. The others were designated as subsidiary or 'incorrect'."

It is interesting to note that some guitarists, such as Ry Cooder, believe that standard tuning arose from the music of Spanish flamenco players; in January 1993 Cooder told UK magazine *Making Music*, "I personally think of EADGBE as a flamenco tuning."

The guitar belongs to a family of related fretted instruments that go back at least 600 years in Western Europe. Tunings for guitar-type instruments have always been a matter of experiment. The precise history of altered tunings is mysterious because it is largely undocumented. As a folk instrument, the guitar had little of its music written down. Perhaps a clue to the development of standard tuning lies with a five-string instrument, which may have predated the guitar, that was tuned ADGBE. A sixth string tuned to E seems to have been added around 1800. In the 20th century blues guitarists used open tunings because of their predilection for the vocalisation effects of slide (bottleneck) guitar. Along with folk players, blues guitarists went for tunings that featured open roots and fifths, freeing the left hand to move around the fingerboard. Experimentation with non-guitar music also acts as a spur. Tunings are invented that allow a player to adapt to the guitar a specific piece that might have originated on another instrument. Thus John Renbourn retuned to arrange Bach cello suites or Elizabethan lute music for the guitar.

The open tunings used by many folk and blues guitarists remained esoteric guitar lore, as their songs were often not written down in any notation. It is true that once the blues and folk singers were recorded in the 50s their tunings could be heard on records, but that did not render them any easier for deciphering. Chet Atkins used open G tuning in the 50s. Various tunings of the American banjo may have been an influence on guitar tuning, with some guitarists trying the banjo's 'sawmill tuning' (GDGCD). The popularity of acoustic blues music boosted the profile of tunings. Electric blues took this further. Tunings originated on acoustic but eventually crossed to electric.

In the 60s the increasing popularity of folk (especially in its 'protest' form) and electric blues boosted the profile of tunings. In his earlier songs Bob Dylan occasionally resorted to an altered string. The few guitar tuition books available (mostly focused toward jazz or classical guitar) dealt only with standard tuning. It is said that British guitarist Davy Graham devised the tuning DADGAD so he could imitate some of the music he heard in North Africa in the very early 1960s, as can be heard on his album *Folk, Blues & Beyond*. Players such as Graham, Renbourn, and Bert Jansch, followed by others including Martin Carthy, Mike Chapman, and Gordon Giltrap, developed the ornate 'folk-baroque' instrumental guitar style that often featured non-standard tunings. Renbourn and Jansch were later part of Pentangle, a group which, through concerts and successful albums, gave 'folk-baroque' guitar an international platform. These guitarists discovered that droning strings and open bass strings suited arrangements of traditional folk melodies, harp tunes, and the like. In the latter half of the 60s it was even a means by which a folk guitarist could imitate the 'hip' instrument of the day, the sitar. One milestone was Jefferson Airplane's second album *Surrealistic Pillow* (1967), which featured a guitar instrumental by Jorma Kaukkonen, called 'Embryonic Journey' in 'drop D' (DADGBE) tuning. For a while having a short guitar instrumental on your band's album became common, an extension of the guitar virtuoso ethic, with examples by Jimmy Page ('Black Mountainside'), Leslie West ('To My Friend'), and Steve Howe ('The Clap', 'Mood For A Day').

By the end of the 60s, headline acts such as Bob Dylan, The Who, The Rolling Stones, Joni Mitchell, Richie Havens, and Crosby Stills Nash & Young were writing and recording songs with altered tunings. There were hit singles such as 'Something In The Air' by Thunderclap Newman (1969), featuring a guitar in an open tuning. The promulgation of tunings also went with a changing approach to the recording studio. As multi-tracking became available and more artistic weight was attached to the making of albums, so the studio became a place where bands made what they intended were permanent artistic statements, rather than a representation of what a band sounded like live. Players no longer assumed that standard tuning was somehow 'proper' and not to be messed with. It became acceptable to tune the guitar to something different for a single song, or even a single overdub. The question of whether such things would translate to the stage was a matter for another time.

Altered tunings as musical identity

Joni Mitchell's music marks an interesting moment in the history of guitar tunings. Many songwriters are conscious of striving for a distinct musical identity. They face the challenge of how to stand out in a world of guitarists, singers, and songsmiths. For a few songwriters and performers it has been altered tunings that have defined much of their music's identity. The distinct sound of the tunings, and the harmony to which they give rise, are a large part of why their songs sound as they do and why listeners are drawn to those songs. Joni Mitchell is a famous example; her hit single 'Big Yellow Taxi' (1970) was probably one of the first chart songs on which the singles-buying public heard the bold assertiveness of an acoustic guitar in an open major tuning. Back then Mitchell's sound was revolutionary because few had heard a chart single with that kind of guitar resonance – all six strings ringing open is something you don't usually hear even in standard tuning; most open chord shapes in standard tuning feature three or four open strings at most. Her popularity in the 70s soon inspired others to seek her guitar chords and tunings. Songwriter and famed alternate tuner David Wilcox said, "I discovered open tunings when I heard this woman playing [Joni Mitchell songs] in the stairwell at college, and to me that really made the guitar an amazing instrument, because it sounded beautiful on its own."

For Joni Mitchell and CSN&Y in particular, altered tunings were crucial to the sound of their music, part of what drew an audience to them. Acoustic singer-songwriters such as Al Stewart, Donovan, and Paul Simon adapted the tuning technique for their own songs. Altered tunings were also crucial to the music of British songwriter Nick Drake, who was writing highly original songs in many tunings of his own devising by 1968, though his fame – and his tunings – was a phenomenon of the late 90s. His songs can be heard on the albums *Five Leaves Left* (1969), *Bryter Layter* (1970), and *Pink Moon* (1972).

The other central case study in the history of altered tunings has to be Jimmy Page. Few guitarists have done as much to popularise altered tunings. He inherited the altered tuning technique from two musical genres: British mid-60s 'folk-baroque' acoustic guitar; and the open G, open A, and open E tunings of American blues guitar songs. The point about Page is that though many guitarists of the 60s and 70s experimented with altered tunings, none sold as many records or reached such a vast audience. Up to a sixth of all Led Zeppelin's songs feature altered tunings, from the drop D of 'Moby Dick' and 'Ten Years Gone', through the open A of 'In My Time Of Dying', to the open C of 'Friends'. Tracks like 'Black Mountainside' and 'White Summer' may owe an awful lot to Davy Graham and Bert Jansch, but through recordings like Led Zeppelin's 'Kashmir' the altered tuning escaped the confines of the folk club and entered the mainstream of popular music. In little over ten years the altered tuning went from Graham's 'Anji' to 'Kashmir' – quite a development.

Led Zeppelin's music and success drew legions of guitar obsessives who wanted to know how Page got his ideas and guitar sounds. Page's use of altered tunings meant that some of the band's mystique rubbed off on the tunings. Gradually, as the accuracy of guitar sheet music and tutorial material improved in the 80s, knowledge of the tunings deployed by Page on Led Zeppelin albums spread. From learning accurate versions of altered tuning songs such as 'The Rain Song' or 'Friends' it was likely that players would compose their own songs in those and other tunings.

When Page and Robert Plant launched the *No Quarter* project in 1994, it was clear that Page himself was aware with hindsight of how important altered tunings had been to Led Zeppelin's soundworld. Some of the Zeppelin songs the pair re-arranged were translated into altered tunings even if they hadn't been that way first time round. Several new songs also featured altered tunings, namely 'City Don't Cry', 'Wonderful One', and 'Wah Wah'.

Jimmy Page had demonstrated that the altered tuning was capable not only of folk-style finger-picked pieces and slide blues but also heavy riff songs played on electric. He almost single-handedly popularised the notion that altered tunings could be played in electric rock because most of the people who bought Led Zeppelin albums had probably not heard electric blues in open tunings from the 50s and 60s.

By the late 80s, guitarists were accustomed to the fact that Jimi Hendrix and Stevie Ray Vaughan had frequently detuned by a semitone, which made sense of otherwise nonsensical riffs and chord sequences that had guitarists scratching their heads, wondering how famous players could get such resonant riffs in E-flat. In the 70s and 80s, tunings were carried forward by fingerstyle solo players like John Fahey, Stefan Grossman, and Leo Kottke, and later Pierre Bensusan, Will Ackerman, David Wilcox, Michael Hedges (who allegedly used over 60 tunings), Alex DeGrassi, and Preston Reed. The Windham Hill record company released many albums of solo guitar that featured altered tunings.

On the electric side the altered tuning gained additional popularity and influence in the 90s because of bands like Sonic Youth, My Bloody Valentine, Smashing Pumpkins, and Seattle grunge bands Nirvana and Soundgarden. Players became noticeably bolder in the kinds of tunings they devised. In Soundgarden's case 11 out of 12 songs on *Badmotorfinger* (1991) and 14 out of 15 songs on *Superunknown* (1994) were in non-standard tuning. Mainstream groups seem more willing to embrace altered tunings than before. Coldplay have used altered tunings on songs like 'Yellow' (EABGBD♯) and 'Trouble' (top E down to D).

Some more technically-minded players wondered whether it would not be better if the guitar were tuned so that every string was the same distance apart, in fifths or fourths. Alan Holdsworth once said he doesn't use altered tunings, but if he had to learn the guitar over again from scratch he would tune it in fourths E A D G C F. This tuning in fourths is used by Stanley Jordan, but he and Holdsworth are primarily instrumentalists. Robert Fripp told *Guitar World* in June 1991 about a tuning of CGDAEG – fifths with a minor third at the top. He was aware that cello and viola are tuned CGDA in fifths, with the violin and mandolin tuned GDAE in fifths also. My view is that such tunings probably hold more for the instrumentalist than the songwriter.

The altered tuning has now permeated the entire field of guitar playing. The advent of MIDI guitar technology means players can use tunings without physically detuning their instruments. MIDI guitar means you can change tunings at the click of a footswitch and store them. This gets around physical problems associated with detuning, such as a lack of string tension and the need to change to heavier string gauges. The popularity of tablature as a notation system has helped because alternate tunings look intimidating in standard notation. Guitar tuners have also made an impact, so people are less wary of detuning if they don't like relying on their sense of pitch to tune.

That, briefly, is the history. In the world of the guitar altered tunings are here to stay. But how do we define an altered tuning?

Defining altered tunings

Tunings can be grouped a number of ways. I define an 'open tuning' as one that makes a simple major or minor chord when no strings are fretted. The six strings sound only the three different notes of a triad, though these may be doubled or trebled at differing octaves. Here's an aphorism to help you remember this: *All open tunings are altered, but not all altered tunings are open.* The term 'open tuning' could be further extended to any tuning that makes a readily identifiable four- or five-note chord type, such as a major seventh, minor seventh, sixth, or ninth. Tunings that do not meet these criteria can be thought of as 'altered' in the broader sense. These include tunings that have been labelled as 'modal', though this name, like others attached to altered tunings, is not very accurate.

In *How To Write Songs In Altered Guitar Tunings* sections 3-9, the selected tunings are organised into seven categories: single-string changes; double-string changes; open major; variant open major; open minor; variant open minor; and modal / hybrid. For a songwriter these categories will provide a rough sense of how much re-tuning might be needed, and what to expect from the tuning itself.

Altered tunings can also be categorised by some of their characteristics. For example, they could be organised on the basis of how many strings get re-tuned. One table in the Appendix provides a list of tunings based on the total number of semitones by which the tuning is changed. They can be grouped according to pitch, in terms of musical family or how far they are from standard tuning, and also by what I term 'harmonic profile' or 'interval profile'.

The 'harmonic profile' of an open tuning is the mixture of roots, thirds and fifths (and possibly other notes from the key scale) it contains. The harmonic profile of open G (DGDGBD) is 515135 and that of open G minor (DGDGB♭D) is 5151♭35. It is not always clear what the harmonic profile of a tuning is, because a tuning may be ambiguous. For example, DADGBD ('double drop D') could be 151461 if D is taken as the root note. But since the top four strings make a G chord, if G was taken as the root note it would have a harmonic profile of 525135.

The usefulness of a harmonic profile, where available, is that it enables a ready comparison with an identical tuning disguised by a different pitch. Open

A is EAEAC♯E, apparently nothing like open G (DGDGBD). In fact, they are both 515135.

The 'interval profile' of an altered tuning is the distance of the strings from each other, proceeding from string 6 up, as measured in tones and semitones. Unlike the harmonic profile, there is no element of subjective interpretation about this: the measurement applies unambiguously because it does not rely on there being a defined root note to the tuning. Standard tuning is 55545: the strings are a fourth, a fourth, a fourth, a major third, and a fourth apart. The intervals between the strings are described as follows:

Minor second = 1
Major second = 2
Minor third = 3
Major third = 4
Perfect fourth = 5
Augmented fourth / diminished fifth = 6
Perfect fifth = 7
Minor sixth = 8
Major sixth = 9
Minor seventh = 10
Major seventh = 11
Octave = 12

In the interval profiles of tunings the numbers one, six, eight, ten, eleven, and twelve are rare. Their presence in an interval profile would alert a songwriter / guitarist to a tuning that might be awkward, physically and musically. The number 12 reveals the presence of two strings tuned an octave apart, which might lead to a deep bass. As with the harmonic profile, the interval profile exposes tunings that are identically configured except for a difference of pitch. Tunings with the same interval profile give the same chord shapes.

When is an altered tuning not really so?

Some alterations to standard tuning need not detain us long. There are many songs where the guitar is re-tuned but remains in standard tuning. Its pitch drops, but its interval profile stays the same. For example, some players detune by a semitone so that they play in E♭ A♭ D♭ G♭ B♭ E♭. This detuning takes some of the strain off the vocalist, deepens the guitar tone, reduces string tension for easier bending, and makes a heavier string gauge feel like a light gauge set. Jimi Hendrix, Stevie Ray Vaughan, Thin Lizzy, U2, Green Day, even The Jam (live) have all done this, and it is endemic among heavy rock bands. The important point is that the layout of the fretboard is unaffected, so the chord shapes and scale patterns you know are unchanged; they are merely a semitone lower. But for songwriters the change of tone which results even from this detuned standard tuning can in itself be inspirational.

Some guitarists take this detuned standard tuning further. Steve Craddock, who played guitar for UK band Gene in the 90s, sometimes tuned down a whole tone. All About Eve's hit 'Martha's Harbour' (1988) was in standard tuning detuned by a tone. The Beatles' 'Yesterday' was played on an acoustic detuned by a tone. Led Zeppelin tuned down a tone for some of the songs they played at their O2 Arena gig in December 2007. Ben and Jason's single 'Air Guitar' makes no guitar sense until you realise they detuned by a tone and a half so that a C shape is an A by pitch. In their quest for riffs that sound as though they have been fished out of ever-deeper canyons of sludge, heavy metal bands take the de-tuning principle even further. Black Sabbath tuned down three semitones for 'Supernaut' from *Black Sabbath Vol. 4* (1972). Their guitarist Tony Iommi was a pioneer of guitar de-tuning. 12-string guitars are often detuned to take the strain off the neck. In the film *Jimi Hendrix*, the guitarist can be seen and heard playing an informal acoustic version of 'Hear My Train A-Coming' on a 12-string which is about two tones down. Leo Kottke detunes his 12-string by three semitones.

On the subject of 12-string guitars, mention should be made of 'Nashville' tuning, where the lower string of each pair is removed, leaving only the high octave strings. This was used on The Rolling Stones' ballad 'Wild Horses'. For R.E.M.'s 'Losing My Religion' Peter Buck added an electric in Nashville tuning (that is, the four lower strings are tuned an octave higher than normal). Steve Craddock of Ocean Colour Scene said the band had a fondness for it: "We used Nashville tuning for some tracks, where you take a 12-string and take off the normal octave strings. It's definitely on 'The Song Goes On'. In fact, we've used it on the last couple of albums ... And it doesn't take up a lot of room in a track."

Conversely, Johnny Marr tuned up a tone on the first album by The Smiths to make the guitar sound brighter and to open a bigger frequency gap between the guitar and the rhythm section. The sparkle can be heard on tracks like 'This Charming Man'. But tuning up runs the risk of strings breaking and increased tension on the neck.

All these tunings affect the sound of the guitar and are worth knowing. But the real subject of this book is what happens when we genuinely leave the patterns of standard tuning behind. This is obviously a step into the unknown, and re-tuning can seem a hassle. Is it worth it?

Why are altered tunings good for songwriters?

- They are a source of inspiration because they defamiliarise the familiar. They recreate the fingerboard, stop your fingers lazily finding the usual sounds in the usual places. They help you escape the limitations of those patterns. As Keith Richards put it, "You just turn a few pegs and get a different tuning and suddenly you get almost like a different instrument."
- They refresh standard chord changes if those have temporarily lost their expressive power for the songwriter by changing their timbre and mix of open and fretted notes.
- Standard chord shapes, with which your fingers are familiar, generate new chords in an altered tuning.
- Altered tunings give the guitar a different timbre through the effects of reduced string tension, with increased sustain and resonance.
- They produce ringing open chords in keys which do not have them in standard tuning.
- Even a single-string change can inspire a song through the device of adding one unusual note to a sequence of simple chords.

- In some tunings a single barre results in one-finger major or minor chords. Single-finger barre chords invite you to be chromatic with your chord changes because there is less physical effort involved in so doing compared to standard tuning.
- They create unique-sounding chords and new types of chord – harmonies that couldn't be found in standard tuning, or not as easily, such as extended chords like sevenths, ninths, elevenths, and so on. The significance of these for a songwriter is that extended chords can complicate a song's emotional content. The extra notes can express the equivocation of 'yes, maybe, but'.
- They give an opportunity to combine open strings with scale figures (octaves, thirds and sixths) that can support a vocal melody.
- They produce sequences where ringing open strings fill the gaps between changes. These over-hanging notes between chord changes can spark melody ideas.
- Altered tunings can potentially broaden the harmony of your songs. Actually, they should do this, because if they didn't it would indicate you weren't taking full advantage of the tuning's possibilities. To go to an open tuning that offers a major or minor chord and then only play with a single-finger barre and play simple majors and minors is not to make the most of its potential.
- They produce chord sequences where a common note changes colour by having a different harmonic function in each chord.
- They make chord sequences over bass pedal notes easier.
- For the solo performer they can produce a fuller accompaniment.
- They are good for finger-picking songs.
- Unisons (two notes of the same pitch) are more frequent than in standard tuning, which can approximate a 12-string effect.
- They give single-finger inverted chords in open major and minor tunings.
- Chord changes which start with a barre can be given extra colour by sounding the open strings between chords. Unlike standard tuning, in an altered tuning this may produce an attractive, if chromatic, chord.

Disadvantages of altered tunings

Altered tunings are not entirely hassle-free, and do have some disadvantages. I think these are outweighed by the songs they can inspire, but consider:

- The need for re-tuning, which can be a problem playing live. David Wilcox puts songs in odd tunings back-to-back in his setlist: "I have to do that if I'm in a place that's really noisy. I'll make the tuning changes in stages, changing one string at a time and gradually changing from one tuning to another, because there are a lot of tunings in between."
- It is harder to incorporate a key-change into a song in alternate tuning.
- Most altered tunings commit you to certain pitches – which is also their joy. They usually have – sometimes, intentionally – a bias toward one particular pitch.
- Intonation can also be a problem, and breaking strings from re-tuning, even when detuning. Joni Mitchell once observed, "The guitar is intended to be played in standard tuning; the neck is calibrated and everything. Twiddling it around isn't good for the instrument, generally speaking. It's not good for the neck; it unsettles the intonation. I have very good pitch, so if I'm never quite in tune, that's frustrating."

- Don't rely on your memory for the chord shapes you find, always write them down. They are hard to transcribe if you forget them, even from a good quality recording or a multi-track where you can isolate the alternate-tuned guitar part.
- Electric guitars with floating bridges don't like being retuned, as changing one string tends to mess up the others. Choose an electric with a fixed bridge. On both electric and acoustic, light gauge strings lose their intonation if detuned. Therefore, some tunings require heavier gauge strings to work effectively. Small intonation problems can, to a point, be compensated for by careful fretting technique.

Before delving into the 30 selected tunings we must first review some basic parts of songwriting technique. This is the subject of the next section.

SECTION 2
ALTERED TUNINGS AND BASIC SONGWRITING

Since this is a book not just about altered tunings but writing songs with them, we must briefly look at what goes into a song. This subject is covered in depth in my other books, but for newcomers to the series (or songwriting) this section is a quick outline of the basic formulas of song structure and harmony. Understanding these concepts will help you get more from the examples in sections 3-9.

There is no set method for writing a song, but songs almost by definition have four main components: words (the lyric) sung to a tune (melody) supported by chords (harmony) played to a beat (rhythm) at a given tempo. You can write a song taking any one of these as the start. Some songwriters favour one method over another; others find that songs arrive in many ways. Occasionally the germ of a new song forms with words, melody, chords and rhythm, when you're away from the guitar. As you get better at hearing music in your head this can be a compositional method in itself. So the writing of a song can begin in the following ways:

1. Write a lyric and then set it to music

A lyric's subject and images may suggest certain things about the mood of the music. The rhythm of the words can evoke a tune. Some people find it inspiring to have words to sing when constructing a melody, instead of merely humming or using nonsense lyrics. Keep a notebook of lyric ideas, including a list of possible song titles. You only need words for one verse and a chorus to compose the basic structure and music – extra verses can be written later.

2. Write a melody and then harmonise it

The beauty of this technique is that it encourages you to compose an effective tune. If a tune sounds good on its own – if it is expressive, with interesting intervals, some pleasing twists and turns, and a catchy 'hook' – it will sound even better harmonised.

3. Write a chord sequence

Construct a pleasing chord sequence and then invent a melody. This is probably the most common approach, especially among guitarists. Strumming chords allows the mind to play with words and melody. Chord sequences – especially in altered tunings – can be inspiring and evoke an emotion that can precipitate out as a melody and a lyric.

4. Write a rhythm track

A classic fault of singer-songwriter material composed on guitar is the lack of rhythmic interest. To avoid this, write chord sequences with a drum machine or drum loops. This can increase awareness of the role of rhythm in your songwriting, and is handy if you write too many slow songs. A further refinement is to add a bass-line to the drum track. The bass reinforces the rhythm, and suggests the harmony. This is important as a technique to use in conjunction with altered tunings because it is easy to be seduced by their often lush harmonies into writing nothing but slow tempo material.

The elements of song structure

The classic popular song structure has three primary sections: a verse, a chorus, and a bridge/middle eight. Possible secondary sections include an intro, a prechorus, an outro and any instrumental solos, links, or riffs that join one primary section to another. A verse lyrically describes a situation and establishes the song's style. Verses are anything from about eight bars up to 24 or more in length, often in a figure divisible by four. Along with 12, 16 bars is the most popular length for a verse section. A 16-bar section can be handled in many ways depending on the amount of repetition. The symmetrical options for structuring the 16 bars are:

- a two-bar phrase played eight times
- a four-bar phrase played four times
- a four-bar phrase played three times with a different phrase for bars 9-12
- a four- phrase played three times with a different phrase for bars 13-16
- an eight-bar phrase followed by a four-bar phrase repeated, or vice-versa
- an eight-bar phrase played twice

Verses of any length can have their own internal structure. If a verse is short, the distinction between verse and chorus can be blurred. There is one song structure that has two sections, A and B, where A is a verse that climaxes with a hook – in other words a 'mini-chorus' is incorporated into it. The Beatles' early albums contain many examples of this A+B structure.

Musically, the chorus is where the 'hook' is located – the notes that lodge in your mind and make you want to buy the song. A hook is a combination of lyric, melody, and chords, often reinforced by backing vocals, counter-melodies, or a riff. The chorus contains the centre of the lyric's meaning; it sums up the central issue and/or expresses the over-riding emotion. Choruses often feature the repetition of words and/or the accompanying harmony. The music intensifies and focuses, and this can be achieved in a variety of ways. Songs often climax with several choruses back to back.

The middle eight or bridge usually comes after the second chorus, though it might be inserted after the second verse as a way of delaying the next chorus. If it is short enough, it can even be included more than once. The term 'middle eight' reminds us that the commonest length for a bridge is eight bars, though it is used regardless of its length to refer to what songwriters call 'the middle bit'. The term 'bridge' reminds us of its function: to connect one part of a song with another. After the second chorus, songs often need to develop a new musical idea. A bridge can break new musical ground in a song, with new chords, withheld from earlier use. One technique is to write the verse and chorus with only chords I, IV, and V, which in the key of G major would be G, C, and D, and save a minor chord (such as Am, Bm, or Em) for the bridge. If the song is in a minor key you could do the reverse and bring in a previously-unheard major chord for the bridge.

The secondary sections include the intro, links, prechorus and outro. A good intro should grab a listener's attention, state a theme, set an atmosphere, potentially get a concert hall jumping. It establishes tempo, key, style, and mood. If clearly audible in the arrangement, an altered tuning can provide striking guitar chords, and melodic figures such as consecutive intervals, with which to make an arresting beginning. A simple chord-change in an altered tuning can establish a powerful atmosphere merely because of its voicing. An intro could instrumentally use material from part of the verse, prechorus, or chorus.

A 'prechorus' is an extension of a verse. It takes a step away from the verse toward the chorus without actually reaching it. The prechorus usually retains the same lyrics from one verse to another, even if the verse changes. In a song that goes verse, chorus, verse, chorus, middle eight, a prechorus provide the transition to the last set of choruses if it is felt that putting in a third verse would delay things too much.

After the chorus, a song must find a return to the verse. You can have no link and go straight to the verse. Whether this works depends on what the melody does at the end of a chorus. Is there enough time between the end of that last phrase and the start of the verse lyric? Does it sound rushed? Does the singer need a bar for taking breath? Does the listener need a break? The faster the tempo, the more likely a link will be needed. In a hard rock song, the guitar riff often functions as the link. You could reprise the intro, perhaps in a shortened form.

At the end of a song, pop tradition is to fade out on repetitions of the chorus. Some outros reprise the chorus instrumentally, with vocal ad-libs or solos, or have another refrain over the music for the chorus, or repeat the intro sequence. The outro refrain could be one for joining in with (the la-las at the end of David Bowie's 'Starman' or T.Rex's 'Hot Love'). Extended instrumental codas can create an engaging mood of their own, as is the case with Roxy Music's 'More Than This'.

These song sections constitute a mould from which a song is formed. The next ingredient is harmony – the chords that fill that mould and that can inspire a melody. Many guitarists write songs without knowing the theory behind the chords they use – they rely on their ears and the principle that if it sounds good, it works. But there is no harm in having a little knowledge about which chords will make pleasing progressions.

Finding chords that fit together

Chords are central to songwriting on the guitar because they are technically easy. Many songwriters who work on guitar write by first creating an interesting chord progression.

It takes little time or practice to learn a handful of guitar chords, which is part of the guitar's popularity. It doesn't take genius to take a few chords and make them into a simple accompaniment to a tune.

Chords in a major key

Here's how to find chords that fit together. Take a guitar-friendly key, C major. The notes of the scale are C D E F G A B. They are separated by a set pattern of intervals: tone, tone, semitone, tone, tone, tone, semitone (whole-step, whole-step, half-step, whole-step, whole-step, whole-step, half-step). In frets this is 2 2 1 2 2 2 1 (easy to remember). It governs all major scales, regardless of the starting note. Choose any note on any string and go up the string playing notes in the 2 2 1 2 2 2 1 pattern. You will hear a major scale.

The chords of C major are formed from the seven notes of this scale. The resulting sequence of seven chords is the same for every major key: major, minor, minor, major, major, minor, diminished. Therefore the main songwriting chords of C major are C Dm Em F G and Am (the diminished can be ignored, as it is rarely used.)

Chords in a minor key

Chords in a minor key are less straightforward as there is more than one version of the minor scale. A natural minor is A B C D E F G A. The pattern of intervals is tone, semitone, tone, tone, semitone, tone, tone (whole-step, half-step, whole-step, whole-step, half-step, whole-step, whole-step). In frets this is 2 1 2 2 1 2 2. The chords formed from the seven notes of this scale generate a sequence true for every natural minor key: minor, diminished, major, minor, minor, major, major. (Once again the diminished can be set aside).

The harmonic minor scale has a raised seventh. A harmonic minor is A B C D E F G♯ A. The pattern of intervals is tone, semitone, tone, tone, semitone, tone and a half, semitone (whole-step, half-step, whole-step, whole-step, half-step, step and a half, half-step). In frets this is 2 1 2 2 I 3 1. This yields a chord on the fifth note which, because of the G♯ on this scale, is major. This chord can be fruitfully combined with the natural minor scale's chords.

The Roman numeral chord system

Chord progressions can be notated without specifying the key or pitch, in a system used for hundreds of years in classical music. This is very handy for a songwriter. Each of the seven chords in a major scale has a Roman numeral: I, II, III, IV, V, VI, VII. In C major I = C, II = Dm, III = Em, IV = F, V = G, VI = Am, and VII = B diminished. Any chord sequence can be notated purely with these numerals, as in I-VI-IV-V (C-Am-F-G in the key of C). Regardless of the major key in which we play this it comprises a major chord followed by a minor and then two majors. In *How To Write Songs In Altered Guitar Tunings* additional abbreviations attached to Roman numerals in sections 3-9 give further detail:

i first inversion (in C major iIV = F with A bass; iVI = Am with C bass)
ii second inversion (in C major iiIV = F with C bass; iiVI = Am with E bass)
m minor version of what would normally be a major chord (in C major IVm = Fm instead of F
^ signals a major version of what would normally in a given key be a minor chord, such as III^
♭ indicates a chord on the flattened note of the scale (♭VII, ♭VI, ♭III)

The Roman numeral system enables you to compare progressions in different keys, and to grasp how a single chord can have a different harmonic function according to which key it is in. For example, the chord Am is II in G major, III in F major and VI in C major – same pitch but different roles.

Which chords belong together in which keys?

Early in the composition of a song the music will naturally coalesce around a key. If we take the five major master-shapes of standard tuning (A, C, D, E, G) as representatives of the major keys we get a table with the chords that belong in those keys.

Master Key Song Chord table for major keys

Major keys

I	II	III	IV	V	VI	♭VII	♭III	♭VI	II^	III^	IVm
E	F♯m	G♯m	A	B	C♯m	D	G	C	F♯	G♯	Am
A	Bm	C♯m	D	E	F♯m	G	C	F	B	C♯	Dm
D	Em	F♯m	G	A	Bm	C	F	B♭	E	F♯	Gm
G	Am	Bm	C	D	Em	F	B♭	E♭	A	B	Cm
C	Dm	Em	F	G	Am	B♭	E♭	A♭	D	E	Fm

It was stated above that a key has six main songwriting chords (I-VI, VII being discarded). In which case, why are there twice as many chords listed for each of these keys? The answer is that in popular music songwriters expand the harmony palette with which they compose by putting a slant on some of the key's main chords. I have analysed these habits and rationalised them with the following terms.

'Flat degree' chords

Chords in columns 7–9 are major chords built on flattened notes of the scale: the ♭VII, the ♭III and the ♭VI. Chord VII is given in its flattened form as a major, because by strict application of the notes of the scale VII should be a diminished chord. The approach to chord VII relevant for songwriting lies with a simple formula: *take the seventh degree of a major scale, lower it by a semitone (half-step), and treat that note as the root of a major chord*. This makes a chord numbered ♭VII, the '♭' indicating that it is built on a lowered degree of the scale. In C this ♭VII chord would be B♭. The ♭VII chord is everywhere in popular music because of the influence of blues harmony and a scale known as the mixolydian mode (C D E F G A B♭) for melodies. Both lower the seventh note by a semitone. The ♭III is a significant blues chord. The ♭VI is also heard in blues, pop and rock.

'Reverse polarity' chords

Columns 10–12 of the Master Key Song Chords table offer other additional chords to the primary I-VI. These are adjusted versions ('reverse polarity') of chords II, III and IV, where what was a minor chord turns into a major and vice versa. These can be substitutes in a primary chord (I-VI) progression. So C-Dm-F-G could be C-D-F-G; C-Em-F-G could be C-E-F-G; and C-Am-F-G could be C-A-F-G.

Chords for a minor key song

If we take the three minor master-shapes of standard tuning (Am, Dm, Em) as representatives of the minor keys and add the barre chords of Bm and F♯m we get a table with the chords that belong in those five minor keys.

Master Key Song Chord table for minor keys

Minor keys

I	♭II	III	IV	V	VI	VII	IV^	V^
F♯m	G	A	Bm	C♯m	D	E	B	C♯
Bm	C	D	Em	F♯m	G	A	E	F♯
Em	F	G	Am	Bm	C	D	A	B
Am	B♭	C	Dm	Em	F	G	D	E
Dm	E♭	F	Gm	Am	B♭	C	G	A

Columns 1–7 show the seven primary chords in songwriting for each minor key. These sound good in any order. As you look *down* the column in the minor keys, notice that:

- I, IV and V are always minor chords
- ♭II, III, VI and VII are always major chords

Whether you use the major or minor form of chords IV and V (columns 8-9) in a minor key depends on the harmony you want and the melody of the song. It is perfectly allowable to combine different minor harmonies in a single song as long as the chord and the melody note match. You can have D and Dm in a song in A minor, but if so the note F in the melody must be sung over Dm (D F A); a D major chord (D F♯ A) requires F♯ in the melody.

Three and four-chord songs

The 'three-chord trick' is the commonest songwriting device that relates to chords. It means a song with chords I, IV, and V of any major or minor key. Here they are in the guitar-friendly keys:

Key	I	IV	V
C major	C	F	G
G major	G	C	D
D major	D	G	A
A major	A	D	E
E major	E	A	B

The distribution of the chords by song section can be anything you wish:

- verse is chord I only, IV and V enter on the chorus
- verse is chords I and IV, V enters on the chorus
- verse is chords I and V, IV enters on chorus
- verse is chords I and V, IV enters on the bridge
- verse and chorus use I, IV, and V; bridge has IV and V only

The three chords work together beautifully, the result a secure architecture to support many musical and lyric intentions. These three chords are used in 12-bar blues, and a vast number of 50s rock'n'roll songs by Elvis Presley, Chuck Berry, Jerry Lee Lewis, Little Richard, Bill Haley, Buddy Holly, and Eddie Cochran. Later rock acts who played 12-bar boogie, like Canned Heat and Status Quo, also use three-chord tricks. This is also the formula for songs such as The Beatles' 'Twist and Shout' and The Clash's 'Should I Stay Or Should I Go?'

Although the classic three-chord trick uses chords I, IV, and V, there are other possible three-chord combinations. Chord I will always be one of the three (if omitted the song will sound harmonically ambiguous and unsettled) but the other two chords could be other than IV and V. Other purely major three-chord tricks using flat degree chords are I-IV-♭VII (in C major C-F-B♭), I-♭III-IV (C-E♭-F), and I-♭III-♭VII (C-E♭-B♭).

Three-chord songs in a minor key

The 'default' for the minor key is assumed to be the natural minor scale and its chords: Am Bdim C Dm Em F and G. In my books F is called VI and G VII, not ♭VI and ♭VII, because on the natural minor scale the seventh note has not been flattened in the way that it can be on the major scale. So in A minor I think of Am-G-F as I-VII-VI, not I-♭VII-bVI, in contrast to A-G-F as I-♭VII-♭VI in A major.

Minor-chord sequences in pop and rock are dominated by I, VII, and VI, moving in either direction. In A minor this is Am G F; in E minor it is Em D C (both easy guitar sequences). It needs to be checked whether in a particular instance this really is in a minor key or is in the relative major key, because Am-G-F could be VI-V-IV in C major, and Em-D-C could be VI-V-IV in G major. (Look up the chords on the Master Key Chord table to get a clearer sense of this.) For example, the verse of Fleetwood Mac's 'You Make Loving Fun' features Gm-F-E♭ as a turnaround. This could lead us to think that the song is I-VII-VI in G minor. However, the chorus starts on a strong B♭ and we realise that actually the song is in B♭ major and the Gm-F-E♭ progression was actually VI-V-IV in B♭. Songs that use I, VII, and VI in the minor key include Phil Collins's 'In The Air Tonight', Dire Straits' 'Sultans Of Swing', Eric Clapton's 'Layla', and Fleetwood Mac's 'Dreams'.

The four-chord song and turnaround

After the three-chord trick, the next significant songwriting technique is the four-chord song. The most popular choice is to add a minor chord – either II, III, or VI – to the I, IV, V of the three-chord trick. Beyond the fact of a song using four chords, there is a specific way of treating those four chords which is important for songwriters. This is the 'turnaround', a short sequence of chords repeated either as an intro, a verse, part of a verse, a chorus, or in a bridge (not to be confused with the lead 'fill' heard in bars 11-12 of a 12-bar blues). The four-chord turnaround is one of the strongest musical hooks going. The turnaround circles its chords, impressing on the listener that it is a unit within itself. It is a progression that loops, or literally 'turns around', many times. Repetition makes a turnaround what it is. It often forms the 'hookiest' point in the song. Four-chord turnarounds gain their power not only from the increase of harmonic colour that a fourth (especially minor) chord brings. They acquire an assertive symmetry because of the number four. Many turnarounds are four chords, four beats each, in a four-bar phrase ... that may even be repeated four times! To be a turnaround the chord sequence should be repeated often enough to form a harmonic and rhythmic unit that feels like a single object. Note that a four-bar turnaround can be made with only three chords, simply by repeating one or more of the chords.

By now you should have some idea about how to choose some chords and connect them by allocating them to a bar or two bars, deciding whether that makes a verse or chorus or bridge, and so on. To turn this into a song you must write some words and then sing them over your chords. Your ear will instinctively tell you if a melody note fits or not. Melodies and lyrics are explained in detail in the books *Melody* and *Lyrics* in this Backbeat series.

Prepare for detuning

We are almost ready to explore the first tunings. There is one practical consideration. Some players may worry about whether they can tune accurately and find their way back to standard tuning. Some electronic tuners allow the guitarist to specify other pitches than standard. Re-tuning can also be calibrated by an octave open string if the note you are heading for has an equivalent in standard tuning. When detuning string 6 to D, string 4 could be used as an octave reference. You can also find the destination note on an adjacent string and then tune down until they match. Notice that I write of tuning *down*. A golden rule of altered tunings is that wherever possible strings should be tuned down. There is less risk of string breakage and tension is not increased on the neck.

As with harmony, it helps if you know a little about how tunings are structured. In sections 3-9 each tuning is introduced in table form, giving at-a-glance information about its characteristics and structure. For an example, let's look at standard tuning catalogued in this way:

Standard tuning	
Changes:	x x x x x x
Pitches:	E A D G B E
Profile:	5 5 5 4 5
3rds	2+3
5ths	-
6ths	1+3, 2+4
Octaves	-
Open triads	Em (1+2+3), Em (2+3+6), G (2+3+4)

This gives some valuable shorthand information about this tuning. It reveals that for standard tuning no changes are needed, that its intervals are fourths with the exception of one third, that none of its strings are a unison, a fifth or octave apart, and that it contains the triads of Em and G on the open strings. Here's more on these categories.

'Changes' is the number of semitones a string has been retuned. A '+' means it has been tuned up; a '-' means it has been tuned down; an 'x' marks a string unaltered from standard tuning. Pluses mean a string tension increase, minuses of a value more than two mean a marked loss of tension in a light-gauge string. 'Pitches' gives the note names. 'Profile' measures the intervals between the strings in semitones; there are five numbers because there are five intervals between six strings. The numbers translate into intervals as follows: 0 = unison (two strings tuned to the same pitch), 2 = major second; 3 = minor third; 4 = major third; 5 = perfect fourth; 7 = perfect fifth; 8 = minor sixth; 9 = major sixth; 12 = octave. Other intervals are possible but do not feature in the tunings presented in *How To Write Songs In Altered Guitar Tunings* because they are better suited to guitar instrumentals than to song accompaniment.

The interval profile of a tuning hints at what it will sound like, and what it is like to investigate for chord shapes. Larger numbers to the left of the profile occur in tunings which have defined bass in their chords; smaller numbers to the left are less defined. 'Unison', '3rds', '5ths', '6ths' and 'Octaves' show which pairs of strings create this interval. So '1+2' means that the top two strings in that tuning are a third apart. This is useful for ideas that involve fretting the intervals and moving them in parallel up and down the fretboard, something which altered tunings often make available. Finally 'open triads' shows if any of the open strings comprise a triad. This information alerts you to which keys or chords the tuning may readily support, and with what fingers a resonant open string chord might be made.

The ability to see triads within a tuning, or how new ones might be created, is a tool for creating new tunings. Working with standard tuning, it is apparent that two triads are already present: the top three strings are E minor (E-G-B); the fourth, third and second are a G major triad (G-B-D). The next step would be to look for major or minor thirds that need one more note to make a triad. B and D only lack an F♯ to make a B minor triad, so if any of the other four strings is detuned to F♯ the tuning would have taken a step toward the key of B minor. E and G need a C to generate a C chord. Next look for roots and fifths that are missing a third to complete them. E and B are one such 1-5 pair that would make an E major chord if there were an open G♯. A and E are a 1-5 pair that would make an A major chord if there were an open C♯ or an A minor if it were a C. D and A are one such 1-5 pair that would make a D major chord if there were an open F♯ or a D minor if it were F. In deciding to make one of these changes select a string that is closest to the target pitch. String 3 G is only a semitone (half-step) above F♯ for that change.

Now it's time to reach for your tuning pegs.

SECTION 3

SINGLE-STRING TUNINGS

If you have only played in standard tuning the thought of retuning the guitar and finding that the chord shapes you knew no longer work can be daunting. In fact, it isn't as bad as it seems. There is an easy method for dipping your toe in the waters of altered tuning: the single-string change. It might seem that re-tuning a single string would not make much difference, but in songwriting that alone can be enough to 'refresh' ordinary chords and the sound of the guitar. A single-string alteration can be effective because it increases the number or position of open strings in chords. Many altered tunings are only a single-string change and yet they can be a quick route to new ideas.

One such tuning is 'drop D', where string 6 is detuned by a tone from E to D. This is what it looks like:

Drop D	
Changes:	-2 x x x x x
Pitches:	D A D G B E
Profile:	7 5 5 4 5
3rds	2+3
5ths	5+6
6ths	1+3, 2+4
Octaves	4+6
Open triads	Em (1+2+3), G (2+3+4)

Altered tunings often have names that are unhelpfully imprecise, when they are not positively folkloric, and 'drop D' is an example. It implies that a D note, or perhaps string, has been 'dropped' (detuned) when it is an E which has gone down to D. Nor does the name differentiate between the E of string 1 and string 6. However, 'drop D' is the name by which it is now known. (Similarly, naming a tuning after a chord is imprecise because there may be more than one way to tune to that chord.)

The beauty of 'drop D' for an altered tuning novice is that it is easy to tune into and back out of. Although it moves the bass note of any chord whose root was on string 6 up two frets, otherwise it doesn't cause much fretboard chaos. All shapes from string 5 up are unchanged. It gives some satisfyingly resonant D and Dm open string chords because the standard shapes can now be struck with all the strings ringing. It exemplifies one of the things about altered tunings that guitarists love: extended bass range. Usually D and Dm are four-string shapes; here they are six and that makes a substantial difference to their sound. Other chords like E, C, Bm, Am can ring over a D bass note, which puts a new slant on them. From a songwriting perspective 'drop D' alters the guitar's standard tuning bias from the keys of E major and minor to D major and minor.

Two groups of songwriters and players in particular are liberated when they find 'drop D'. Folk guitarists like it because it has an open-string D octave between the fourth and sixth strings, good for an alternating-thumb finger-pick. Heavy rock players like it because the three bass strings produce D5 and with a one-finger barre E5, F5, G5, and so on. It is used for writing lower-pitched D riffs, notably on Led Zeppelin's 'Moby Dick'. Notes on this detuned string 6 bend easily because of the decrease in string tension.

Drop D features on Led Zeppelin's 'Ten Years Gone', The Move's 'Brontosaurus', The Darkness's 'Growing On Me' and 'The Best Of Me', Smashing Pumpkins' 'Hummer', Bon Jovi's 'Let It Rock', Guns N' Roses' 'The Garden', The Byrds' 'Everybody's Been Burned', and CSN&Y's 'Carry Me'. Nirvana's 'Heart-Shaped Box' and Smashing Pumpkins' 'Jellybelly' are both drop D plus a semitone (half-step) lower.

The low D makes heavy blues-rock riffs inviting, especially when fifths can be held down with a single finger (many open tunings have a fifth on strings 6-5-4). A single barre finger is responsible for most of the chords in CD track 1: D5 (at open and XII position), F5, G5, and C5. Notice the change in contrast between the 'dark' low-pitched fifths and the brighter five-string chords of G5 and F9add13 that flare out in bars 5-6. You could take advantage of this in song terms by singing over bars 1-2 or 3-4. One way of thinking about this idea is to see it as a 16-bar verse with the second D riff as an extra four-bar section. The G13 adds a little extra colour before the second D riff comes in. This riff contrasts with bars 1-2 because it is scale-based (one note at a time) in contrast to the chordal riff of the verse. The heavy blues-rock sound is achieved by the combination of the drop D tuning, the fifth chords, the absence of any minor chords and the ♭III and ♭VII (assuming the song is in D major).

Songwriting tip 1

The ♭III 'flat degree' chord voiced as a fifth or a major contributes to a toughening of a chord progression.

In CD track 2, notice the contrast in musical style from the heavy blues-rock of CD track 1 even though we are in the same tuning. This is a relaxed verse and hook that uses the low D as a pedal note over which triads move on the top three strings. Some of the chords could be re-named if the low D was taken as the root note rather than a separate pedal note. Em/D would be an implied

CD track 1: DADGBE

I				IV				II				III			
D	/	/	/	G/D	/	/	/	Em/D	/	/	/	F♯m/D	/	/	/

I				IV				II				III		V	
D	/	/	/	G/D	/	/	/	Em/D	/	/	/	F♯m/D	/	A/D	/

IV						VI		I				Vm			
Gadd9	/	/	/		/	Bmadd4	/	D6	/	/	/	Am7/D	/	/	/

IV						VI		I			II		♭III		
Gadd9	/	/	/		/	Bmadd4	/	||:D	/	Dmaj7	/	Em	/	Fmaj9	/ | Fmaj9:||

D13 (no 3rd), F♯m/D would be Dmaj7, A/D would be D9 (no 3rd), and Am7/D would be D11 (no 3rd). This last chord provides an expressive contrast to the A/D.

Listen for the typical add note chords that are so readily available in an altered tuning – the Gadd9, Bmadd4, D6. Notice the subtle change in the movement of the chords in bars 9-10, 13-14, where the Gadd9 is given six beats – that avoids having every bar filled with one chord. A quickened feeling of chord movement characterises the hook, where the Fmaj9 is an example of a ♭III chord (III in D is F♯m, so ♭III is F) where the blues inflection it would have in other contexts has been diluted by making it a more complex chord.

CD track 2
DADGBE

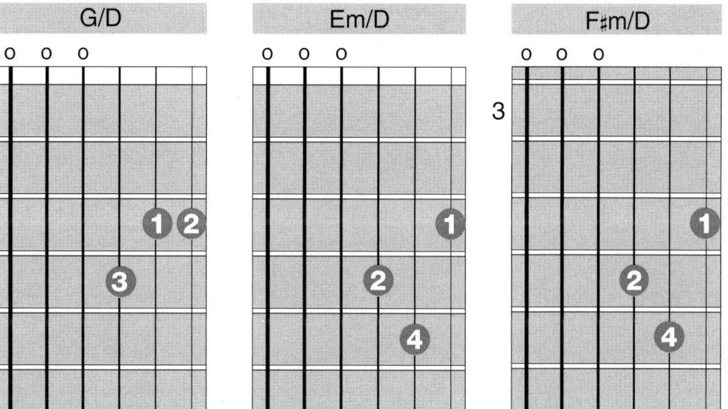

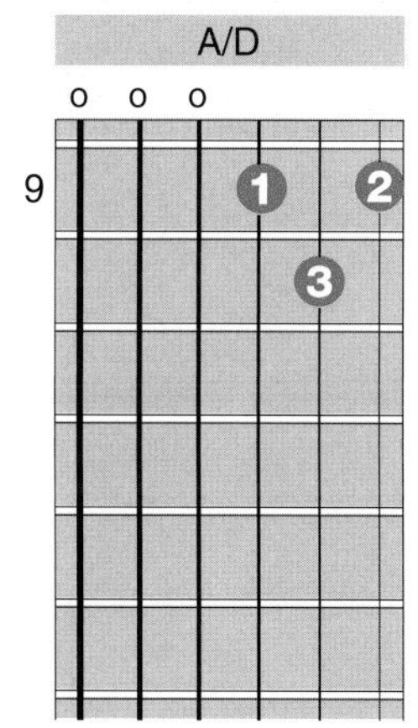

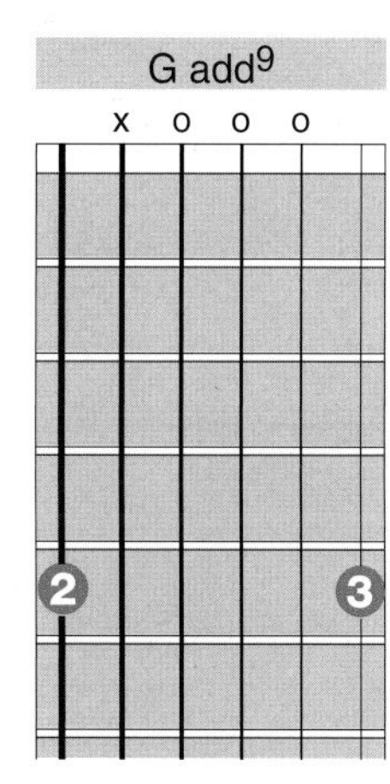

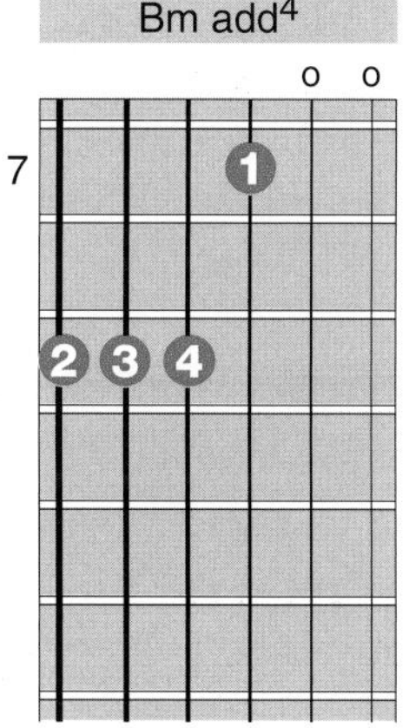

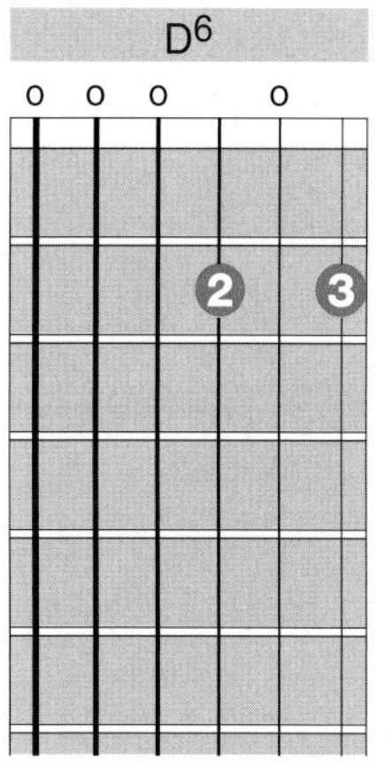

CHORDS: CD track 2
DADGBE
(continued over page)

CHORDS: CD track 2
DADGBE

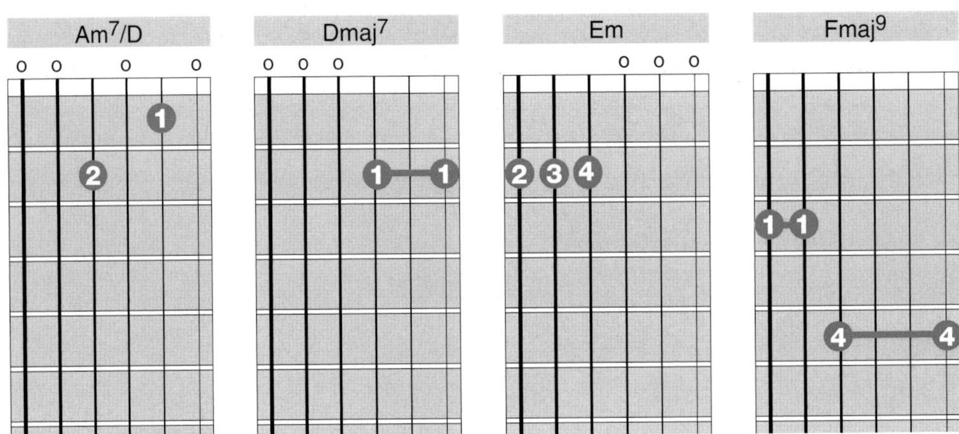

Songwriting tip 2

Check the rate at which the chords in your song change. Are they all changing on the first beat of a bar and taking a bar? Introduce variety of movement by having a chord last for six beats or two bars, or only two beats.

Half drop D♯	
Changes:	x x x x x -1
Pitches:	E A D G B D♯ (E♭)
Profile:	5 5 5 4 4
3rds	1+2, 2+3
5ths	-
6ths	2+4
Octaves	-
Open triads	G aug. (1+2+3), G (2+3+4) Em (2+3+6)

This is a less conventional idea for a tuning, and 'half drop D♯' is my suggestion for a label. With the guitar in standard tuning take string 1 down a semitone (half-step) from E to D♯. Hold D♯ at the fourth fret of string 2 and tune the top E down until the two are the same. If you now play standard chord shapes, unlike in the case of top drop D, it seems almost everything sounds peculiar and dissonant. Your first reaction might be to think nothing good can come from this tuning. To make it yield some great musical effects you need to consider how it can work. This is a matter of identifying which chords or keys feature the note D♯. D♯ is:

- the root (1) of the chords D♯ and D♯m
- the third of the chord of B
- the fifth of the chords G♯ and G♯m
- the major seventh of Emaj7
- the sixth of F♯ and F♯m6
- the second of C♯sus2
- the add ninth of C♯add9 and C♯madd9

Most of these chords belong in the keys of B major or G♯m, so that is the key in which to start songwriting in this tuning. In standard tuning this key involves either barre chords and/or a capo, so straight away the tuning opens up the possibility of writing in B major. The open strings E, A, B, and D♯ all work in this key. A and D can be treated as a blue (flattened) note in certain kinds of material.

CD track 3
EADGBD♯

I		IV	
B / / /	Bmaj7 / / /	Emaj7 / / /	/ / Emaj7add13 / :‖
II	V	II	VI
C♯m9 / / /	F♯13 / / /	C♯madd9 / / /	G♯m / / / ‖
II	V	♭VII	
C♯m9 / / /	F♯13 / / /	A9♯11 / / /	/ / / / ‖
I III	IV V	VI	V I
‖: B / D♯m /	Emaj7 / F♯13 / :‖	G♯m / / /	F♯13 / / / B ‖

The gentle verse of CD track 3 has a four-bar I-IV change in B major played twice. The rich major sevenths have an extra ring in this tuning in comparison to playing them as barre chords in standard tuning. In bars 4 and 8 the Emaj7 is furthered coloured with an add13. The II-V change in bars 9-10, 13-14 has additional colour moving from C♯m9 to F♯13, with the verse coming to a

CHORDS: CD track 3
EADGBD♯

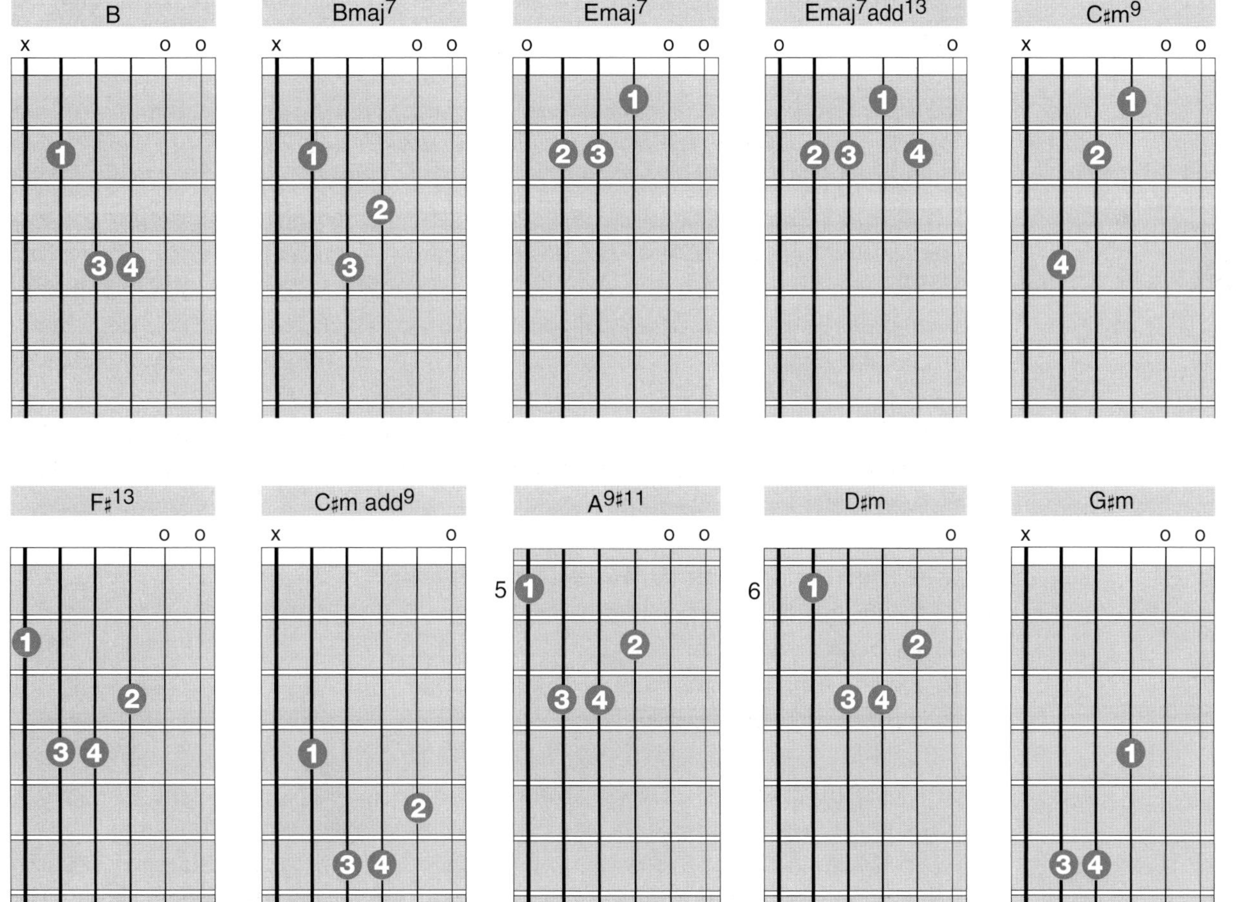

harmonic pause on a non-blues ♭VII voiced as A9♯11. The shapes (below) reveal that the complexity of a chord in an altered tuning often bears little relation to how easy it is to play, whereas in standard tuning, more often than not, a complex chord requires a tricky fingering (often a barre) and does not flow easily to the next complex chord. In altered tunings complex chords have resonance but also ease of movement when changing one to another.

What could be a chorus idea is a four-chord turnaround I-III-IV-V with a VI-V-I change to finish. The B chord is played with the same shape as the F♯13 and A9♯11 but at the seventh fret. This minimises the distance to the D♯m. Listen out for how in the B, D♯m, and G♯m chords the D♯ of the altered open string 1 blends in. This is because D♯ belongs to all three chords. In other chords D♯ will stand out. This is a general effect in altered tunings – open strings blend into chords where they are a root, third, or fifth, but stand out in other types. (This effect also happens in standard tuning but is not so pronounced.)

One of the guitar parts on the audio was recorded with a tremolo effect. This guitar processing effect makes the chords shimmer, strengthening the open string resonance. It is a successful effect with many open tunings because, unlike distortion, it doesn't blur the notes within the chords.

Songwriting tip 3

The effect of a turnaround four-chord sequence is heightened if the chords are moving quickly. If the song has a fast tempo this will happen naturally. If the slow has a medium to slow tempo (as here) giving each chord only two beats will achieve the same result.

The musical potential of an altered tuning is shaped not only by its pitches but how you interpret them, and what you consider their musical meaning to be. This is important whenever a tuning has a sharp/flat note as an open string. These can be considered as two different notes which point to contrasting key-centres and harmony. EADGBD♯ is also EADGBE♭. Thinking of the tuning as the former you might compose a song in B major (CD track 3) or E major; thinking of it as the latter you can instead compose a song in E♭ major or C minor. Every sharp note (A♯ C♯ D♯ F♯ G♯) is also a flat (B♭ D♭ E♭ G♭ A♭). We can analyse the song potential of this detuned string by thinking of it as E♭, not D♯. E♭ is:

- the root (1) of the chords E♭ and E♭m
- the third of the chords C♭ and Cm
- the fifth of the chords A♭ and A♭m
- the seventh of the chords F7 and Fm7
- the sixth of the chords G♭6 and G♭m6
- the second of D♭sus2
- the add ninth of D♭add9 and D♭madd9
- the fourth of B♭sus4

The open strings D, G, and E♭ belong in E♭ major or C minor. Interpreted this way the tuning leads the songwriter to a different set of chord shapes.

In CD track 4 (right) the music is finger-picked in E♭, instead of strummed in B major. You would hardly think it was the same tuning as CD track 3. The

CD track 4 EADGBE♭

final chord shapes are a good example of how your fretting hand technique needs to be strong and precise so you don't unintentionally stop notes sounding. This is always more noticeable when finger-picking than when strumming. The finger-picking pattern is a traditional syncopated one in which the thumb plays any note with a tail going downwards (an 'alternating thumb'). This amounts to the four quarter notes that mark the beat. Fingers pluck the other higher-pitched notes.

The main chord change goes from I-V in E♭ for two four-bar phrases. Then two minor chords appear, which emotionally take the sequence somewhere else, though the A♭maj7 softens the sadness and brings a hint of resolution. Notice how the A♭maj7 chord in bar 11 creates a contrast of timbre because there are no open strings in it. The chorus sequence is I-II^-♭VII-I with the chord voicings lending interest to the three major chords, and the second time the IVm chord enters to bring the musical idea to a romantic conclusion.

The chord voicings create some typical effects brought out by finger-picking an alternate tuning. One is the proximity of notes sounding a semitone or tone apart. In bar three there is an F and G sounding a tone apart, and above them a D and an E♭. The semitone of D-E♭ sounds in bars 5-6 as part of the Cmadd9 chord and in bars 7-8 as part of Gm6.

Thus we have potentially written two songs, one in B and one in E♭, from a single-string semi-tone change.

Songwriting tip 4

Turning chord IV into a minor just before a song concludes is a traditional romantic musical gesture.

Top drop D	
Changes:	x x x x x -2
Pitches:	E A D G B D
Profile:	5 5 5 4 3
3rds	1+2, 2+3
5ths	1+3
6ths	2+4
Octaves	1+4
Open triads	G (1+2+3) Em (2+3+6)

The next single-string tuning can be reached by continuing downward a semitone (half-step) from the previous. Having taken E down a semitone to D♯ we take it one more semitone to D. My suggested name for this tuning – 'top drop D' – distinguishes it from 'drop D' where string 6 is involved. This tuning is a good illustration of the principle that higher string changes function as an added note to familiar chord shapes; changes to strings 5 and 6 are more likely to be root notes.

To get a feel for this tuning, play standard tuning shapes and listen to how the chords are changed by the alteration of any note they include on string 1. As you change from one shape to another the top open D remains the same but its function as a note in relation to the rest of the chord changes. Play the sequence of chords A C D E G. The top D becomes an add fourth, an add ninth, a second, a seventh and a fifth. This is also a good tuning for 'raga-rock' droning effects, moving chord shapes up the neck but leaving string 1 open. Other standard tuning shapes change as follows: Am = Amadd4; Cmaj7 = Cmaj9; E = E7; Em = Em7; Emadd9 = Em9; Fmaj7 = F6; G6 = G.

In CD track 5 the sophisticated sound of extended chords such as 13s and 9s creates a different effect to a plain E-F-C (I-♭II-♭VI) in standard tuning. The first change, suitable for a song intro, is just on two variants of E, with a relaxed feel. The second phrase is edgier and bluesier because of the two extended

CD track 5
EADGBD

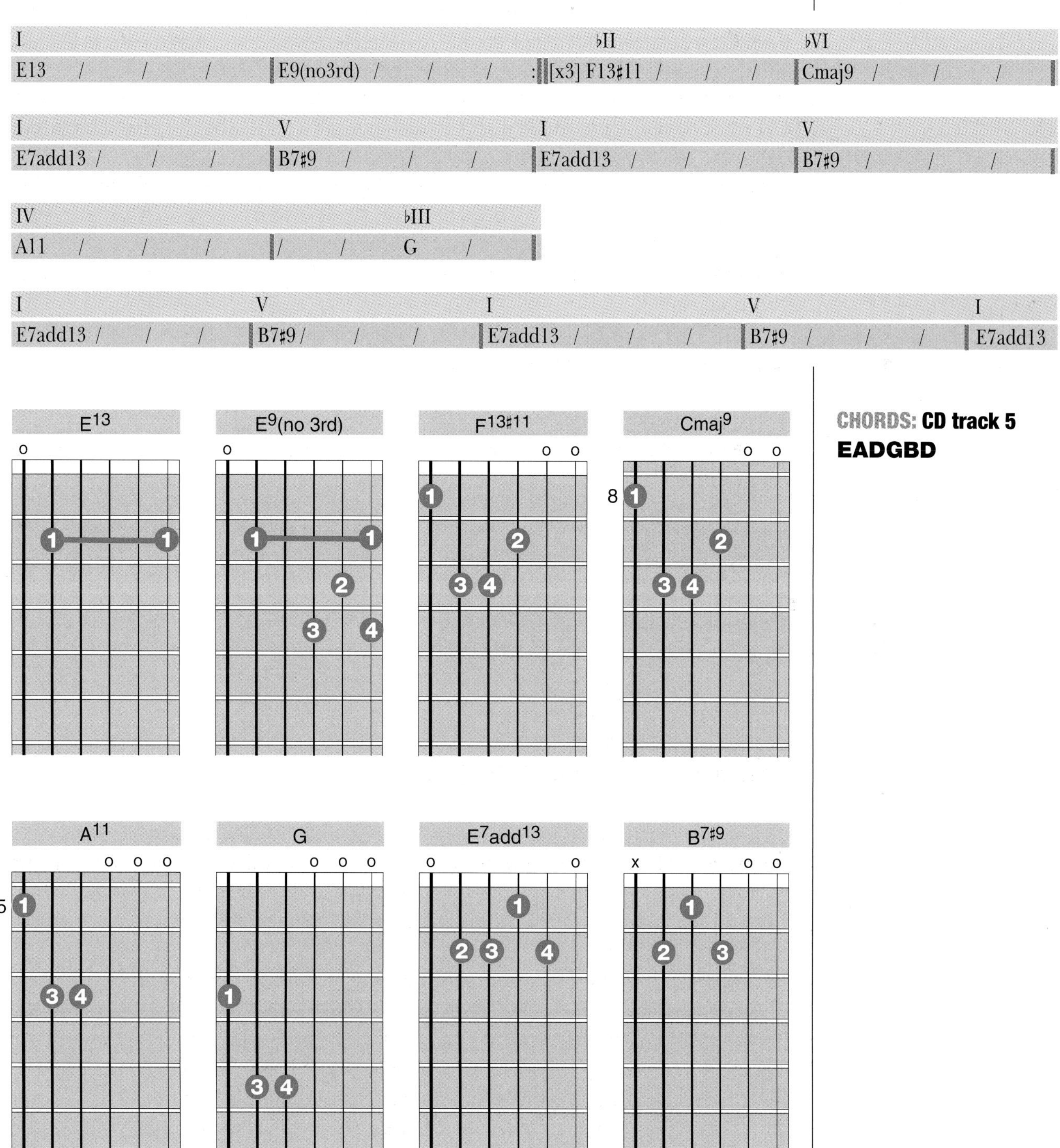

I		♭II	♭VI
E13 / / /	E9(no3rd) / / / :‖	[x3] F13♯11 / / /	Cmaj9 / / /

I	V	I	V
E7add13 / / /	B7♯9 / / /	E7add13 / / /	B7♯9 / / /

IV	♭III
A11 / / /	/ / G /

I	V	I	V	I
E7add13 / / /	B7♯9 / / /	E7add13 / / /	B7♯9 / / /	E7add13

CHORDS: CD track 5
EADGBD

dominant sevens – E7add13 and B7♯9. The E7add13 is an interesting voicing because the top two notes are a semitone apart. The latter is the chord now known in rock circles as the 'Hendrix chord' because of his use of it in songs like 'Crosstown Traffic'. Its spiky quality is here modified by the open string of the altered tuning. The blues effect is also down to the IV-♭III (A11-G5) change. Notice the overall harmonic toughness is also a consequence of the absence of minor chords.

Songwriting tip 5

If writing a song without minor chords replace them with 'flat degree' chords (♭III, ♭VI, ♭VII) or one or more of the 'reverse polarity chords' (II^, III^ or VI^).

CD track 6
EADGBD

CD track 6, in the same tuning, is in 6/8 and so has a distinctive rhythmic lilt of One…two…three, One…two…three. The first sequence is a turnaround of I-II-VI-V, but in contrast to standard tuning each of the chords is decorated by the

I	II	VI	V
G / / / / /	Amadd4 / / / / /	Em7 / / / / /	D5 / / / / / :‖

VI	V	IV	V	I
‖:Em7*/ / / / /	D13 / / / / /	C9 / / / / /	D13/ / / / /	G:‖

CHORDS: CD track 6
EADGBD

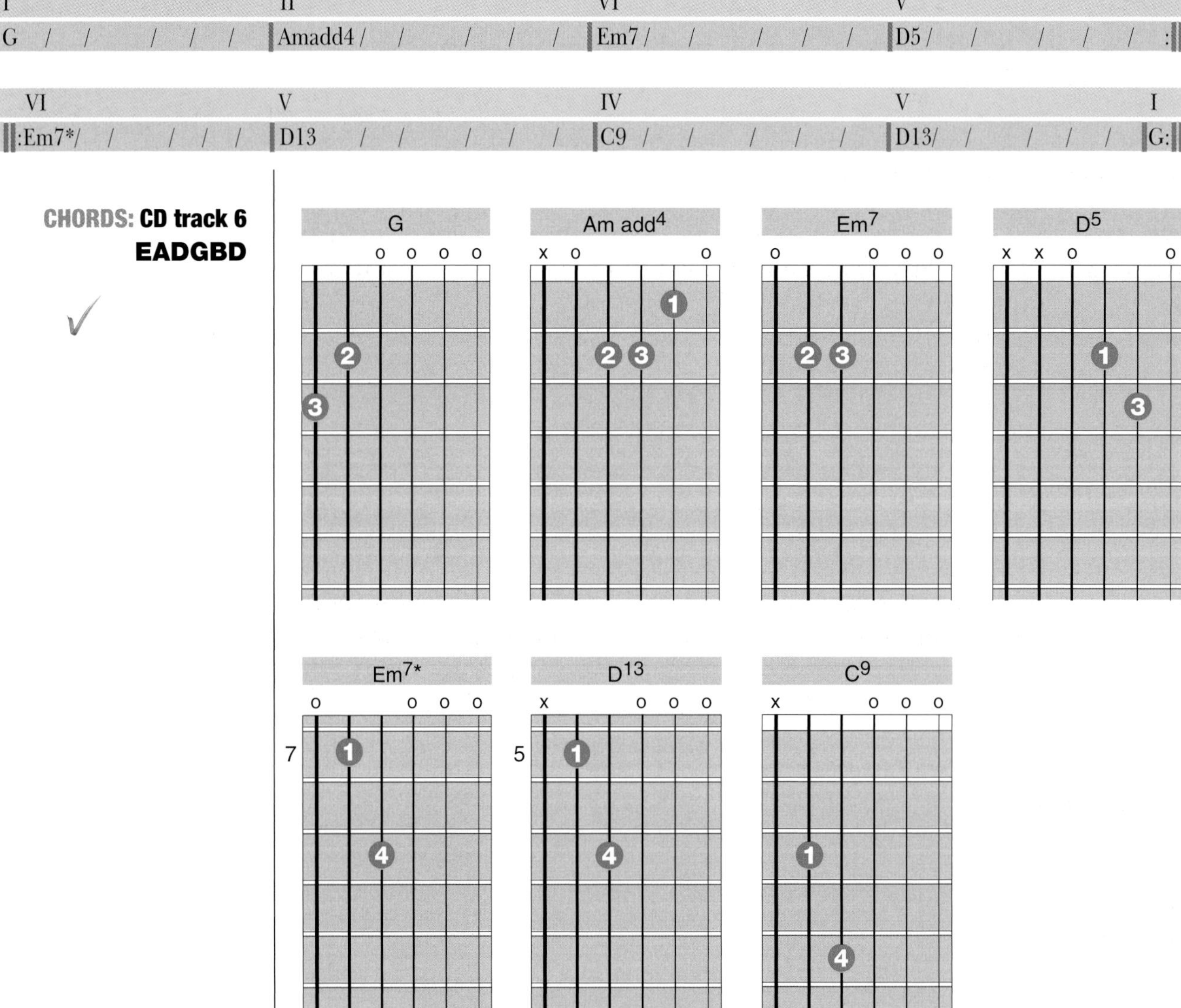

open string D at the top. In each bar the harmonic value (and therefore the effect) of that open D changes: in bar one it is the fifth of G and blends in; in bar two it is the fourth of Am and sticks out; in bar three it is the seventh of Em and half-blends; and in bar four it is the root of D and completely blends without tension. Then a second sequence is generated by moving a perfect fifth shape from the seventh fret to the third fret. (The asterisk added to the Em7* is to differentiate it from the Em7 played earlier.) Listen for the bar in which there is a chord change to D on the third beat to add variety of movement.

Songwriting tip 6

Instead of always writing songs in 4/4, experiment with the dance-like rhythm of 6/8 or 3/4. These could be used for an intro even if the rest of the song is in 4/4.

Lute tuning

Changes:	x x x -1 x x
Pitches:	E A D F♯ B E
Profile:	5 5 4 5 5
3rds	3+4
5ths	-
6ths	2+4, 3+5
Octaves	-
Open triads	Bm (2+3+4), D (3+4+5)

With the guitar in standard tuning this experiment involves detuning string 3 (G) a semitone to F♯. Play F♯ at the fourth fret of string 4 to check that it is in tune. This gives EADF♯BE. If you view E as the root note of the tuning the open strings make a chord of Em11. Interpreted thus it would encourage a songwriter to develop a song in E minor (or possibly A minor or B minor, where this chord is important). The tuning got its name because it approximates the intervals used in tuning a lute, except to get the pitch the same a capo is placed at the third fret as the lute was tuned a minor third higher. Classical guitarists adopt lute tuning to make it easier to finger lute and vihuela music of the 16th century. This was a tuning that Pete Townshend apparently tried in some songs by The Who in the 60s.

The chord boxes show how, as with the previous two tunings, familiar chord shapes have now changed their content (G is now Gmaj7, and so on). Any chord which features F♯ prominently is going to be easier to voice. Most notable are the wonderful B and Bm chords with open strings. F♯ is:

- the root of the chords F♯ and F♯m
- the third of the chords D and D♯m
- the fifth of the chords B and Bm
- the seventh of G♯7 and G♯m7
- the major seventh of Gmaj7
- the sixth of A and Am6
- the second of Esus2
- the add ninth of Eadd9 and Emadd9
- the fourth of C♯sus4

Not all these chords belong in the same key, so they won't all mix. The chords D, Emadd9, Esus2, F♯m, Gmaj7, A6, and Bm do go together, and otherwise the key of B major works well.

CD track 7 begins with a slinky four-bar phrase using the chords of a three-chord minor trick (I-IV-V). Bars 1-2 show how to get extra use out of a chord by simply changing the type of chord built on that root note, rather than going to a different chord. The appearance of the major form of chord V in bar nine

CD track 7
EADF♯BE

I		IV	iiV
Bm / Bm11 /	Bm / Bm11 /	Em / Esus2 /	F♯m7/C♯ / / / :‖
iiV^	VII	iiV^	ii♭VI VII
F♯7/C♯ / / /	A6 / / /	F♯7/C♯ / / /	G6/D / A /
I	IV	I	IV
B / / /	Eadd9 / / /	B / / /	Eadd9 / / /
ii♭III	iiVm	I	
Dmaj7/A / / /	D/A / F♯m7/C♯ /	B :‖	

CHORDS: CD track 7
EADF♯BE

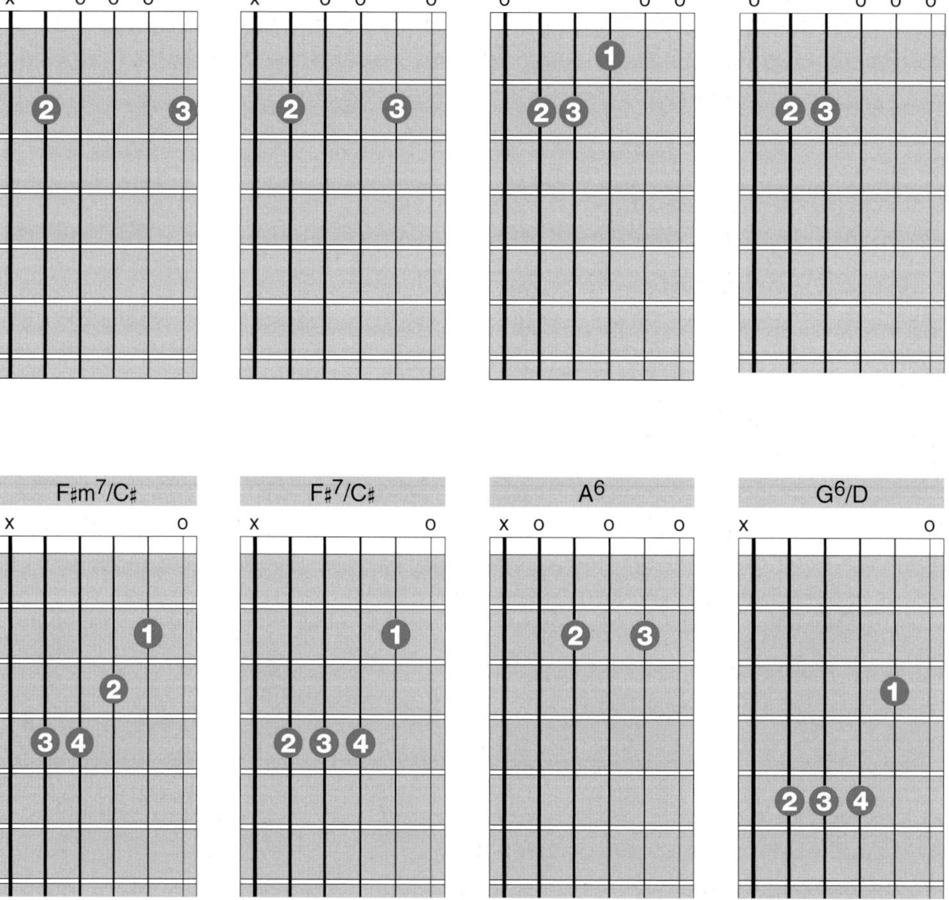

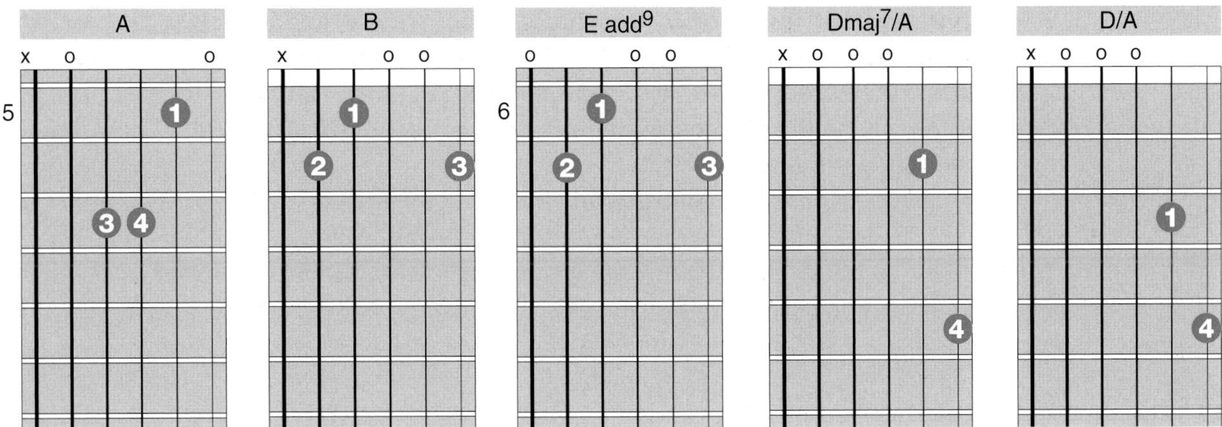

CHORDS: CD track 7
EADF♯BE
(continued)

indicates the music is going somewhere else. This four-bar idea leads to a change of key from B minor to B major for the last six-bar idea which is suitable for a chorus. Having the verse of a song in a minor key and the chorus in its tonic major (the same root note) can be a fine contrast (The Beatles' 'Fool On The Hill' does it the other way round, with the verse in D major but the chorus in D minor). Remember that if these audio examples were developed for a song various sections and chord changes would be extended.

Songwriting tip 7

Going from the minor version of chord V to the major in a minor key song creates a moment of optimism, and can also act as a door to the tonic major key and a contrasting positive mood.

Drop A	
Changes:	x x x x -2 x
Pitches:	E A D G A E
Profile:	5 5 5 2 7
3rds	-
5ths	1+2, 2+4
6ths	1+3
Octaves	2+5
Open triads	-

So far we've detuned string 1 by a semitone (half-step) and a tone (whole-step). The same approach could be taken with string 2. Of the two options, going a whole-step down to A from B is more likely to be musically productive. This tuning, which I've called 'drop A', leans toward A minor, A major, G major, D major, and E minor. Billy Corgan of Smashing Pumpkins used this tuning for 'Farewell And Goodnight' and 'Muzzle', tuned down a semitone (half-step). An A is threaded through standard open chord shapes as an extra note, extending their harmony. An open fifth sounds at the top of the tuning, whilst there is only a tone (whole-step) between strings 2 and 3, opening up the possibility of 'harp' effects if a finger is fretted higher enough on string 4. 'Harp' effects in altered tunings result when there are three notes on separate strings whose pitch is close together. In this tuning fretting F♯ at fret four on string 4, and playing strings 4, 3 and 2 creates a run of notes (F♯-G-A) that span only three semitones (half-steps). Such note-clusters are hard to find in standard tuning, but are a hallmark of many altered tunings. For the songwriter they can suggest a fragment of melody.

A tone cluster is a chord in which notes are close in pitch. Chords with notes a tone or semitone (whole-step or half-step) apart have a colour all of their own. They are difficult on the guitar, but as the easiest way to make them is with an open string it is not surprising that they are easier to find in altered tunings. They include some of the sixth, suspended second, and add ninth chords, where the extra note is only a tone or semitone away from one of the triad notes. But this extra note might not be adjacent. One of the paradoxes of music is that the semitone (the minor second), one of the most dissonant sounds, has a role in some of the most beautiful chords. In extreme cases a guitar chord has a cluster of three notes within a small span of three to five semitones, as though they were extracted from a scale. These are sometimes likened to the sound of a harp. Semitones and tones that feature low down in a chord can give that chord a distinct 'chill' which is sometimes right for sinister effects.

CD track 8
EADGAE

V																
E5	/	/	/	E7sus4	/	/	/	E5	/	/	/	E7sus4	/	/	/	:‖

I		II^		♭VI			♭VII	I		♭III		♭VI		Vm		
A	/	B7add11	/	Fmaj7	/	/	G6/9	A	/	C6	/	Fmaj7	/	Emadd4	/	:‖

I		II^		♭VI			♭VII	I		♭III		IV				
A	/	B7add11	/	Fmaj7	/	/	Gadd4	A	/	C6	/	D6/9	/	/	/	‖

				I
/	/	/	/	A :‖

The first four bars of CD track 8 show how the E chord can be altered to create musical interest without going to another chord immediately. Neither of these shapes gives a hint of the distinctive open A string 2 of this tuning. That is held in reserve for the first A chord and B7add11. The unsettling flavour of this progression is the result of several flat degree and reverse polarity chords from the scale of A. B7add11 has replaced Bm (II^), C6 has replaced C♯m (♭III instead of III), Fmaj7 has replaced F♯m (♭VI instead of VI) and there's a ♭VII (D6/9). However, the chord voicings – using sevenths, sixths, ninths – make the emotional effect of the harmony less bluesy than it would have otherwise been. This could be the verse of a hard rock song, but if so it is post-70s hard rock. The main sequence shows how in an altered tuning you can sometimes get a substantial progression by moving one shape up and down the fretboard.
Of the ten shapes, five are the same one played in five different positions. Like the open top D in the previous example, the open string 2 forms different harmonic relationships inside the chords: as the root it blends with A; it adds tension as a seventh in B7add11; it blends as the third of Fmaj7; it adds

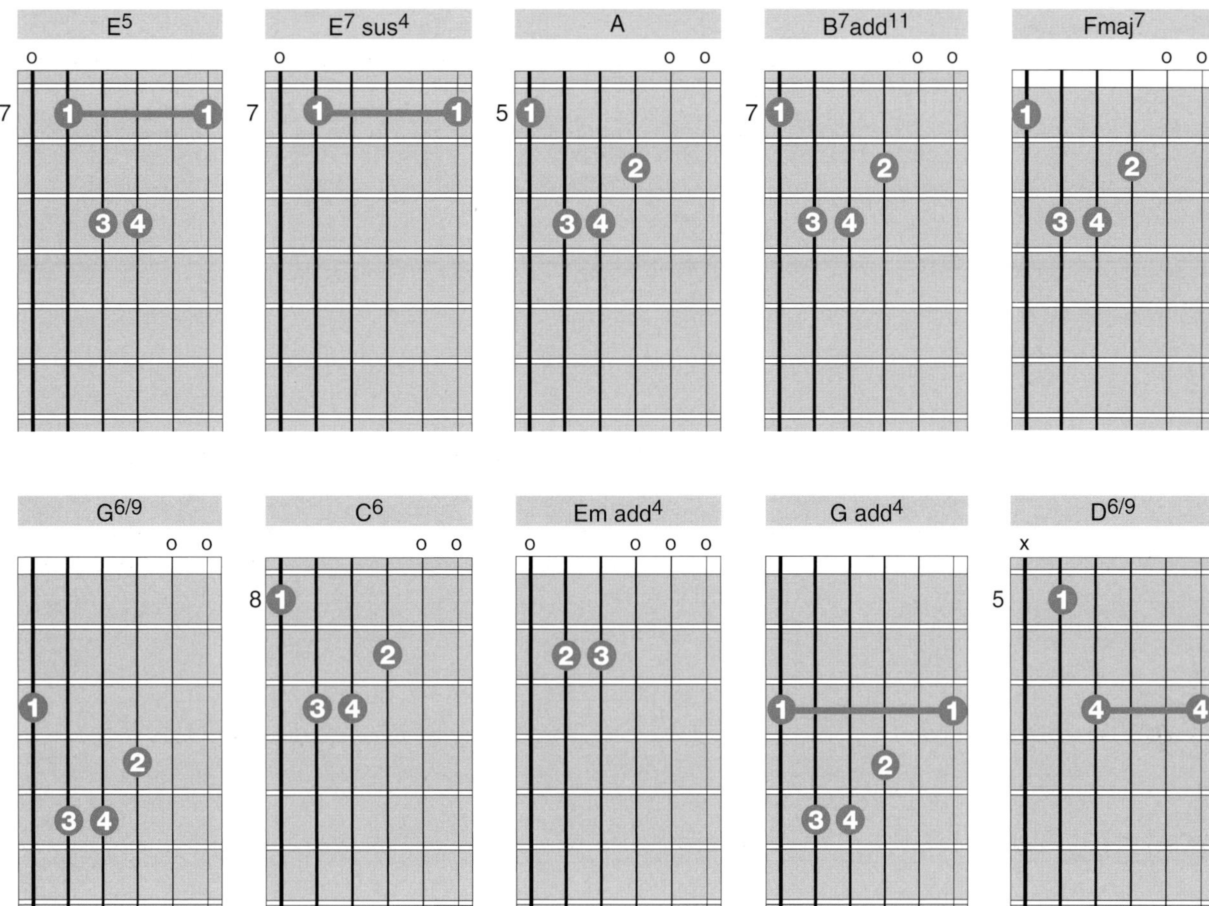

tension as the ninth of G6/9; it half-blends as the sixth of C6; it adds tension as the fourth in Emadd4.

CHORDS: CD track 8
EADGAE

Songwriting tip 8

A common note can link otherwise unrelated chords and make them more acceptable to the listener. When a chord or progression is felt to be acceptable to the ear it also becomes emotionally explicable; that is, it is more likely the listener will find an emotion evoked by that sound.

CD track 9 (next page) is an arpeggiated idea in the same tuning which could be a link, an intro, or even a verse. The chord names are in brackets because they are implied rather than overt, and other chords could be placed under these notes. Look and listen for moments where the same note is sounded as a fretted note and an open string in close proximity. At times this produces an impression of a note echoing, without actual echo being applied to the guitar. In the B7sus4 chord this even leads to three instances of the same note played in succession. Listen also for adjacent notes that are only a semitone apart and generate a dissonant shimmer in the music.

CD track 9 EADGAE

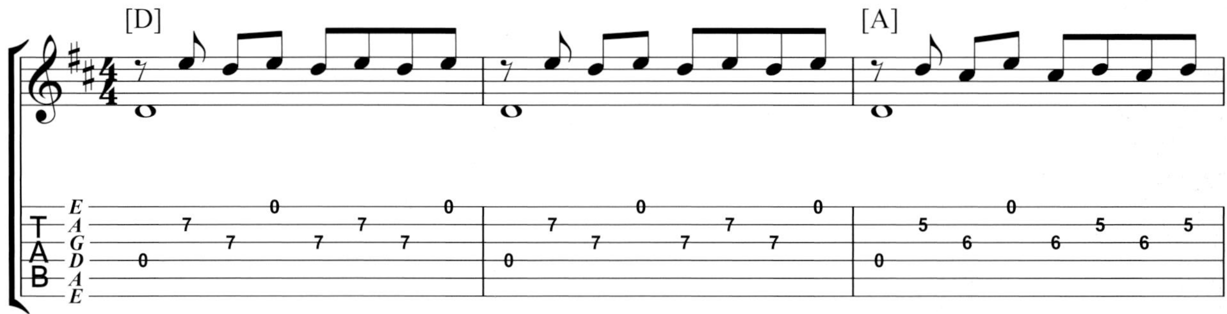

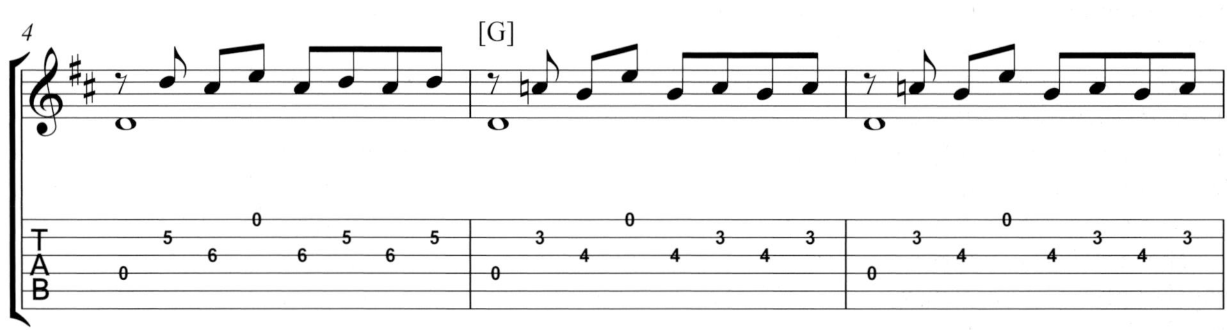

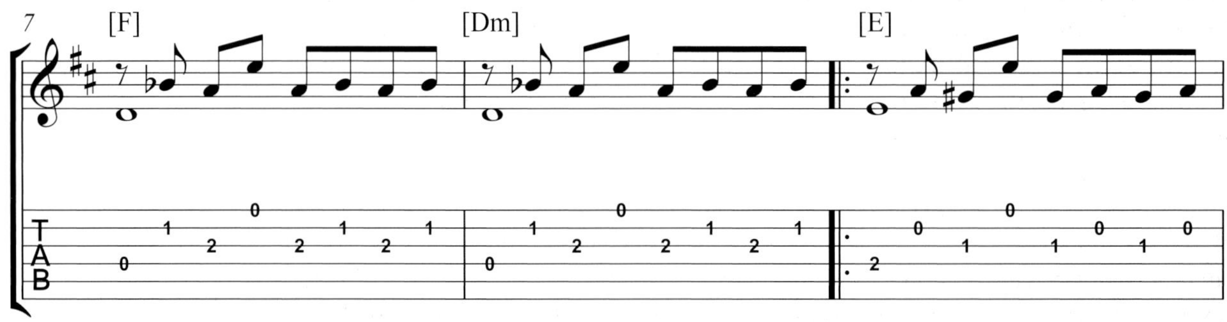

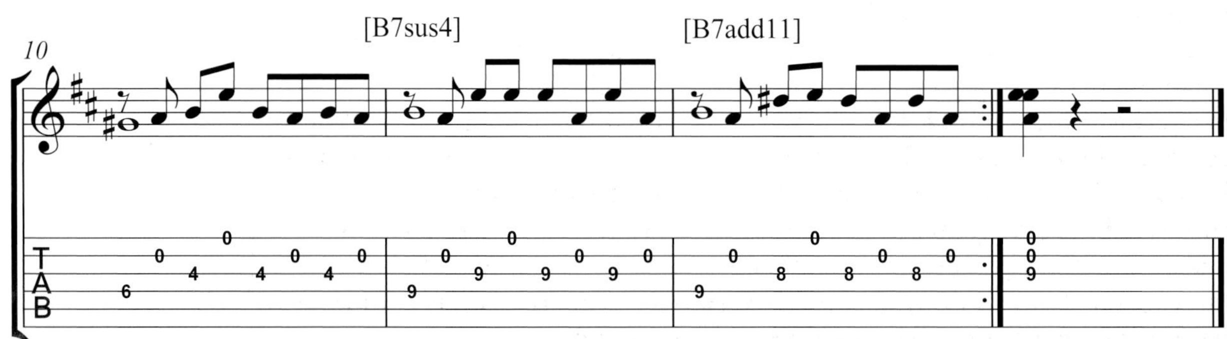

Songwriting tip 9

Arpeggio passages are a way of creating melodic interest out of chords during non-vocal links, intros, outros , and so on.

Drop C

Changes:	-4 x x x x x
Pitches:	C A D G B E
Profile:	9 5 5 4 5
3rds	2+3
5ths	-
6ths	1+3, 2+4, 5+6
Octaves	-
Open triads	Em (1+2+3), G (2+3+4), C (1+3+6), Am (1+5+6)

From standard tuning 'drop C' advances on the idea of the first tuning we looked at in this section, 'drop D'. This time string 6 has gone down two tones (whole steps) to a C an octave below the C at the third fret on string 5. At a push, this could be characterised as an open C9add13 tuning. Bob Dylan used this tuning for 'It's All Over Now, Baby Blue', and John McGeoch for Siouxsie & The Banshees' 'Green Fingers'. Some bands have written material where string 6 goes down further to B, as with Soundgarden's 'Holy Water' and 'Rusty Cage'.

The low C has a powerful gravitational effect, magnified by the perceived gap between it and string 5. Test this gravitational power by strumming a standard C shape and moving to a standard D shape; hit all the strings in both instances. The low C is so strong it makes the D chord sound less like D/C (or a third inversion D7) but C13♯11, where the As are 13ths, the D a ninth and the F♯ a ♯11. Similarly, a normal Em shape finds itself turned into a Cmaj7. In both instances standard shapes are lent a new colour by the detuned string 6.

The songwriter will immediately be pulled into C major, with the open C-string acting as a pedal note. Fingering chords that have their root on string 6 is tricky, though first and second inversions present possible substitutes. An inversion is a chord whose root is no longer at the bottom. In a major or minor chord if the lowest note is the third it is called a first inversion. If the fifth of the chord is at the bottom it is called a second inversion. The number of inversions is always one less than the number of notes in a chord, though complex chords may generate a different root chord if they are inverted. A first inversion tends to sound as though it wants to move up or down. A second inversion is either used as a default substitute for a root chord or in slower tempo songs as a dreamy version of the basic chord.

In this tuning the songwriter might write a sequence where the chords of C major are played over a continuous C pedal note. Shifting to chords whose root note is on string 5 removes the presence of that low C, so that when it is heard again its effect is refreshed. Chords over this C pedal might create a summery ballad or, in a rock arrangement, drama by postponing the arrival of root chords. The ballad genre suggests itself because the tuning produces strong major sevenths and 13th or 11th effects. If these were treated chromatically (moving one fret at a time) in movable shapes and played loud with drums the result might be progressions reminiscent of Jeff Buckley.

For the more intrepid, a move into the key of C minor is another option. However, this is hindered by the open E-string, which is out of key. It is not easy to find effective Fm and Gm and A♭ shapes, though E♭ is not so bad. Tuning the top string down to E♭ (CADGBE♭) might help if you wanted to write in the key of C minor. The E♭11 barre shape gives a contrast of tonality to the dominant pull of C.

Unlike drop D there is no easy power-chord on strings 6-4 but you can generate a grunge-type riff, one in single notes and one using fifth shapes above the C bass string. There is also no open string octave for finger-pickers, but the Fm9-Dm9 change is fruitful with a picking approach.

CD track 10
CADGBE

I	♭III	II^	iiIV
C / / /	E♭/C / / /	Dadd4/C / / /	F/C / / /

I	♭III	II^	V
C / / /	E♭/C / / /	Dadd4/C / / /	G / / /

iVI		♭III	iiV
Am/C / / /	/ / / /	E♭maj7 / / /	/ / G7/D /

I	II	iiIVm	I
‖:Cmaj7 / / /	Dm6/9 / / /	:‖[x3] Fm/C / / /	/ / / / C:‖

In CD track 10 the first four-bar phrase puts the chords over a C pedal note. The first eight bars of this example are played with a single shape. The E♭/C could also be interpreted as Cm7. The very low string-6 C gives the progression an additional colour and tension. Notice the change of chord in bar eight compared to bar four, with G replacing F/C, the open string 6 muted, and the fact that this has emphasis as a root chord. Am has impact as the first minor chord to appear. The last change, which might be a chorus, is a I-II change enriched by the low bass, with a romantic IVm coming in toward the end. The combination of the pedal note with the extended chord voicings of eleventh, major seventh, sixth/ninth, gives the harmony sophistication. This example might lend itself to a soul ballad (the I-II change in a major key was a favourite of Smokey Robinson's).

Songwriting tip 10

A low pedal note lends fresh colour to a chord progression sounded above it. This is also quick route to giving a progression tension. Many classic Who songs feature pedal notes in standard tuning – listen to the F♯ pedal that runs through the intro of 'Pinball Wizard' or the D pedal that carries the chords of the chorus of 'Substitute'.

CHORDS: CD track 10
CADGBE

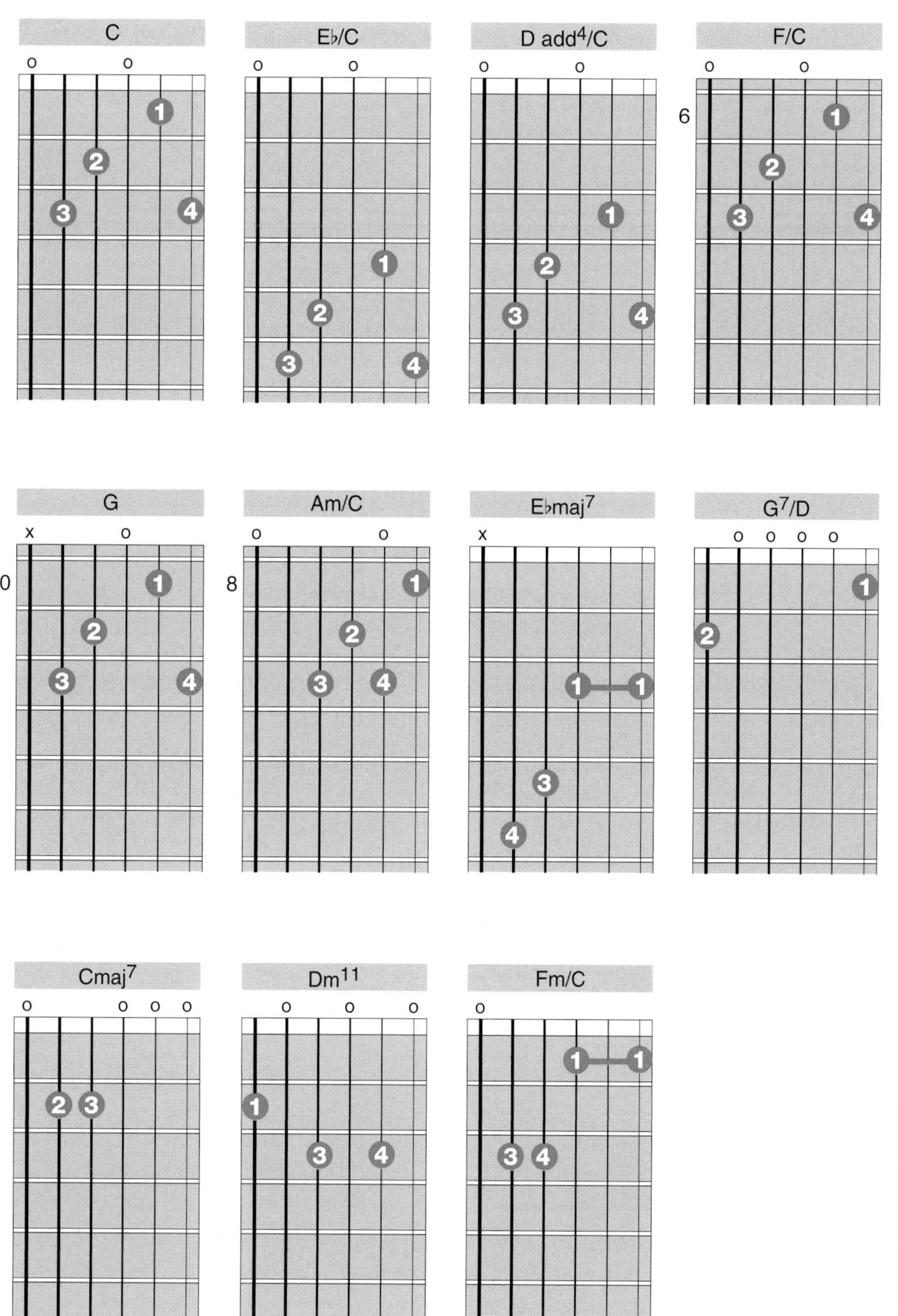

SECTION 4
DOUBLE-STRING TUNINGS

Having experimented with the single-string change, in this next section we move to tunings that involve altering two strings. Some of these ideas are combinations of tunings featured in Section Three, as if they had been overlapped. Like those, these tunings are relatively quick to change into. If you write a song with a single-string change it can be easy to re-tune one more string and move to one of the following.

Double drop D

Changes:	-2 x x x x -2
Pitches:	D A D G B D
Profile:	7 5 5 4 3
3rds	1+2, 2+3
5ths	1+3, 5+6
6ths	2+4
Octaves	1+4, 4+6
Open triads	G (1+2+3), G (2+3+4)

This tuning combines the two single-string drop D alterations from **Section Three**. The lower three strings make a D5 and the upper three a G major triad. This signals that the tuning is pitched between D major or minor and G major. It is also comfortable to write in the keys of B minor or E minor. The tuning offers the deep bass of 'drop D' but the unusual 'add note' effect of 'top drop D'. Fingerings on the middle four strings are unchanged from standard tuning. Additionally, it is only one string adjustment away from the open G tuning we will meet in **Section Five**. Neil Young's 'Cinnamon Girl', R.E.M.'s 'Ignoreland', Stephen Stills' 'Bluebird', Led Zeppelin's 'Going To California', and The Darkness's 'Holding My Own' are in this tuning.

CD track 11 is a bluesy folk idea, halfway perhaps between *Led Zeppelin III* and The White Stripes unplugged. The blues style is created partly by the structure of the verse, which is derived from a 12-bar pattern, and also by the flat degree chords in D: C (♭VII), B♭ (♭VI), and F (♭III). Minor chords are saved

CD track 11
DADGBD

I		♭VII I	I	i♭VI		♭VII	
Dadd4	/	Cadd9/D	Dadd4	Bb6/D	/	Cadd9/D	D :‖

♭III	iiIV	♭III	iiIV	♭VI	iiIV	♭III	
F6/9/D	G/D	F6/9/D	G/D	B♭6/D	G/D	F6/9	/

I		♭VII I	I	i♭VI		♭VII	
Dadd4	/	Cadd9/D	Dadd4	B♭6/D	/	Cadd9/D	D

♭III				V			
F6/9	/	/	/	A7add11	/	/	/

I		Im		Vm		IVm		I
‖: Dsus2	D5	Dm7	/	Amadd4	/	Gm7	/ :‖	Dsus2 ‖

to the last phrase. Bars 1-2 amount to a two-bar chordal riff, repeated for bars 3-4. Just as in a 12-bar, we would expect a change of chord and sure enough the chord riff is transposed up a fourth and heard once (bars 5-6), the B6/D chord played 12 frets higher than its first appearance. This is followed by the first riff again (bars 7-8). The F6/9 in bar 9 is a different shape to the earlier one, closing off the open string 6, as does the A7add11 chord that comes after

CHORDS: CD track 11
DADGBD
(continued over page)

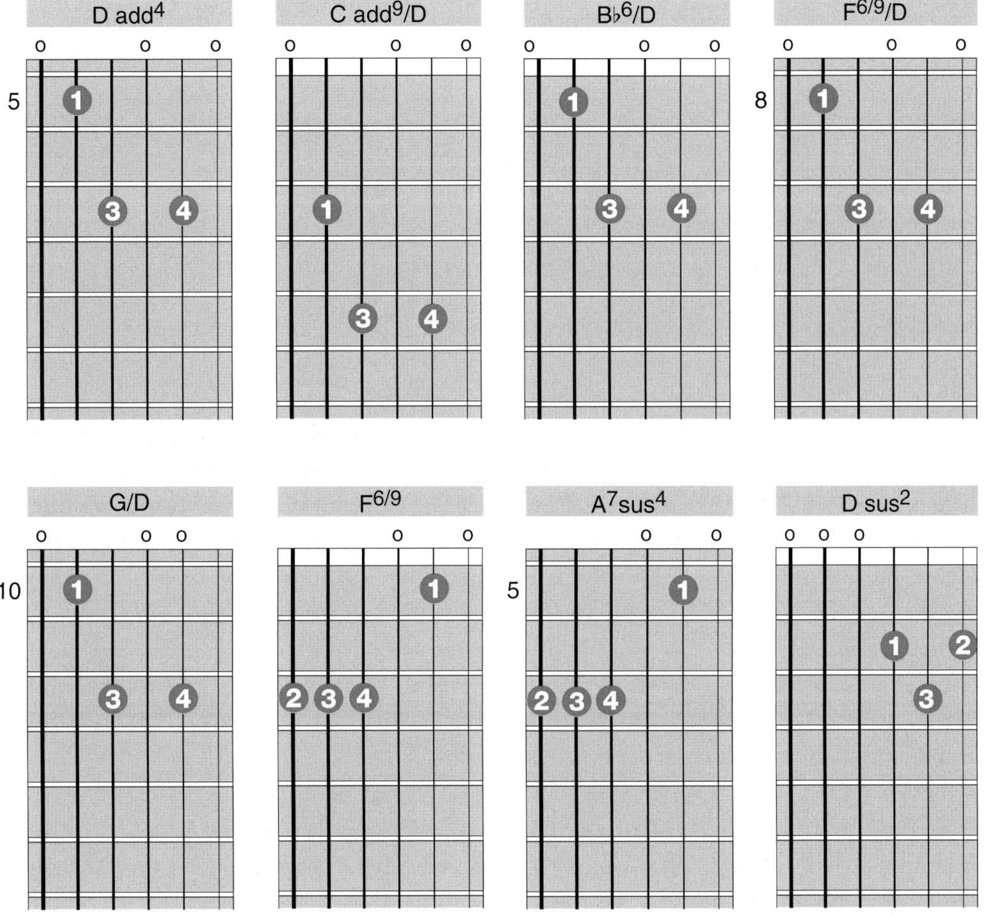

CHORDS: CD track 11
(continued)

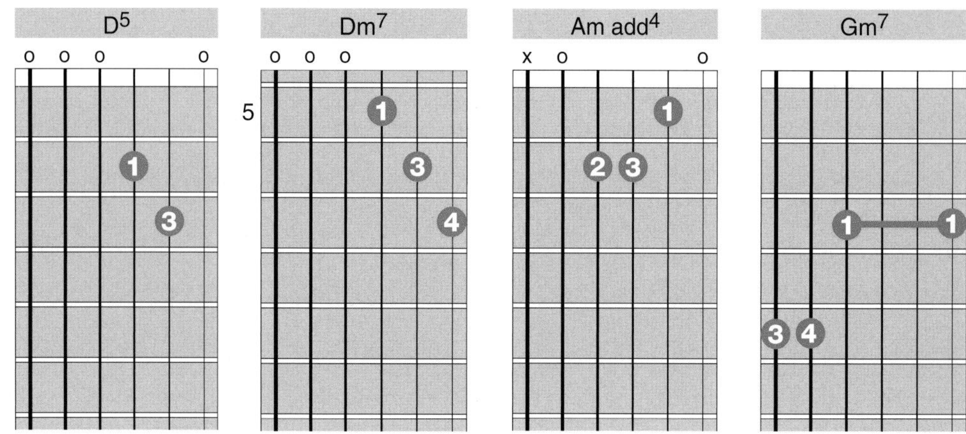

with the same shape. Thus far we have a ten-bar verse. A new two-bar chordal hook rounds things off, extending the structure to 14 bars.

A more predictable 12-bar verse could have been written if bar 9 used some form of A, if bar 10 returned to the G/D shape, and if bars 1-2 formed bars 11-12. Chords arranged in any pattern could make 12-bars; it could result in repeating a four-bar phrase three times; or it might be created from an eight-bar phrase added to a four-bar phrase. However, '12-bar' often implies a set form for the chords. The 12-bar is one of the most frequently-used structures in popular music. From blues it passed to 50s rock'n'roll, then to 60s pop and soul, regaining its blues roots in the psychedelic rock that was influenced by the blues revival (Hendrix, Cream, Free, Led Zeppelin). It is still used today. The 12-bar form can feature in any part of a song – a verse, chorus or bridge – and you do not have to be writing a blues song. It is now such a familiar structure that listeners recognise it and know where it is going. The 12-bar can contrast with sections that are less formulaic.

Songwriting tip 11

The emotional effect of a minor chord is heightened if it is the only one in a song or section. This is doubly true of a minor version of chord I in a song in a major key.

CD track 12 is a second example from the same tuning, but this one requires playing individual strings (it can be fingerpicked or played with pick and fingers). A triad shape is held down on the top three strings and gradually descends the fretboard, and in each bar the open top string is the last note in the sequence. The sequence is long enough that at this tempo it could be a verse. The part is not so busy as to distract attention from any vocal melody placed on the top. (If a guitar accompaniment gets too intricate it can seem more interesting than the melody, which in a song is not desirable, and of course makes the song hard to play and sing at the same time.) Listen for the close-interval 'harp' effects in many of the bars where notes sound simultaneously only a tone or semi-tone apart.

Songwriting tip 12

A song can mix arpeggiated or finger-picked passages, where there is singing, with strummed sections for dynamic contrast.

CD track 12 DADGBD

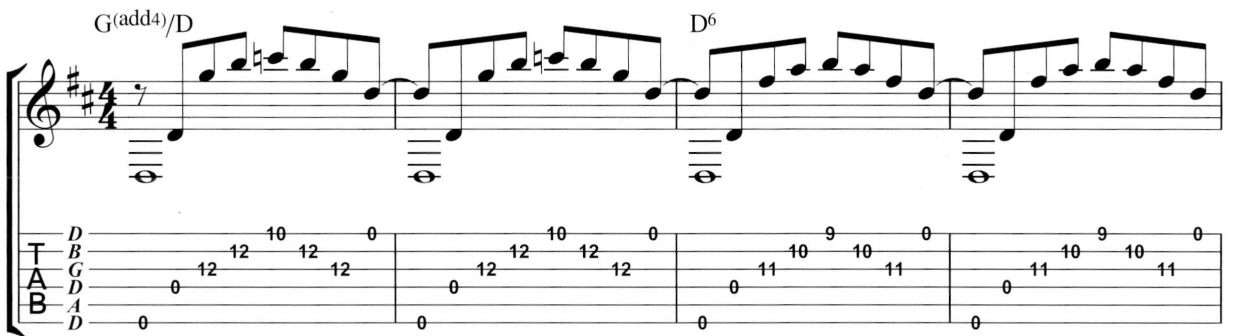

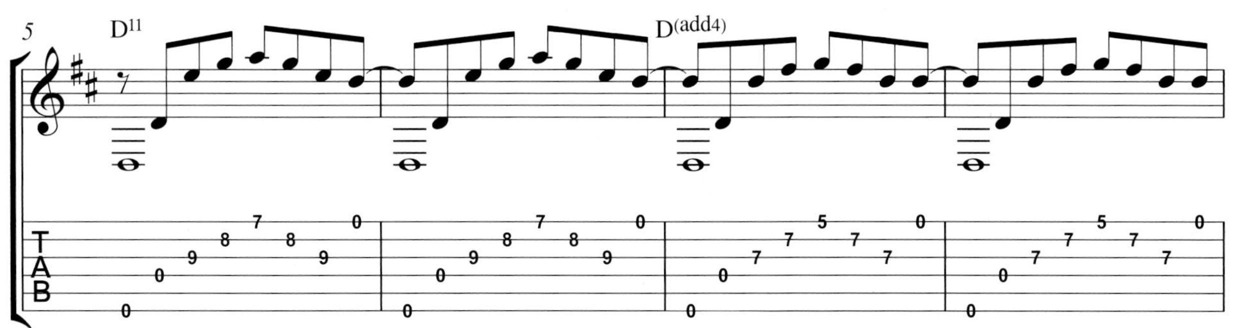

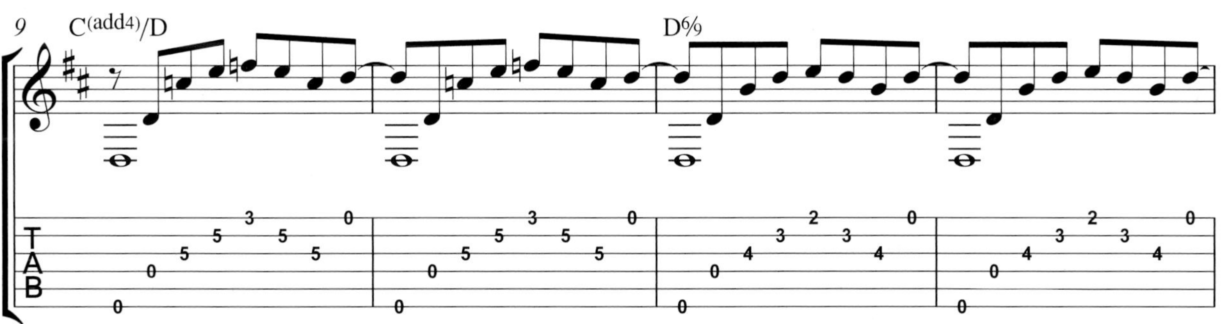

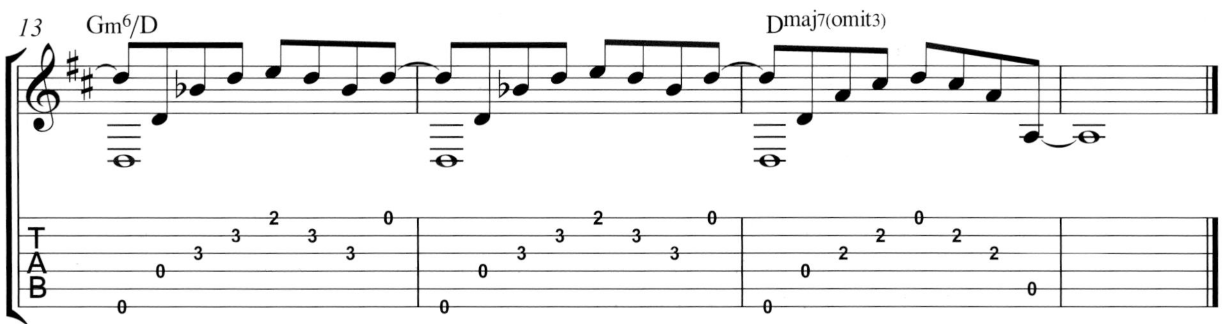

CD track 13 DADF♯BE

Lute drop D

Changes:	-2 x x -1 x x
Pitches:	D A D F♯ B E
Profile:	7 5 4 5 5
3rds	3+4
5ths	5+6
6ths	2+4, 3+5
Octaves	4+6
Open triads	Bm (2+3+4), D (3+4+5)

This tuning combines the 'lute' tuning and 'drop D' tuning alterations from **Section Three**. The open strings feature a Bm triad and D; the lower three strings make a D5. This signals that the tuning is pitched between D major, B minor, but E minor and G major will be fruitful keys. It can also be considered a variation on open D tuning and has a sweet and pleasing sound.

CD track 13
DADF♯BD

CD track 13 begins with a change from the open-string sound of the first D chord to the entirely barred F6, with the top note staying in position. The Cmaj7 is typical of altered tuning chords in having a unison within it – the two Bs, one the open string 2 and the other fretted on string 3. Unisons add 'ring' to chords. A few altered tunings (we will meet several in this book) actually have an in-built unison because they have two bass strings tuned to the same note. Chord voicings also occasionally occur with three notes at the same pitch.

The intro sequence is I-♭III three times, followed by II-♭VII, a progression nicely balanced between a blues-inflected harmony and major key harmony. What could be a verse starts with another typical altered tuning technique: constructing a melody or accompaniment figure from a sequence of parallel intervals with the lower strings as a drone support. The likeliest intervals for this purpose will be thirds, sixths, and octaves. With thirds or sixths (which characterise vocal harmony) you could sing one of the notes and have the guitar harmonise with the other. In example 13 there are two bars on D during which thirds move up and down on strings 1 and 2. Each time this phrase is followed by a bar of Gm and then an A, giving a I-IVm-V sequence (a romantic variation on the I-IV-V three-chord trick). The altered tuning facilitates the interval melody phrase and the colouration of the IVm and V as extended chords.

The sound changes when we reach the Bmadd4. In bars 9-10 the fretting hand forms the shape of a perfect fifth with a hint of the open strings above it. The fifth has a bare, stark sound which contrasts with the sweeter chords previously heard. Experiment with hitting the open strings above such a fifth shape and moving it around. Bars 11-12 move up the neck on another 'fifth' shape, first at XII on D, then descending via the X and IX positions. During these bars the open string 3 F♯ resounds as a common note. The progression is rounded off with a reprise of the rising third idea. This third idea could be further developed by moving it higher up the neck.

Songwriting tip 13

Melodies which move up and down by scale-steps lend themselves to being harmonised by thirds, whether as backing vocals or on an instrument.

CD track 14 EADF♯BD

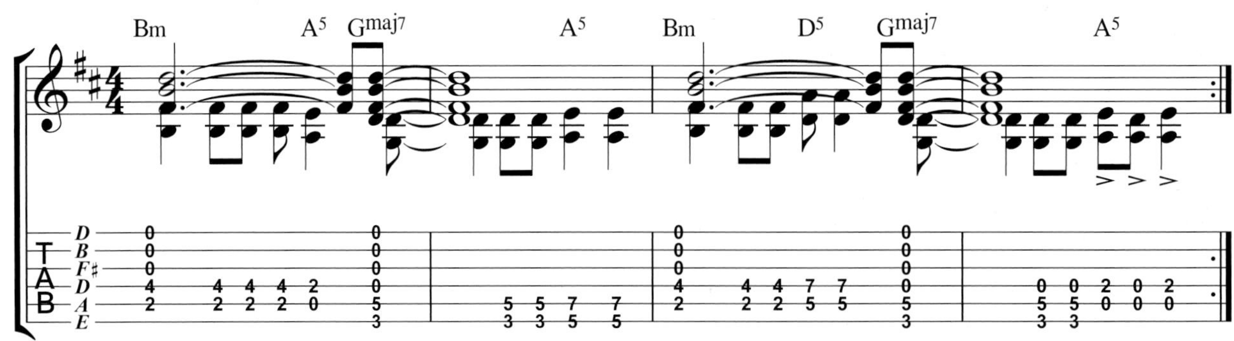

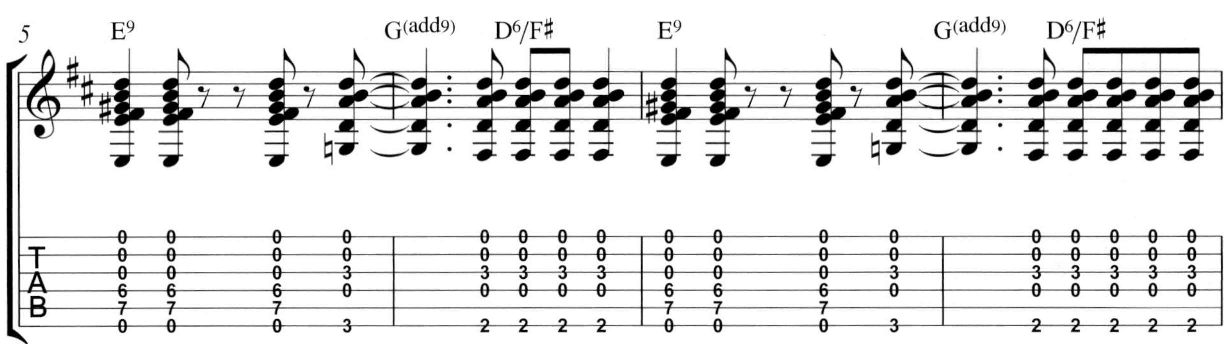

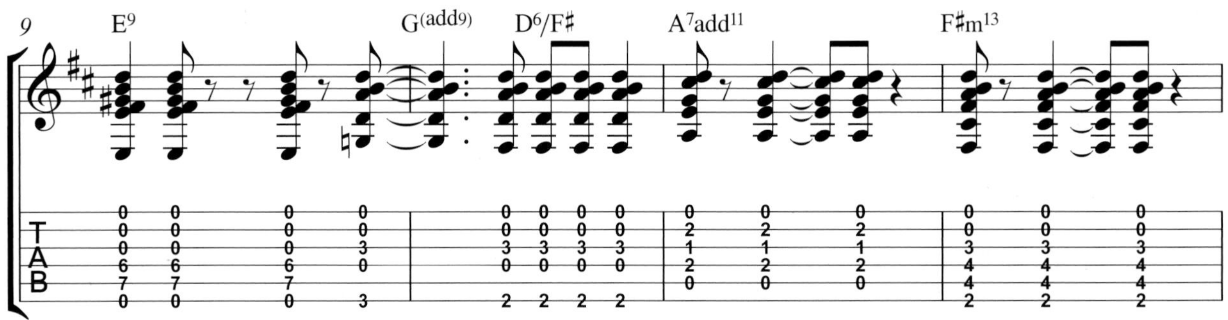

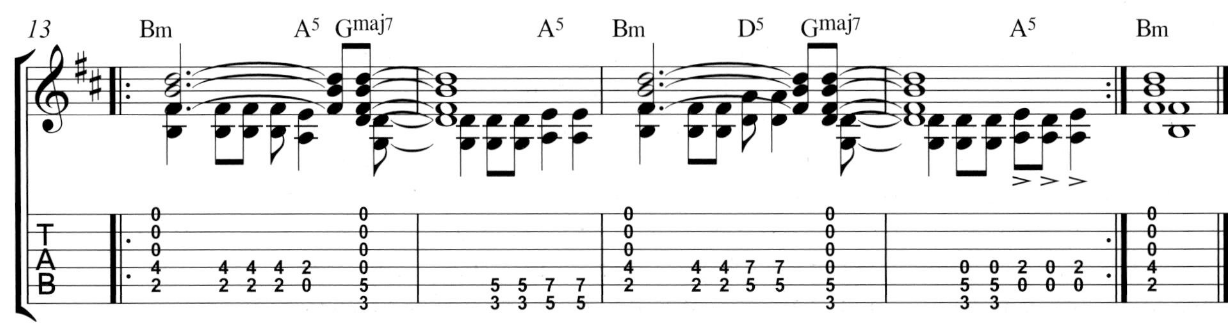

Lute top drop D

Changes:	x x x -1 x -2
Pitches:	E A D F♯ B D
Profile:	5 5 4 5 3
3rds	1+2, 3+4
5ths	-
6ths	1+3, 2+4, 3+5
Octaves	1+4
Triads	Bm (1+2+3), Bm (2+3+4), D (3+4+5)

This tuning combines 'lute tuning' with 'top drop D'. Unlike the previous tuning, this one is more rooted in E major or minor, or B minor, than D because of string 6 still being E. It will also create some expressive chords and changes if you treat the two changes to the tuning as new notes in old shapes, as well as building new ones around them. A single finger at the second fret of string 5 turns all six strings into an add ninth (no third), which can then make an easy barre shape for this type of chord.

In a similar manner to CD track 13, CD track 14 provides another instance of taking a standard fifth shape and moving it around, hitting the upper strings occasionally and letting them ring. The basic progression is I-VII-VI (in B minor: Bm-A-G), which is a very common sequence, especially in melodic rock songs. What the tuning does is give this almost cliched sequence a f resh sound. Bars 5-12 could be a verse, if 1-4 are considered the main riff/chorus. Harmonically the music takes a new slant with the E9 chord (IV^ in a minor key). As this section stays with major chords until the last bar, the F♯m chord, which enters in bar 12 to lead back to the riff, is more striking. It makes good use of the top two open strings to add a sixth and an eleventh to the chord.

Songwriting tip 14

The progression I-VII-VI in a minor key is one of the most frequently used in rock. If you write a song with it, give yours more character by inserting another chord into the sequence on some of its repeats.

CD track 15
EADF♯BD

CD track 15 is a different way of using this tuning. This chord progression takes advantage of the fact that a barre 'E' shape, which in standard tuning would provide a major chord, here creates a minor seventh chord. In bars 1-4 this chord is moved about to create a mildly jazzy sequence. In an altered tuning, barre chords invite you to be chromatic in your chord changes because there is less effort involved compared to in standard tuning. Notice that on the last beat of each of bars 1-4 the finger is lifted just to enhance the chord with the top two open strings (B and D) before the change to the next minor seventh.

The key at this point is slightly ambiguous; I have chosen to hear the Am7 chord as a chromatic chord in B minor. At bar five the music could be interpreted as having changed key to G (Em is IV in B minor but VI in G major and forms a stepping stone), a change strengthened by the more relaxed feel of the sixth/ninth and major seventh chord types. Notice also that these shapes have open strings in them, unlike bars 1-4. At bar 8 the extended F chord takes the sequence back into B minor with a highly unorthodox change. The chords do at least have a common note: the root note of Bm is the ♯11 of F.

CD track 15
EADF♯BD

Songwriting tip 15

Use minor seventh chords instead of minor to dilute the gloom and sadness of having several minor chords in a progression.

I	V	VIIm	IV [VI]	
Bm7 / / /	F♯m7 / / /	Am7 / / /	Em7 / / /	:‖ [x3]
IV	I	IV	♭VII	
Cmaj9 / / /	Gmaj7 / / /	Cmaj9 / / /	F13♯11 / / /	‖
I	V	VIIm	V	I
Bm7 / / /	F13♯11 / / /	Bm7 / / /	F13♯11 / / /	Bm ‖

CHORDS: CD track 15
EADF♯BD

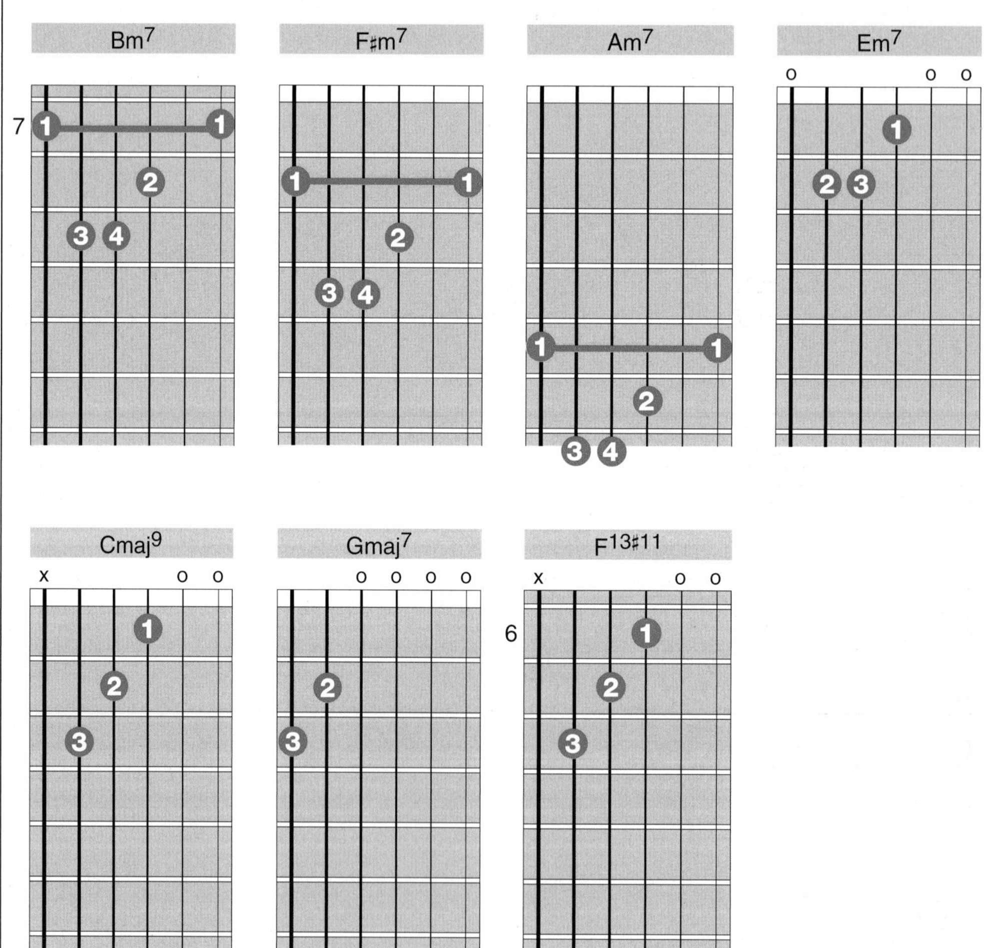

Em7add11

Changes:	x x x x -2 -2
Pitches:	E A D G A D
Profile:	5 5 5 2 5
3rds	-
5ths	1+3, 2+4
6ths	-
Octaves	1+4
Triads	-

This tuning brings the top two strings down a tone from standard tuning. It results in an open Em7add11 chord, the same as standard tuning, except the fifth of the chord (B) is missing. This tuning transforms many chord shapes for playing in the keys of C major, E minor, A minor, and G major. The absence of the open F♯ present in the previous two tunings makes it marginally harder to write in B minor or D major. As the altered notes are at the top of the tuning conventional chord shapes from standard tuning are given a new identity by the addition of A and D.

CD track 16 is another instance of the arpeggiation of an open tuning to generate an accompaniment or a link passage. Arpeggiation (playing the notes of a chord one at a time instead of together) emphasises the flavour of the

CD track 16
EADGAD

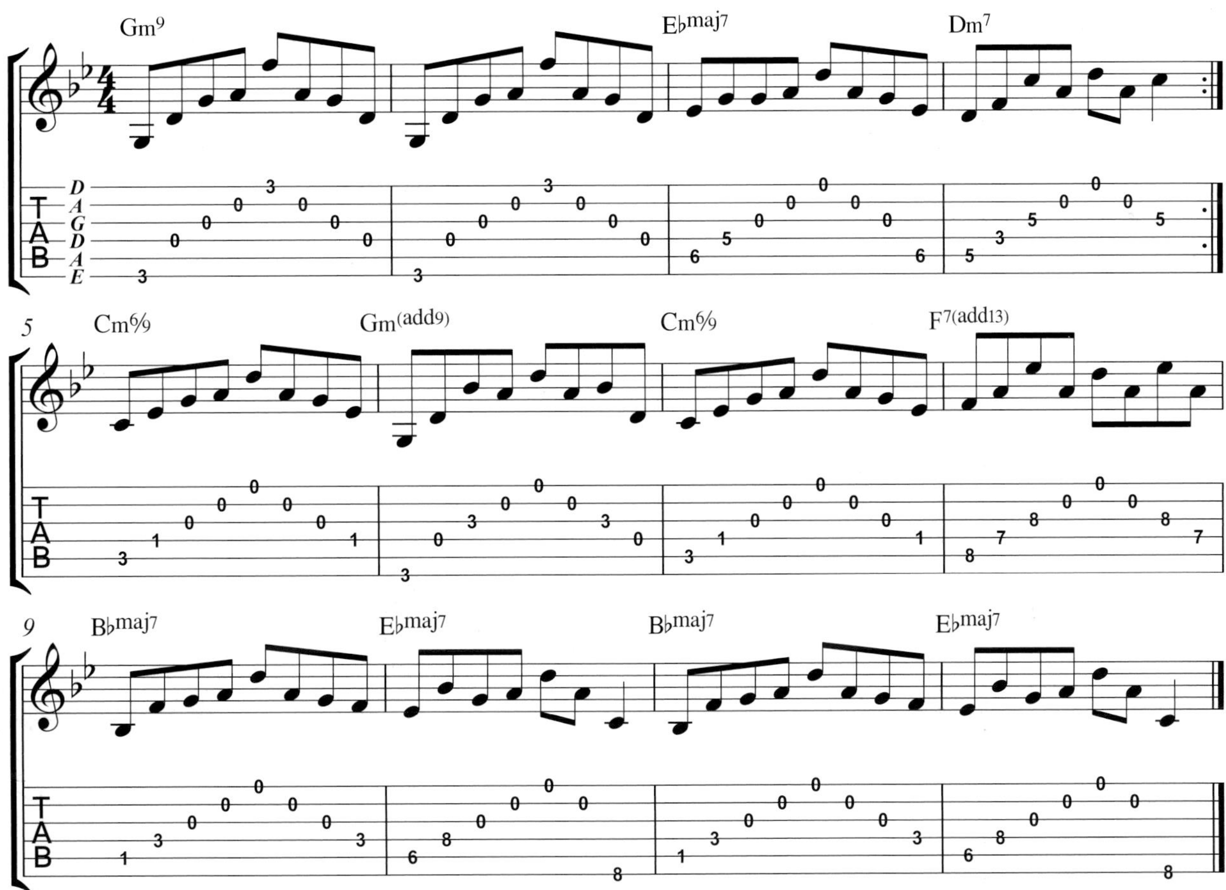

individual combination of strings in a tuning. Bars 1-4 are I-VI-V in G minor, then the progression goes IV-VI-IV-V-I-IV-I-IV in B♭ major. The chords sound edgy and sinister in G minor but the I-IV change at the close is altogether warmer because of the major sevenths.

Songwriting tip 16

Increase the contrast between one song section and another by selecting a predominance of one type of chord in one section – such as sixths and ninths – and a different type in another section – such as major sevenths.

CD track 17
EADGAD

I	IV	Vm	♭VII
E7add11 / / /	Asus4 / / /	Bm7 / / /	D/F♯ / / /

I	IV	V	♭III
E7add11 / / /	A11 / / /	B11(no3rd) / / /	Gadd9 / / / :‖

I ♭VI	I ♭VI	I ♭VI	V	I
‖: E7add11 / C6/9 /	D/F♯ / C6/9 /	E7add11 / C6/9 /	B11(no3rd) / / / :‖	E7add11 ‖

CD track 17 is a strummed sequence using some simple shapes with plenty of open-string resonance. The type of chord creates a pleasing tension and drama. The absence of simple majors and minors means there is a feeling throughout of things not being resolved (and there's a possible topic for a lyric). The first section of eight bars would make a verse and the second section of four bars repeated would make a suitable chorus. The first section is a blues-inflected E major (notice the prominent E7add11) with chord V unusually featuring as a minor. This is an example of what in *How To Write Songs On Guitar* I term the 'mixolydian song', with a minor chord V and a ♭VII chord appearing with the usual chords in a major key. Notice how the B11 is a full barre which closes off the open strings providing a contrast of guitar sound. I think of such a shape as a 'masking' chord because it masks the open string sound that identifies that particular open tuning.

Songwriting tip 17

Inversions such as D/F♯ help to create movement in a chord progression, because the bass note is keen to rise a step or fall a step to the bass note of the next chord.

CHORDS: CD track 17
EADGAD

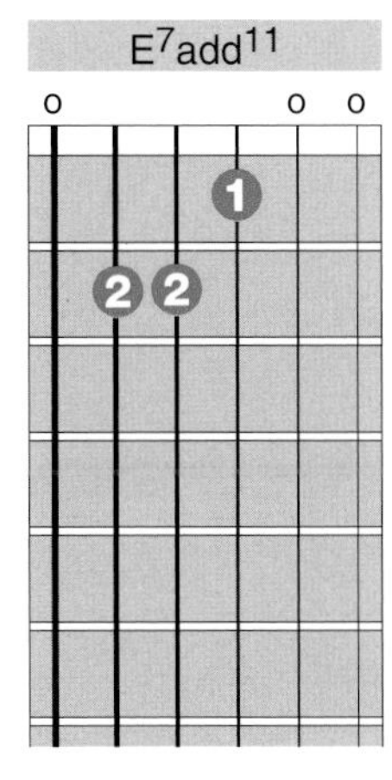

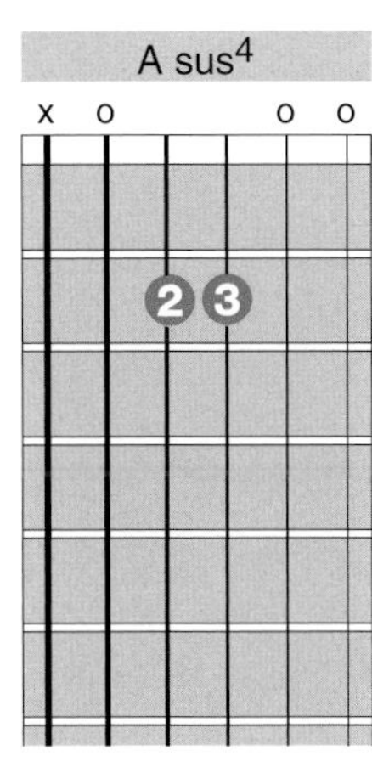

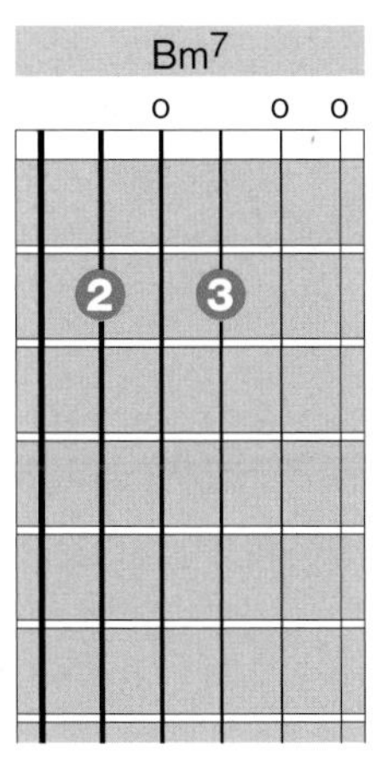

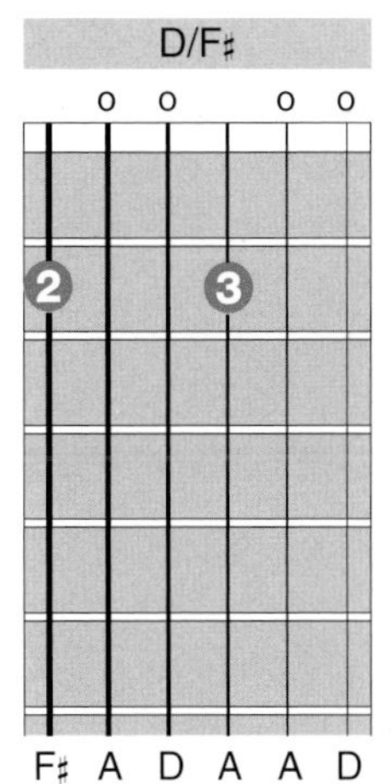

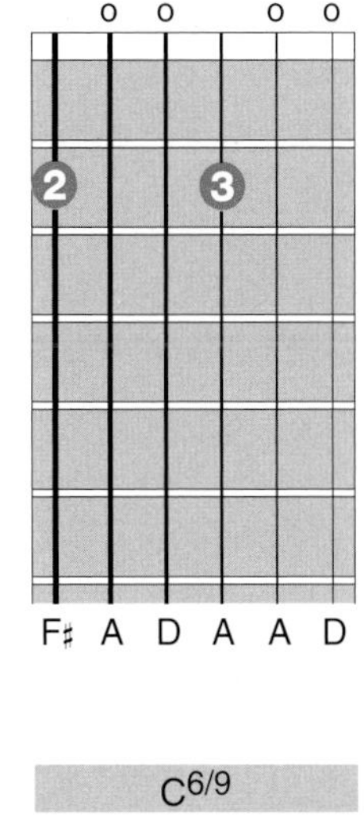

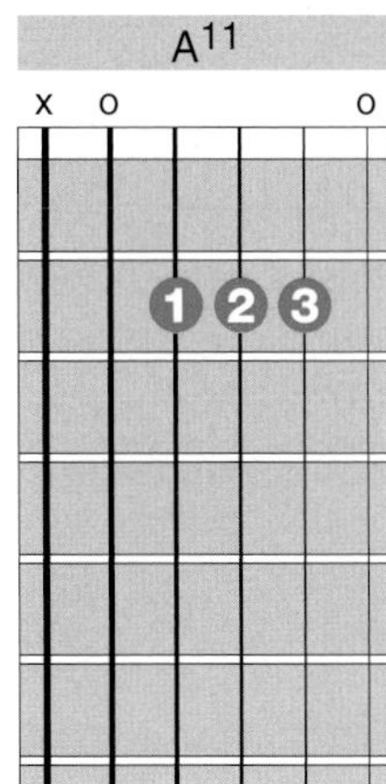

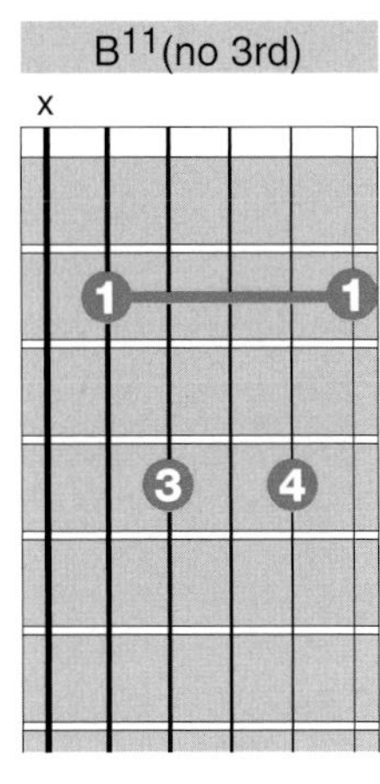

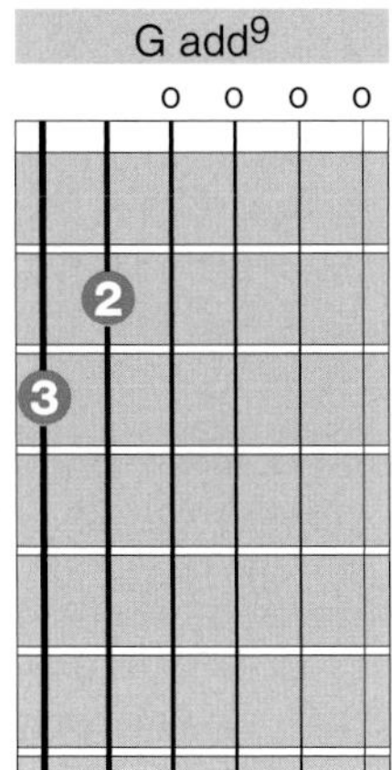

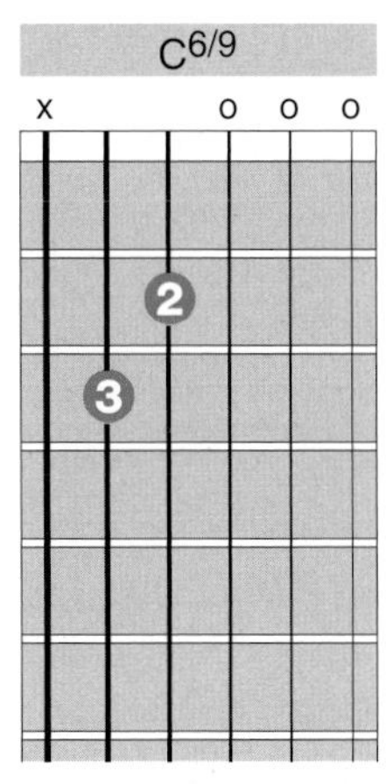

SECTION 5
OPEN MAJOR TUNINGS

"You're twiddling and you find the tuning. Now the left hand has to learn where the chords are, because it's a whole new ballpark, right? So you're groping around, looking for where the chords are, using very simple shapes. Put it in a tuning and you've got four chords immediately – open, barre five, barre seven, and your higher octave, like half-fingering on the 12th. Then you've got to find where your minors are and where the interesting colours are – that's the exciting part." (Joni Mitchell)

In the previous two sections we've seen that changing one or two strings can result in a guitar tuning sufficiently different from standard to spark new ideas. Now it's time to go one step further, into a group of tunings which for many guitarists define what altered tunings are about. An open tuning can be defined as one which, when you strum the strings, sounds a major or minor chord. The most popular open tunings are major. This section features six such major open tunings.

Open tunings share certain properties regardless of pitch. The first thing to grasp is that a barre with finger 1 will, in an open major tuning, give a major chord at each fret. This means between the open strings and fret 12 a major chord is available as a barre for every note. Not all of these major chords are of equal importance to the songwriter because they do not all belong in the key(s) suggested by the tuning. In any open major tuning the following chords are available and these are the ones a songwriter will be drawn to:

0	1	2	3	4	5	6	7	8	9	10	11	12
I		II^	♭III	III^	IV		V	♭VI	VI^	♭VII		I
G		A	B♭	B	C		D	E♭	E	F		G

If the tuning is taken as the key the open strings and fret 12 give chord I, the key chord. At fret five there is chord IV and at fret seven chord V. These three major chords comprise the songwriter's 'three-chord trick'; they are also the three chords used in a 12-bar blues or rock'n'roll song. So by simply playing a barre at the fifth and seventh frets, plus using the open strings, you can write a three-chord song. Of the remaining chords those at frets three, eight, and ten are flat degree chords – chords not truly in key but possible in songwriting, especially for songs with a blues or rock character. They combine well with the three major chords.

For an instant blues riff in a major open tuning strum the open strings, then barre at the fifth fret, then barre at the third fret (the sequence is I-IV-♭III). For more of a classic pop sequence combine any of the reverse polarity chords (marked ^ at the second, fourth and ninth fret) with the three normal majors of the key. A I-II^-IV-V sequence can be played with frets zero-two-five-seven; a I-III^-IV-V with frets zero-four-five-seven; and a I-VI^-IV-V with frets zero-nine-five-seven. These reverse polarity chords are the three which, to be correctly in key, should be minor. They might still be found in their minor form in a major open tuning but they cannot be played as minors with only a barre, and it is typical of open major tunings that minor chords are not always to hand. (It is often easier to find an extended minor like a seventh, ninth or 11th, than a plain minor.) All of these chords work when playing with a bottleneck; the bottleneck acts as a finger 1 barre. Play at frets three, five, seven, ten and 12 for a blues feel, and instead of strumming all the strings, play limited combinations of them. These chord relationships and positions in an open major tuning transcend factors such as the pitch of the strings, the harmonic mix of roots, thirds and fifths, or the interval profile.

A small drawback to what initially seems the brilliant simplicity of an open major tuning is that such chord voicing is ruled by parallel motion. When you go from one chord to another with a barre all notes move in the same direction, which is functional rather than elegant. However, the inner movement of notes within chord-changes on the guitar even in standard tuning tends to be inconsistent at the best of times with full chord shapes, rather than the pared-down voicings of jazz guitar. The inelegancies of parallel motion largely go unnoticed beneath a voice, other instruments, and on top of a beat.

The next step is to see what can be done to decorate or add notes to this one-finger barre to get other chord shadings. This leads into various riffs which, in open G and open E, are a mainstay of the guitar-work of Keith Richards (with The Rolling Stones), Ron Wood (with The Faces), and Joni Mitchell when she plays in open D. Several of this book's CD tracks make this evident. Another technique is to hold down the lower three strings with fingers 2, 3, and 4 at the same fret. As you move this shape from fret to fret the top three open strings make new harmonic relationships, and therefore a different type of chord, with the three fretted notes.

Open G	
Changes:	-2 -2 x x x -2
Pitches:	D G D G B D
Profile:	5 7 5 4 3
3rds	1+2, 2+3
5ths	1+3, 4+5
6ths	2+4
Octaves	1+4, 3+5, 4+6
Triads	G (1+2+3), G (2+3+4)

To take the guitar into open G from standard tuning strings 6, 5, and 1 are detuned, each by a tone (whole step). (An open G tuning could also be made by taking string 6 up to G, string 5 up to B, and string 1 up to G, but string 1 might break and the increased tension would be bad for the guitar neck.) If you write a song in G, chord I is the open top five strings or a barre at fret 12; chord IV (C) is at fret five, and chord V (D) is at fret 7. Two other chords significant for blues / rock are the ♭III major chord at fret three (B♭) and the chord on the flattened seventh at fret 10 (F). Primed with these chords and a bottleneck you should get some authentic blues riffs going.

As the root note of this tuning is on string 5 rather than string 6, some players leave string 6 as E (an open Em7 tuning, a variant on the open Em7 featured later) or, as in the case of Keith Richards, take the string 6 off altogether. Another option is a 'high bass' version of open G tuned GBDGBD, in which string 6 has been tuned up three semitones to G, and string 5 two semitones up to B. This is sometimes called 'Dobro open G'. Stone Gossard of Pearl Jam sometimes plays a variation of open G in which string 6 is tuned up to a G in unison with string 5.

Famous songs that use open G include many by The Rolling Stones including 'Honky Tonk Women', 'Moonlight Mile', 'Brown Sugar', 'Start Me Up' (key centre C), 'Tumbling Dice' (key centre B, capo IV), as well as The Black Crowes' 'Hard To Handle', Bad Company's 'Can't Get Enough of Your Love', and Jeff Buckley's 'Last Goodbye'. Open G is a favoured tuning for folk-style playing, of which Paul McCartney's 'Blackbird' and Led Zeppelin's 'That's The Way' (though that was detuned a semitone to G♭) are instances. Led Zeppelin's 'When The Levee Breaks' was recorded in open G tuning and then slowed down to put it in F; to play along with the CD would mean tuning to an open F major of CFCFAC.

If open G is tuned up a tone it produces open A, a popular electric tuning (EAEAC♯E). This was used for Led Zeppelin's version of 'In My Time Of Dying', and the guitar parts for their 'Celebration Day' include a slide guitar tuned to open A.

Open G lends itself to good-time rock'n'roll. It has been an integral part of Keith Richards' rhythm playing for The Rolling Stones, defining the sound of their music from the late 1960s on. One of the milestones for most guitarists is the first time they put the guitar into open G and hit the chords to 'Brown Sugar' or 'Start Me Up'. Both songs are actually in the key of C not G, an example of what is called 'cross-tuning', where the tuning is to another chord in the key you compose in, often chord IV or V. Ry Cooder played 'Tattler' from

CD track 18 DGDGBD

his *Paradise And Lunch* album in the key of D in open G tuning. David Wilcox uses open C to play in the key of G, or G in DADGAD. Wilcox has said, "I think that there are some wonderful voicings you get when you play in an open tuning outside of its tonic centre, and I really love using a major-key open tuning but playing it so that the song is in the key of the chord that's maybe on the second fret, so it comes out in a sort of modal, minor, fun thing."

CD track 18 shows some classic rock rhythm ideas in the key of G in open G. The form is an extended 12-bar. The first ten bars are what you would expect from a 12-bar but it is extended by four bars to 14, with four more bars of riff following. These shapes also work on acoustic.

Songwriting tip 18

When linking chords into song sequences think rhythmically as well as harmonically. Don't always settle for a regular strum-pattern. Play the chords with rhythmic emphasis, accent some, leave gaps between them. Such rhythmic elements can be a hook in themselves.

CD track 19
DGDGBD

I		iiIV				iiIV	
G /	G9 /	Gmaj7(no3rd) /	Cadd9/G /	G /	G9 /	Gmaj7(no 3rd) /	Cadd9/G /

V	II	VI	IV	V
‖: Em9 / / /	A13 (no 3rd) / / /	Em9 / / /	Cmaj7 /	D / :‖

I							
G /	G9 /	G6(no 3rd) /	G9 /	G /	G9 /	G6(no 3rd) /	G9 / ‖

For contrast, CD track 19 is an acoustic chord sequence in open G. The chords in bars one and two are made by moving the interval of a sixth, on strings 2 and 4, down from the seventh fret over a G pedal note. These are three colourations of a G chord, and a second inversion C. After the first four bars the Em9 enters as a strong contrast. Chords IV and V lead the progression back to the opening sequence (the D chord takes advantage of the detuned string 6), except in this case the bass guitar plays different root notes under those shapes to give them a different quality. The bass plays G-D-C-D which implies a I-V-IV-V sequence.

CHORDS: CD track 19
DGDGBD

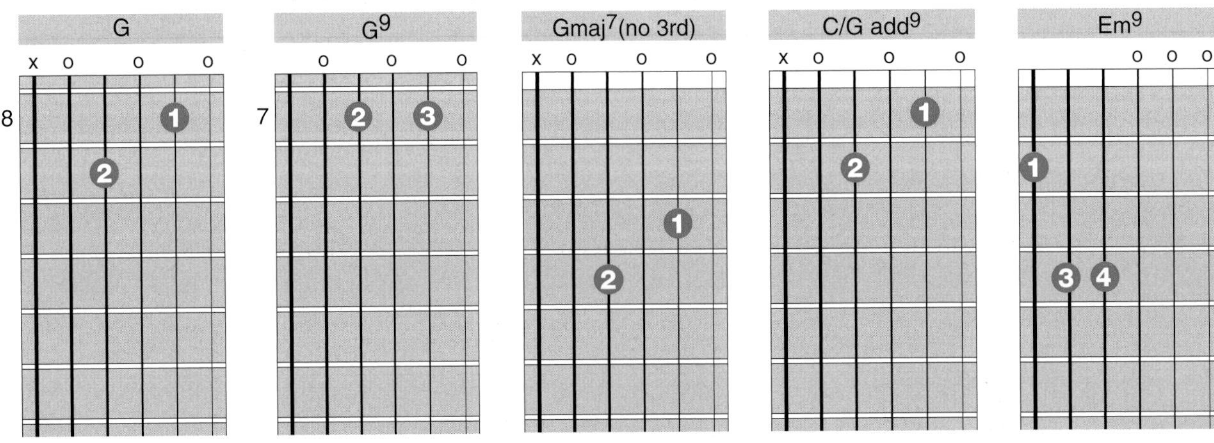

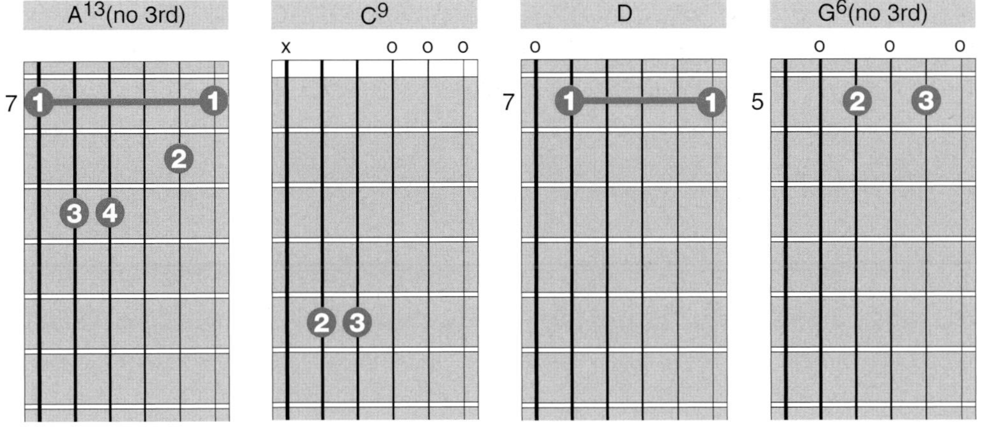

Songwriting tip 19

A chord progression can be given additional musical life by changing the bass notes underneath it.

Open D

Changes:	-2 x x -1 -2 -2
Pitches:	D A D F♯ A D
Profile:	7 5 4 3 5
3rds	2+3, 3+4
5ths	2+4, 4+6
6ths	1+3, 2+4
Octaves	2+5, 4+6
Triads	D (1+2+3), D (2+3+4), D (3+4+5)

This is probably the next most popular open tuning after open G. Open D has a characteristic deep sound which is more pronounced than open G owing to the fact that the root position open major chord has six notes. The open E form (a tone higher, EBEG♯BE), also known as 'Sebastopol' tuning, occurs frequently in blues / rock material, including The Black Crowes' 'She Talks To Angels', The Police's 'Next To You', Pearl Jam's 'Even Flow', 'Garden', and 'Deep' from their *Ten* album, and The Allman Brothers' 'Little Martha'. Other songs transcribed as open D are Stephen Stills' 'Love The One You're With', and Joni Mitchell's 'Big Yellow Taxi' (capo II as open E) and 'Both Sides Now'. In terms of slide guitar, open A has been characterised as 'rural' in sound and open E 'urban'.

An interesting variation on this tuning is to tune a semitone higher as open E♭: E♭ B♭ E♭ G B♭ E♭ (-1 +1 +1 x -1 -1). This requires more detuning than going from standard to open D but the distances are smaller.

CD track 20 follows on from track 18, except this time it uses the rock rhythm shapes found in the playing of Ron Wood. He does this type of playing in open E in songs like 'Stay With Me' (The Faces), a tone higher than open D. The 'on-off' shapes are similar to those in open G but occur one string lower. The opening four bars also reveal that this tuning has lyrical possibilities too, before the rock rhythm comes in on a C chord at tenth position. Bars one to four could therefore be developed in another direction, into a song more like a

CD track 20 DADF♯AD

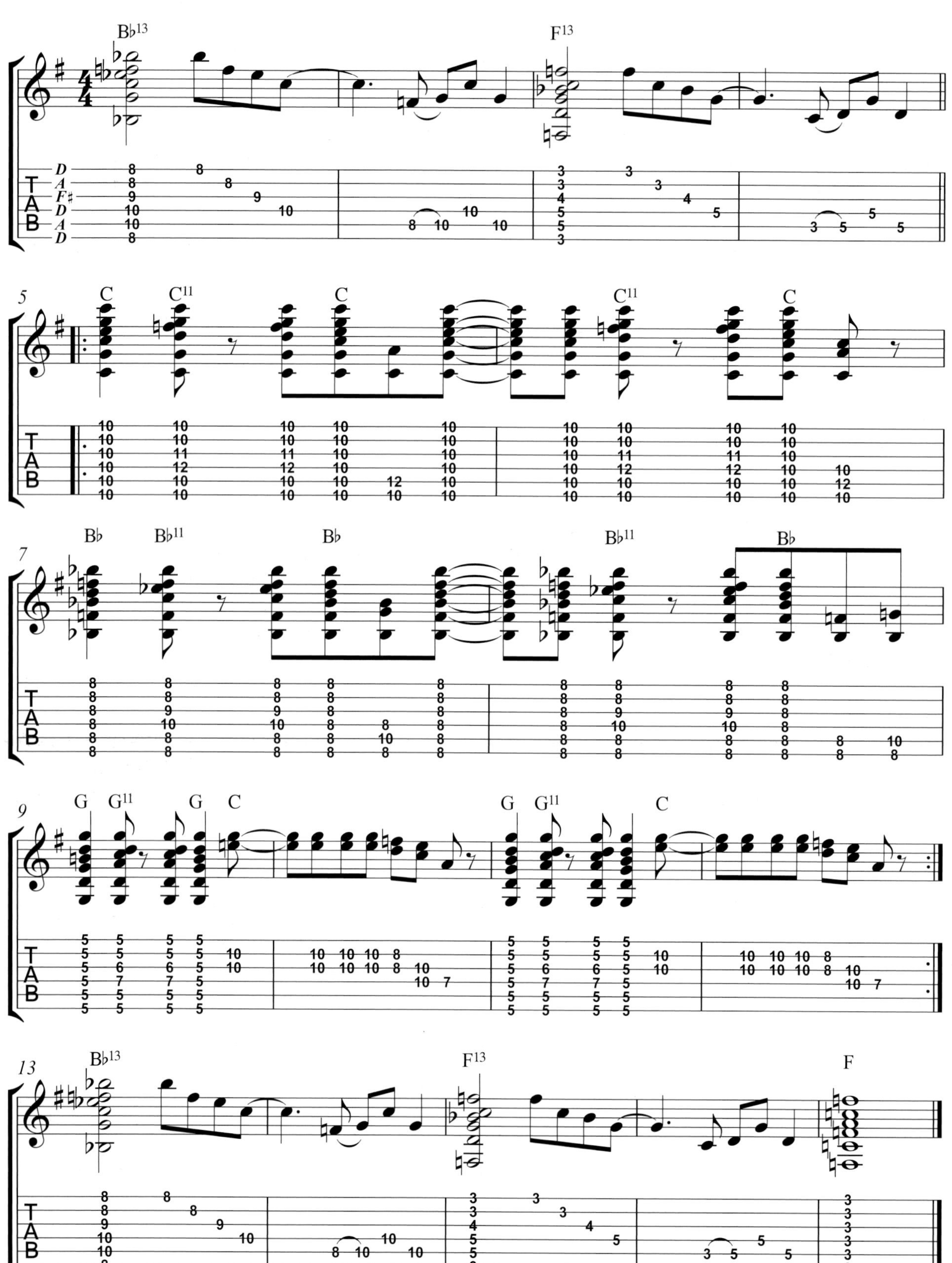

ballad. The blues-rock sound is also achieved by the IV-♭III-I progression (C-B♭-G). (You'll find more guitar like this on Rod Stewart's album *Never A Dull Moment* and The Faces' *A Nod's As Good As A Wink …*)

Songwriting tip 20

Open major tunings offer the chance to contrast straight majors with more complex chords not customarily heard in a rock context. The harmonic contrast of the chord types is strengthened by the gradations of timbre between simple chords entirely fretted and others that mix open strings with fretted strings.

CD track 21
DADF♯AD

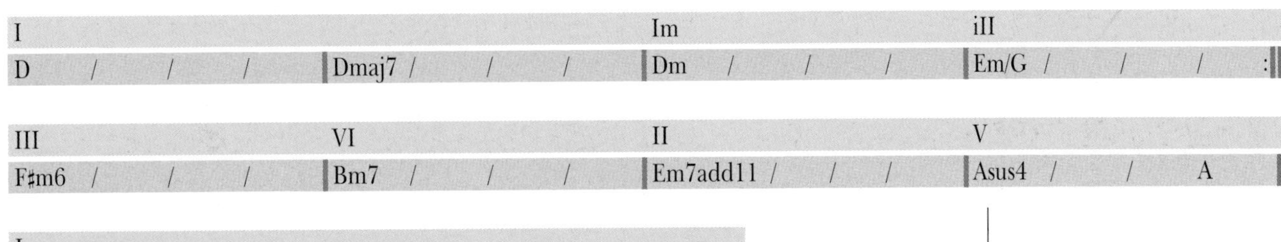

I		Im	iII
D / / /	Dmaj7 / / /	Dm / / /	Em/G / / / :‖
III	VI	II	V
F♯m6 / / /	Bm7 / / /	Em7add11 / / /	Asus4 / / A
I			
‖: D11 / D* /	D13(no 3rd) / Dmaj7* / :‖ [x3] D ‖		

CD track 21 draws on the deep resonance of open D tuning. Try it on a clean-sounding electric guitar with a touch of chorus effect, reverb and echo, and you'll hear how the tuning makes a full sound. The minor chords in particular are deeper and more colourful in open D. Notice the sudden darkening of the progression with the Dm at bar 3 and the switch to fretted notes in bar 4. The A chord in bar 8 is a masking chord. (Asterisks distinguish two versions of the same chord.)

Songwriting tip 21

Allow chromatic changes to a single note, going up or down one semitone at a time, within a chord to create a progression. This can be carried through several bars with changes from a plain major or minor chord to its sevenths and sixth.

CHORDS: CD track 21
DADF♯AD
(continued over page)

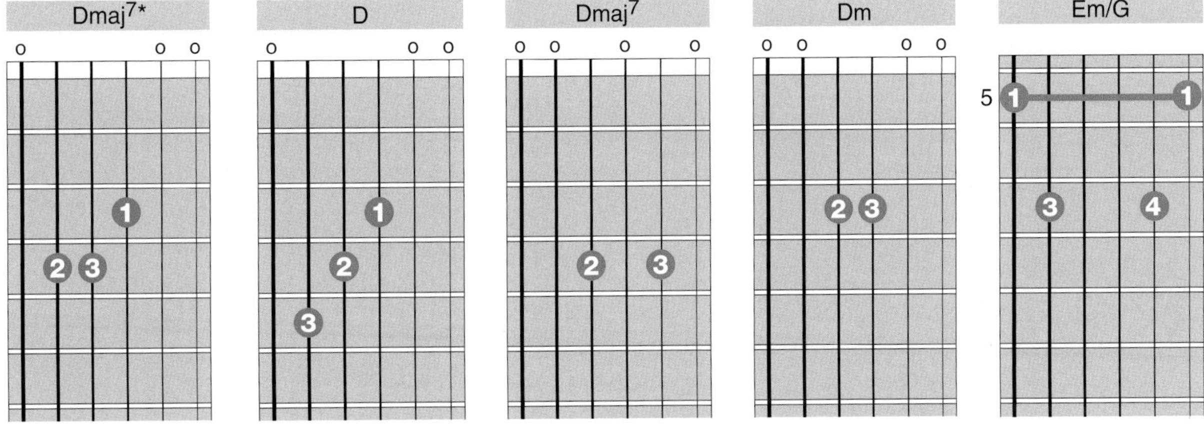

CHORDS: CD track 21
(continued)

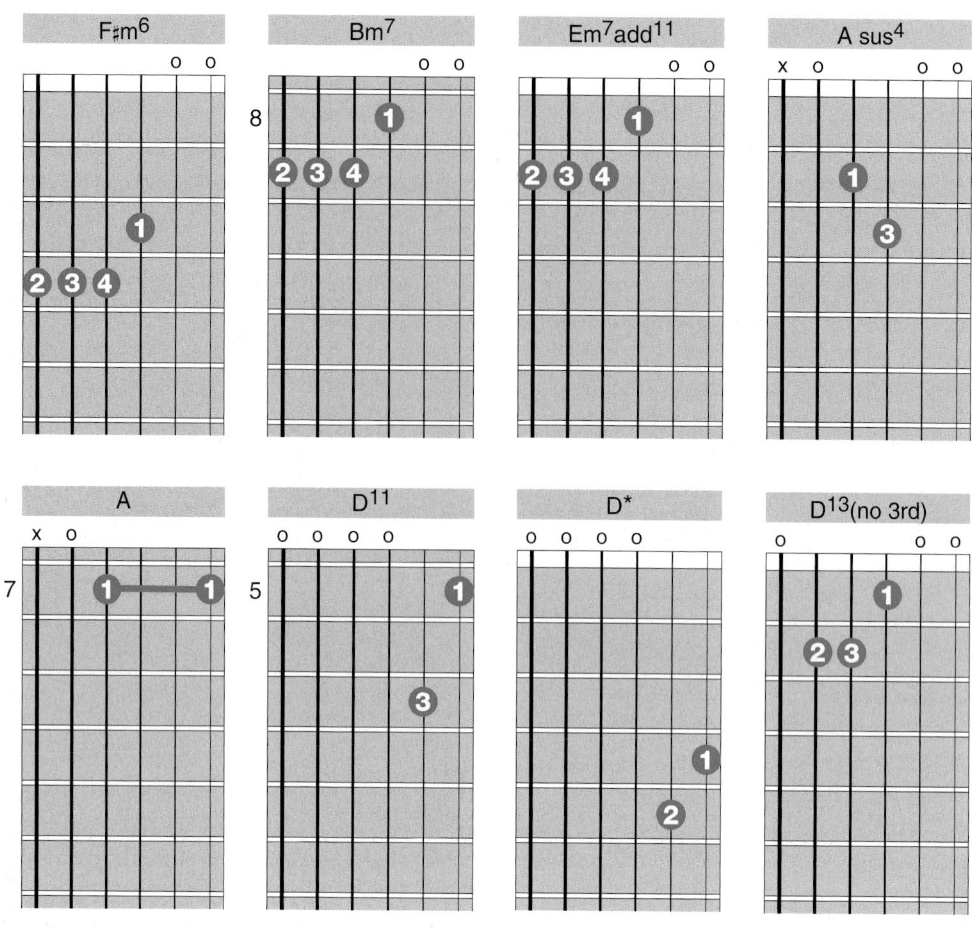

Open C

Changes:	-4 -2 -2 x +1 x
Pitches:	C G C G C E
Profile:	7 5 7 5 4
3rds	1+2
5ths	3+4, 5+6
6ths	1+3
Octaves	2+4, 3+5, 4+6
Triads	C (1+2+3)

Open C is a tuning full of character but which does not entice with immediate rewards in the manner of open G or open D. It was used on two Led Zeppelin songs, 'Friends' and 'Poor Tom', and a track on the Page/Plant album *Walking Into Clarksdale*, 'Most High'. Its identity is determined by two factors: first, the low C string 6, making it sound very deep, and second, the fact that the third of the chord (E) – the note determining whether the tuning is major or minor – is string 1. To my ear that high-placed third lacks sufficient presence to counter-balance the stark effect of the roots and fifths sounding from strings 2-6. This can be compensated for if you add a fretted E on one of the central strings, such as the fret four on string 4. Another approach might be to re-tune to a variant open C tuning such as CGCEGC, as used on the song 'Amelia' by Joni Mitchell, where the third is lower-pitched.

CD track 22 CGCGCE

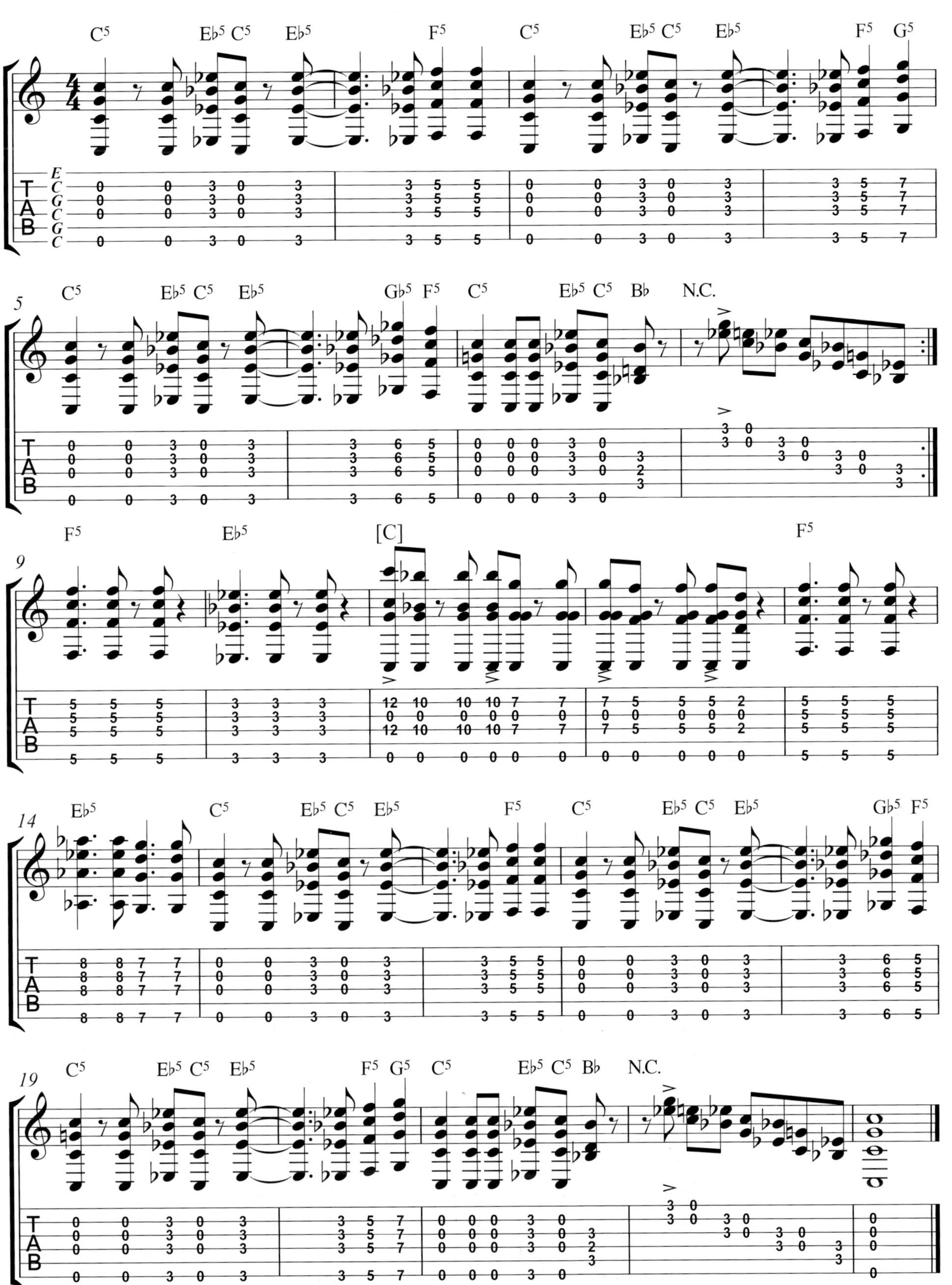

CD track 22 (previous page) utilises the dark tone of the open C tuning through a blues approach. The fingering means that almost all the chords are fifths because the top string isn't being played, which is where the third of each chord is. The opening chord progression is a classic blues I-♭III-I-♭III-IV, with a chromatic ♭V chord on G♭ appearing in bar 7 just before the guitar fill. In bars 11-12 what would have been a straight chord I is made more of a feature by using a C octave figure on strings 2 and 4 descending from the 12th fret.

Songwriting tip 22

Chord changes and riffs can be shaped by the '3+1' formula. Across eight bars this means that bars 1, 3, and 5 contain the same chord or riff component. Bars 2, 4, and 6 are slightly different ways of answering the first idea. Bars 7 to 8 complete the sequence with a new chord or variation; bar 7 might be a variation (for example, in timing) of bar 1.

I		V	VI	
C* / / /	C13* / / /	G / / /	Am7 / / /	
IV	iII	I		
F / / /	Dm/F / / /	C13 / / /	C / / / :‖	
III	IV	III	IV V	
Em7 / / /	Fmaj9(no3rd) / / /	Em7 / / /	Fmaj9(no3rd) / G /	
I			II	
C / / /	C13* / / /	C / / /	/ / C13 /	C ‖

CD track 23
CGCGCE

By contrast with track 22, here the open C tuning yields a melodic major/minor progression. The first eight-bar phrase could easily be a verse, using a I-V-VI-IV-II-I sequence. The four bars that follow could be a pre-chorus and the last four bars the hook of the song. Notice how bars 9-12 avoid chord I in order to make its return for the hook fresh, and how chord voicings modify the C in bar 2. Asterisks differentiate different voicings of the same chord. In an open tuning there is always an abundance of voicings for the chord after which the tuning is named. Alternate tunings also raise puzzles concerning the naming of

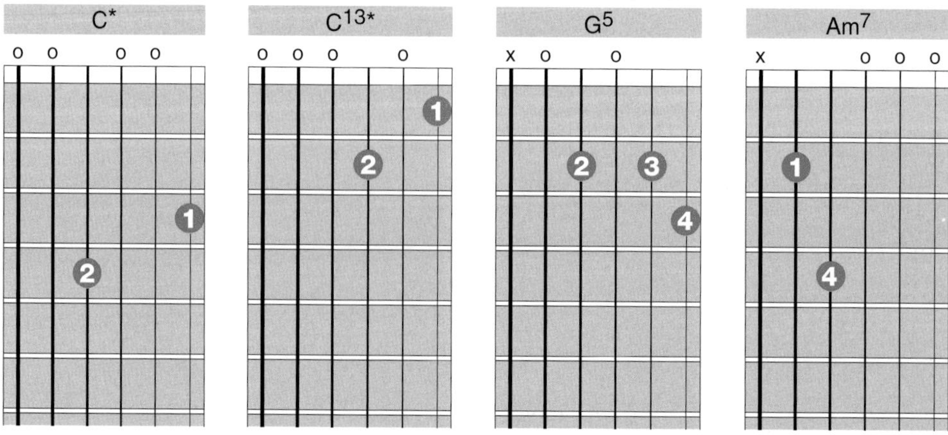

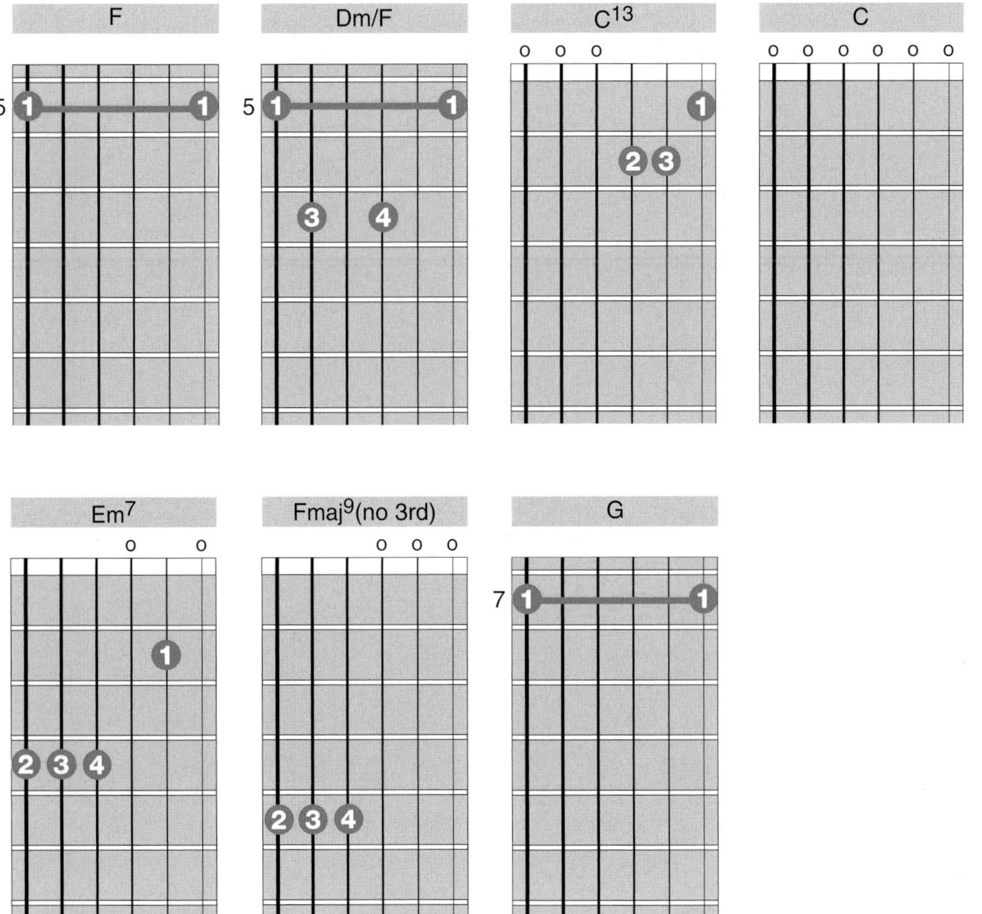

a chord, and show how naming chords sometimes depends on interpretation about what the music is doing. The C13* in bar two (CGCACF) and the C13 in bar seven could alternatively be thought of as an F triad and a Dm triad over a C5 pedal. (As 13ths they are both incomplete, but that is often the case with 13th voicings on the guitar).

Songwriting tip 23

Beginning and ending a verse or verse section with chord I in a major key creates a feeling of arrival, security, coming home. A prechorus to such a verse would be advised to avoid chord I, so that it can be heard with renewed power on its return in the chorus.

'Slack' open A

Changes:	x x -1 -3 -2 x
Pitches:	E A C♯ E A E
Profile:	5 4 3 5 7
3rds	3+4, 4+5
5ths	1+2, 3+5
6ths	2+4, 4+6
Octaves	1+3, 2+5, 3+6
Triads	A (2+3+4), A (3+4+5)

The traditional way to construct an open A tuning is to tune the guitar EAEAC♯E. This is the same interval profile as open G but a tone higher. Alvin Lee of Ten Years After had a variation of this in which string 6 E was tuned down to A giving an octave difference between strings 5 and 6. This open A is acceptable on electric guitar but I would not recommend it for acoustic guitar because of the additional string tension. Alternatively, to get an open A tuning you could capo open G at fret 2 to get the shapes of this tuning. David Wilcox used a variant open A major tuning of EAC♯EAC♯ but that was devised to facilitate playing an instrumental Bach piece, not a song.

Instead of the high tension open A tuning, which would only reproduce the interval profile of open G, I've included a variant 'slack' open A I devised for myself on acoustic guitar, in which the third of the chord (C♯) is on string 4, not string 2, giving a moodier quality than the usual open A. This tuning was used on Pearl Jam's 'Deep'. It generates some effective voicings for F♯m and C♯m, which in standard tuning tend to be barre chords. Notice that strings 6, 5, and 1 remain the same as in standard tuning. This means that the bass root notes of chords will be in the same positions as they would be in standard tuning.

I	VI	IV
A* / / / | A9 / / /	F♯m7 / / /	Dadd9 / / /

I	VI	IVm
A* / / / | A9 / / /	F♯m7 / / /	Dmadd9 / / /

I	VI	iIVm
A* / / / | A9 / / /	F♯m7 / / /	Fmaj7♯5 / / /

V ♭VII	IV	V ♭VII	IV ♭VI
E / G/E /	D/E / / /	E / G/E /	D/E / C6 /

V ♭VII	IV	II	V
E / G/E /	D/E / / /	Bm7 / / /	E11 / / /

I	♭VII	I
‖: A / / /	G6/9 / / / :‖	[x3] A ‖

CD track 24
EAC♯EAE

CD track 24 is a more relaxed set of chord changes taking advantage of the resonant voicings available in this tuning for F♯m, D, and Bm. Notice how the three opening phrases have a different type of D chord in bars 4 and 8. Then for contrast, at bar 13 we get E, G, and D major chords over an E bass note (the G/E could also be interpreted as an Em7). The barre shape in bars 13-17 temporarily masks the ringing open strings heard earlier. Two flat degree chords (D and C) are also used. The A and G variant chords are created by the simple movement of one shape.

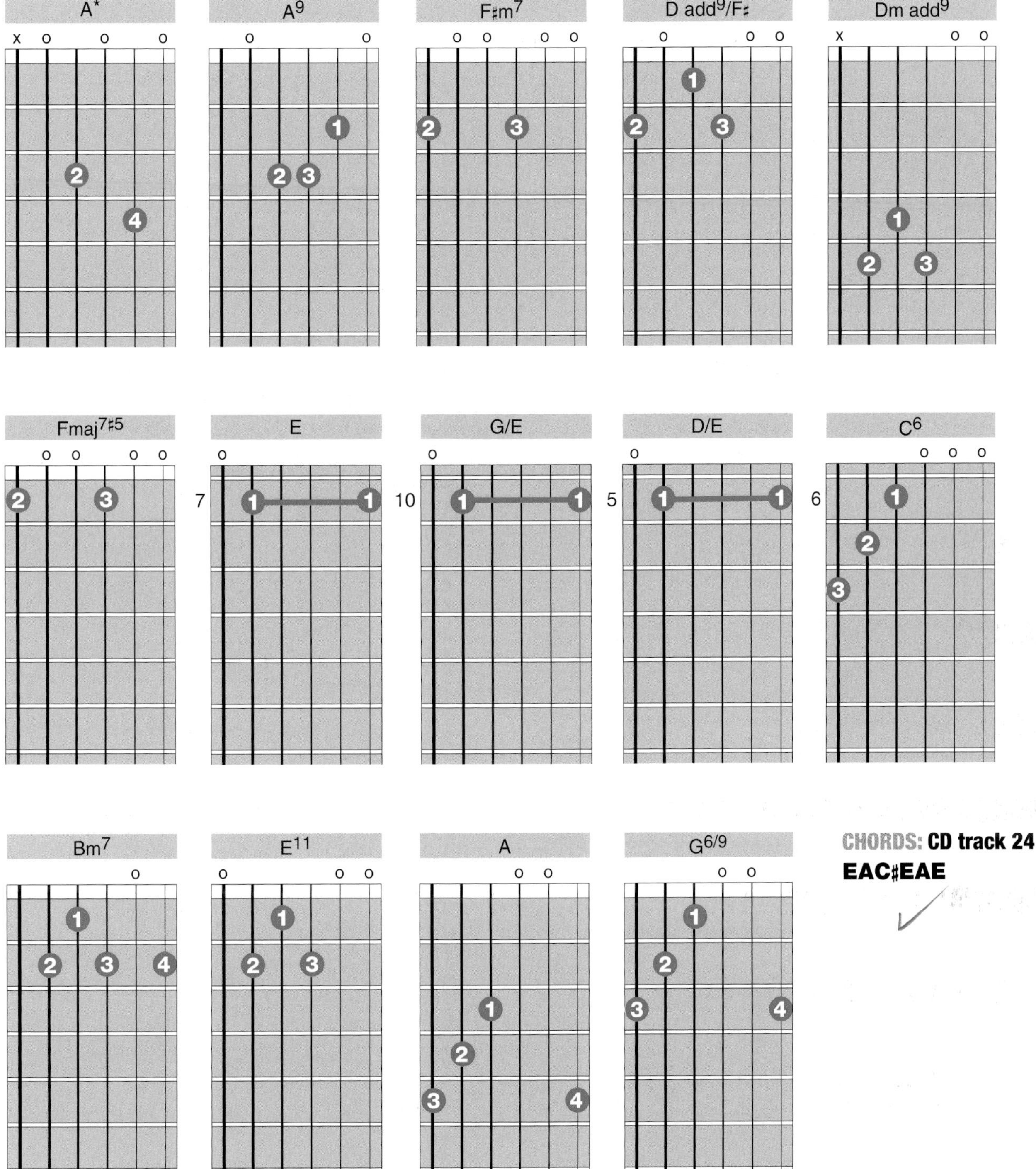

CHORDS: CD track 24
EAC♯EAE

Songwriting tip 24

If the root note of chord V in an open tuning is the open string 6, a song section where chord V is prevalent can be made more interesting by moving a single-finger barre to and from the seventh fret (where chord V will occur) with string 6 as a constant bass. This is an easy method to generate implied chords like elevenths.

'Slack' open E	
Changes:	x -1 -3 -3 x x
Pitches:	E G♯ B E B E
Profile:	4 3 5 7 5
3rds	4+5, 5+6
5ths	2+3, 4+6
6ths	3+5
Octaves	1+3, 2+4, 3+6
Triads	E (3+4+5), E (4+5+6)

This tuning demonstrates the same approach as the previous example to the problem of avoiding increased string tension. The traditional open E tuning is EBEG♯BE (the tuning used by Ron Wood and Chris Rea, mentioned earlier). This has the same interval profile as open D but a tone higher. The blues guitarist Tampa Red used open E and capoed to be in a key favourable to a keyboard player, such as F major. This open E is fine for electric guitar but is risky for acoustic guitar. One solution is to capo open D at the second fret to get the shapes of this tuning at the desired pitch. Alternatively, I devised a variant 'slack' open E where the third (G♯) is on string 5, not string 3. It has an even moodier quality than the 'slack' open A tuning because the third is lower in pitch again. It generates some effective shapes for G♯m and C♯m, which in standard tuning tend to be barre chords.

CD track 25 begins with a four-bar phrase using C and Am (♭VI and IVm in E major). The main phrase from E to C♯m creates a melodic phrase from octaves. The last bar of this four-bar phrase is subject to a variation the second time when an A chord replaces the second bar of C♯m. This leads to a chromatic link over four bars which includes two bars of 'masking' chords without open strings. The example ends with the shape which created the C chord in bar 1 descending through third, second and first positions to create a second chromatic sequence. The three fretted notes on the lower strings comprise a major triad, but the upper three open strings form different harmonic relationships with it each time the shape moves down.

Songwriting tip 25

Never underestimate the songwriting power of the I-VI change. At a basic psychological level changes from major to minor and back express something profound about our experience of the light and dark of life. An altered tuning often brings out this power when I-VI in standard tuning temporarily sounds uninspiring to your ears.

CD track 25 EG♯BEBE

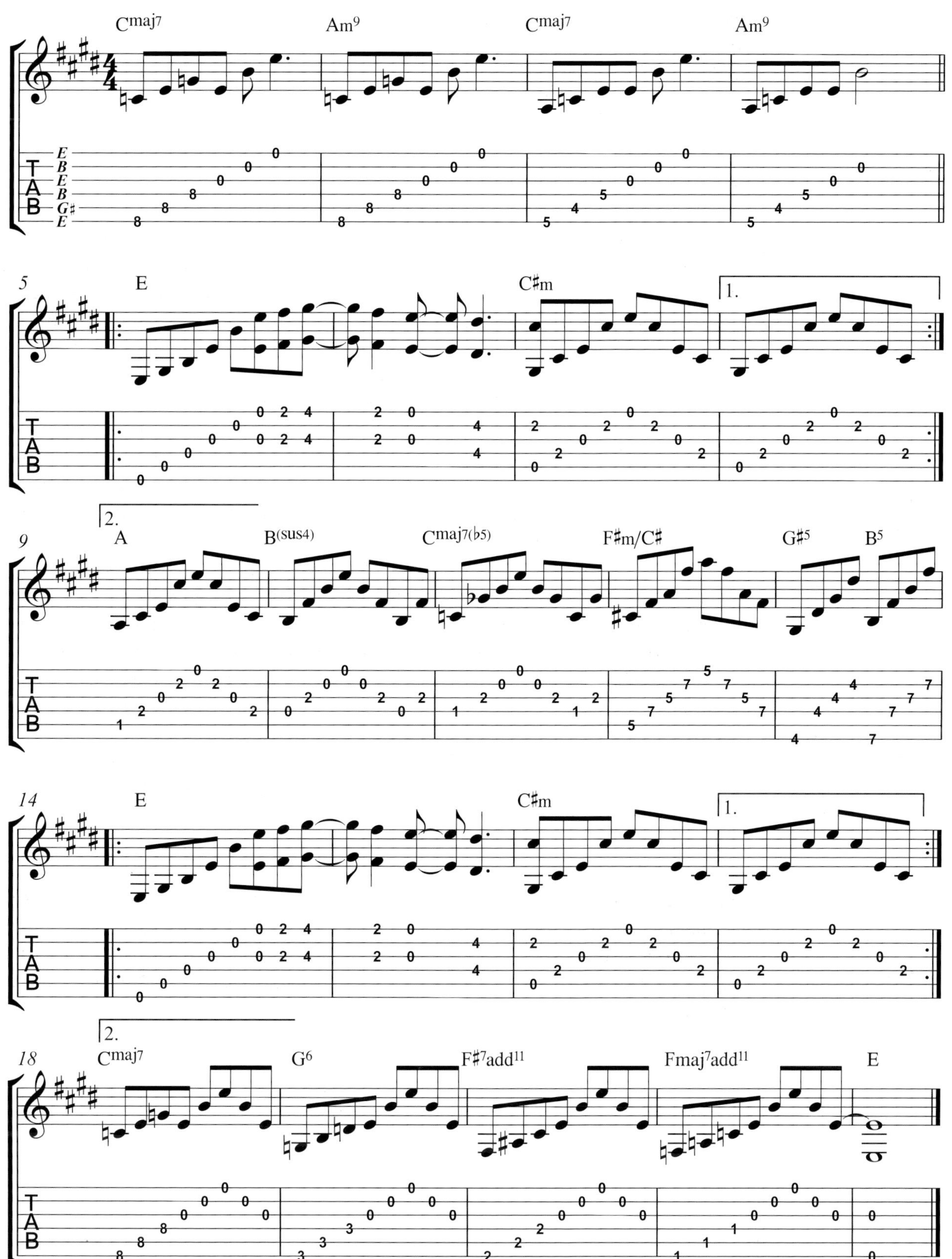

Open B♭

Changes:	-2 +1 x -2 +1 -2
Pitches:	D B♭ D F B♭ D
Profile:	8 4 3 5 4
3rds	1+3, 3+4, 4+5
5ths	3+5
6ths	1+3, 2+4, 5+6
Octaves	1+4, 2+5, 4+6
Triads	B♭ (1+2+3), B♭ (2+3+4), B♭ (3+4+5)

To conclude **Section Five**'s survey of open major tunings, let's go for something unusual. It is theoretically possible to invent an open major or minor tuning for any note. The constraints of the guitar mean some are hard to configure in ways that work physically on the instrument (because of string tension). I thought it would be interesting to choose a key guitarists often ignore (unless armed with a capo), namely B♭ major. Can we invent an open B♭ tuning?

In standard tuning most of the chords a songwriter would try in B♭ major are barre chords; in B♭ major the guitar is not very resonant, playing fills is hard, and the fretting hand gets tired, and then the chords don't come out cleanly. The sonic rewards of B♭ major on the guitar appear meagre. To construct an open B♭ major tuning we look first for any open strings in EADGBE that can remain as they are. The answer is yes, in the case of string 4, since it is a D. A B♭ major chord has the notes B♭-D-F. Step two is to detune other strings to the nearest note of those three. E goes down to D, G goes down to F, B goes down to B♭ and E goes down to D. That leaves string 5 (A) to go

CD track 26
DB♭DFB♭D

I				IV		V		I				IV		V	
B♭5	/	/	/	E♭	/	F	/	B♭5	/	/	/	E♭	/	F	/

I								VI							
[[: B♭5	/	/	/	B♭7	/	/	/	Gm	/	/	/	/	/	/	/ :‖

III^				I				II^				IV			
D	/	/	/	B♭5	/	/	/	C9	/	/	/	E♭	/	E♭9♯11	/

E♭	/	/	/

II				V				IV				III			
Cm9	/	/	/	F	/	/	/	E♭maj7	/	/	/	Dm6	/	/	/

II				V				IV							
Cm9	/	/	/	F	/	/	/	E♭maj7	/	/	/	/	/	/	/

I		V		IV		V		I
‖: B♭	/	F	/	E♭	/	F	/ :‖	[x3] B♭ ‖

up a semitone to B♭. Although it is desirable to avoid tuning strings up, it is essential for the tuning to be successful that there is a low B♭.

The result of this re-tuning (five strings, no less) is an open B♭ major: DB♭DFB♭D. It has a different interval profile to any of the major tunings in this section, so it isn't an easier tuning disguised at this pitch. The mix of roots, thirds and fifths is not optimum – three Ds (the third of the chord) is frankly excessive. Having more than one third is often a challenge; generally one is

CHORDS: CD track 26
DB♭DFB♭D

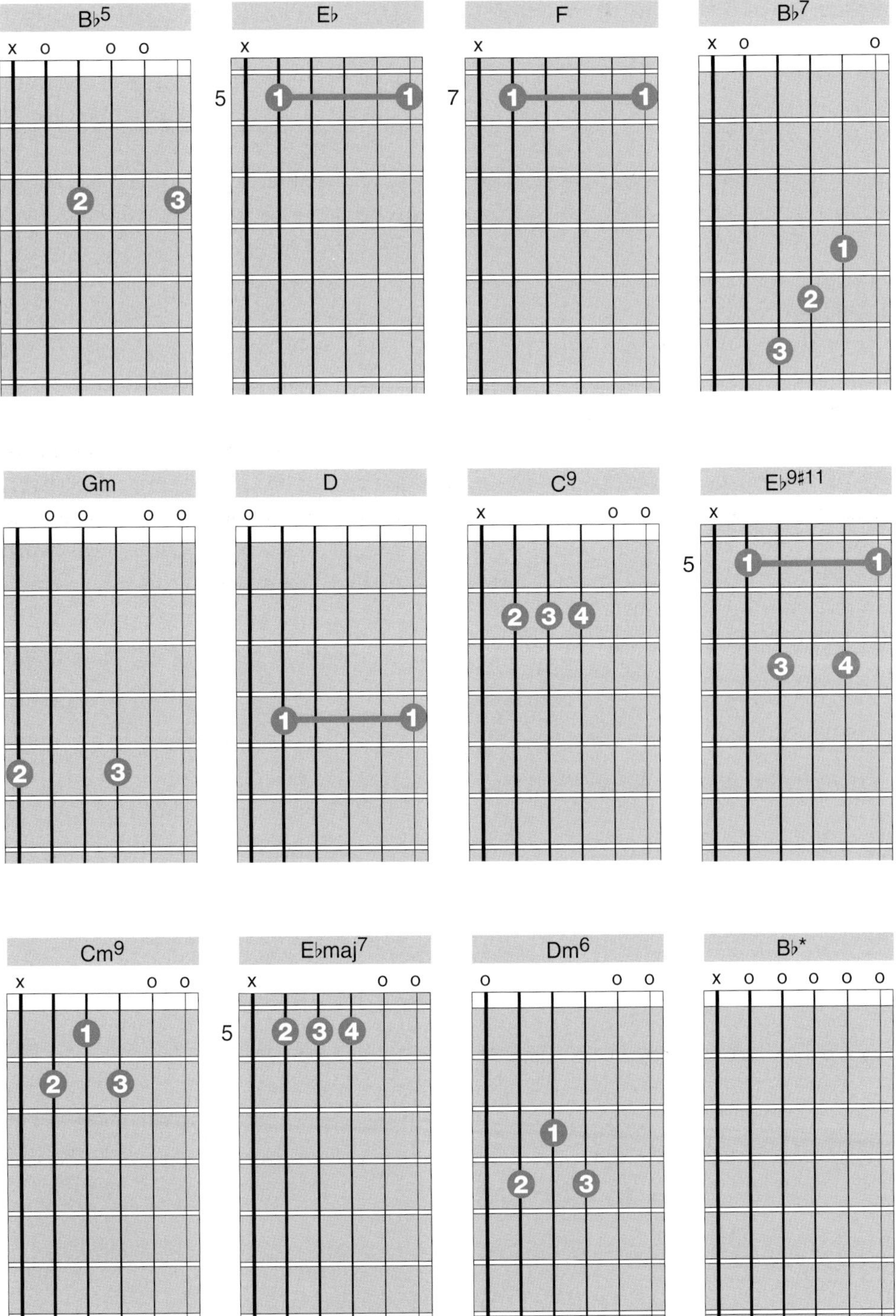

enough in both open majors and minors. It would be better if one of these thirds were a fifth, so a variant that achieved this is FB♭DFB♭D, where string 6 is tuned up a semitone. Nevertheless, I have found the tuning DB♭DFB♭D leads to some expressive voicings for Dm, E♭ and Gm.

An open B♭ major tuning can also be obtained by capoing open G at the third fret, open D at the eighth fret, and any open A tuning at the first fret. CD track 26 starts with an intro idea featuring accented I-IV-V chords. What could be a verse is built from a repeated I-VI change, completed with an additional four bars which promise, via the III^ of D, a key-change to G minor which doesn't happen. Notice also the other reverse polarity chord of II^. What could be a chorus avoids chord I altogether, instead following a strong II-V-IV-III-II-V-IV sequence. The song idea is finished with a version of the intro. What has changed is that the bass guitar is not playing root notes under the E♭ and F but instead those chords' thirds, so they are changed into first inversions. This is an effect you can employ at any time with a chord progression to give it a fresh character.

Songwriting tip 26

Get fresh inspiration by writing in a different key to those you normally inhabit. If the chord shapes are awkward, use a capo or re-tune, as in this example of B♭ major.

In contrast to the upbeat spirit of the previous example, CD track 27 is in a sombre style and is finger-picked with a swing rhythm. As a general point a tuning doesn't reveal its full identity until it has been strummed *and* finger-picked. The whole progression springs from the idea of an alternating bass figure fretted on string 6 and 4, or 6 and 3, played by the thumb, with the open strings chiming various harmonic colours above. The lesson to take from this track is that a great chord shape in an altered tuning should be tried at many different frets to reveal its potential. Listen also for the repeated B♭ in bar 4 that results from that note being an open string and a fretted note, such as a unison.

The opening progression is a popular descending bass-line which takes the progression one semitone (half-step) at a time (B♭-A-A♭-G) from chord I to chord VI. This type of sequence is not always easy to play in standard tuning. After the repeat the bass-line goes down even further. Listen for the unusual chromatic chord in bar 8. To finish, there's a nicely-voiced and resonant I-II change. The first two ideas would suit a verse and the last six bars a chorus or hook.

Songwriting tip 27

A little touch of asymmetry every now again can stop your songs sounding too predictable, and too similar to each other and everyone else's. In this case, it is the five-bar extension to the verse, rather than the more expected four or eight bar extension, that does the trick.

CD track 27 DB♭DFB♭D

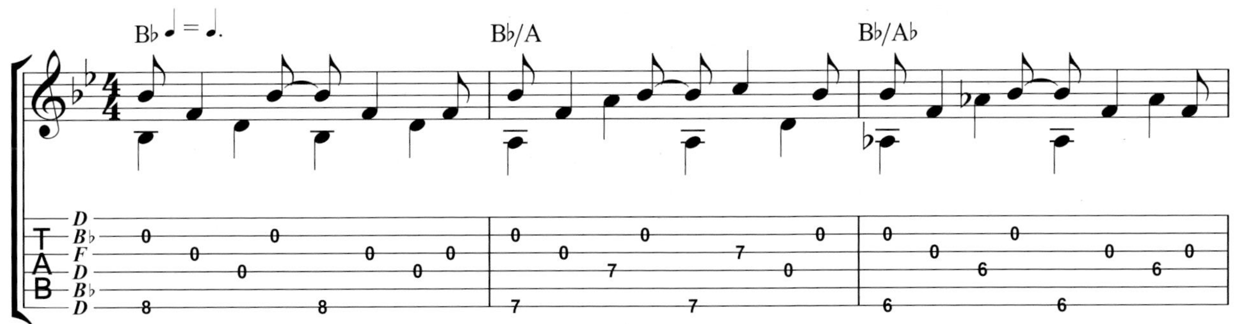

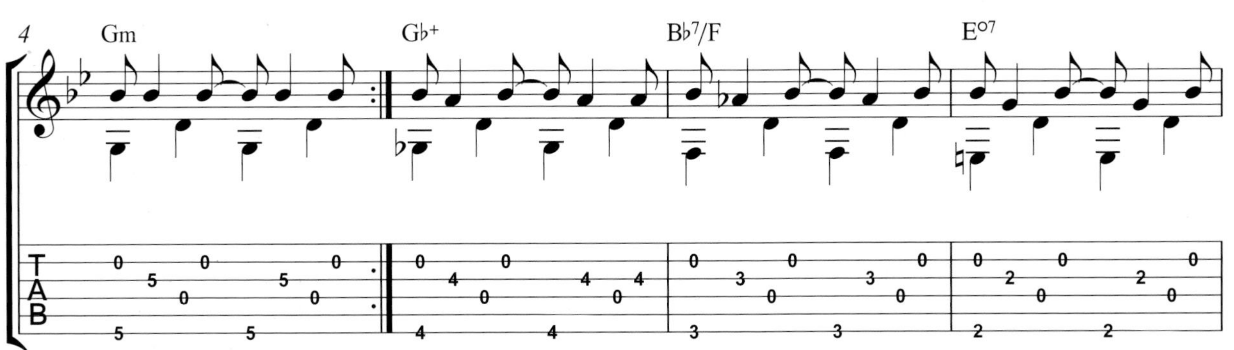

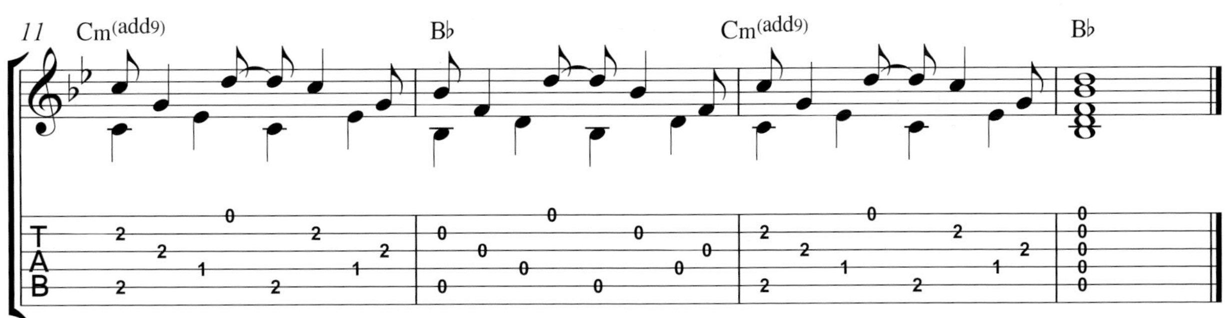

SECTION 6

VARIANT MAJOR TUNINGS

"I had one that was for playing in B, B minor, or B modal, which was EG♯C♯F♯BE. The fingering down the bottom was very simple but the chords were very rich. But you wouldn't go far out of the mode. It's not the sort of thing you would use for something in E-flat." (John Renbourn)

Can open major tunings be taken any further? The answer is yes, by having four or even five different notes present instead of three. Sometimes a songwriter takes this option, having part-composed a song in a plain open tuning, because he or she finds one or two chords simply won't make themselves available where needed in the progression, or because a particular shape has a wrong note in it. A string is re-tuned to provide the shape or remove the undesired note, and as a consequence there is a new tuning.

One method for devising new sounds from a major tuning previously used in writing a song is to alter one of the upper notes, especially if that note is doubled elsewhere in the tuning. This can be the root, the third or the fifth, but you must leave one third in the tuning, otherwise it will no longer be major. One of the notes of the major triad is changed to another note on the scale – the second, fourth, sixth, seventh, or flattened seventh. The result is a tuning with four notes instead of three. Four-note tunings often result in open chords such as a major sixth, seventh, major seventh or add ninth. When a single-finger barre is applied at the frets mentioned earlier the same chords are available but they are voiced as a seventh or a sixth, and so on.

In one genre of guitar such tunings are essential to the identity of the music, and that is in Hawaii. For decades guitarists there developed a tradition of playing in what they term 'slack-key tuning', the word 'key' here referring to the tuning peg. This approach first reached a wider audience via the album *Leonard Kwan And His Slack-Key Guitar* (1960). As the secrets of the tunings were shared by more players the style gained in popularity. There are now instruction books, recordings, and festivals that celebrate it. It has been speculated that open guitar tunings in Hawaii started because immigrant Mexican cattlemen who brought guitars with them left those instruments behind when they emigrated home. These guitars came into the hands of beginners and inexperienced players who, not knowing any better, tuned them so the strings made an attractive chord.

If tuning by ear and without musical theory or training, it is plausible that you will tune strings so that the instrument makes a chord without any fingers fretting. Most Hawaiian tunings require tuning down, hence the term 'slack-key'. It has been said that no other folk guitar tradition uses so many tunings. The most common are open G, Cmaj9 (C Wahine, CGDGBD), Dmaj7 (D Wahine, DADF♯AC♯), Gmaj7 (G Wahine, DGDF♯BD), C6 Mauna Loa, CGEGAE. ('Wahine' refers to a tuning with a major seventh in it.) The Mauna Loa tunings are based on a major chord with the top two strings tuned a fifth apart; some of these (such as G Mauna Loa, DGDDGD) lack the third of the chord and could be associated with the 'modal' tunings discussed in **Section Nine**.

The principle of extending a tuning can be taken further with five-note tunings such as Cmaj9 (CGDGBE). You might think this is a long way from standard tuning. In fact, in this instance the top four strings are unchanged from EADGBE but the two lowered bass strings result in a radically restructured tuning powerful in C major and A minor or G major and E minor.

Outside of the Hawaiian tradition, other players have found their way to variant open major tunings. Chet Atkins played a variation of open G (DGDEBD) with string 3 lowered to E to make a G6 tuning for Jerry Reed's 'Steeplechase' in the 1970s. CACGCE was used by Jimmy Page for the Led Zeppelin instrumental 'Bron-Y-Aur'. John Renbourn and Richard Thompson have used a G6 tuning DGDGBE, which is standard with strings 5 and 6 lowered. DAEF♯AD is a D major variant of Joni Mitchell's.

Open A6

Changes:	x x -1 -1 -2 x
Pitches:	E A C♯ F♯ A E
Profile:	5 4 5 3 7
3rds	2+3, 4+5
5ths	1+2
6ths	2+4, 3+5
Octaves	2+5
Triads	F♯m (2+3+4), A (1+2+4), A (4+5+6)

This tuning is related to the slack key open A in **Section Five**. String 3 has been tuned up to F♯; the loss of the open E does not unbalance the tuning because there is an E on the top string.

Another way to open up this tuning is to look at how it would be approached from standard tuning. String 3 goes down a semitone, which gives lute tuning (EADF♯BE); that is followed by adjustments to strings 4 and string 2. The tuning is balanced between the keys of A and F♯ minor. Taken from string 5 upward it gives an A6 chord, so a barre at frets five and seven will give a D6 and an E6.

IV	V	♭VII	Vm
D6 / / /	E6 / / /	:‖ [x3] G6 / / /	Em7 / / /

I	VI	II	IV
A5 / / /	F♯m / / /	Bm7 / / /	Dadd9 / / /

I	VI	II	III
A5 / / /	F♯m / / /	Bm7 / / /	C♯m / / /

IV	V	VI	
Dadd9 / / /	E6 / / /	F♯m / / /	F♯m ‖

CD track 28
EAC♯F♯AE

This tuning possesses many rich open-string chords, especially for F♯m, D and Bm. For the songwriter major sixth and seventh tunings give a melodic and mellow feel. Slower songs come naturally in this tuning, so CD track 28 shows how the tuning responds to a quicker tempo. This track could be a light funk/soul idea but the chord voicings are unorthodox because of the tuning. It opens with a IV-V change using the sixth chord available under a single barre in this tuning. The addition of the open string 6 in bar 4 turns the previous bar's G6 into an Em7. As you work with altered tunings be sensitive to when

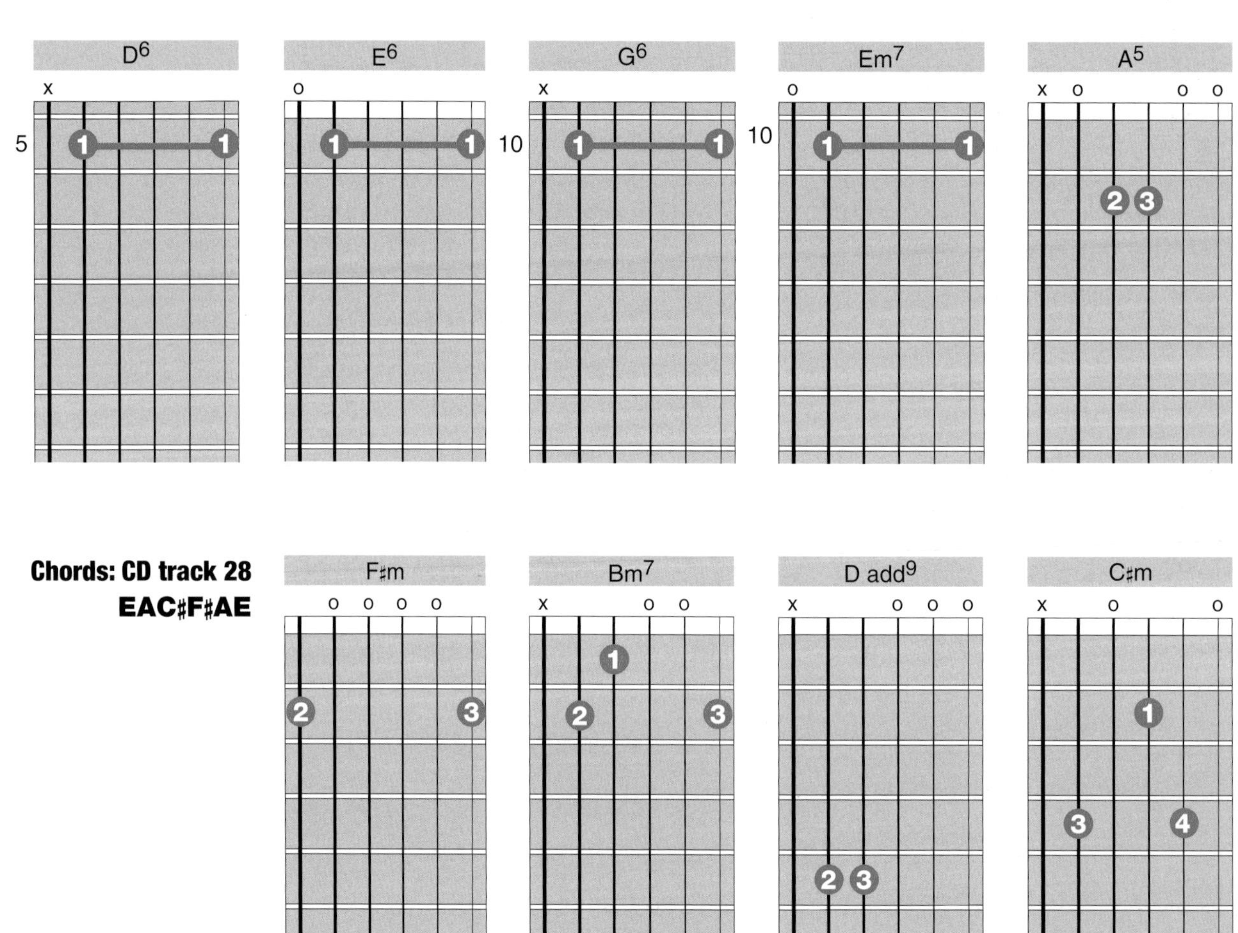

bringing in or taking out a bass string can change the harmonic identity of a single shape. This makes an eight-bar intro.

The verse could begin with the A5 chord. Resonant fifth chords in open tunings are easy to get; it is a matter of locating which open strings are tuned to the third of the chord and fretting them at the third fret from the barre. This A5 could have been an A major, but after the richness of the sixths this bare fifth is a welcome break. It is a mistake to overwhelm the listener with a stream of richly-voiced chords; if you choose too many their emotional impact is reduced. Playing through these chords notice how the shapes are easy changes. Only the C♯m requires particular attention to ensure the unison root notes on the fretted string 5 and open string 4 sound together. Notice the variation whereby I-VI-II is completed by a IV first and then a III.

Songwriting tip 28

Consider the timing of the first appearance of chord I in the song progression. Delaying it can heighten expectation. It can also be delayed by sounding it as a fifth chord.

Open Bmaj7

Changes:	x +2 +1 -1 -1 -1
Pitches:	E B D♯ F♯ A♯ D♯
Profile:	7 4 3 4 5
3rds	2+3, 3+4, 4+5
5ths	2+4, 3+5
6ths	1+3
Octaves	1+4
Triads	D♯m (1+2+3), D♯m (2+3+4), B (3+4+5)

Unlike the previous tuning this is not a variant of one of the major tunings from **Section Five**, but rather a tuning constructed from scratch. Starting from standard tuning the top three strings have gone down a semitone, with string 4 going up a semitone. The bass notes on string 5 and 6 are unchanged.

This tuning has an interesting in-built ambiguity for a songwriter. It leans both to the key of B and secondarily to E major. Working in B major the top five strings sound a Bmaj7 chord. Put your finger on the first fret of string 2 and it becomes B major. With the root note on string 5 the tuning is comparable to open G in that respect. A barre across these five strings results in Emaj7 at the fifth fret and F♯maj7 at the seventh. The latter is not in key for B major (it should be F♯7), but this can be fixed by turning the barre into a straight major by fretting string 2 one fret up from the barre. This replaces the seventh of the chord with the root note.

I think of this as an 'overlap' tuning, a tuning that contains a major (B) and a minor triad (D♯m) and the open bass notes to maximise working in either. The identity of the tuning depends then on whether you view string 6 (E) or string 5 (B) as its root note. Most effective tunings are founded on a root note on string 5 or 6. Any higher than that and the tuning becomes unbalanced, with many of the simple chords needed for a song turning into unwanted inversions. It is rare to find an altered tuning with its root note on string 4.

Treating this tuning as a version of E major generates some interesting chords but one challenge – the A♯ open string 2 does not belong to the scale of E major, which should have an A. This challenge can be met either by removing that note from any chord to which it does not belong, or intentionally making its dissonance a feature of the music. There is a scale (the lydian mode) which is almost the same as a major scale except for having the fourth note raised by a semitone (half-step). E lydian is EF♯G♯A♯BC♯D♯. This tuning would lend itself to a song using that mode, but will have an unusual sound to most people. Of course, any chord that would normally be used by a songwriter in E major which happens to have an A♯ in it can take advantage of the open second string A♯. Such chords would be F♯ (II ^), and possibly D♯ if changing key to G♯m.

I		IV	
B / / /	Bmaj7 / / /	Emaj7add13 / / /	Emaj9 / / / :‖
V	VI	III	VI
F♯7add13 / / /	G♯m / / /	D♯m / / /	G♯m / / / ‖
II	V	I	IV
C♯m6/9 / / /	F♯7add13 / / /	‖: B / Bmaj7 /	Emaj7 / / / :‖

CD track 29
EBD♯F♯A♯D♯

CD track 29 uses the tuning in the key of B major. The romantic flavour of the major sevenths in this piece suggest a Burt Bacharach ballad in the making. The opening four-bar phrase arises from two basic shapes: a fifth on the top two strings which, taking the approach of moving intervals around, is moved to the fifth fret where a major seventh is created. Two separate exotic voicings of E are played with a single shape at the third and then first position. The F♯7add13 is unusual for a complex guitar chord in that all its notes are in ascending order (often impossible in standard tuning because of fingering difficulties). Listen for the unison top two strings in G♯m and strings 2 and 3 in D♯m. The D♯m shape creates a haunting C♯m chord if it is moved down with string 2 left open; in this instance there is a note fretted on string 2, but try it without anyway. The 'masking' chord – the one providing a break from the open strings – is the Emaj7 in the final bar, a simple barre with the open string 6 as the bass note.

Songwriting tip 29

Two major sevenths a fourth apart makes a romantic chord change that will launch any ballad with clear intent.

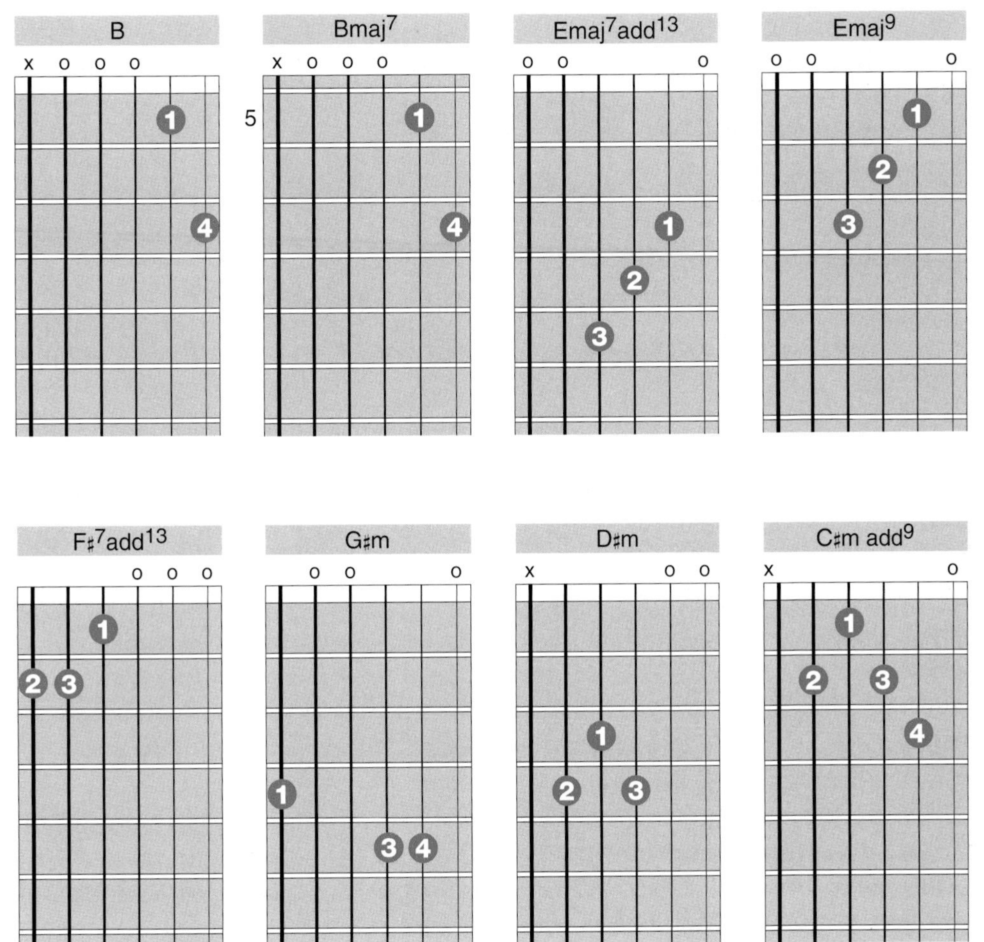

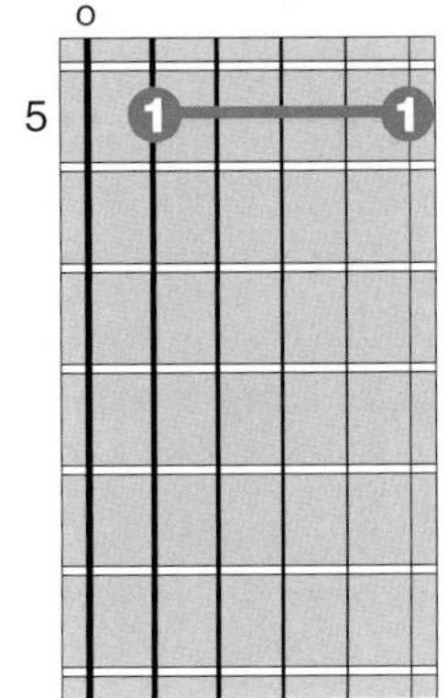

CHORDS: CD track 29
EBD♯F♯A♯D♯

SECTION 7

OPEN MINOR TUNINGS

If the guitar can be tuned so that its open strings sound a major chord, it must also be able to produce a minor chord by the same method. The minor open tuning is one in which, when you strum all the strings, a minor chord is heard. This section features five such minor open tunings. Any major open tuning can be turned into a minor by locating the third of the chord and tuning that note (or notes) down by a semitone (half-step). As with the open majors, a barre with finger 1 gives a minor chord at each fret. Minor tunings are sometimes called 'cross-note' tunings.

For most minor key songs only two fretted positions are of practical use: the fifth fret where chord IV can be found, and the seventh fret for chord V, if a songwriter wants I, IV and V as minor chords. At the open fret and fret 12 there is chord I, the minor key chord. These three minor chords comprise a minor-key version of the songwriter's three-chord trick, and often feature in a minor-key 12-bar blues or ballad. So with two one-finger barres at the fifth and seventh frets plus the open strings you can write a three-chord song in a minor key.

But what of the remaining frets? It is difficult to fit any of the other minor chords into a minor key song based on I-IV-V unless deliberately seeking a song with a feeling of alienation.

What is needed instead are the major chords that belong to the minor key. These would occur at frets one, three, eight and ten, and also at five and seven because in a minor key chords IV and V can occur as majors. The important point about getting songs from a minor tuning is that a songwriter still needs major chords even when writing in a minor key.

This apparent lack of majors is easily remedied. Contrary to what you might imagine, it is typical of open minor tunings that major chords are easy to find. They can be played merely by fretting a note in addition to the barre. Locate which string or strings has the third of the tuning and raise this note or notes by a semitone. With a single-finger barre minor chord this means adding a finger or two to the shape. In open G minor tuning (DGDGB♭D) there is one third, on string 2. The B♭ chord in open G minor tuning can be played with a barre at the third fret with finger 2 fretting string 2.

In any open string minor tuning these minor and major chords are available to the songwriter (taking open G minor as an example):

0	1	2	3	4	5	6	7	8	9	10	11	12
I	♭II		III		IV (IV^)		V (V^)	VI		VII		I
Gm	A♭		B♭		Cm (C)		Dm (D)	E♭		F		Gm

These chord relationships and positions remain true for an open minor tuning regardless of the pitch of the strings, the harmonic mix of roots, thirds, and fifths, or the interval.

Every open minor tuning lends itself to functioning in the key of the dominant; that is, the chord found at the seventh fret. An open E minor tuning, where chords I, IV and V are at frets zero, five, and seven, can also be a tuning for the key of B minor, where the same I, IV, V chords are found at frets seven, zero, and two. Minor tunings where the root note is on string 5 also invite composing in the minor key a fifth away – such as from open G minor, D minor – if string 6 is the fifth of the tuning's chord. In addition, minor tunings lend themselves to either the tonic major (in the case of open G minor, G major) or the relative major (B♭ major).

The general balance and position of the root, third, and fifth in a chord is crucial in shaping the sound of a tuning, whether major or minor. EBEG♯BE is open E major. Letting string 3 down a semitone to G gives an open E minor, EBEGBE. This is the minor tuning played a semitone higher as F minor by bluesman Albert Collins. A barre with a finger added to string 3 gives a major chord. However, we could also get an open E minor tuning by altering the strings to EGBGBE, or tuning to open D minor (DADFAD) and then applying a capo at fret two. In EGBGBE there are two thirds in the tuning, so when we play a barre fingers have to be added on string 3 and 5 to raise both Gs to G♯s. The same thing would happen in open F♯m (F♯AC♯F♯AC♯).

The position of the third in a minor tuning has another aural consequence. The lower it is the darker the tuning sounds. This is especially true if the root note of the tuning is on string 6 and not 5. If the tuning has a root on string 6 but a lone third on the top string the effect can be unbalanced and harsh, the third too weak to colour the chords whose bass roots and fifths overwhelm it. This is my assessment of open C minor when it is arranged CGCGCE♭. The effect is less pronounced when the root note of the tuning is on string 5.

Open G minor	
Changes:	-2 -2 x x -1 -2
Pitches:	D G D G B♭ D
Profile:	5 7 5 3 4
3rds	1+2, 2+3
5ths	1+3, 4+5
6ths	2+4
Octaves	1+4, 3+5, 4+6
Triads	Gm (1+2+3), Gm (2+3+4)

CD track 30 DGDGB♭D

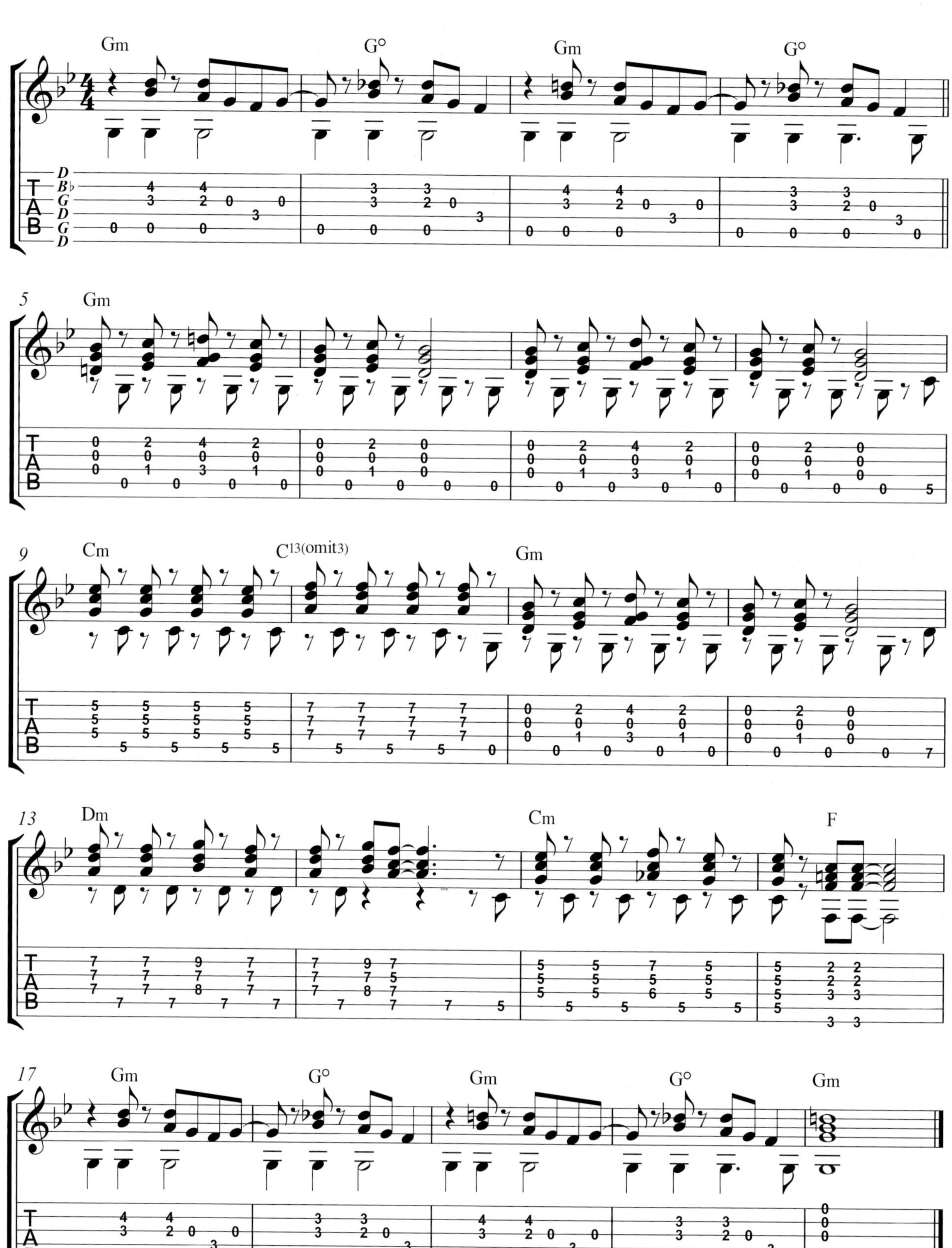

This tuning is derived from the open G featured in **Section Five**, the difference being that string 2 is detuned a semitone lower from B to B♭. A barre at the fifth and seventh frets gives Cm and Dm. These three chords are suitable for playing some folk material built with the three-chord trick in a minor key. If we add a finger to the barre on string 2 a major chord results. Try playing the open strings, then a barre at the fifth, then a barre at the seventh with the extra finger to get Gm-Cm-D (I-IV-V^), a common minor sequence.

The British singer-songwriter Michael Chapman wrote an instrumental in this tuning, 'Kodak Ghosts,' released on *Fully Qualified Survivor* (1970). At the end of the tune he hits the open Gm chord in harmonics at fret 12 with a single strike and while the notes sustain grabs the tuning peg and tunes string 2 up from B♭ to B while it is sounding – a neat trick, transforming the last minor chord into a major and setting up the guitar for a song in open G.

To write a song in a different open-tuned G minor, capo open D minor at the fifth position, or open E minor at the third position.

CD track 30 is a finger-picked treatment of open G minor in which fingers and thumb grab the chord. This is based on a 12-bar idea but is in a minor key. Listen for the sinister effect of the D♭ in bar 2 of the opening riff. It would have been easy to have played another D-natural, but the D♭ adds edge to the riff. At bar 5, which might be the start of a verse, the progression features sixths moving on strings 2 and 4. These could be exploited further up the neck if you like the sound and wanted more of that type of idea. Four bars later, in keeping with most 12-bars, the music moves to chord IV (Cm), but notice how that chord is extended in bar 10 to an implied C11 (Dm/C). At bar 13 there is the expected chord V (Dm) and in bar 14 Cm again, but both are decorated with extra notes. The progression concludes with a rhythmic and harmonic pause on an F chord in bar 15 before the riff returns.

Songwriting tip 30

12-bar songs don't have to be major-key blues. A 12-bar progression can be used in a minor key and can be extended by doubling the number of bars in the 9-12 section as well as by introducing a fourth chord.

CD track 31 (next page) demonstrates that minor-key tuning songs do not have to be slow. This one begins with a four-bar intro based on two unusual voicings of Cm, the second resulting from a single finger moving with the barre held in place at the eighth fret. Altered tunings can tempt the songwriter to luxuriate in the barred happiness of straight majors or the gloom of minors. From the songwriter's point of view, if you find one can your ears accept a dissonant chord and see it as a possibility? Can you resolve it? Can you use it dramatically? What kind of emotion does it arouse? What kind of lyric would that lead to?

The verse kicks off with the high Gm which changes into a fifth shape to find the next two chords. On the repeat of this idea a new bass note on string 6 changes the E♭maj7add13 chord into a Cm9. I've interpreted the music as changing key when the B♭6 appears, along with the fifth shape, this time in first position. The G7 chord is musically interesting given this example is in G minor tuning. This is a good indication of how an open minor tuning need not

IV			
Cm7♭5 / / /	/ / / /	Cm11♭5 / / /	/ / / /
I		VI	
Gm / / /	Gm7/F / / /	E♭maj7add13 / / /	/ / / /
I		VI	IV
Gm / / /	Gm7/F / / /	E♭maj7add13 / / /	Cm9 / / /
I	♭VII	VI^	
[[: B♭6 / / /	A♭13♯11 / / /	G7sus4 / / /	G7 / / / :‖
III^		III [V]	
Dadd9 / / /	/ / / /	Dmadd9 / / /	/ / / /

I VII	VI	V
‖: Gmadd9 / F13(no 3rd) /	E♭maj9 / / / :‖	[x3] Dm9 ‖

CD track 31
DGDGB♭D

trap a songwriter into its root minor key. The open strings are masked by the appearance of the Dadd9 and Dmadd9 chords, both making effective use of a low D on the open string 6. The idea is finished with a re-statement of the Gm-F-E♭ progression from earlier, this time with only two beats to the first two chords and new voicings. The Gmadd9 should be examined carefully. If played one string at a time it becomes apparent that it contains a note cluster of G-A-B♭ and D. If you decide you don't like the 'jagged' quality of chords with note-clusters (often invisible at first) it is a simple matter to change one of the notes or find a different Gm shape – such as the open strings.

Songwriting tip 31

An exotic, mildly dissonant chord can make a good intro because the dissonance grabs the attention, creates drama and tension, and can be resolved at the beginning of the verse. This is a means of using an exotic chord that would be hard to sing over if featured in a verse.

CHORDS: CD track 31
DGDGB♭D

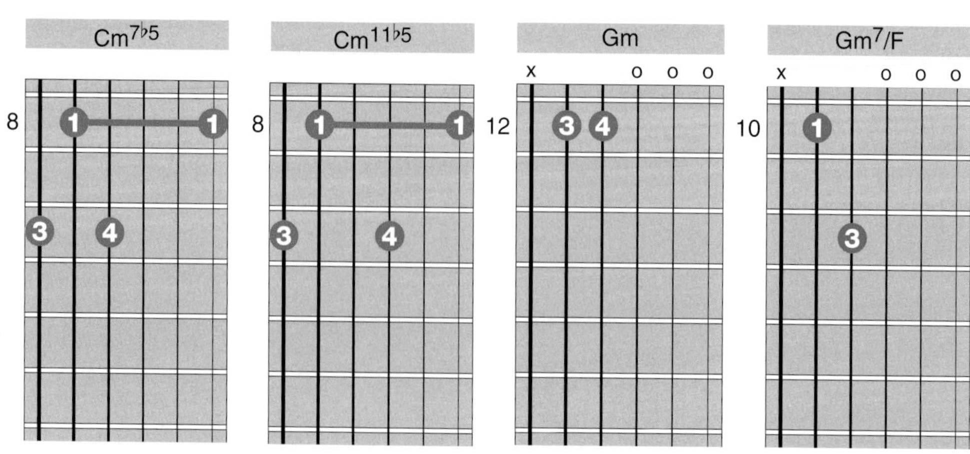

CHORDS: CD track 31
DGDGB♭D
(continued)

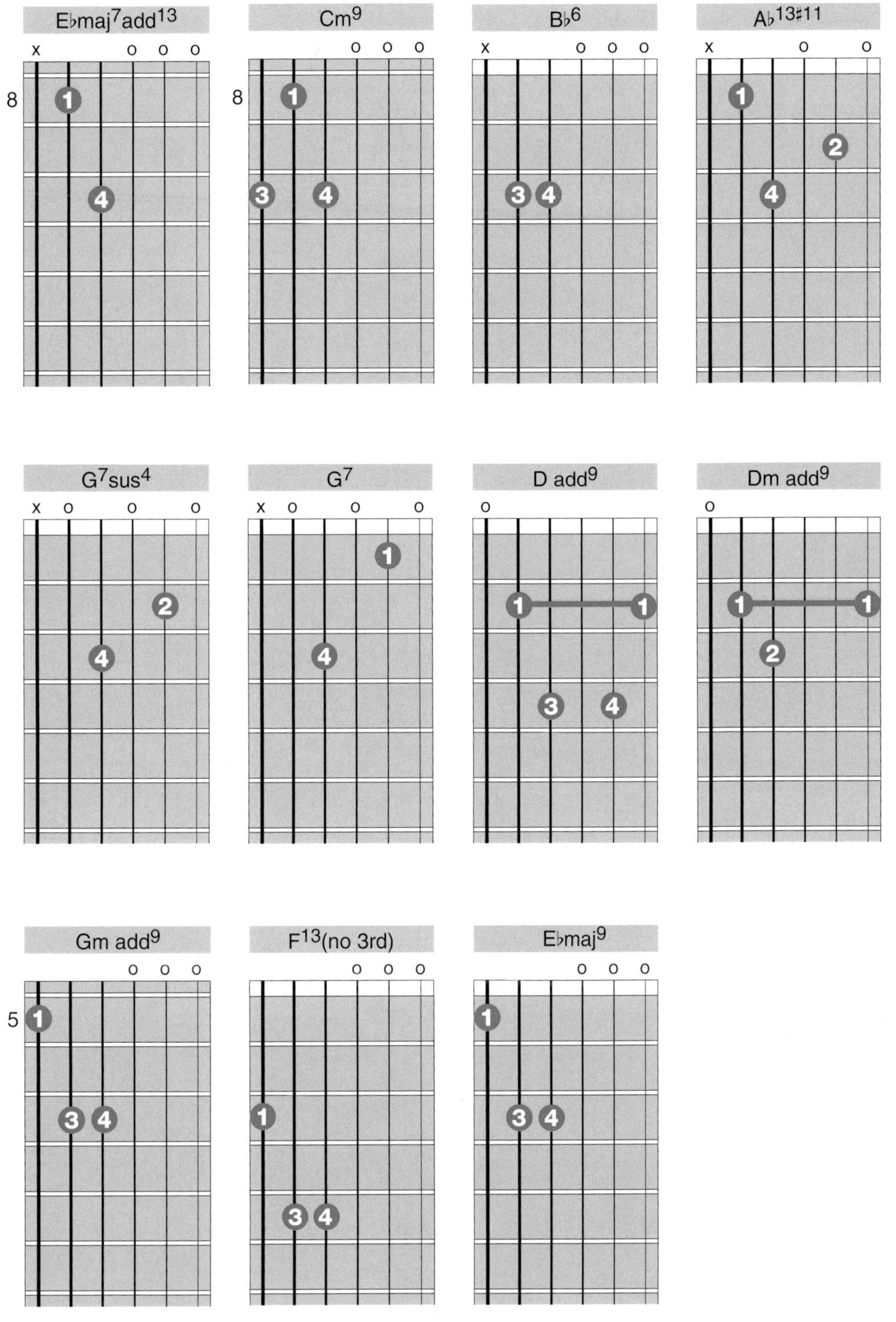

Open D minor

Changes:	-2 x x -2 -2 -2
Pitches:	D A D F A D
Profile:	7 5 3 4 5
3rds	2+3, 3+4
5ths	2+4, 5+6
6ths	1+3
Octaves	1+4, 2+5, 4+6
Triads	Dm (1+2+3), Dm (2+3+4), Dm (3+4+5)

This tuning is a close relative of open D, the difference being that string 3 is lowered a semitone (half-step). A barre at the fifth and seventh frets gives chord IV (Gm) and chord V (Am). As with any minor open tuning, these three chords suit folk material which uses the three-chord trick (I-IV-V) in a minor key. If we add a finger to the barre on string 3 the chord becomes major. Open D minor is a notably deep-sounding tuning, more so than open G minor. This is the consequence of the tuning's root note being the detuned string 6, and the third of the chord F being on the detuned string 3 (a fourth below string 2's B♭, which featured in open G minor.)

CD track 32: DADFAD

I		IV	IVm	I		♭II	
Dmaj7 / / /		Gmadd9 /	Gm / :‖	Dmaj7 / / /		F6/9 / / /	

♭VI	♭VII	V	Vm	I	Im	I	Im
B♭ /	C /	A /	Am /	Dmaj7 /	Dm7add11 /	Dmaj7 /	Dm7add11 / ‖

CHORDS: CD track 32 DADFAD

To again demonstrate that minor tunings can be more flexible than you might imagine, CD track 32 is a song idea with a slow blues feel centred on D major despite being in open D minor tuning. The detuned nature of open D minor tuning means even happy chords like major sevenths take on a moody character compared to how they sound in standard or less slack tunings. Listen for the contrast of the chords with open strings and those chords that have none. As the last couple of bars show, this key/tuning combination contains the possibility of a powerful contrast of major and minor key and chords on the

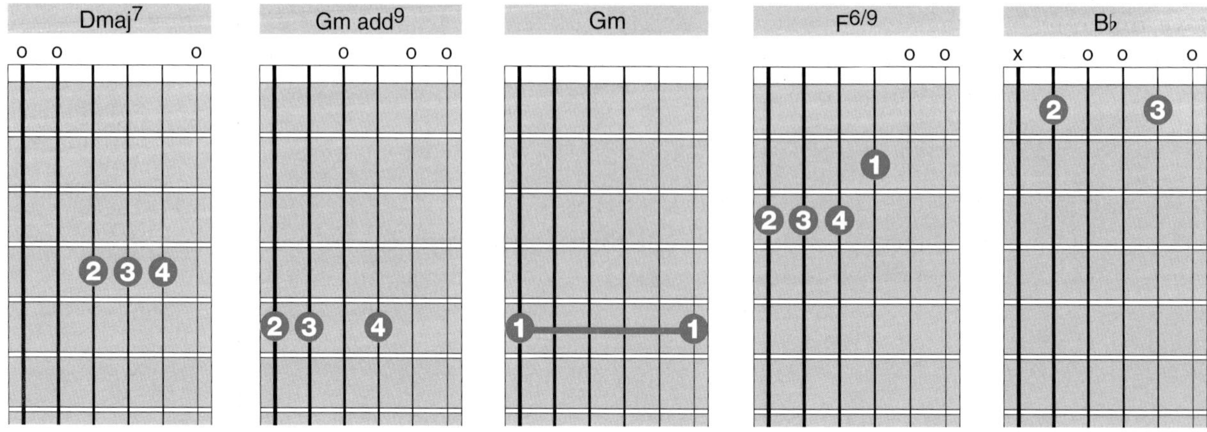

CHORDS: CD track 32
DADFAD
(continued)

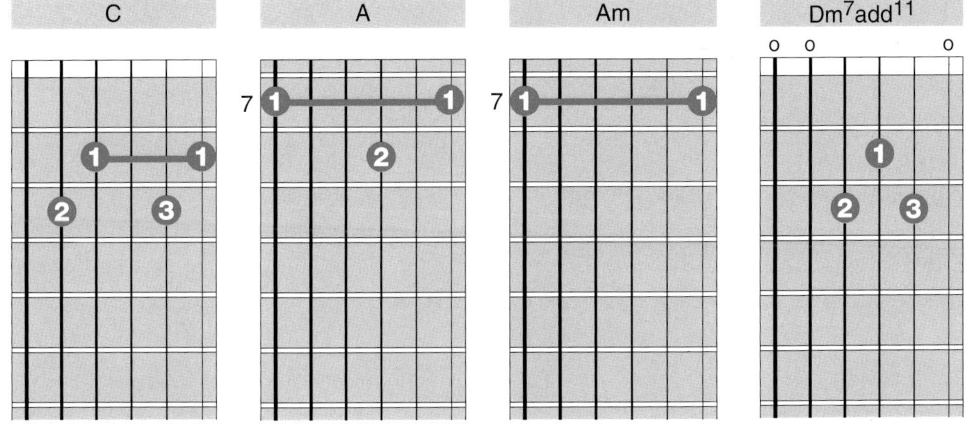

same note. This track does not start with a four-bar click; it comes straight in with solo drums.

Songwriting tip 32

Instead of a standard intro, why not launch a song with a solo drum intro to establish a rhythmic feel and create anticipation for the entry of the first chord. Listen to David Bowie's 'Five Years' for an understated example of this approach.

Open A minor

Changes:	x x -2 -3 -2 x
Pitches:	E A C E A E
Profile:	5 3 4 5 7
3rds	3+4, 4+5
5ths	1+2, 3+5
6ths	2+4, 4+6
Octaves	1+3, 2+5, 3+6
Triads	Am (2+3+4), Am (3+4+5), Am (4+5+6)

CD track 33 EACEAE

This tuning is a slack-key version of A minor which doesn't put too much tension on the guitar neck. The standard approach would be to take open A tuning (EAEAC♯E) and lower string 2 C♯ to C, giving EAEACE (x x +2 +2 +1 x). Notice there is only one third in the tuning and it is an octave lower than string 2's C in the raised open A minor. These two versions of open A minor have different interval profiles and harmonic make-up. To write a song in another open-tuned A minor capo open G minor at the second fret, or open D minor at the seventh. Writing a song or song section in C major might work well with this tuning.

In CD track 33 sixths are used as a prime melodic feature of the guitar part in the opening four-bar phrase. This opening phrase's Am and Em harmony insists on its minor character, so a contrast is provided at bar 5 where the chords change to F, C, and G. The top notes of each chord, with the top string sounding on its own, might suggest a melody.

CD track 33 EACEAE

Songwriting tip 33

It is helpful when writing a melody to develop awareness of its ascending and descending features. The more aware a songwriter is of the curve and shape of a melody, the more he or she can see the potential in even a short phrase.

Open B minor

Changes:	-2 +2 x -1 x -2
Pitches:	D B D F♯ B D
Profile:	9 3 4 5 3
3rds	1+2, 3+4, 4+5
5ths	3+5
6ths	1+3, 2+4
Octaves	1+4, 2+5, 4+6
Triads	Bm (1+2+3), Bm (2+3+4), Bm (3+4+5)

There is no commonly agreed open B minor tuning. Songwriters who want to work in that key are reasonably well-served by standard tuning, and an open B minor could be achieved by using a capo on open A minor tuning at the second fret, or fourth fret in open G minor. However, devising a stand-alone B minor open tuning seems worthwhile, since all the strings in standard tuning belong to its scale, and two notes (D and B) are in the chord of B minor.

This suggested tuning requires mostly tuning down, but it is a necessity to tune string 5 up to B to ensure there's a low root note. Remember that ideally you want an altered tuning to have a root note on string 6 or 5 so as to have an effective bass in the harmony.) This tuning could have been F♯BDF♯BD but its interval profile (513513) is close to that (513515) of the open A minor we have just tried. Tunings that have the fifth of the chord as the lowest open string yield a resonant shape for chord V in that minor key; if the third of the chord is there instead this will be harder.

This tuning produces a number of effective chords for both B minor and D major. Since the root note is on string 5 this tuning can be treated as a five-string open tuning.

CD track 34
DBDF♯BD

I	VI	II	IV
Dmaj7 / / /	Bm / / /	Em7 / / /	G / / /

I	VI	II	V
Dmaj7 / / /	Bm9 / / /	Em7 / / /	A11 / / /

iIV	iV	Im	iII iIII
G/B / / /	A/C♯ / / /	Dm / / /	Em/G / / F♯m/A /

VI^		II^	♭VII
‖: Bsus4 / / /	B / / /	:‖ E7 / / /	Cmaj9 / / /

I	VI	I	VI
Dmaj7 / / /	Bm / / /	Dmaj7 / / /	Bm ‖

The first chord change contrasts a seventh-fret barre chord with a five-string Bm chord that has four open strings. The G chord in bar 4 is unusual because it contains two unison pairs. Notice how bar 8 completes the I-VI-II-IV sequence with I-VI-II-V. Two inversions appear in bars 9 to 10 leading to an unexpected minor version of chord I that benefits from string 6 (D). Chord VI appears in major form (VI^), suggesting there may be a key-change to E or E minor, but the E7 prevents this (E7 suggests we could be heading for A or A

CHORDS: CD track 34
DBDF♯BD
(continued over page)

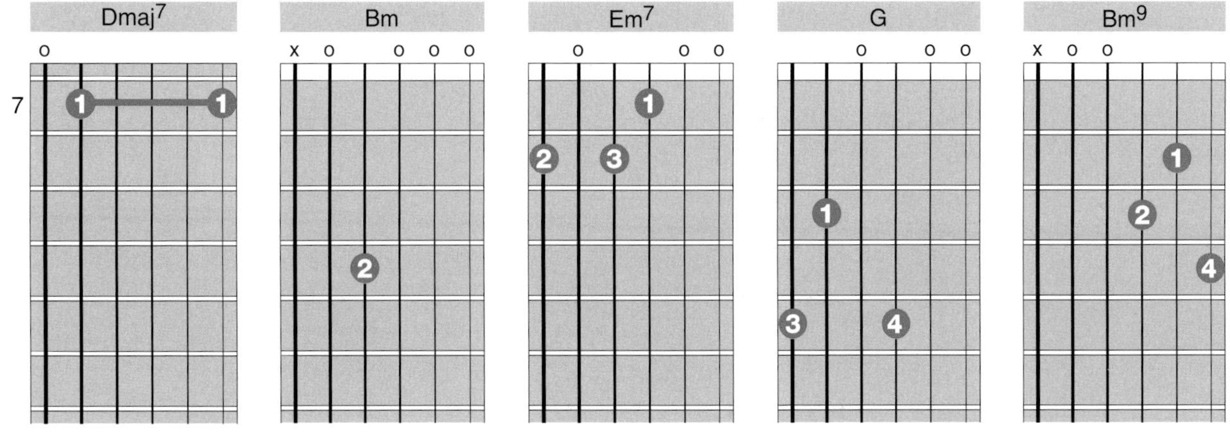

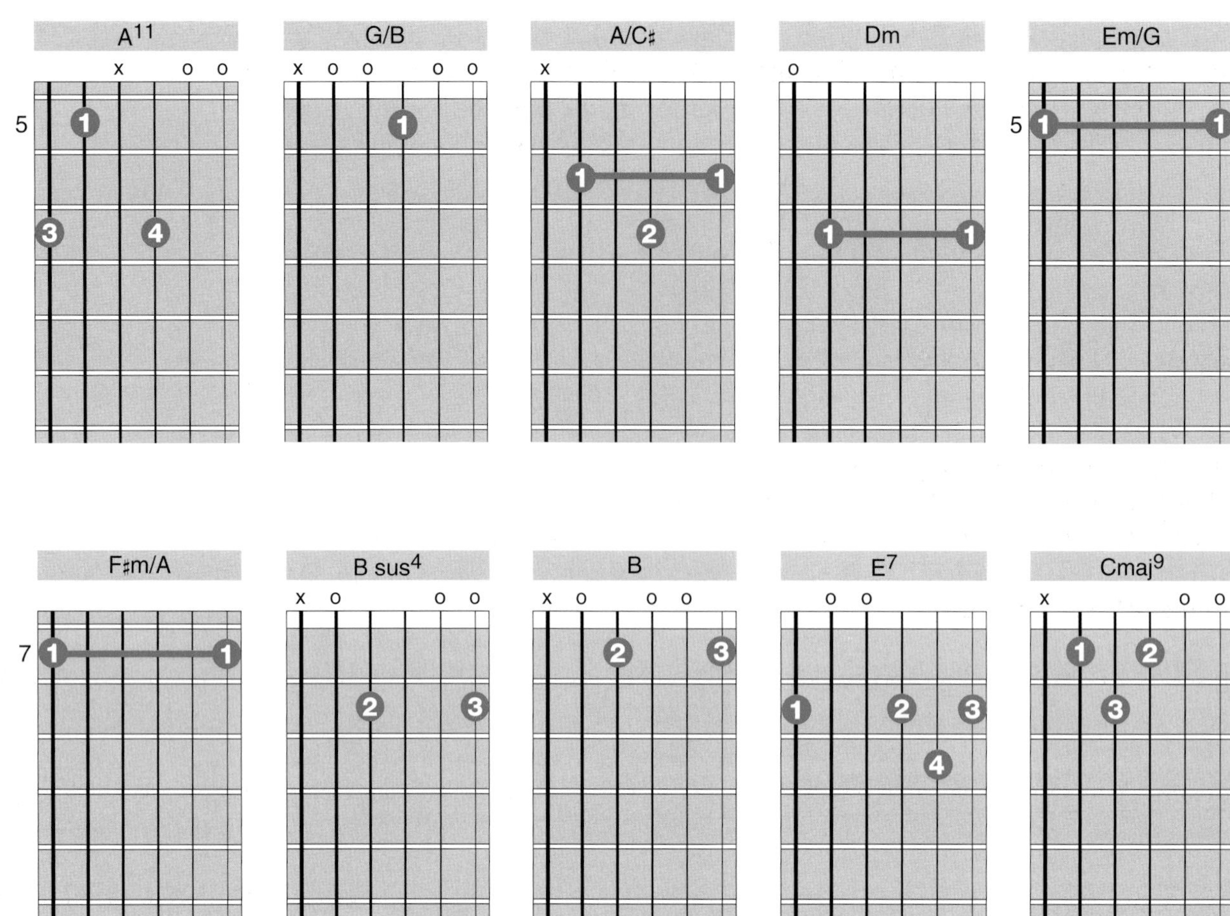

CHORDS: CD track 34
DBDF♯BD
(continued)

minor, as it is chord V for both). This II^ turns out to be only a reverse polarity chord in the original key of D (E instead of Em). Following the Cmaj9 (♭VII) with Dmaj7 (I) makes for an interesting contrast since the latter contains a C♯.

Songwriting tip 34

A sequence of rising first inversion chords creates movement and can effectively lead to the root note of an unexpected chord. Get the bass to double the lowest guitar note in the guitar's first inversions to emphasis the effect.

Open E minor

Changes:	x -2 -3 -3 x x
Pitches:	E G B E B E
Profile:	3 4 5 7 5
3rds	4+5, 5+6
5ths	2+3, 4+6
6ths	3+5
Octaves	1+3, 2+4, 3+6
Triads	Em (3+4+5), Em (4+5+6)

An open E minor tuning is simplicity itself to create on guitar because standard tuning has a bias to E minor. Strings 6-3-2-1 make an E minor chord, with string 4 a seventh and string 5 an 11th. If tuning up is permitted open E minor can be EBEGBE, with strings 4 and 5 going up a tone. However, this has the same interval profile as open D minor (DADFAD) and could therefore be reached merely by applying a capo to fret two. As an alternative, this slack-key E minor tuning is formed by tuning down. The result is a minor tuning with a different interval profile to the others we have explored. With the root note on string 6 and the third on string 5 the tuning has a deep character. The metaphorical shadows of the tuning have deepened in comparison to open G minor. This may be what you want for certain types of song or lyrics.

Every minor tuning lends itself to either the tonic major (in this case E major) or the relative major (in this case G major). It is easy to find G and C chords and their extended forms in this tuning. Chords such as G6, Gmaj7, Cmaj7, Cmaj9 present themselves straight-forwardly. The lack of an open D on string 6 is sometimes felt in this tuning (which could be remedied by tuning it to the hybrid DGBEBE).

I				V				IV							
Em	/	/	/	Bm	/	/	/	Am	/	/	/	Amadd9	/	/	/ :‖

III								IV				I^			
G	/	Gmaj7	/	G6	/	Gmaj7	/	Amadd9*	/	/	/	E	/	/	/

VI				V		V^		VI				IV		VII	
Cmaj7	/	/	/	Bm	/	B	/	Cmaj7	/	/	/	Am	/	D	/ ‖

CD track 35
EGBEBE

This verse sequence starts with I, IV, and V in E minor played with a single-finger barre. In bar 4 the Amadd9 adds additional shading to the plain Am of bar 3. The second idea illustrates how instead of changing chord, a progression can move through various voicings of a single chord, in this case G. A single note changes within it: G drops to F♯ for the maj7, then to E for the G6, and then climbs back up. This song idea also shows how the two forms of chord V

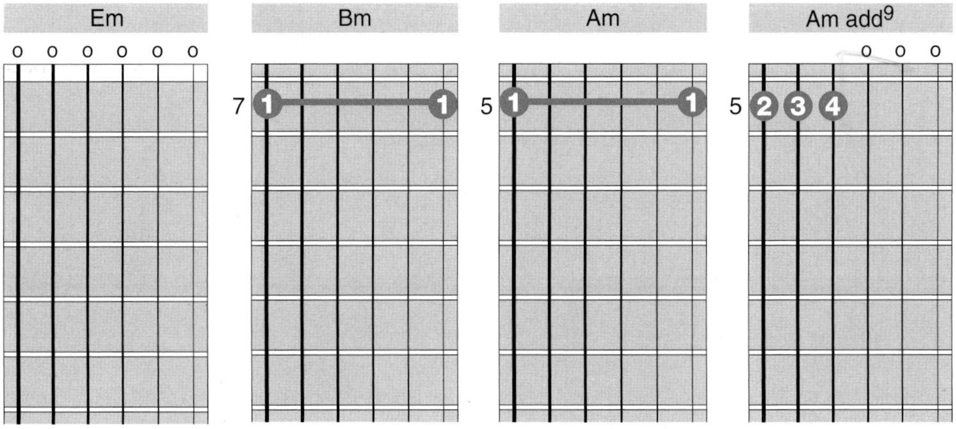

Em: o o o o o o

Bm: 7 — barre 1

Am: 5 — barre 1

Am add^9: 5 — 2 3 4; o o o

CHORDS: CD track 35
EGBEBE

(continued over page)

CHORDS: CD track 35
EGBEBE
(continued)

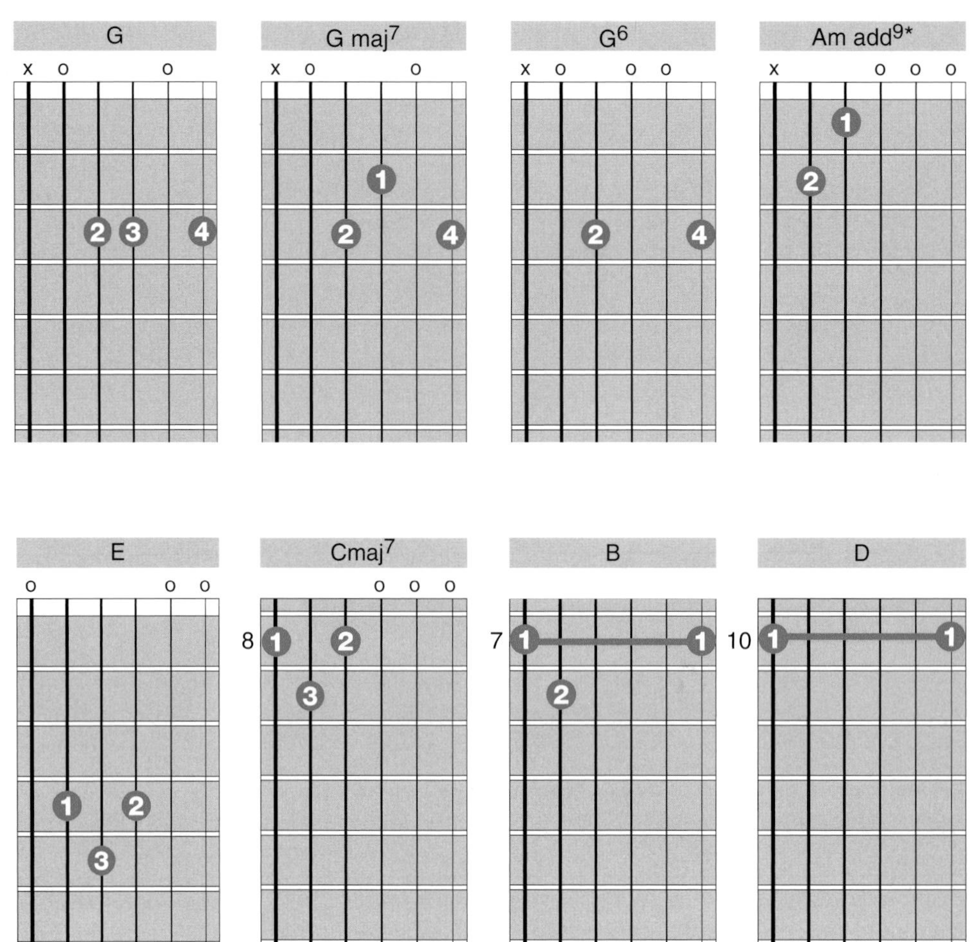

can fit in a song and how the application of a single fretting finger to the barre minor works to sharpen the third, turning a minor chord into a major one.

Songwriting tip 35

Alteration of a major chord through its seventh and sixth can also include the dominant seventh between the major seventh and the sixth. On an A chord this would be the sequence A-Amaj7-A7-A6.

SECTION 8
VARIANT MINOR TUNINGS

In this section we can have a brief look at the possibility of adjusting a minor tuning so it has more than three different notes in it. For a songwriter a minor seventh tuning could be a more attractive option than a plain minor, given the feeling of emotional oppression that an open minor tuning can induce. Since minor chords themselves produce a gloomy effect in plain minor form, many songwriters change at least one or two minor chords in a song into minor sevenths to dilute their sadness. In an open minor tuning this can be done either by looking for the open string shapes that create them, or making a further adjustment to the tuning and introducing a seventh.

The easiest way to achieve this is to de-tune one of the root-note strings. Not the lowest, as that is essential for giving the chords their identity, but a root note on the upper strings. Open G minor DGDGB♭D could be retuned as open G minor seventh (DGDFB♭D, see Section 12 for chord boxes for this tuning) by taking string 3 down a tone to F. Hey presto! With a single-finger barre you now have a set of minor seventh chords that can be restored to minor with the addition of a finger on string 3, turn into majors with an additional finger on string 2, and dominant sevenths (G7) with a finger on string 2 only. This is a flexible set-up; in fact, from a songwriting angle it offers more options than an open major tuning.

Other minor variants might be to include a sixth or a ninth, or possibly an added fourth (not a suspended fourth). The Smashing Pumpkins song 'Mayonnaise' features an unusual tuning of E♭B♭B♭G♭B♭D, which makes an E♭m/maj7 chord. Swervedriver's 'Kill The Superheroes' used FADADE, a Dmadd9 tuning. Notice that if a ninth is introduced into the minor tuning it may intensify its sadness. Try, for example, open Gmadd9 (DGDAB♭D) or open Dmadd9 (DADFAE). The minor add sixth will also be edgy and dark, as with open Gm6 (DGDGB♭E). The minor seventh tuning is emotionally less burdened. Consider how in genres such as soul music and New Romantic pop, as well as much singer-songwriter material, minor seventh chords in standard tuning are common. The open minor seventh tuning suits soul and jazzy progressions, especially when it lends itself to moving a semitone (half-step) at a time, in chromatic minor seventh chords. Here are two examples of an extended open minor tuning.

Open Em7

Changes:	x +2 x x x x
Pitches:	E B D G B E
Profile:	7 3 5 4 5
3rds	2+3, 4+5
5ths	5+6
6ths	1+3, 2+4, 3+5
Octaves	2+5
Triads	Em (1+2+3), G (2+3+4), G (3+4+5)

This tuning is actually a single-string change, string 5 going up a tone, from standard tuning. Standard tuning is very close to making an Em7 chord. Another possibility is EGDGBE, EGDGBD or even EBEGBD – there are many options. With the tuning EGDGBD, if you take G as the root note this makes the top five strings make the chord of G and interpreted thus it would encourage you to write a song in G major (or possibly C major or D major, where this chord is important). I've chosen EBDGBE partly because it is only one string change from standard tuning and because it often works better to have a fifth at the bottom of the tuning rather than a third. The plain minor is restored with one finger on string 4 two frets from the barre, which removes the seventh. The shape that in standard tuning would produce a major chord yields here a major sixth chord. (Handy for confusing guitarists in your audience as they wonder why a shape they recognise doesn't sound as it should.)

With E unambiguously the root note of the tuning, it draws the songwriter to write in E minor (or possibly A minor or B minor, where this chord is important). CSN&Y's songs 'Compass', 'Déjà Vu', and 'Guinnevere' were played in a variation of open Em7 which is also a variation on standard tuning: EBDGAD.

CD track 36
EBDGBE

V	VIIm	IV		V	VIIm	IV	VI
Bm7 /	Dm7 /	Am7 / / /		Bm7 /	Dm7 /	Am7 /	Cm7 /
V	VIIm	IV	♭V	V	VIIm	IV	VI
Bm7 /	Dm7 /	Am7 /	B♭m7 /	Bm7 /	Dm7 /	Am7 /	Cm7 /
III		IV^		I		IV^	
G6 / / /		A6 / / /		Em7 / / /		A6 / / /	
V^		VI	VII	I			
‖: B / / /		C/B /	D/B /	:‖ [x3] Em7* / / /		/ / / /	Em7 ‖

CHORDS: CD track 36
EBDGBE

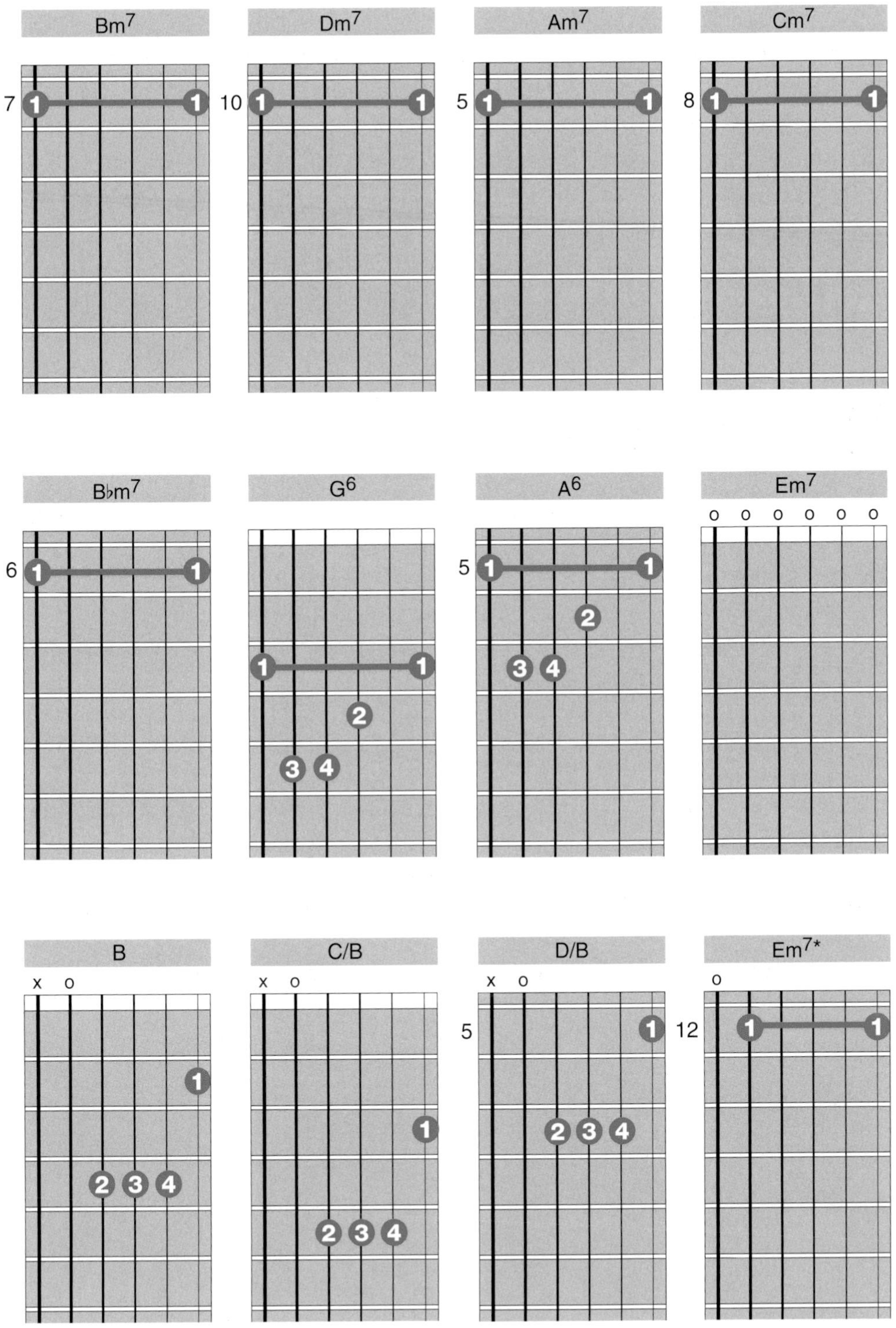

CD track 36 makes plentiful use of that basic feature of open tunings – that a single-finger barre makes a chord. The first eight bars can be played with that one shape, but because each is a minor seventh chord, and because the changes themselves are chromatic, the overall sound belies the simplicity of its execution. In other words, if you only heard this progression on guitar I suspect you would think it involved more complicated chord changes. Sixths such as

CD track 37 EBDGBE

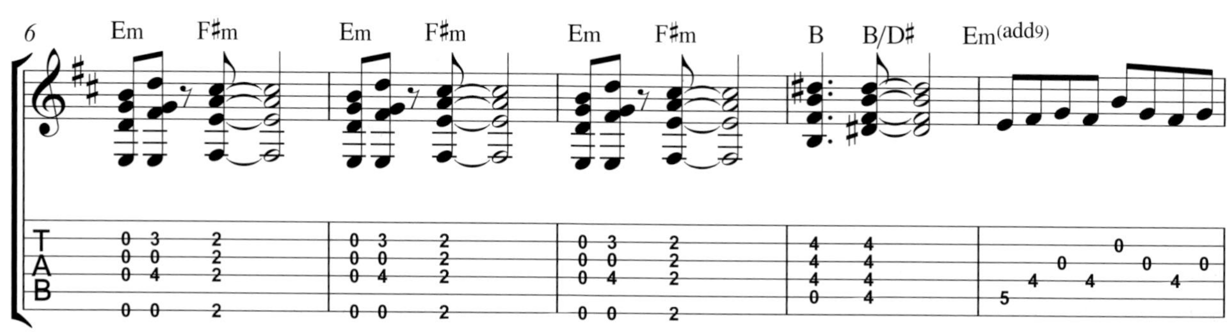

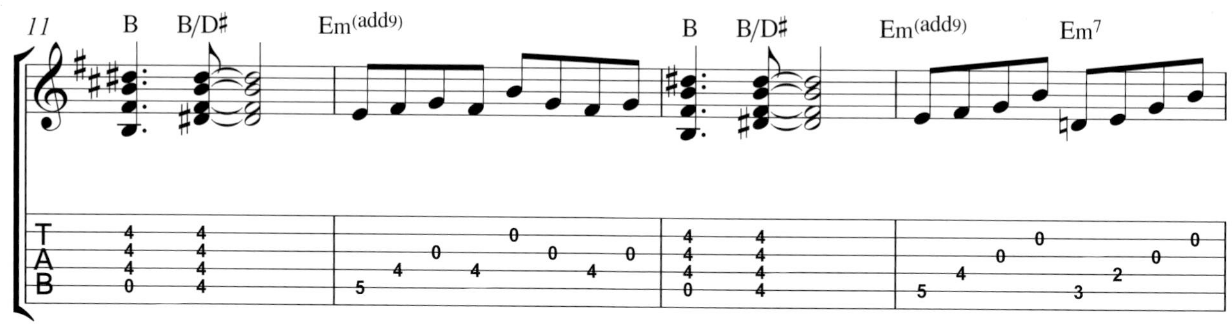

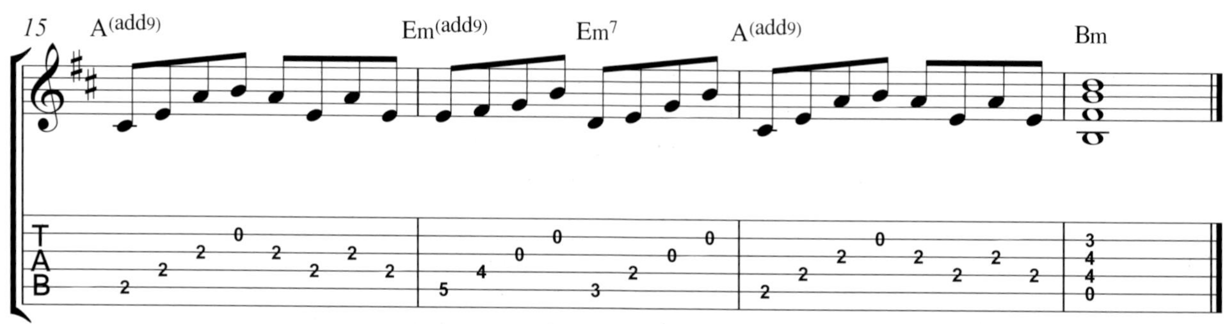

G6 and A6 make a good complement to minor seventh chords. A third idea introduces more tension and drama. String 5's B is treated as a pedal note, with the chords of B, C and D moving above it. All chord shapes that would work in standard tuning on the upper four strings are unchanged in this tuning. The final Em7 is not quite a full barre at fret 12. The finger lets string 6 remain open to give a deep root note E.

CD track 36 is a little ambiguous when it comes to its key, so for the sake of clarity I've interpreted the entire progression as being in E minor.

Songwriting tip 36

To get a combination of musical breeziness and oddity, move between minor seventh chords three semitones apart. No major or minor key ordinarily contains both, though the major key can if reverse polarity produces II-IVm (in C major Dm-Fm, hence Dm7-Fm7).

CD track 37 is another approach to the same Em7 tuning. This takes string 5's B as the root note and is a progression in B minor. It could almost be played in standard tuning, but the fingering would be harder, and the absence of the open B bass string would change its sound. Notice the sixths moving on strings 2 and 4 as a melodic riff idea. There are also several bars where 'harp' effect arpeggios with close-pitched notes are played. If you play this example be careful to let the strings sustain as much as they can and allow the notes in the arpeggio figures to bleed into one another. This produces a halo of sound as you move to the next chord.

Songwriting tip 37

Use consecutive sixths if you want a melodic accompaniment idea which is less 'sweet' than thirds.

Open F♯m7	
Changes:	+2 -3 -1 -1 -2 x
Pitches:	F♯ F♯ C♯ F♯ A E
Profile:	0 7 5 3 7
Unison:	5+6
3rds	2+3
5ths	1+2, 4+5, 4+6
6ths	2+4
Octaves	3+5
Triads	F♯m (2+3+4), A (1+2+4)

This tuning is probably the oddest in the book so far because the two lowest strings are tuned to the same note. This results in an emphatic F♯ drone at the bottom of the tuning if you move shapes around the fretboard on the upper four or five strings. Chords can be moved around on the top five strings to create chords over a single F♯ pedal, or string 6 can be ignored if a chord with its root on string 5 is needed. Taking this idea of bass strings tuned to the same note further, there are some tunings where the root note is on string 5 and it is doubled an octave down on string 6, as in the case of open A minor (EACEAE)

I	♭VII	V	I^
‖: F♯5 / / /	E/F♯ / / /	:‖ [x4] C♯m / / /	F♯ / / / ‖

V	I^	V^	iVI [IV]
C♯m / / /	F♯ / / /	C♯7 / / /	Dadd9/F♯ / / / ‖

I	II^	IV	V
‖: A / / /	B7sus4 / / /	Dadd9 / / /	E11(no3rd) / / / :‖

III	II	III	II [IV]
C♯m7 / / /	Bm7 / / /	C♯m7 / / /	Bm7 / / / ‖

I			
F♯5 / / /	F♯m / / /	F♯5 / / /	F♯m / / / :‖

CD track 38
F♯F♯C♯F♯AE

where string 6 could go down to A, or open B minor (DBDF♯BD) where string 6 could go down to B. At light gauges this will of course result in very slack strings.

Track 38 is in F♯ minor, but the first F♯ that appears is neither major nor minor but a bare fifth. This first chord shows off the drone quality of the tuning, with the E chord that follows suspended over the F♯ bass. In playing the C♯m care must be taken not to strike either string 5 or 6. It is followed by three surprising harmonic twists: an F♯ instead of F♯m, a C♯ major chord, and a first inversion Dadd9. This D chord is chord IV in A major. There is a feeling that the music has changed key to A major for the I-II^-IV-V turnaround. I think the C♯m7-Bm7 change is still heard as being in A major, but the Bm7 functions as chord IV of F♯ minor to return the music to F♯ minor for the final bars. Notice with the chord shapes how there is a contrast between the barre chords and the open chords, and how when constructing chords you have to allow for the presence of two notes at the same pitch on the bass strings. This takes a little getting used to.

Songwriting tip 38

In a song with many extended chords a bare fifth chord acts as a refresher, giving the listener a deliberately plain stark sound to enhance the richer chords when they occur.

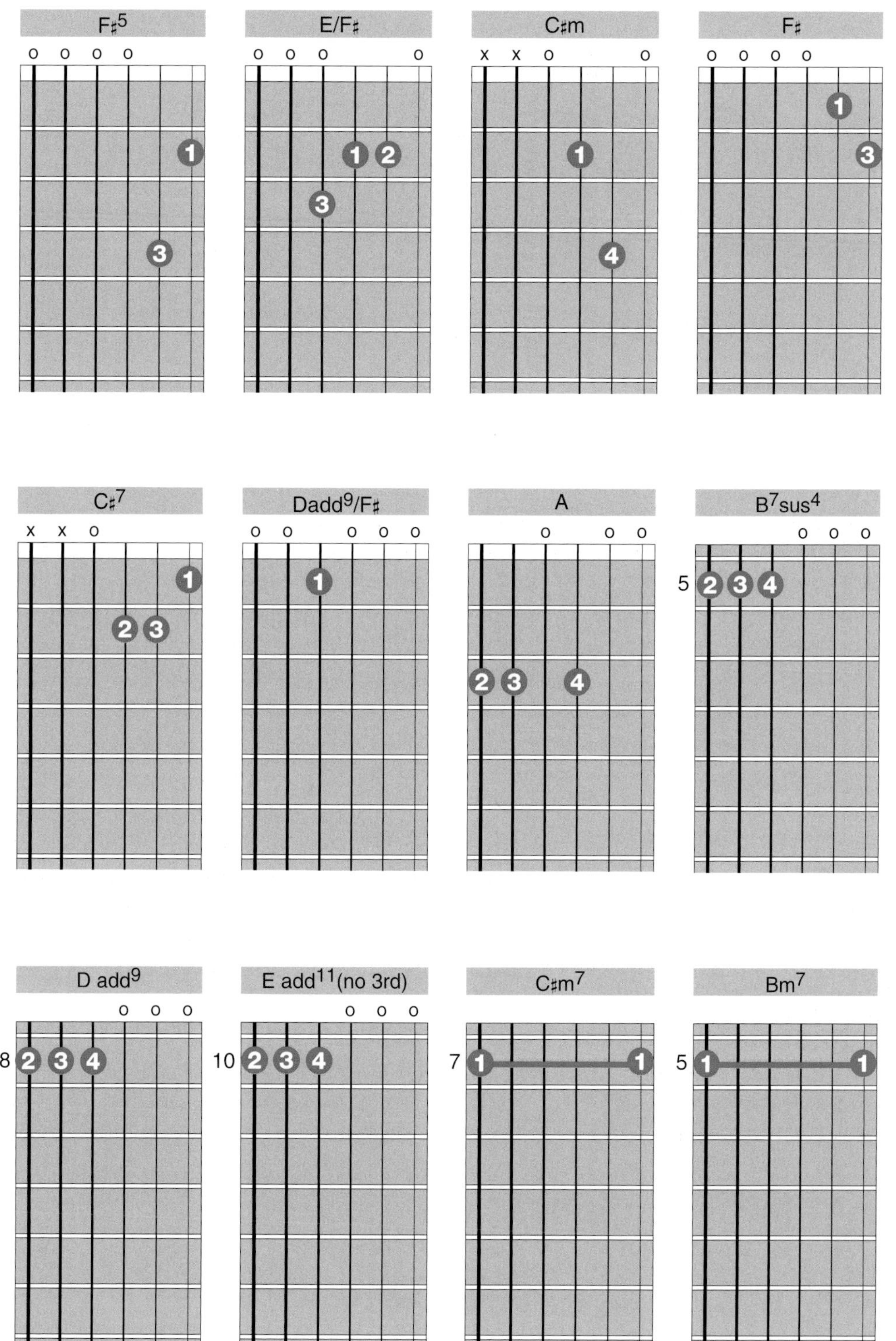

CHORDS: CD track 38
F♯F♯C♯F♯AE

SECTION 9

'MODAL' AND HYBRID TUNINGS

"I stayed with a session player, a Los Angeles guy, long time back, and he heard me playing in DADGAD and just flipped. He wanted to learn it because he thought it was a new sound for sessions. So I left him with it. He sat up all night. The next day he said, 'I've cracked it!' Every key – he could do the whole lot. I said, well you've just made it 100 times more difficult for yourself 'cause that's not the point at all!" (John Renbourn)

So far we have looked at single-string and double-string tunings, open major tunings (with variations), and open minor tunings (with variations). This final section of tunings looks at those that don't fit in any of these categories. It primarily focuses on an intriguing group of tunings that are neither major nor minor. They have become known as 'modal' tunings.

The term 'modal' tuning is slightly misleading, but the label has stuck. It came about because some of these tunings were devised for the playing of folk melodies drawn, not from the conventional major or minor scale, but from older scales called modes. In their simplest form the common modes are the scales heard if you choose a white note on the piano and play only white notes until you reach the same note one octave higher. The mode on D, for example, is called the dorian mode. Its notes are D E F G A B C. Compare this with D major (D E F♯ G A B C♯), D harmonic minor (D E F G A B♭ C♯) or D natural minor (D E F G A B♭ C), the latter being a mode in itself – the aeolian transposed onto D.

Modal tunings tend to avoid the third of the chord. Often this is replaced either by the fourth or second of the scale. A tuning consisting of root, second and fifth makes a sus2 chord; a tuning with root, fourth and fifth makes a sus4 chord. The daddy, or should I say 'Dad-gaddy', of them all is the tuning DADGAD, where the open strings sound a Dsus4 chord. This tuning can be reached from open D by tuning string 3 up a semitone from F♯ to G (heading therefore back in the direction of standard tuning). According to musical legend, this tuning was invented by British guitarist Davy Graham at the turn of the 60s. Graham was a key figure in the 60s British folk clubs, and is remembered chiefly for his guitar instrumental 'Anji', once a finger-picking rite of passage that every aspirant folk guitarist needed to learn. He devised DADGAD while playing with Moroccan musicians – which is ironic, given its later history.

The tuning was thereafter taken up by John Renbourn and Al Stewart. Bert Jansch recently said he didn't play 'Black Waterside' on *Jack Orion* in DADGAD, but many, including Al Stewart, thought he had. Stewart in turn showed it to Jimmy Page, who was already enthusing over the *Jack Orion* album. Even before Led Zeppelin were formed Page devised a guitar instrumental called 'White Summer', an improvisation based on the traditional song 'She Moved Through The Fair' in the form recorded by Graham in the early 60s. Page put his version of 'Black Waterside' on Led Zeppelin's debut album in 1969, with the title 'Black Mountainside'. Page also composed 'Midnight Moonlight' (on The Firm's debut LP) in the tuning. But the apotheosis of DADGAD tuning was the riff for Led Zeppelin's epic 'Kashmir'. This song, more than any other in the Zeppelin catalogue, was responsible for Page and Plant teaming up with Moroccan musicians for their *No Quarter* CD, at which point the DADGAD wheel had gone full circle. This tuning probably encouraged Page to look for similar tunings that were neither major nor minor. One other tuning he devised that belongs in this section was for 'The Rain Song' (DGCGCD, live version a tone higher).

Comparable 'modal' tunings include EADEAE (Asus4) used by Davy Graham and Martin Carthy, Michael Hedges' DADEAB (for 'The Naked Stalk'), Nick Drake's CGCFCE, often with a capo at V ('River Man'), and DGDDAD (for 'Road'), John Renbourn's DAEGBE, CGDGAD, CGCGCF, Alvin Lee's DADDAD, Pete Townshend's DADADE, Richard Thompson's DADEAD and FGDGCD. Other tunings in the group include DADGAE, DACGCD, DAEGAD, and DGDGCD. For The Police hit 'Every Little Thing She Does Is Magic' Andy Summers played in DGDGAD. Duncan Sheik uses EBEF♯BE, an Esus2.

'Dadgad' or Dsus4

Changes:	-2 x x x -2 -2
Pitches:	D A D G A D
Profile:	7 5 5 2 5
3rds	-
5ths	1+3, 2+4, 5+6
6ths	-
Octaves	1+4, 2+5, 4+6
Triads	-

One of the purposes of an altered tuning is to increase the role the open strings make to the overall guitar sound. This is especially important if you perform your songs solo. CD track 39 was written to have absolutely minimal work done by the fretting hand. Every shape requires only one finger to hold a single

CD track 39 DADGAD

note. This allows the maximum amount of resonance from the open strings. Let them ring, and notice how when changing chord the sustain overhangs from one chord to the next. This gives the progression a sense of smoothness and flow.

Songwriting tip 39

First and second inversions of major chords in slow tempo ballad songs can sometimes be more expressive than root position chords, and as such a half-way house between major and minor.

Dsus2

Changes:	-2 x x -3 -2 x
Pitches:	D A D E A E
Profile:	7 5 2 5 7
3rds	-
5ths	1+2, 2+4, 5+6
6ths	-
Octaves	1+3, 2+5, 4+6
Triads	-

Like DADGAD, this tuning is related to open D, but the third has been replaced by a second (E) which is doubled an octave higher with string 1 tuning up from D to E. Notice that like DADGAD its open strings do not contain any triads. It is a tuning in which melodic ideas might come from playing octaves, of which there are three pairs. In a sus2 tuning a minor chord can be restored by raising the seconds by a semitone, and a major chord by raising them by a tone. This is easier to do than in DADGAD where the fourth would have to come down a semitone or a tone to get the major and minor chords. This can't be done without losing the single-finger barre chord shape, as the desired notes lie behind the barre on the relevant strings. In Dsus2 the relevant notes are in front of the barre; it simply means fretting them with two fingers.

CD track 40
DADEAE

I		♭IIIm
D /	Dmaj7 /	Fm9add13 / :‖ [x3]

I	II^	IV	II^
Asus2 / / /	B7 / / /	D7 / / /	B7 / / / ‖

I	♭VII
Asus2 / / /	Gsus2 / / / ‖

I			Im	Vm	IV	♭III
‖: D /	Dmaj7 /	D9 /	Dm9 /	Am /	G6/9 /	Fmaj7 / / / ‖
/ /	IV Gsus2 /	:‖				

I		♭IIIm
‖:D /	Dmaj7 /	Fm9add13 / :‖ [x3] D ‖

CHORDS: **CD track 40**
DADEAE

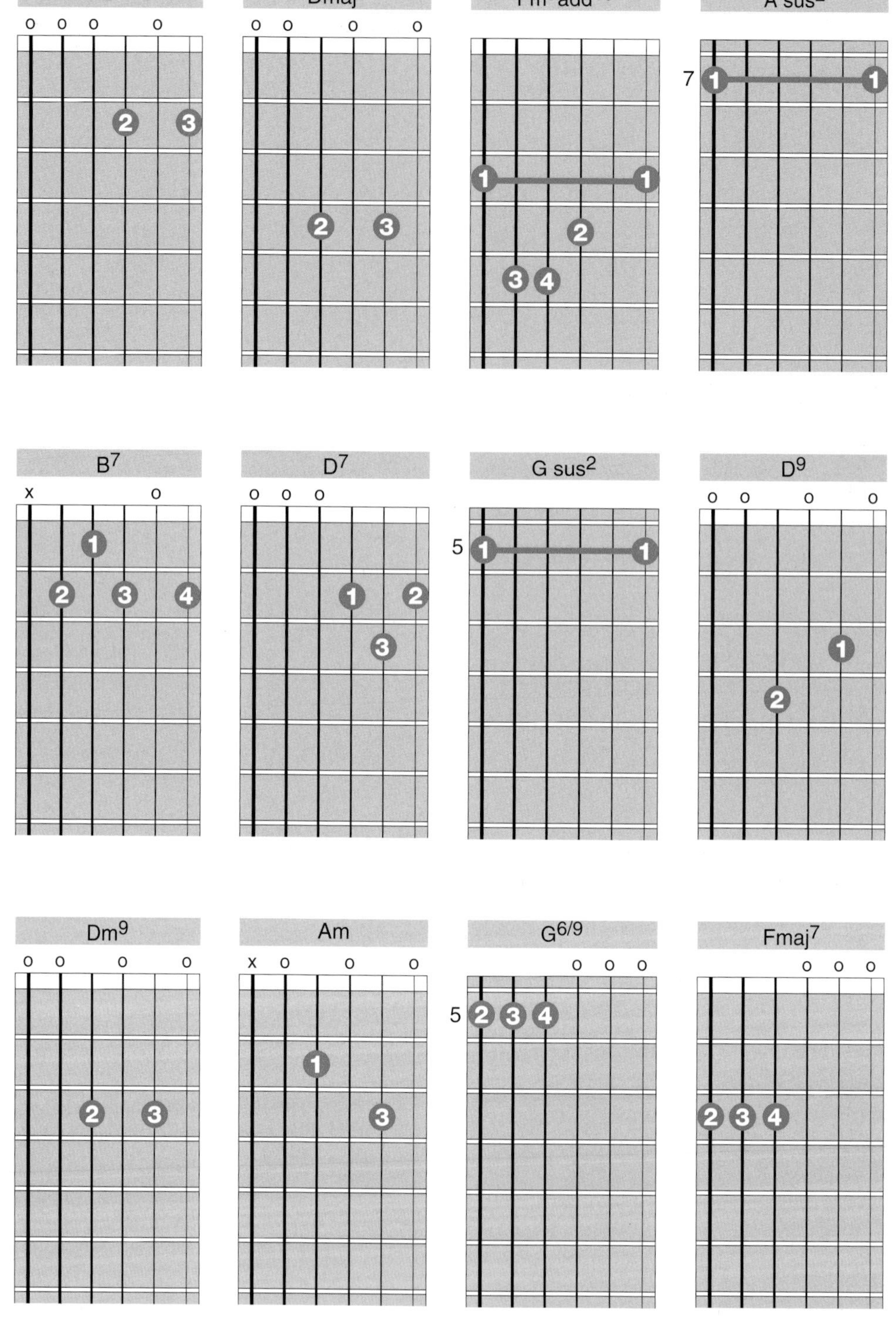

Track 40 (previous page) shows once more that a single type of tuning can express highly contrasted musical styles and emotions. Track 39 in DADGAD (Dsus4) was the foundation of a lyrical finger-picking ballad. Track 40 in Dsus2 tuning is a contemporary rock progression with changing time signatures and angular chord changes. It starts with a six-beat three-chord idea spread over a 4/4 and a 2/4 bar with an unusual change from D to Fm. Then it settles into

4/4, with a six-bar verse idea that, aside from one D7, avoids D. The third idea is a descending sequence of chords whereby D is modified from major to minor, clearly related to the intro idea. The shapes fall nicely under the hand, so it's easy to play but gives a big, resonant sound.

Songwriting tip 40

Create interest in part of a song by adding an extra beat or two beats to a chordal phrase, such as a 5/4 bar or a bar of 2/4 on the end of several 4/4 bars.

Asus4	
Changes:	x x x -2 -2 -2
Pitches:	E A D E A D
Profile:	5 5 2 5 5
3rds	-
5ths	2+4, 3+5
6ths	-
Octaves	1+4, 2+5, 3+6
Triads	-

This tuning has the lower three strings of standard tuning but the top three detuned, giving an Asus4 chord. Again, there are no triads on the open strings. As with both previous tunings the presence of two strings only a tone apart makes it possible to achieve note-clusters. These are not always attractive as strummable chords, but if arpeggiated may suggest melodic phrases. Octaves are strongly supported by this tuning. It is worth noting that in these 'modal tunings' moving an octave pair to the right position on the neck can result in four strings (two fretted, two open) sounding the same pitch in two octaves. This is a characteristic sound of alternate tunings generally but especially those that are open chords or 'modal'.

CD track 41 (next page) is a gentle finger-picked sequence that allows the open strings to ring out in the chords. This could also be played with a pick. Notice that the pitch order of the notes does not always coincide with their physical sequence on the guitar – a sometimes bewildering feature of chords in alternate tunings where some notes are fretted and some not. Track 41 features a descending chord progression popular among songwriters who write on the piano. It can be hard to perform in standard tuning, but in this alternate tuning it gains resonance from the open strings and ease of fingering.

If string 2 were tuned up a tone to B we have EADEBE, a tuning used by the British singer-songwriter Roger Brooks. Roger's catchy lyrics and songs were a cut above the average in the folk clubs of the 70s, though wider success sadly eluded him. This tuning could also be reached by going from standard to 'lute' tuning, and then a further tone (whole-step) down on string 3. From this tuning it is only a single-string adjustment to return to standard.

Songwriting tip 41

When arpeggiating chord sequences in altered tunings listen for hints of what could be vocal melody within the chords, and between chords, caused by 'harp' effects, such as notes moving step-wise.

CD track 41 EADEAD

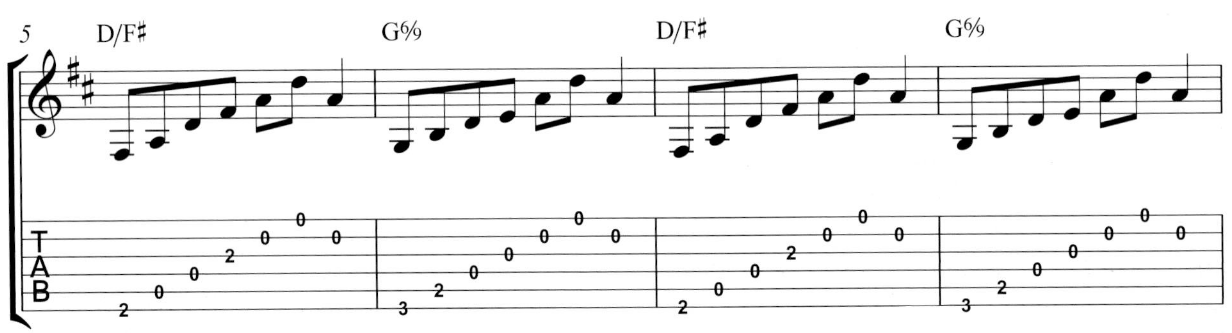

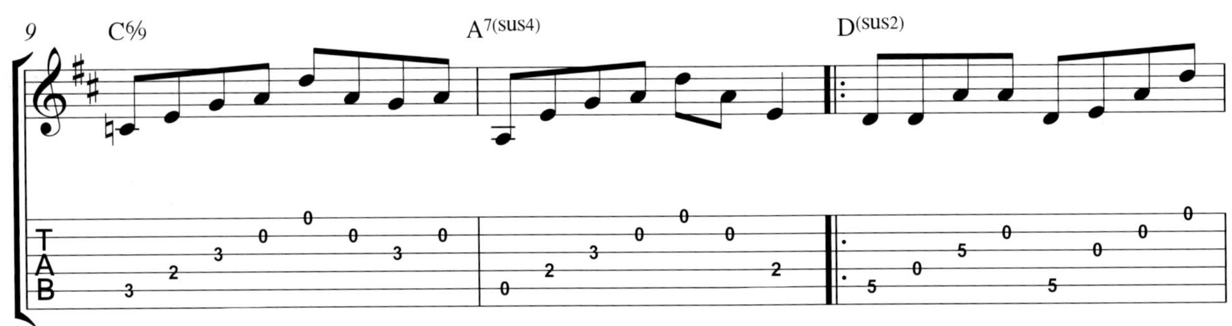

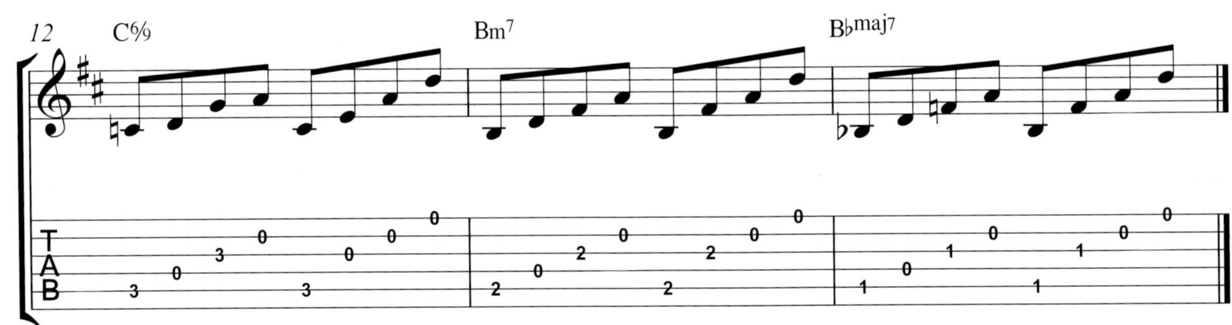

Csus2

Changes:	-4 -2 x x +1 -2
Pitches:	C G D G C D
Profile:	7 7 5 5 2
3rds	-
5ths	1+3, 4+5, 5+6
6ths	-
Octaves	1+4, 3+5, 2+6
Triads	-

Our third example of a sus2 tuning derives it from open C tuning (CGCGCE) by detuning the top string to D and raising string 4 to D. Fretting both those strings at the first fret creates a C minor chord; at the second fret a C major chord. These two shapes can be used with a barre to make major or minor chords at any position on the fretboard.

CD track 42 starts with four bars moving between an extended E♭ chord and C. The verse is through-composed, meaning it does not include any repeated changes. It begins with a G11 (no third) and an Fm that quickly leads the chord sequence toward the flat side of things, culminating in the Cm chord's hint of a change of key. The Gsus4-G change prepares the way for the chorus, an open tuning version of a chord sequence involving the key chord and its sus2 and sus4, often heard in standard tuning (think of The Searchers' 'Needles And Pins', The Who's 'So Sad About Us', The Beatles' 'I Need You', Cat Stevens' 'Can't Keep It In', John Lennon's 'Happy Xmas' (War Is Over)'.)

CD track 42
CGDGCD

♭III		I	
E♭maj7add13 / / /	/ / / /	C / / /	/ / / / :‖

V		IVm	
G11(no 3rd) / / /	/ / / /	Fm / / /	/ / / /

♭VII		II	
B♭ / / /	/ / / /	Dm7 / / /	/ / / /

Vm	Im
Gm7 / / /	Cm / / /

Vm	Im	V	
Gm7 / / /	Cm / / /	Gsus4 / / /	/ / / /

G / / /	/ / / /

I			V	I
‖: C / Csus2 /	Csus4 / C /	C / Csus2 /	Csus4 / G11 / :‖	C ‖

CHORDS: **CD track 42**
CGDGCD

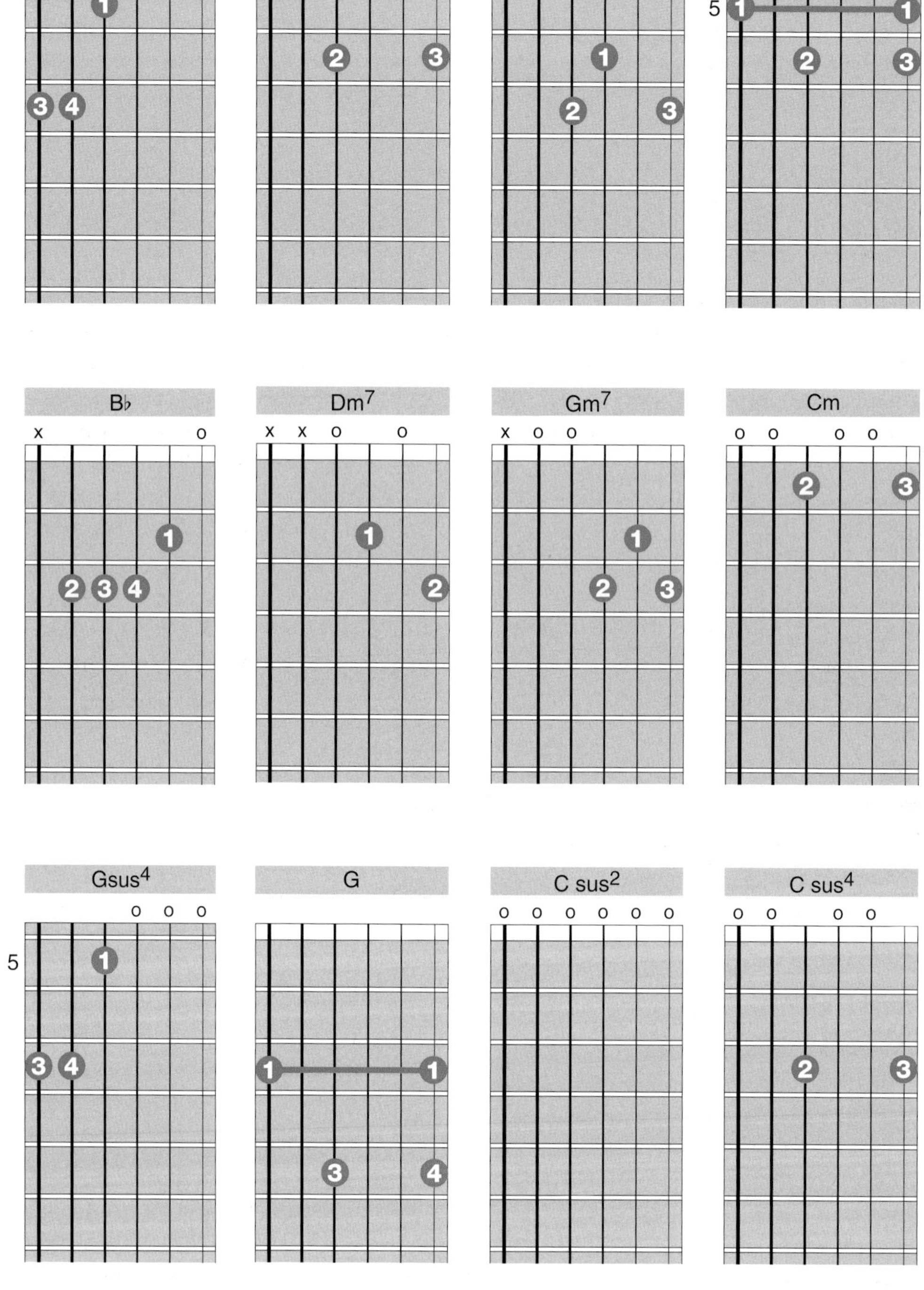

Songwriting tip 42

Try writing a verse in which there are no repeated chord changes. Save those for the chorus and/or the bridge. That way the song has a powerful structural contrast between those sections.

E5

Changes:	x +2 -3 -3 x x
Pitches:	E B B E B E
Profile:	7 0 5 7 5
Unison:	4+5
3rds	-
5ths	2+3, 4+6, 5+6
6ths	-
Octaves	1+3, 2+4, 2+5, 3+6
Triads	-

One method for devising a radical tuning is to tune the strings to only two notes, usually a root note and a fifth. Since standard tuning contains two Es and a B the nearest such tuning would be an E5. How many strings are the root and how many the fifth depends on the pitches you choose and how much detuning is required to get the six strings to one note or the other. In this E5 there are three of each, but another option is to have a unison of two Es rather than two Bs (EBEEBE). A fifth tuning can be derived from an open major if the third of the tuning is tuned up to the fifth. Open D major (DADF♯AD) would become DADAAD with strings 3 and 2 in unison. Open G (DGDGBD) indicates the problems this can pose, as tuning the B string up to D to get DGDGDD risks breaking it. The same risk presents itself with open C (CGCGCE) where tuning the E string up to G might cause it to snap. An A5 tuning could be EAEAAE (x x +2 +2 -2 x) or AAEAAE (-7 x +2 +2 -2 x).

CSN&Y used this type of tuning on some of their songs, including 'Suite: Judy Blue Eyes'. Soundgarden's 'My Wave' from *Superunknown* takes this to a further level with a tuning of EEBBBB with the top three strings in unison. One of Nick Drake's favourite tunings was BEBEBE and 'Man In A Shed' is said to be in DGDGDG, though if the top 2 strings are tuned up to those notes it risks string breakage (if you want to try that one I'd recommend tuning CFCFCF and adding a capo at the second fret).

A tuning which comprises only a fifth lends itself to droning effects and 'raga-rock' songs. It will take a fair amount of distortion. Octave melodic playing and pedal-note ideas are easily achieved. Barre major and minor chords can be found by locating a third on one of the upper strings. However, it seems slightly perverse to be in a tuning like this and try to stick to conventional chord harmony.

CD track 43 (next page) shows the opportunity with an E5 tuning for a heavier rock song. It starts with a classic blues-rock riff of I-♭III-IV. This idea returns at the end with a guitar fill. At bar nine a classic rhythm figure that most guitarists will know in standard tuning is given a fresh slant by the tuning, as the notes are coloured and supported by the droning upper strings above. The effect is thicker than it would be in EADGBE. This verse idea is presented through a variation on the 12-bar form. Notice in bars 19-20 that the top three strings are sounded open, making chords that contrast with the sound of the previous fifths.

CD track 43 EBBEBE

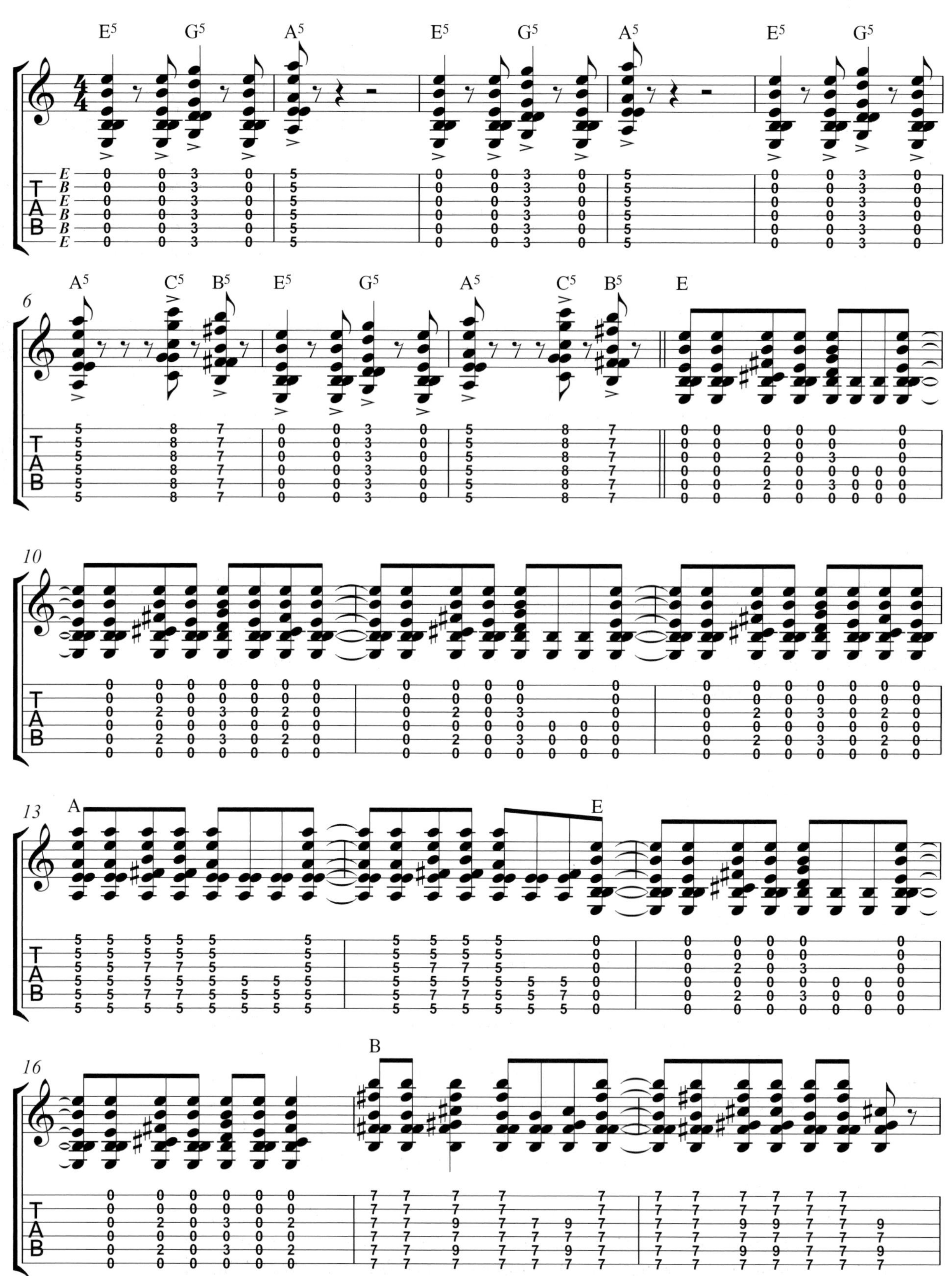

CD track 43 (continued)

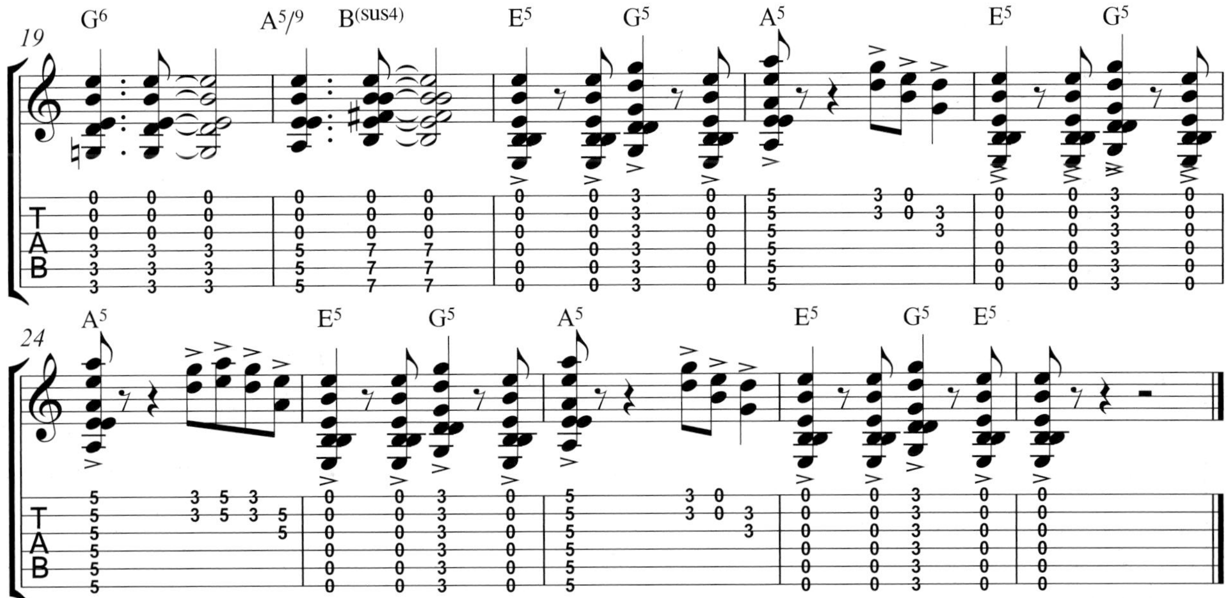

Songwriting tip 43

The chord on the ♭V (heard as B♭ in bars six and eight of track 42), especially in its form as a fifth, has a dark and unsettling effect in a chord progression, though it is less obtrusive as a chromatic passing chord between IV and V provided it is voiced as the same type of chord. So if they are majors, it is major; if they are minor sevenths, it is a minor seventh.

Fmaj7

Changes:	x x -2 -2 -2 x
Pitches:	E A C F A E
Profile:	5 3 5 4 7
3rds	2+3, 4+5
5ths	1+2
6ths	2+4, 3+5
Octaves	2+5
Triads	F (2+3+4), Am (1+2+4), Am (4+5+6)

This tuning is the result of an experiment which was fruitful but not in the manner I anticipated. I had been thinking about creating a bespoke open F major tuning. F major is a key little used in standard tuning because a full barre F is a tiring chord to play and other important chords in the key such as Gm, B♭ and E♭ are also barre chords. Many guitar songs in F major default to a capo at fret three (playing as if in D) or fret five (playing as if in C) where the chord shapes are open.

An F major tuning could be pitched from open D with a capo at fret three, or by detuning open G a tone, or taking an open E tuning and capoing up a fret. But I was looking for something that would sound different. What I hit upon was this tuning which I constructed around an easy shape for a mostly open-string F chord at the first fret. Unfortunately, as the chord boxes show, the other chords in the key a songwriter would want were elusive as effective shapes, nor did I have the compensation from the tuning of a one-finger barre major chord. However, inspiration struck when I found some exciting chords for A major, including a couple with an unusual mix of notes. What had turned into a problem was now a songwriting opportunity. The solution was to put the verse into F major and play whatever shapes were okay in that, and then change key for a chorus in A major. It's not a tuning I would want to spend a lot of time with but it has its good points.

CD track 44
EACFAE

I Ω	VI	I	VI
F / / /	Dmadd9 / / /	F / / /	Dmadd9 / / / ‖
V	II	V	II
C / / /	Gm7 / / /	C / / /	Gm7 / / / ‖
I	VI	♭III	
F / / /	Dmadd9 / / /	A♭11♭9 / / /	/ / / / :‖
I V	VI	I V	VI
‖: A / E11 /	F♯m9 / / /	A / E11 /	F♯m9 / / / ‖
I V	VI	♭III	i♭VII
A / E11 /	F♯m9 / / /	C / / /	G6/9/B / / / ‖
IV			
Dadd9 / / / :‖ Dadd9 ‖			

Track 44 is an upbeat song with some harmonic twists. The verse has classic I-VI, V-II changes but the verse (of 12 bars) has a surprise at its end, which is the A♭11♭9. This chord is a fine instance of the principle that one method for finding interesting chords in a new tuning is to play familiar shapes from standard tuning and see how they come out. I held down a standard tuning barre minor shape and this monster was the result. It was then a matter of adjusting the pitch so that the root note of this chord made sense in the overall progression, as a chord in F and occupying a position leading to the key-change into A at the chorus. Enharmonically all but one of the flat notes in this A♭ chord are sharp notes on the scale of A major. The F♯madd9 has a different bass note under it on the third time C♯ which changes the chord into a C♯m6 chord – this is because of its ambiguity in the first instance.

Songwriting tip 44

A key-change into a chorus in a major key can be uplifting, especially following a verse that was in a minor key.

CHORDS: CD track 44
EACFAE

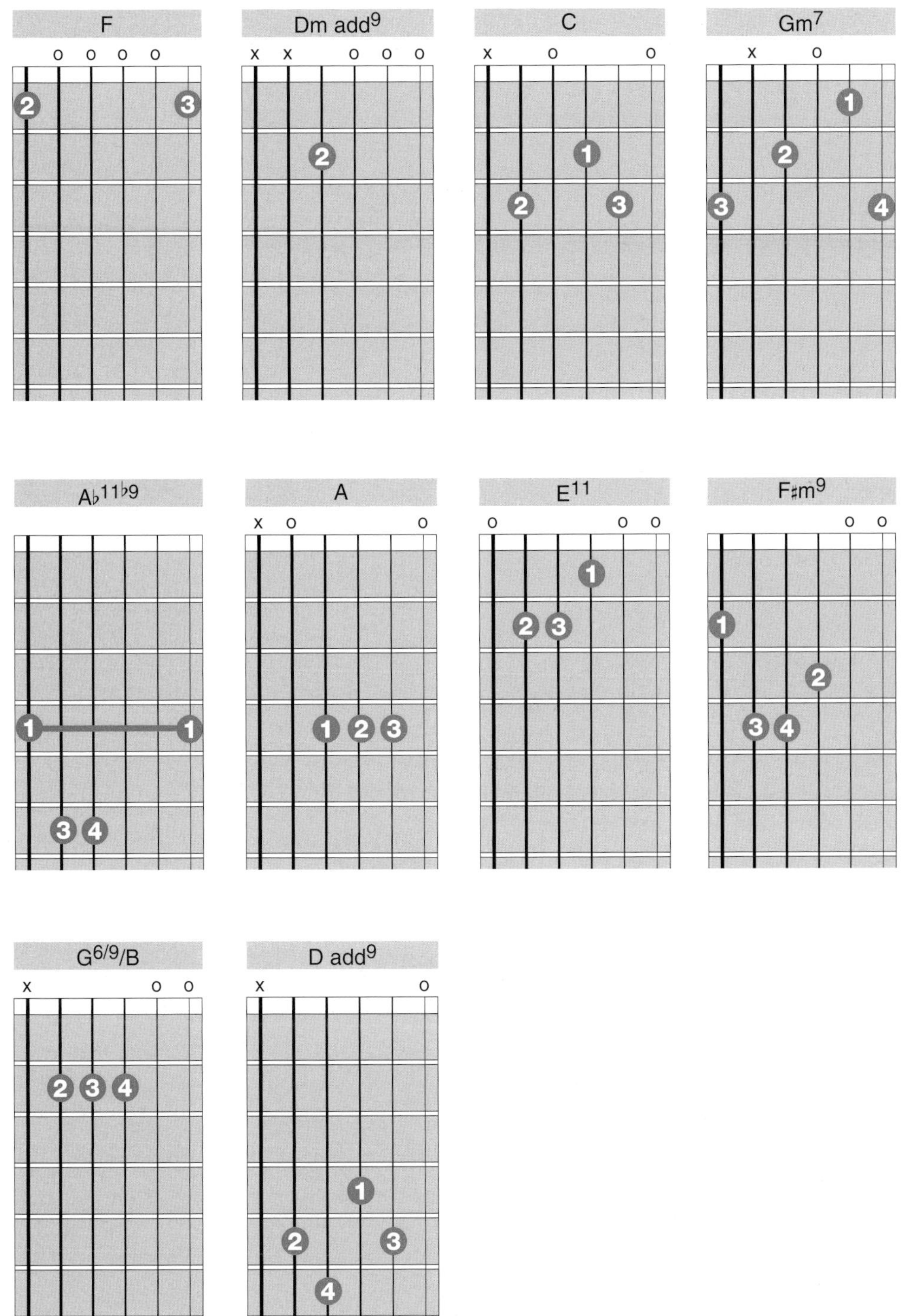

This concludes our journey into the world of altered tunings. There are many other tunings to be discovered or invented, but these are more than enough to give you a feeling of whether you can write songs with them. Remember that for each tuning there are ready-selected chord shapes in the chord dictionary in **Section 12**. Following 30 tunings it would be understandable if you didn't have a few questions you wanted answered. I'll try to anticipate some of them in the next section.

SECTION 10

FAQs FOR ALTERED TUNINGS

How exactly do I go about exploring a new tuning with a view to finding song ideas?

My own approach is to simply play and initially not think too consciously about what I'm doing. I passively allow a mood to creep over me as I listen to the new chords. Emotion-charged harmony is often the start of a song. Otherwise:

- I play shapes from standard tuning and listen for how they have changed in the new tuning. If a chord shape is nearly acceptable but has one 'wrong' note I locate it and turn it into something more acceptable by adjusting my fingering.
- If the tuning makes an open chord I hold a first-finger barre and add fingers to it.
- I check the intervals between strings, find octaves, thirds or sixths, move them up and down and let the other strings sound as drones. This might provide a riff or a melodic idea, but it can also locate chords.
- I experiment with fifths on the lower strings, again with the open strings as drone notes.
- I use theoretical knowledge to look for a tuning's potential to work in certain keys. In some tunings if you have a great chord where you're holding down the lower three strings and the top three are open you can find a different type of chord as you move up the neck. This is effective because it changes the harmonic value of the open strings, which in an altered tuning risk being monotonous.
- If the altered tuning has a particular note(s) that dominates I look for a chord that temporarily removes that note during part of the song to refresh the tuning.
- If I write a song in one tuning I try to write another in it based on a different key centre with different chords. I may also use a capo on the tuning.
- If a tuning is not happening I sometimes tweak a string within it. This could mean adding a seventh to an open major or minor, or taking the third out and going to a so-called 'modal' tuning. I might add a sixth, which has the effect on an open major tuning of making it closer to the relative minor (see the A6 tuning in Section Six).

Once I have purchase in a territory and a song idea for a verse or chorus, I look for contrasted chord voicings. I'll want an effective shape for chords I-VI, and some of the flat degree and reverse polarity chords. If I get a pleasing sequence with rich major/minor sounds I may then seek chords to build a key contrast round, or dissonant chords to add toughness – dominant sevenths and ninths are good for that. You don't need that many chords to write a song – six or seven is often enough.

My friend says that altered tunings are a cheat. Is he right?

In a word, no. Altered tunings are not a cheat. We play instruments to make music. If an altered tuning furthers that aim, then it is valid. Furthermore, if an altered tuning actually creates music with its own character, then it couldn't be played in anything else but that tuning. If it enables you to write songs you otherwise would not have written, that also is valid. The only negative aspect of altered tunings is if they were a substitute for learning enough technique to be able to play in standard tuning. Then they could restrict someone's development as a guitar player and conceivably as a songwriter. But many players don't learn that many chords in standard tuning anyway; if you don't want to progress as a player beyond the rudiments, the tuning you play in may be immaterial.

Finally, ask your friend if he considers a song like Led Zeppelin's 'Kashmir' or Joni Mitchell's 'Amelia' a 'cheat'!

I've not been playing guitar very long. Is it correct to say that altered tunings are only for advanced players?

Not really. Advanced players have the theoretical knowledge and fretboard experience to create and explore altered tunings with rapidity and seize the opportunities they offer faster than less experienced players/songwriters. But you don't need to be skilled as a guitarist to find a few chord shapes that spark a song. Guitar technique has little to do with the ability to write a memorable song on the guitar, as the history of chart hits demonstrates over and over. Remember that some beginners started in an open tuning because nobody showed them EADGBE. The only aspect that might cause anxiety to the less experienced guitarist is the business of tuning and pitching notes. These days technology takes care of that, because even if your ear isn't that good an electronic tuner does the job.

Do I need a special set of strings to work in altered tunings?

Not initially, provided you're not venturing too far from standard tuning. But the lighter the gauge the sooner a de-tuned string loses tone, feels too slack, and acquires intonation problems when fretted. The heavier the gauge the more head-room there is when you slacken the tension before such problems arise. Light to medium gauge strings on an acoustic will cope with string detuning of roughly up to about four semitones. Lighter gauge strings on an electric with a low action will not respond to detuning so well, with fret-rattle one result. Guitarists who want to do heavy electric detuned riffs usually re-string with a heavier gauge. If you can afford it, it can be helpful to have a second acoustic guitar strung with heavier strings for detuning.

Are altered tunings more effective on the acoustic than the electric?

My personal view is yes, but it's a marginal thing. I would say that altered tunings function with greater ease, clarity, and immediacy on acoustic guitar. On electric guitar light-gauge strings make many altered tunings less effective because of a loss of tension and tone in the strings. Press too hard on a detuned string, or strike it too forcefully, and it goes sharp. Pull it a little up or down, same thing. Having said this, provided there isn't a problem with string tension, I personally like the sound of some open-tuned riffs with slight distortion – as in Neil Young's 'Cinnamon Girl' (tuned DADGBD).

What about using effects with altered tunings?

The problematic effect for altered tunings is undoubtedly distortion/overdrive, which makes the tunings sound mushy, partly by boosting complex overtones, and thus can mask the subtleties of their chord voicings (though fifth chords and tunings are not so bad). In a way distortion is counter-productive, because the point of re-tuning the guitar is to create those voicings. Clean guitar effects – chorus, phasing, reverb, and echo – sound good with altered tunings on both acoustic and electric.

I've noticed that open tunings rarely feature flat notes. Why is this?

Keys on the 'flat side' of things, from F major to C♭ major, (yes, there really is such a key) require more re-tuning if standard tuning is the start point. This was demonstrated in **Section Five** by the creation of an open B♭ major tuning:

Standard	E A D G B E
Tuning	+1+1 x -2 -1 -2
Result	F B♭ D F B♭ D
Profile	5 4 3 5 4

Five of the strings have changed pitch and the tuning has two thirds, which is often troublesome. To remove either of them involves considerable re-tuning up or down of string 1 or 4. Similar issues arise when tuning to extreme sharp keys. How about creating an open F♯ major?

Standard	E A D G B E
Tuning	+2 +1 -1 -1 -1 -3
Result	F♯ A♯ C♯ F♯ A♯ C♯
Profile	4 3 5 4 3

In this case all six strings have changed pitch and again the tuning has two thirds.

So is it possible to create an open major or minor tuning for any note?

Possible, yes, but whether desirable or easily achievable is another thing. Many altered tunings are based on the notes A, C, D, E, and G, but not B, F, or the five sharp/flat notes (C♯/D♭, D♯/E♭, F♯/G♭, G♯/A♭, A♯/B♭). The decisive factor has to do with the guitar's open strings in standard tuning. Do any of these fit in the new tuning? If not, how much re-tuning is needed to get all the strings to the right pitch? How feasible is it to get the root note of the tuning on the open string 5 or 6? This isn't to say that there aren't interesting flat/sharp open tunings to be explored, but the simpler route if pitch concerns you (perhaps for vocal reasons) may be to choose the nearest common open tuning – like open D or E, G or A – (or their minor equivalents) and let a capo raise the tuning to the desired pitch.

What are the unison notes marked on some of the chord boxes in Section 12?

Unison notes are a feature of altered tunings – you get more of them than in standard tuning. Unison notes are notes that share the same pitch. They enhance the resonance of an open-string chord. This can result in a chord sound reminiscent of a 12-string, since 12-string guitars have their top two (or three) pairs of strings tuned to the same pitch. Unisons happen more often when the guitar is in non-standard tunings, and unison chords work well on acoustic guitar. The precise effect of any given unison chord depends on:

1. Whether the unison involves adjacent strings.
2. Whether both strings are open or one is fretted.
3. Whether the note pair is the root, third, fifth, or something else of the chord. Doubled roots and fifths tend to make the strongest impression.
4. How high or low in the chord the unison is positioned.
5. How many unisons there are.

Harder to spot are sneaky 'hidden' unisons. These are notes at the same pitch but not adjacent and therefore less obvious. They sometimes crop up in altered tuning open chords higher up the neck. In rare instances a chord can have even have two unison pairs.

How do I invent my own tunings?

When you re-tune a guitar it doesn't take long before, just by messing about, some great sounding chords will present themselves. The challenge is to get past the point at which you have the initial burst of inspiration and then hit a temporary zone where it seems you have struck the limits of that particular tuning. Sometimes this is because you can't find a certain chord needed in a progression. That is why it is useful to find good movable shapes to cover the simple majors and minors, as they will often plug such a gap. To really get to know an altered tuning takes longer. This may not be of concern to songwriters, because if you get enough from a tuning to write a song then your mission is accomplished. Instrumentalists, however, may take longer to get to know a tuning. This can also apply to songwriters who wish to write a number of songs in the same tuning. If you wish to do that you may want to use a capo to vary the pitch but also consider how many key centres that tuning allows you to play in effectively.

There are other points to consider when you move past haphazardly playing shapes and marvelling at the sounds. Identify those strings that are tuned in octaves, thirds, or sixths, as these are the intervals for melodic ideas and riffs. Identify the mix of roots and fifths in the basic open chord and locate (if there is one) the third. That is crucial because it tells you something about how to change chords from major to minor or vice versa. You can also try to find the 12 basic songwriting chords for that key, though in my view this takes one too close to things one might do in standard tuning. Remember that each movable shape will give you chords for each pitch.

When you re-tune the guitar a good immediate approach to finding sounds by ear is to play a number of simple shapes from standard tuning and see how different they sound. Run through the master-shapes – A, C, D, E, G, Am, Dm, Em – first. Then try their respective sevenths. If a note sounds wrong, see where it is. It will often be the case that a single-string alteration tuning flavours common chords with a foreign note and that is enough to make a sequence sound exciting. You will also want to take out a drone note where one exists in a tuning. So in EADGBD it is possible to play through a sequence of chords with the top string open. This might become monotonous if sustained through a whole song. So find some shapes where a finger placed on that string will temporarily mask it. The drone note changes colour – that is, harmonic function – with each chord.

The easiest method is to start with EADGBE and then re-tune only one or two strings. To make this effective these alterations can't really be random. More musical results follow either de-tuning a string to a note of the key you want to play in, or to a natural note that will to some extent blend with those of standard tuning. Another approach is to create a new major or minor triad within EADGBE (see the opening of **Section Three**). Always tune down rather than up.

Tunings with adjacent strings only a semitone (half-step), tone (whole-step), or third apart work well in finger-picked or arpeggiated songs, but not so well in strumming because they may not have enough effective chord shapes; strumming is more productive in tunings where the chord shapes are straightforward.

If you want to create an open major or minor tuning consider the mix of roots, thirds and fifths. Aim to have one third, preferably in the upper strings (though not on the top string which in my experience has a weak sound – as in open C, CGCGCE). There should be two strings apiece for the root and the fifth. Ideally the root note should be the open string 5 or 6. It is desirable to have wider intervals (fourths and fifths) at the bottom of the tuning than at the top.

The kind of open tuning is related to the style of the song you want to write. Open major tunings or hybrid ones made out of 5ths only, or even some 'modal' tunings like DADGAD, are good for blues, rock, and riffs. Open major tunings lend themselves to slide playing if you write blues songs. Tunings with octave bass strings are good for finger-picking songs. Open major and minor variants (see **Sections 6** and **8**) lend themselves to ballads and more emotive material, with less or no blues influence.

Can I play a guitar solo during a song in an altered tuning?

Yes, though this is when the player experiences the defamiliarising effect of altered tunings at their strongest. The fastest way to take your lead guitar soloing back to the drawing board is to attempt a solo in an altered tuning.

Depending on the tuning, few notes may be where they were, and it only takes one note out of place to mess up a familiar scale pattern. But you never know, that might be a good thing. Start by running up and down patterns you usually solo with. It may be you will strike lucky and find some good phrases. If you get notes that sound wrong, adjust the pattern until they fit. Another approach is to solo up and down a string instead of across the fretboard; that way you can take advantage of droning open strings. The potential gain is that unfamiliar finger patterns can produce unexpected melodic ideas, and slacker strings can mean wilder bends.

When it comes to re-fingering scale patterns for playing lead the rule is this: for every semitone a string is detuned the notes on that string move up one fret.

If I'm working in altered tunings, don't I need to know how are chords made?

You don't have to, but it helps you name the chords you find. Take the scale of C major (we could use any major scale but C will do as it has no sharps or flats):

C	D	E	F	G	A	B	C	D	E	F	G	A	B	C
1	2	3	4	5	6	7		9		11		13		

Each degree of the scale is given a number. Notice that the scale has been extended past the octave (C to C) and that the numbers eight, ten, 12, 14, and 15 are missing. In simple harmony terms this is because those notes do not exist in ways that make a difference to the formation and naming of chords. They duplicate notes lower down. Eight and 15 would be heard as the same as one, ten would be heard as the same as three, 12 as the same as five, and 14 the same as seven. In the context of chords the ear can't hear any meaningful harmonic difference between such pairs. So the only numbers that count are one to seven, nine, 11 and 13.

To make a chord we take these notes in order and stack them. So notes 1-3-5 make the chord of C major. This is known as a triad because it has three notes. To make a 'seventh' we would add a B; to make a 'ninth' add a B and D, and so on. Variations of chords are also created by lowering or omitting the third, lowering the seventh, raising or lowering the fifth or ninth.

What determines how many roots, thirds, or fifths I put in a tuning?

A triad is a three-note chord. There are four foundation triad types: major, minor, augmented and diminished. Each involves two intervals or gaps measured in semitones (half-steps), in a combination of three and/or four semitones. They exist on any of the 12 notes. Here they are on the note C with the interval measurement in-between.

Triad of C major	C	4	E	3	G
Triad of C minor	C	3	E♭	4	G
Triad of C augmented	C	4	E	4	G♯
Triad of C diminished	C	3	E♭	3	G♭

All the chord shapes are created on these basic triad types. A simple major or minor only needs three notes. Since the guitar has six strings it makes sense to double or treble these notes. Doubling or trebling means adding more roots, thirds, and fifths. It does not involve adding any different notes if the chord is a simple major or minor. Take the open A major chord, for example, in standard tuning:

6	5	4	3	2	1
x	A	E	A	C♯	E
	1	5	1	3	5

It has two roots, a third, and two fifths. In most cases the lowest sounded note in a guitar chord should be the root note, that is, the note after which the chord is named. So with this A major chord you should avoid hitting the low E string. Open major and minor tunings are constructed along triadic lines.

Can I combine a guitar in altered tuning with one in standard?

Yes, and on a recording or performance with more than one guitar this can give extra depth and texture, as long as the shapes are pitched in the same key. On recordings by The Rolling Stones, if Keith Richards is in open G, Ron Wood will usually be in standard tuning. If Guitar I is in standard tuning, simple options for Guitar II include:

- 'Lute tuning', third string down to F♯. Good for songs in D and B minor.
- Top string down to D. Good for songs in C, G, D, A, and E, A minor, E minor, B minor.
- Fifth string down to G. Good for songs in G, G minor, or E minor.
- 'Drop D', sixth string down to D. Good for songs in D or D minor.

The pitch and key of any of these can be further modified by a capo. After this it might be a matter of choosing an open tuning to match the key in which Guitar I is played.

What happens when I capo an altered tuning?

Here are some options for combining a capo with an altered tuning:

- A capo can raise the pitch of an open or altered tuning to the desired key. This is a sensible way to take the strain off the neck. Open A (EAEAC♯E) and open E (EBEG♯BE) are popular open tunings on electric guitar, but they require tuning a number of strings above standard pitch, risking string breakage. Many players avoid this on an acoustic with heavier strings. Tuning to open G and open D (the equivalents a tone down) with a capo at the second fret is a good compromise.
- A capo can bring a second guitar in open tuning up to the correct pitch for a song that is played with Guitar I in standard tuning. For a song in E, Guitar I plays standard open shapes, Guitar II is in open D tuning with a capo at the second fret.
- If you like open tunings and play live, a capo is one method to get several songs from the same tuning but varying the key and without slowing your

performance by constant re-tuning. The first song could be in open G, second song could be in A (open G tuning, capo II) and third song might be in C (open G tuning, capo V).

- A capo can help you cheat in the studio if you have a song in an altered tuning and want to do a key-change. Imagine a song in open E tuning and half way through the song it changes key up a semi-tone to F. The problem is that the E major section uses distinctive open-string chords and these cannot be replicated with barre shapes. So another guitar part is recorded for the second half of the song with the capo at the first fret. You still have the open tuning but it is now sounding in F. Unfortunately, this will not be reproducible live – unless you take a pause from playing guitar to put the capo on.
- Capos help with transposing the key of a song for the sake of a singer. This applies to altered tunings as well. Let's say you have a song in open G tuning (DGDGBD) and that's a good key for you to sing but not for the new vocalist who has joined your band. She wants to sing it in C, a fourth higher. Perhaps the song might be moved into open C tuning (CGCGCE). You try this and find some of the best chord shapes are lost. Instead, the solution might be to go back to open G and capo at the 5th fret.

Is it possible to use altered tunings on a twelve-string guitar?

It certainly is, but it needs patience for one simple, practical reason: that's an awful lot of strings to re-tune! Plus there's the risk of snapping the high G octave on string 3, even coming down. Also, the barre-chords you might play in an open major or minor require more strength and better positioning to make them sound clean. Of course live, when you have reached your desired tuning with the 12-string and played your song, no audience is going to be happy sitting waiting for you to tune back! So for live gigs it is a non-starter unless you have a 12-string which stays in one tuning for the gig and is only played for a couple of numbers. A capo would yield more songs from the same tuning in different keys, but even then would need re-tuning between numbers once you put the capo on or move it.

In the studio, it's a different matter. A 12-string naturally amplifies the chorus-like effect of an altered tuning, and where a tuning includes chords with unisons they become doubled – so you can find chords with four or even five strings sounding the same note.

Sometimes I find a promising chord in an altered tuning but it isn't quite right. How can I adjust the sound of chord shapes in altered tunings?

Check for unwanted doubling of thirds, thirds that are too low, adjacent bass strings that are only a tone apart, and unwanted unisons if a vital note is missing from the tuning and could be fretted and replace one of those unwanted doubled pitches. Favour wide intervals (fourths and fifths) between the lower strings rather than small intervals (thirds and seconds). Aim to have the extra notes of extended chords, if they are part of the tuning, higher in pitch on the upper strings. For example an open Emin9 tuning of EF♯DGBE would be less effective than EGDF♯BE.

What can I do with harmonics and altered tunings?

Harmonics sound good in an altered tuning, often because there are more useful ones available at a given fret. If you're not already familiar with them, harmonics are high, soft notes created by touching a string, instead of pressing it down, at certain points on the neck. To create a harmonic, touch the string right over the metal fret, not behind it. Strike the string and pull your finger away to let the string ring. The strongest harmonics are at frets 12, seven, five and four or nine in both standard and altered tunings. They pitch as follows:

- Fret 12 gives the note an octave above the open string.
- Fret seven gives the note an octave and a fifth above the open string.
- Fret five gives the note two octaves above the open string.
- Fret four or nine gives the note two octaves and a major third above the open string.

To get these harmonics when you have a capo on the fretboard simply add on to the above fret positions how many frets the capo has been placed.

- In an open major tuning, the strings' harmonics give chord I (frets 12 and five), chord V (fret seven), and chord III^ (fret four or nine). In open G: chord I = G, chord V = D, chord III^ = B. In open G minor: chord I = Gm, chord V = Dm, chord III^ = Bm.

For the songwriter, harmonics can be useful as a musical punctuation point during a chord progression.

I recorded a song in an altered tuning with my band. Once we overdubbed two other guitars and a keyboard I couldn't hear the tuning anymore. What happened?

This happens in a band arrangement because the sonorities of altered tuning chords are easily obscured. What makes the altered tuning sound the way it does is a combination of guitar timbre and chord voicing. If you record a solo demo with one guitar the guitar part is unobstructed and clear so you hear the effect of the tuning. Once other harmonic instruments are overdubbed the chord voicings of the alternate tuning are blurred. The more instruments placed around an altered tuning guitar part, the more the character of that tuning is lost. This does not in itself invalidate them for full arrangements. To retain their identity, multi-track several guitars in the same tuning, playing the same chord voicings, but different types of instrument, that is, acoustic and electric, six-string and 12-string. The flavour of the altered tuning can be strengthened if melodic voice leading within the chord changes (the motion of one note in a chord to the next) is doubled by single-note melodic figures in other instruments. If you hear short melodic phrases resonating from the chord changes, transcribe those notes and then get another instrument to play that melodic phrase at that point.

You may need fewer guitar parts than you think, as altered tunings can occupy a lot of aural space in an arrangement, especially if distorted. Such a track may not need many harmonic instruments on it.

How do I know to which key a tuning lends itself?

Always look for hidden chords within a tuning's open strings. This will be a pointer to which chord shapes to construct. Triads within an altered tuning are useful for second guitar fills, decorative arpeggios, harmonic gap filling (where you can't find a decent shape for a specific major or minor chord), harmonics, and slide guitar. When trying to work out which keys/chords an altered string leans toward, refer to the scales in which it occurs, especially where it occurs as the first, fourth, or fifth of the scale. Analyse the new note like this:

New detuned note D is the:

- root of D and Dm
- second of C and Cm
- third of B♭ and Dm
- fourth of A and Am
- fifth of G and Gm
- sixth of B♭ and Bm
- flattened seventh of E
- minor seventh of Em
- major seventh of E♭

I can find a few chords in a new tuning, but how do I get more from altered tunings?

One way is to think intervals. In an altered tuning it is often possible to play melodic phrases in intervals such as thirds, fourths, fifths, and octaves. These can be accompaniment figures, heard at the end of a vocal line, or phrases used for an intro or a link to a chorus, or an instrumental bridge. They can be enhanced by pulling one or other finger off onto the open string each time after playing them. These intervals follow certain patterns up and down the neck depending on the precise scale you want to use. This is normally the major scale for the key of the open tuning, but it might be minor if the tuning is minor, and it might also be a modal scale such as the mixolydian if your chord progression tends that way.

On any given pair of strings, octaves keep the same fretting shape as they move up and down the fretboard. Thirds and sixths utilise two shapes – a minor third, a major third, a minor sixth, and a major sixth, which result in a change of fretting position. Such interval-based figures are handy for solo performers as they allow for melodic content in the guitar-playing with the background support of the open strings.

Sometimes you can create a progression with a single shape. In most of these positions the open strings form added notes, sometimes tense, but there may be one position where the open strings suddenly are simply the root, third, or fifth of the chord. This creates a significant shift of colour – I call this the 'resolution chord'.

For an example take 'top drop D' (EADGBD) tuning and the shapes 355000, 133000, 577000, and 799000. Sometimes it is a matter of choice as to how you voice a chord to achieve a certain effect. Compare the shapes in that tuning: x35000 and x35500. They are both versions of a C9 (no 3rd). The first is xCGGBD, where there is a unison G; the second is xCGCBD, where there is a note-cluster on the top three strings, each note being next to each on a C major scale. If finger-picked it will produce a 'harp effect'.

What is the difference between an 'add4' and a 'sus4' tuning?

In an add4 chord the third is still present; in a sus4 chord the third is missing. Aadd4 is AC♯ED (root-third-fourth-fifth); Asus4 is ADE (root-fourth-fifth). The add4 chord can be either major or minor; the sus4 chord is tonally neutral, although context may colour it. Play an Asus4 after Am and resolve it to Am several times and the Asus4 starts to sound as if it were in some way minor. The reverse happens with the sus4 following and resolving to a major chord.

What is the difference between an 'add9' and a major or minor 9 tuning?

The add9 chord lacks a seventh and only has four different notes. Cadd9 is CEGD (1-3-5-9); C[dominant]9 is CEGB♭D (1-3-5-♭7-9); Cmajor9 is CEGBD (1-3-5-7-9); Cmadd9 is CE♭GD (1-♭3-5-9); Cm9 is CE♭GB♭D (1-♭3-5-♭7-9). Of these, the add9 chord is the most popular in standard tuning. Altered tunings make examples of the minor add9 and minor 9 more playable than in standard tuning.

I've looked on the web and seen long lists of tunings and felt overwhelmed. Do I really need to know them all?

No you don't. There has been an amazing spread of tunings because people who compose on the guitar experiment continuously in pursuit of new sounds. What counts is knowing a small number in which you can write your songs. So find a couple of tunings you like and make them distinctively yours by seeing how much you can get from them. That's better than knowing dozens and dozens but being unable to make them creatively function. An interesting challenge is this: can you write an album of songs (that is, about ten numbers) in only two tunings, allowing the use of a capo to change the keys? It is also the case that songwriters are drawn to different kinds of chords and sequences. This means they get different sounds from a common tuning. There are songs to be written in open G that don't sound like The Rolling Stones, and songs in DADGAD that don't sound like Led Zeppelin. It's up to you.

SECTION 11

FAMOUS SONGWRITERS TALK ALTERED TUNINGS

BERT JANSCH

Drop D is my favourite. I find that with DADGAD you can get a certain flavour out of it but unless you want that flavour it's limiting. I think all tunings are limiting really. Most of my playing is in standard tuning. My favourite is to just drop the bottom E down to D … I think then the whole scale of D opens up. It goes right down. The whole range is wider than normal tuning … If you capo up you lose the depth. Sometimes I do it for vocal reasons.

JOHN RENBOURN

If you take DADGAD, it's fine if you're playing in related scales round D, right? Or close ones – you could play in a mode on A. Pierre Bensusan plays quite a lot in C using DADGAD. But it seems you're making things more difficult for yourself if you want to use an open tuning and play the same type of harmonic music that would be suitable for EADGBE. The opposite applies, too. If you're in standard and you want to play something that's purely in one mode or has an even more limited note grouping then sometimes you have notes that are inessential in the tuning. So why have them?

I can just about manage to sing an octave in B. So if I want to sing a certain folk song I adjust the tuning. If I drop the G to F♯ ['lute tuning'] that helps. I could then play things effectively. You begin the process of changing one string. Then you think, "Ah well, this piece has got a strong C♯ in it so why don't I just drop the D string a semitone?" Then you find you've got a nice accompaniment for the words and a few guitar phrases that roll together and sound good without you singing them. Then you begin to find your way round the tuning. But it has gone a hell of a long way. I mean guys like Alex diGrassi and Michael Hedges. They take the British influence and make what they call New Age guitar music – that's nearly always in non-standard tuning. A lot of it I really like.

Most of the tunings I use are neither major nor minor. If I use open G, open

D, one in A, or open C it is just to play pieces that are specifically in a major key and fit.

PAT KIRTLEY

Not every player will be comfortable with the prospect of making a drastic break with the familiar. Going into a new tuning is like walking into an unfamiliar forest with no trails or markings. Of course a walk into the forest may lead to an adventure.

One tuning equals one tune is not a very productive use of my resources.

ALAN HOLDSWORTH

I may have used them on acoustic many years ago. You could write so many different things you'd need a guitar for each song, so I stayed away from it.

RITCHIE HAVENS

It just happened. I couldn't get anybody to teach me how to use my fingers, so I tuned to a chord, set the guitar on my lap, barred it with my thumb, and played it like a dulcimer. [Open D] … which I sometimes turn into a minor or a minor seventh. I'll tune string 3 a whole tone down, which makes it a minor [such as DADFAD], and I'll tune the high E down, which makes it a seventh [such as DADF♯AC♯ or DADFAC].

PETER BUCK, R.E.M.

Sometimes I'll tune to something bizarre like all Ds with an A in there to jumpstart my creativity.

[Recalling the early Athens music scene] Take Randy Bewley from Pylon, who was the greatest player I'd seen back then. He played in this really weird tuning. It went BDCGDA, and that was all he knew. He quit, saying he ran out of ideas, and so I bought one of his guitars and when I tried to play that way, I couldn't play anything that didn't sound like Pylon. He got it all.

MICHAEL CHAPMAN

I remember one album with 14 songs and they were all in different tunings, starting off in one and finishing up in some really weird stuff. Tonight I used first a strange C tuning. From the bottom it's GGCGCC. I don't know how I came across it. I've been using it for a long while, then there was just G, G minor, DADGAD and normal … I use different tunings to find out new chord sounds anyway, and new voices and harmonics.

DUNCAN SHEIK

The real beauty of alternate tunings is that things are given to you as gifts that you never would have come up with consciously on your own.

LED KAAPANA, HAWAIIAN SLACK-KEY PLAYER

Sometimes I'm at home. It could be like two or three o'clock in the morning – and I just hear this tuning in my head. When I start tuning the guitar, sometimes it sounds weird; but after you do the tuning, then the fingerboard is all changed and you have to find your own fingerings. And when I find the fingerings, some of the chords are so outrageous, they sound so beautiful, that I say, "Wow, what a tuning."

PETER FRAMPTON

I have a Trans-Performance Les Paul [which creates instant tuning changes]. It's phenomenal. I've always written in open tunings, ever since I heard Joni Mitchell for the first time; things like open D and G. Then I might make a mistake tuning, or a string gets knocked, or it's drifted way down. Then I don't know what tuning I'm in so I make it up as I go along - which adds different sounds. 'Show Me The Way' was in open G – it starts with the D at the seventh fret.

JONI MITCHELL

The chords I heard in my head I couldn't get with my left hand so I just retuned the guitar. I have about 50 different tunings ... If any of you are typists ... imagine your typewriter letters: somebody comes in and puts them in a different place every day. It takes a lot of rehearsing to get your left hand accurate because some of the shapes are similar and your hand could go like a horse to the barn, you know, in the wrong direction at any moment ... But, as a compositional tool, it coughs up very fresh, melodic movement. It seems to me that it's infinite. So musically, I'm as excited as I was as a kid, maybe more.

In the beginning, I built the repertoire of the open major tunings that the old black guys came up with ... It was only three or four. The simplest one is D modal [DADGBD]; Neil Young uses that a lot. And then open G [DGDGBD] with string 5 removed, which is all Keith Richards plays in. And open D [DADF♯AD]. Then going between them I started to get more "modern" chords, for lack of a better word.

ERIK MONGRAIN

The first tunings I learned I got from Soundgarden, the grunge band; they use a dropped D. And then I heard a Canadian band called The Tea Party; they had a song called 'Winter Solstice' which used open C tunings [CGCGCE], and I used to play that a lot on a twelve-string, and that was a lot of fun. That was the first tuning I got into, and from there I decided I could create my own tunings. So I experimented, moving tunings to a sharp or flat to get different textures and tones. From there I picked up the DADGAD which lots of people know, and then I discovered the Don Ross F-tuning [FACFCF], and I used the tunings that it showed me, and then I started to develop my own.

DON ROSS

I don't like to rely on the same tuning too much because there is a sameness of sound; that's why I use so many tunings.

MARTY POSEN

When I write an open tuning it's like having a blank canvas in front of me ... I write by sound, feel, inspiration ... it's a deeper kind of creativity. It's got to be creative.

ARRANGER ROBERT KIRBY ON NICK DRAKE

I used to sit then with him and go through exactly how he played his chords, because he always detuned his guitar. He used strange tunings, not proper guitar tunings, and not the ones like people use in D tunings. He had very complicated tunings ... Sometimes a low string would be higher than the string above.

JIMMY PAGE, LED ZEPPELIN

[On devising the tuning for 'The Rain Song'.] I altered the strings around so that I'd have an octave on the A notes and an octave on the D notes, and still have the two Es. Then I just went to see what finger positions worked.

I think C was the first tuning I explored, though people often associate me with DADGAD. I used to call DADGAD my CIA tuning – Celtic/Indian/Arabic – 'cause that's what it was. DADGAD was something going round the folk scene during the 60s, and it was when I first started playing that that I became really interested in Arabic and Indian music.

PETE TOWNSHEND

Sometimes with standard tuning, your head gets in a rut. If you're writing and using open tunings, you can be taken somewhere you've never been before. It can make you feel like you're learning guitar all over again.

While I'm a great believer in practice, I really don't do it anymore. I play purely for pleasure. When I sit around at home, I'll pick up some small-bodied acoustic, tune it to some wacky Scottish open tuning, and just search around until I find something entertaining.

DAVID WILCOX

What I aim for is to always have the beginner's mind-set, to be always starting. The thing that the guitar gave me was a sense that I wasn't just playing it, I was listening to it, and it was playing things I couldn't play. I love that feeling. I like to get lost and find a new way home, and that's why any time I start to know my way around a tuning, I change it.

I think that if you know what you like and have a way of creating interesting mistakes that will give you new variations – for me it's the open tunings – then the laws of probability are in your favour.

LEE RANALDO, SONIC YOUTH

Our whole thing isn't about searching for new tunings anyway. We utilise them when they're appropriate. I mean, I find new tunings every time I sit down and play guitar. Some of them stick around and some don't.

THURSTON MOORE, SONIC YOUTH

[On the album *Sonic Nurse*] I wrote a couple of songs using the Brother James tuning (GGDDD♯D♯) – and the Death Valley tuning (F♯F♯F♯F♯EB). I may even have used the Expressway tuning (EG♯EG♯EG♯) on 'Paper Cut Exit'. Basically those three and the one I used on 'Murray Street' (CGDGCD).

DAVE MUSTAINE OF MEGADETH

With 'Youthanasia' we got a couple of songs down half a step, and it really messed up the stuff live because I was used to singing a half step lower and I'd try to sing it live. I wouldn't be off by much but I would be kind of sharp a little bit.

MARK KNOPFLER, DIRE STRAITS

I nearly always write with an acoustic, but if it's tuned to an open chord you will obviously have to write something different. I think if you've got the creativity to write in the first place, you just need to change, not so much the instrument, but maybe change the tuning or the pitch. Then you might find you write something different.

KELLY JONES, STEREOPHONICS

On the new record [*Just Enough Education To Perform*], yeah, there are a few open G tunings and there are a lot with drop tunings. It's not through trying to be arty or clever, it's just trying to find the right keys for certain songs. I use the capo a lot. I'm just trying to use different shapes. I try to start with new chords to make the songs sound different, otherwise each album sounds the same.

RON WOOD, THE FACES AND THE ROLLING STONES

I really stumbled on open tunings myself – I thought, "Well, if you were playing a chord already on the open strings what would it sound like?" I didn't know anyone who played in open tunings or anyone who played slide so I just worked it out for myself. I think open E was the first thing I came across and it's always been the main one I've used … for a couple of songs I'll detune the sixth string to D – I did that for 'Cut Across Shorty' with Rod [Stewart] just to get those couple of extra notes at the bottom end.

ANDY SUMMERS, THE POLICE

I find that a lot of the open-tuning stuff is very pretty, but my ear gets tired of it. Some of the tunings are interesting, but to me they're not as significant as real harmonic knowledge and real chord progressions on standard tuning. Standard tuning is absolutely infinite. My language is standard tuning. It takes a lifetime to learn it, and then you get there and you don't really want to give it up.

JOHN MCGEOCH, PIL AND SIOUXSIE AND THE BANSHEES

Tunings are a good way of keeping your approach to the guitar fresh – it gives you a different angle.

MARTIN SIMPSON

If you think about it, tunings like D, G, and C all contain root, fifth, root, one other interval, and then a repetition of the fifth and the root. So if you think about open D major, it's DAD (root, fifth, root, F♯ (third), then fifth and root again. G major just moves over, so you get fifth, root, fifth, root, third. Now if you get that in your head and then say "OK, what do I do to tunings to alter those?" Well almost every time you're going to alter the third, so DADGAD has an absolute equivalent in G which would be DGDGCD, so if I can play in DADGAD I can play in the G equivalent or the C equivalent.

PIERRE BENSUSAN
A lot of people playing in alternate tunings are stopping at the moment where they should in fact start. If you really want to master your instrument, get into a tuning in the same way that you would enter into standard tuning.

STONE GOSSARD, PEARL JAM
[In an altered tuning] the simplest thing will sound fresh and new, which is perfect for songwriting.

KEVIN SHIELDS, MY BLOODY VALENTINE
There are occasional moments of panic when we go to play a song and I've forgotten to write down the tuning.

A lot of the chord progressions in our songs are quite basic. But they're done with open tunings, which leaves a lot of room for strange versions of the basic chords.

DAVID CROSBY
If you are a tuning freak like I am, you just fool around. Take a tuning you've had for years and tweak one string one whole note and all of a sudden it's a different world. It's endless what you can do.

KEITH RICHARDS, THE ROLLING STONES
I'd gotten a bit bored, and I was getting a bit stale with playing everything on a concert tuning – you know, the regular six-string thing – and I'd had the time to sit around and fool around and figure some of those old blues tunings and things like that; which I think is another reason why *Beggars Banquet* suddenly had a slightly different sound to it, because that's what tunings and tonalities will do for you ... But to me it rejuvenated my enthusiasm for playing guitar, because you'd put your fingers where you thought they'd go and you'd get accidents happening, and you wouldn't have done on regular tuning, because you'd know it too well.

RICHARD THOMPSON
Any modal tuning offers a slightly elusive quality that blurs the edges of the key you're playing in. They really add a haunting quality to British traditional music, which is often performed unaccompanied. When you investigate a traditional song, it's not always clear what tuning you should use ... A modal tuning makes it possible to keep that elusive nature, and retain a pleasing ambiguity ... I like to use open tunings to keep the modal quality and mystery alive.

CHRIS CORNELL, SOUNDGARDEN
A lot of the weirder ones I came up with were based on trying to get to one note I couldn't reach. So I'd just tweak one string and get it where I wanted it.

KIM THAYIL, SOUNDGARDEN

The low E is tuned to a B, which mandates that you use a really heavy string. The heavier gauge tightens the slack.

We like to goof around with tunings, and sometimes a song just wouldn't have come into being if we hadn't been playing around with something weird. It often facilitates a riff that you might not otherwise have played.

MARY MCCASLIN

[Referring to Joni Mitchell's 'Nathan La Franeer' in open G on the album *Song to a Seagull*] ... it became obvious to me that Joni Mitchell was not playing 'Nathan La Franeer' in standard tuning. There was no way to duplicate the incredible chords she was playing in standard tuning ... Having figured out that 'Nathan La Franeer' was in the key of 'G', it was only logical to try open G tuning. This time, it was as if all those beautiful chords stepped out of hiding and the door to a whole new world opened up.

Over the years I've used 'A' tuning ['drop A', EADGAE] for lots of songs, it's a favourite. The chords I've found ... are beautiful and haunting – there are many more chords yet to be discovered. I learned this wonderful tuning from Steve Gillette way back in the 1960s.

BILLY CORGAN, SMASHING PUMPKINS

Different tunings, like effects, will make the guitar seem like a whole new instrument. James [Iha] wrote 'Mayonnaise' [on *Siamese Dream*] after just screwing around with tunings until he came up with something he liked (E♭, B♭, B♭ [same octave], G♭, B♭, D). Using this tuning, he stumbled across an E♭sus2/Cm/A♭ chord progression, which ultimately shaped the song.

SECTION 12

THE ALTERNATIVE CHORD MASTER

Here is a chord dictionary for the tunings featured in *How to Write Songs In Altered Guitar Tunings*. There are many chord dictionaries for standard tuning (see my *Chord Master*) but few for altered tunings. Although discovering new chords is part of the fun of alternative tunings, sometimes you might want a head start, or to know what the chord is you've found. A traditional chord dictionary lets you look up an unfamiliar chord, as a dictionary provides the meaning of an unfamiliar word. For each tuning I've provided a selection of chords that a songwriter would be likely to use and that show off the musical qualities of that tuning. Some chord shapes are included which may not have an especially open sound but common song progressions often feature them. These can be useful to the songwriter.

There is no attempt to provide a chord on every note, let alone every chord type on every note – that would lead to hundreds of chord shapes for every single tuning! Many chord books contain hundreds, if not thousands, of chords. But the harmony of popular music is limited. Since many songs only use about six chords most tunings reveal at least six effective shapes. For more information about the use of particular chords in songs see *The Songwriter's Sourcebook* and *How To Write Songs On Guitar*. The chords selected are based around the pitches and keys that each tuning first presents to a songwriter who goes into that tuning and looks for song ideas. Many of the chords are open-string shapes, but there are also a few movable shapes, handy for 'masking' the open strings.

Chord boxes for alternative tunings function in the same manner as those for standard tuning. The strings are the vertical lines. On the left is the thickest, lowest-pitched string, bottom E (string 6). On the right is the thinnest, highest-pitched string, top E (string 1). The horizontal lines are the frets. The top of the box is always the nut, the piece of plastic or metal with the grooves in it in which the strings sit as they pass on toward the machine heads. The exception is if there is a number written to the left, which signals a fret further up the neck.

Above the nut are 'o' and 'x' symbols. The 'o' is an open string which is played; the 'x' is a string not played. To avoid playing an 'x' string, mute that string with an adjacent fretting finger. Allow the fretting finger to lean over a little so it touches the string marked with an 'x', to stop the string vibrating. If the bottom E is the string that needs damping, touch it lightly with the thumb of your fretting hand. Fretting fingers are numbered 1-4. If a 1 or 4 extends over more than one string it is a 'barre'. A barre is always assumed to go flat on the fretboard from its lowest note across to the right, though it is only written in on the strings whose notes are actually sounded.

A number on the left of a chord box indicates when finger 1 lines up with a fret position away from the nut. Remember that barres are drawn in the chord boxes where they are holding a sounding note or notes. But they are understood to be physically flat on the strings behind notes that are on higher frets.

Underneath the chord box the harmonic degrees (one, three, five, seven, nine, 11, 13) reveal the note combination of the chord and where added notes (other than one, three and five) are located. Any string that shows as a '3' or '♭3' determines whether the tuning is major or minor. Re-tune it to shift from major to minor or the other way round. These numbers show notes that can be altered or missed out to vary the chord. Find which string has the third and omit it to make the chord tonally neutral. Raise or lower the fifth to create an 'altered' chord. Miss out a ninth to turn an 11th chord into a seventh add11. Miss out a seventh to turn a ninth into an add nine, and so on. In some cases these numbers are one of a couple of possible interpretations of what the chord is. Notes that are functioning as a pedal are not given a number. Along with these numbers you can read the letter-names of the pitches involved.

The ●—● symbol on the boxes reveals where two strings are a unison, sounding at the same pitch. Unisons are a characteristic of alternate tunings.

CHORD DICTIONARY CONTENTS

DADGBE

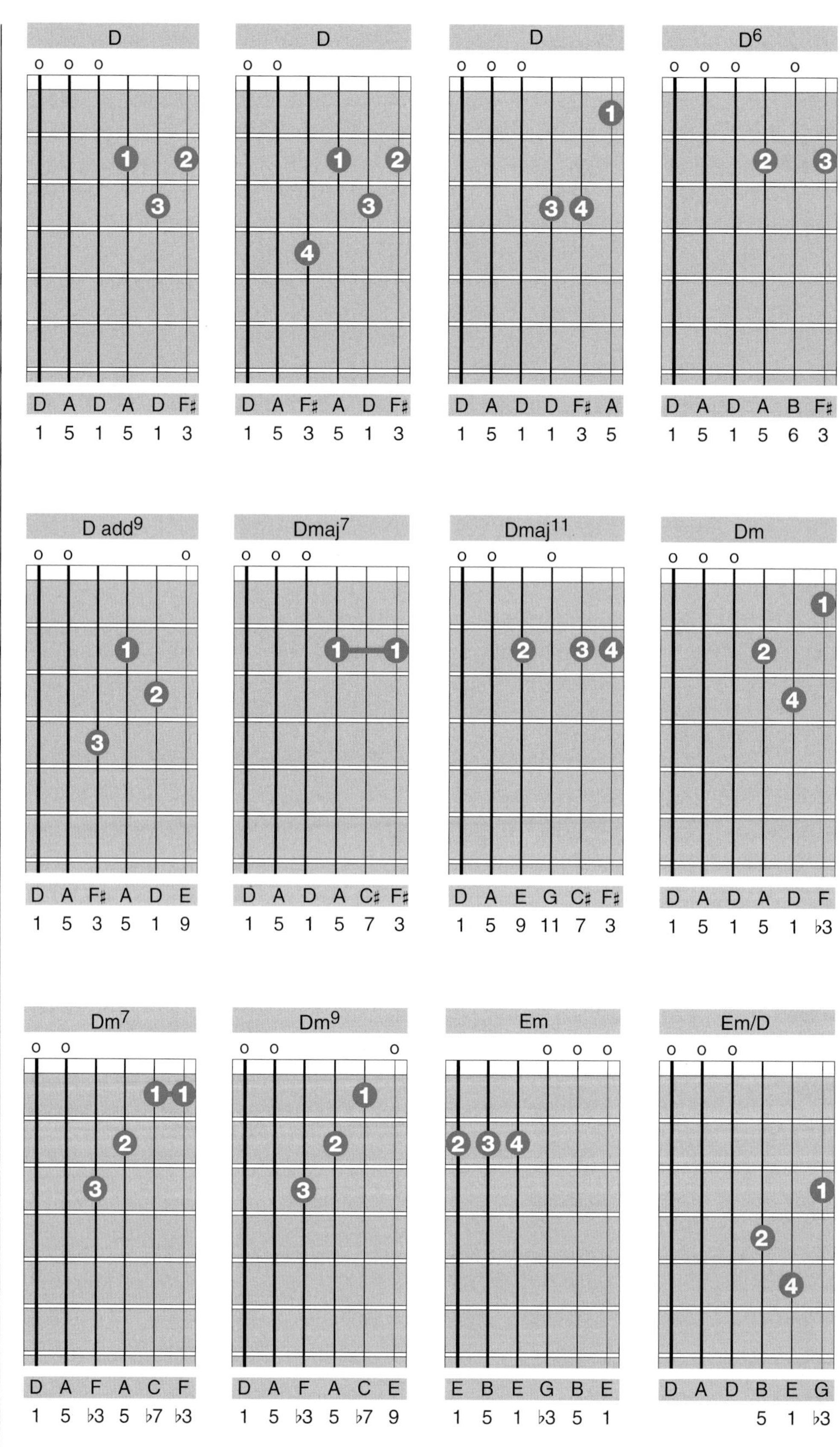
D
D A D A D F♯
1 5 1 5 1 3
D
D A F♯ A D F♯
1 5 3 5 1 3
D
D A D D F♯ A
1 5 1 1 3 5
D6
D A D A B F♯
1 5 1 5 6 3
D add9
D A F♯ A D E
1 5 3 5 1 9
Dmaj7
D A D A C♯ F♯
1 5 1 5 7 3
Dmaj11
D A E G C♯ F♯
1 5 9 11 7 3
Dm
D A D A D F
1 5 1 5 1 ♭3
Dm7
D A F A C F
1 5 ♭3 5 ♭7 ♭3
Dm9
D A F A C E
1 5 ♭3 5 ♭7 9
Em
E B E G B E
1 5 1 ♭3 5 1
Em/D
D A D B E G
5 1 ♭3

DADGBE

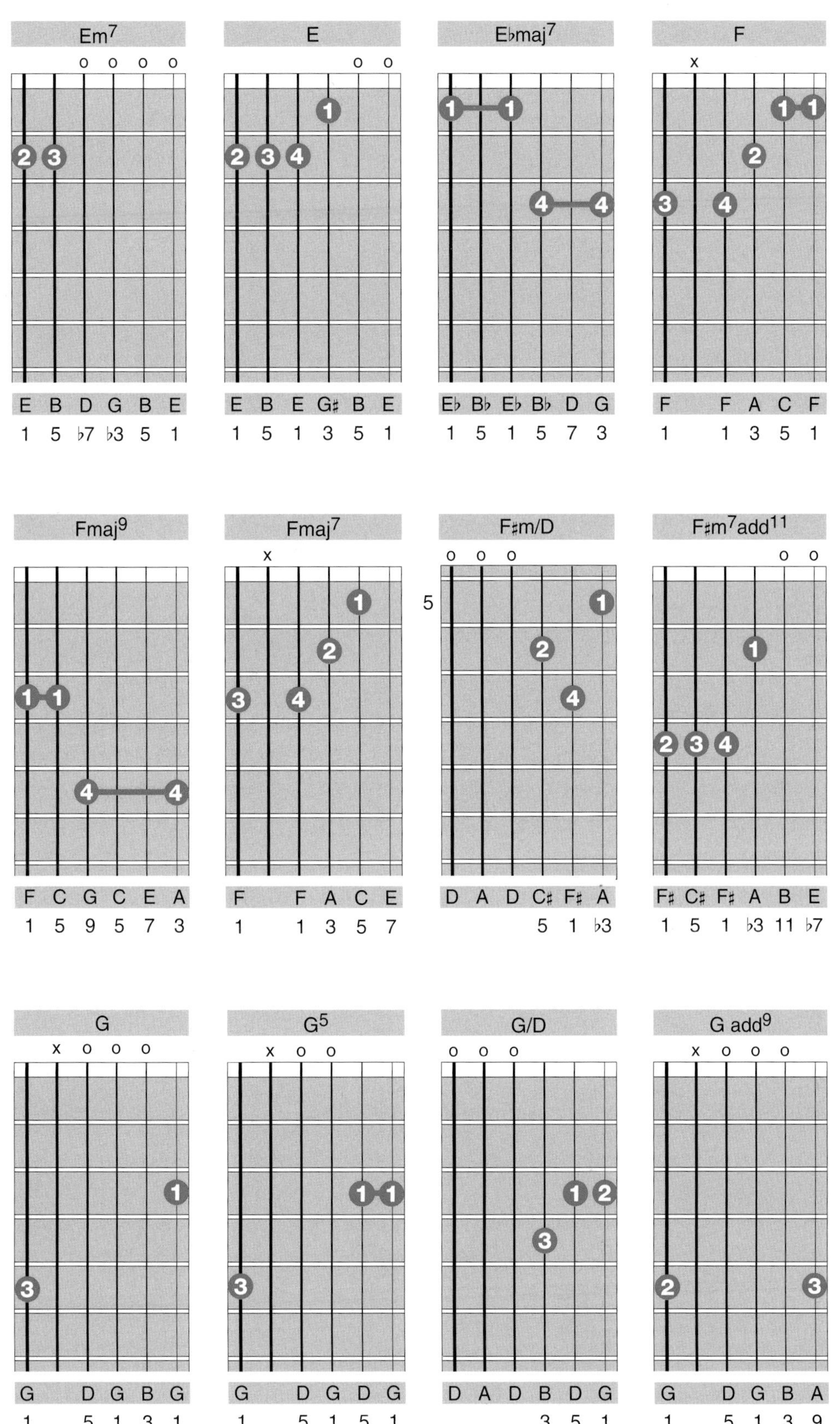
Em7
E B D G B E
1 5 ♭7 ♭3 5 1
E
E B E G♯ B E
1 5 1 3 5 1
E♭maj7
E♭ B♭ E♭ B♭ D G
1 5 1 5 7 3
F
F F A C F
1 1 3 5 1
Fmaj9
F C G C E A
1 5 9 5 7 3
Fmaj7
F F A C E
1 1 3 5 7
F♯m/D
5
D A D C♯ F♯ A
5 1 ♭3
F♯m7add11
F♯ C♯ F♯ A B E
1 5 1 ♭3 11 ♭7
G
G D G B G
1 5 1 3 1
G5
G D G D G
1 5 1 5 1
G/D
D A D B D G
3 5 1
G add9
G D G B A
1 5 1 3 9

DADGBE

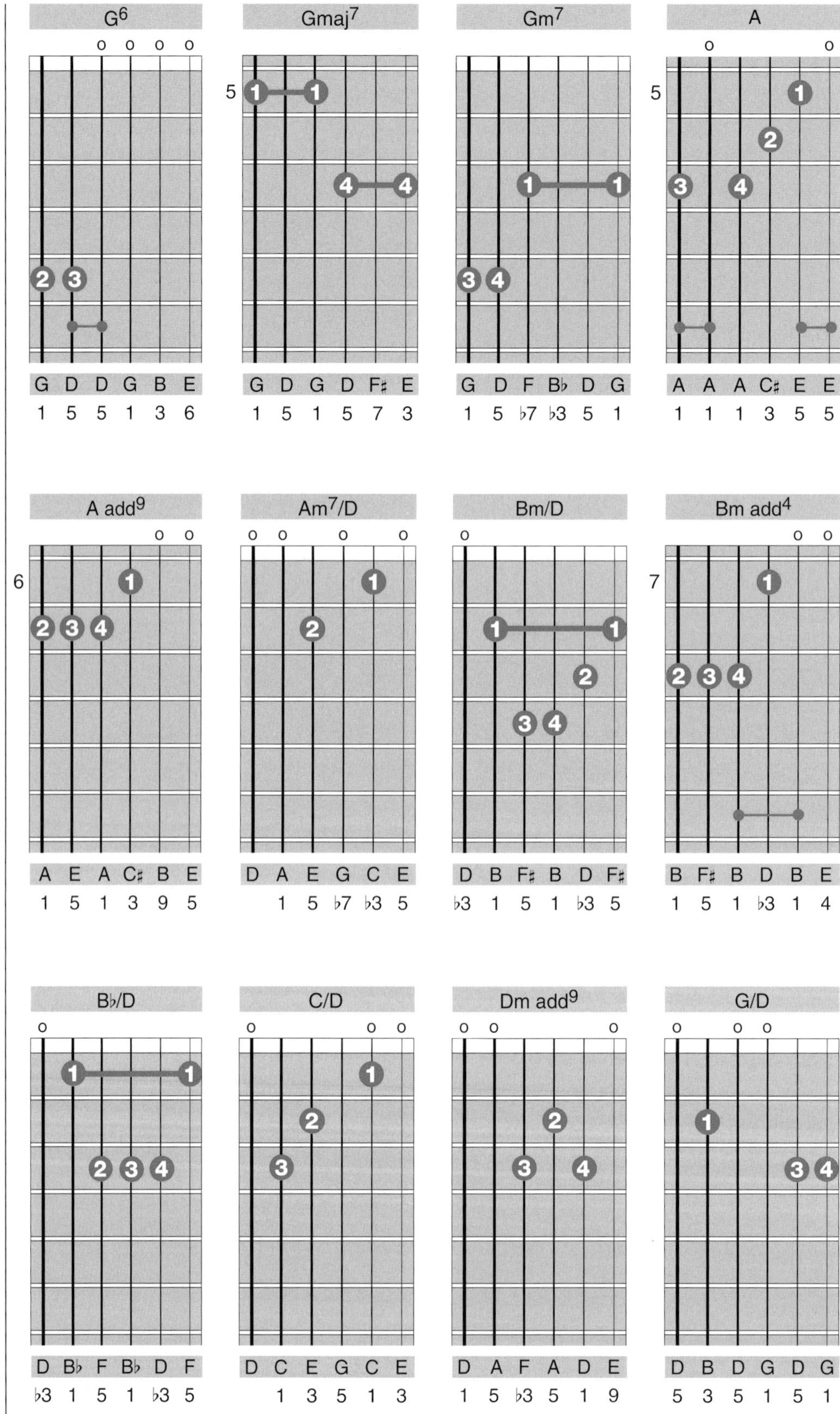
G6
G D D G B E
1 5 5 1 3 6
Gmaj7
5
G D G D F♯ E
1 5 1 5 7 3
Gm7
G D F B♭ D G
1 5 ♭7 ♭3 5 1
A
5
A A A C♯ E E
1 1 1 3 5 5
A add9
6
A E A C♯ B E
1 5 1 3 9 5
Am7/D
D A E G C E
1 5 ♭7 ♭3 5
Bm/D
D B F♯ B D F♯
♭3 1 5 1 ♭3 5
Bm add4
7
B F♯ B D B E
1 5 1 ♭3 1 4
B♭/D
D B♭ F B♭ D F
♭3 1 5 1 ♭3 5
C/D
D C E G C E
1 3 5 1 3
Dm add9
D A F A D E
1 5 ♭3 5 1 9
G/D
D B D G D G
5 3 5 1 5 1

EADGBD♯

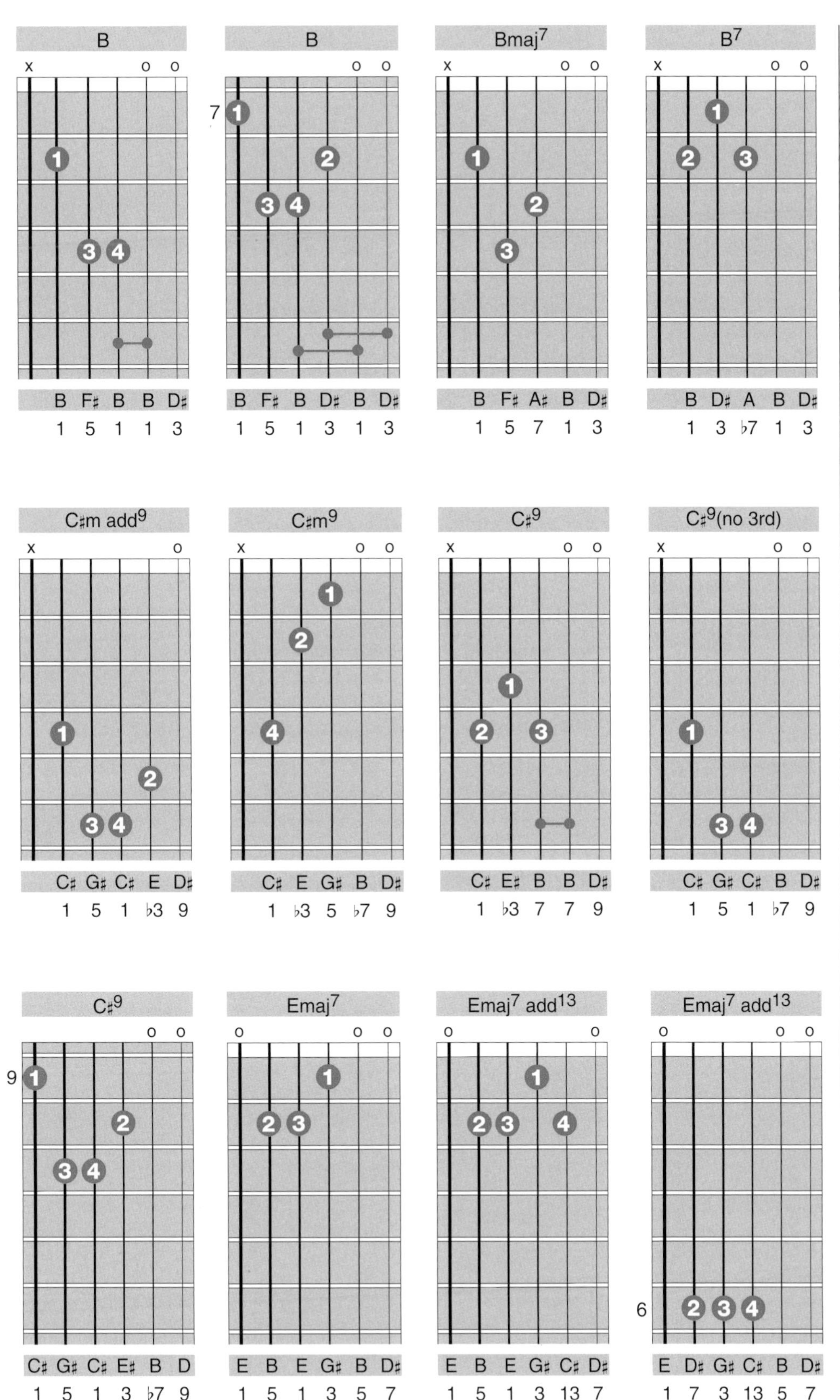
B
x o o
B F♯ B B D♯
1 5 1 1 3
B
7
B F♯ B D♯ B D♯
1 5 1 3 1 3
Bmaj7
x o o
B F♯ A♯ B D♯
1 5 7 1 3
B7
x o o
B D♯ A B D♯
1 3 ♭7 1 3
C♯m add9
x o
C♯ G♯ C♯ E D♯
1 5 1 ♭3 9
C♯m9
x o o
C♯ E G♯ B D♯
1 ♭3 5 ♭7 9
C♯9
x o o
C♯ E♯ B B D♯
1 ♭3 7 7 9
C♯9(no 3rd)
x o o
C♯ G♯ C♯ B D♯
1 5 1 ♭7 9
C♯9
o o
9
C♯ G♯ C♯ E♯ B D
1 5 1 3 ♭7 9
Emaj7
o o o
E B E G♯ B D♯
1 5 1 3 5 7
Emaj7 add13
o o
E B E G♯ C♯ D♯
1 5 1 3 13 7
Emaj7 add13
o o o
6
E D♯ G♯ C♯ B D♯
1 7 3 13 5 7

EADGBD♯

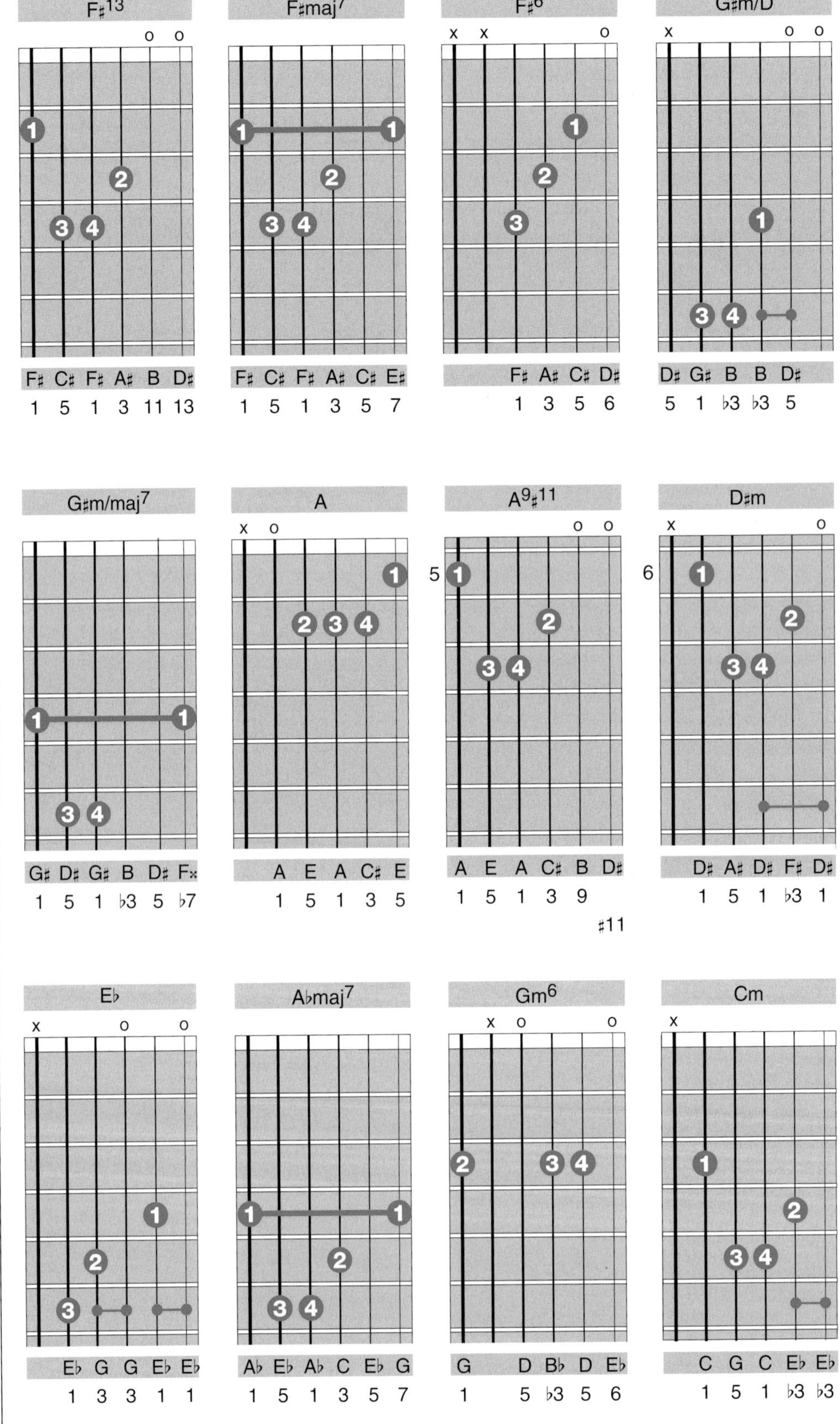
F♯13
F♯ C♯ F♯ A♯ B D♯
1 5 1 3 11 13
F♯maj7
F♯ C♯ F♯ A♯ C♯ E♯
1 5 1 3 5 7
F♯6
F♯ A♯ C♯ D♯
1 3 5 6
G♯m/D
D♯ G♯ B B D♯
5 1 ♭3 ♭3 5
G♯m/maj7
G♯ D♯ G♯ B D♯ F𝄪
1 5 1 ♭3 5 ♭7
A
A E A C♯ E
1 5 1 3 5
A9♯11
5
A E A C♯ B D♯
1 5 1 3 9 ♯11
D♯m
6
D♯ A♯ D♯ F♯ D♯
1 5 1 ♭3 1
E♭
E♭ G G E♭ E♭
1 3 3 1 1
A♭maj7
A♭ E♭ A♭ C E♭ G
1 5 1 3 5 7
Gm6
G D B♭ D E♭
1 5 ♭3 5 6
Cm
C G C E♭ E♭
1 5 1 ♭3 ♭3

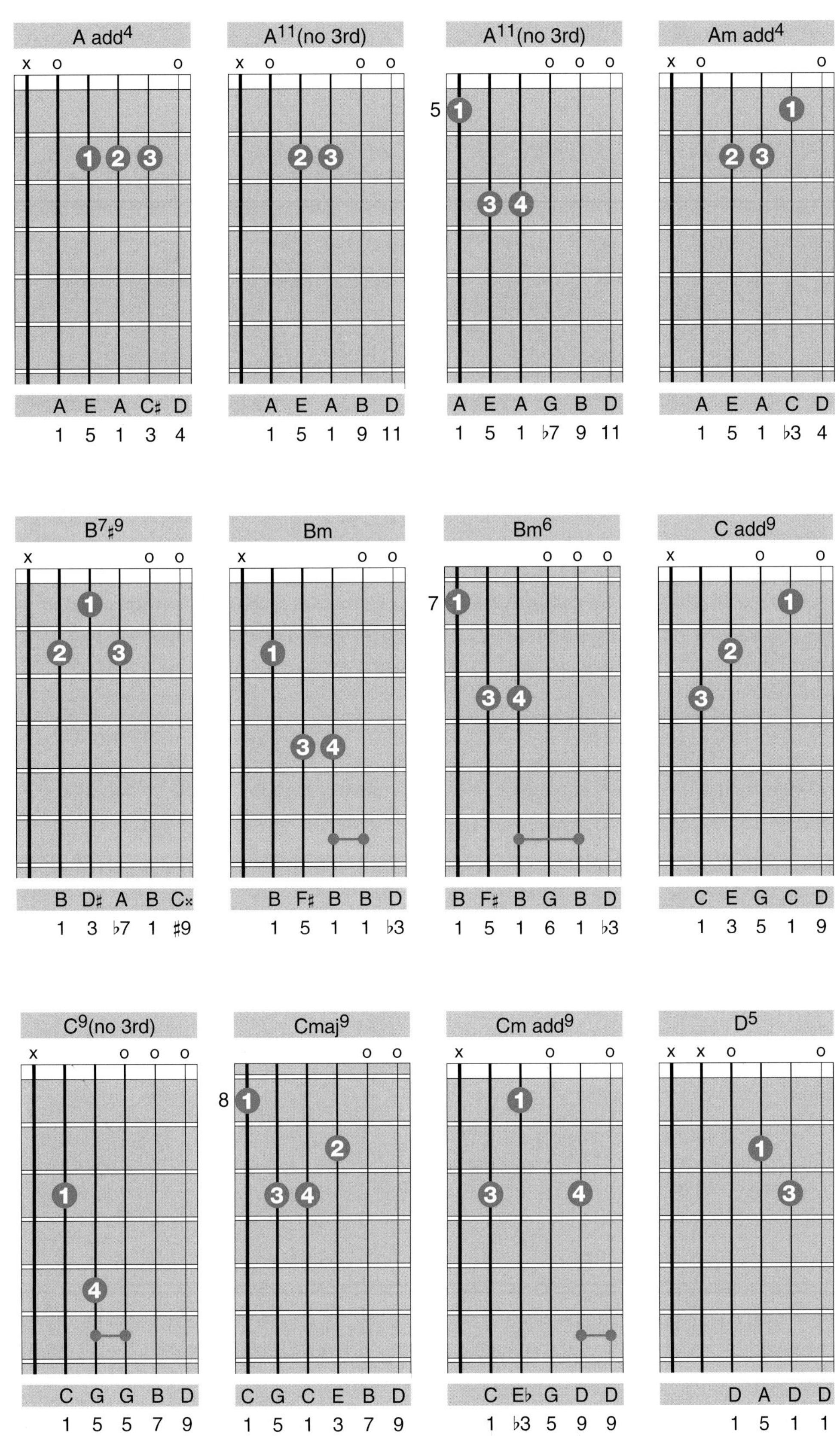
A add4
x o o
A E A C♯ D
1 5 1 3 4
A11(no 3rd)
x o o o
A E A B D
1 5 1 9 11
A11(no 3rd)
o o o
5
A E A G B D
1 5 1 ♭7 9 11
Am add4
x o o
A E A C D
1 5 1 ♭3 4
B7♯9
x o o
B D♯ A B C𝄪
1 3 ♭7 1 ♯9
Bm
x o o
B F♯ B B D
1 5 1 1 ♭3
Bm6
o o o
7
B F♯ B G B D
1 5 1 6 1 ♭3
C add9
x o o
C E G C D
1 3 5 1 9
C9(no 3rd)
x o o o
C G G B D
1 5 5 7 9
Cmaj9
o o
8
C G C E B D
1 5 1 3 7 9
Cm add9
x o o
C E♭ G D D
1 ♭3 5 9 9
D5
x x o o
D A D D
1 5 1 1

EADGBD

EADGBD

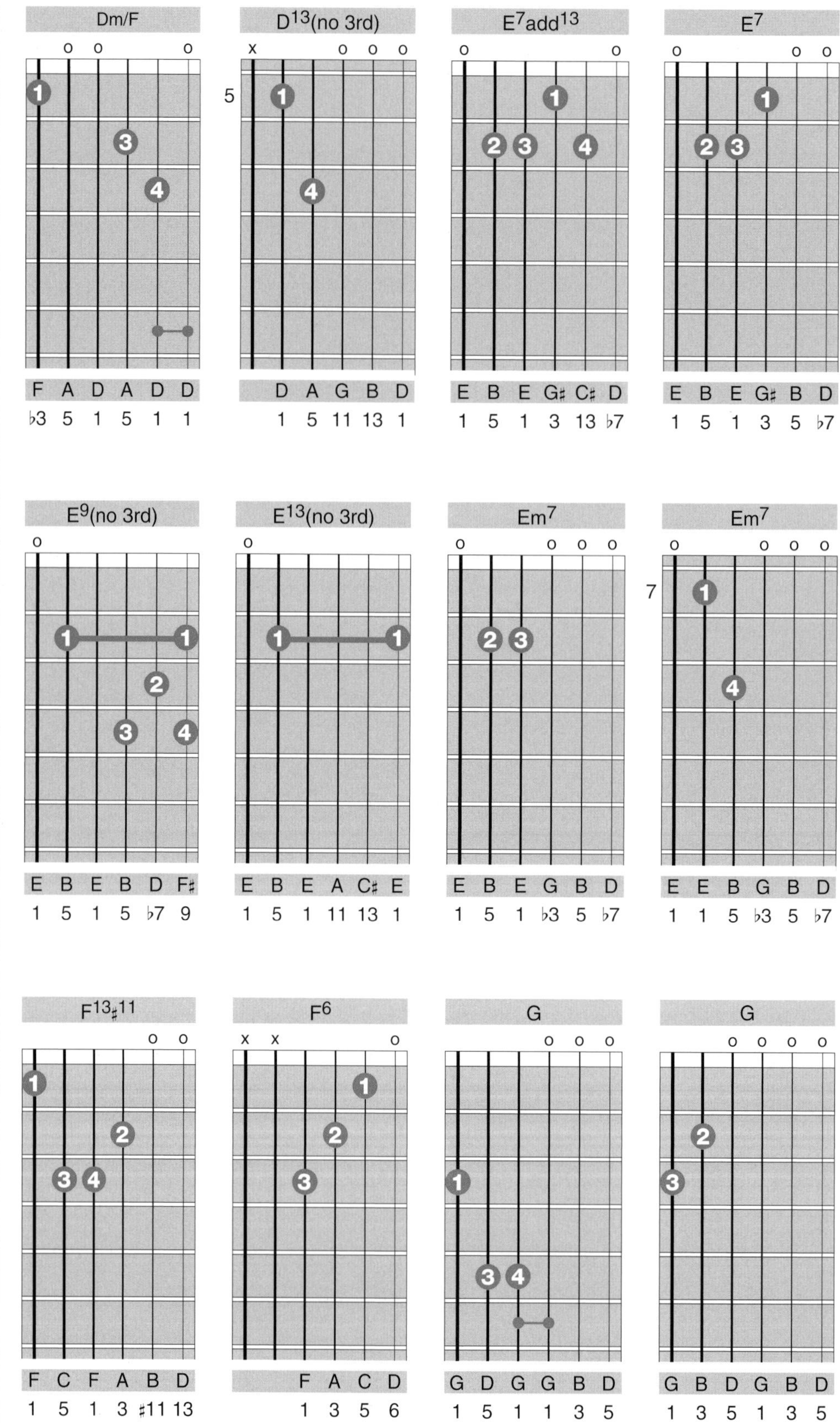
Dm/F
F A D A D D
♭3 5 1 5 1 1
D13(no 3rd)
5
D A G B D
1 5 11 13 1
E7add13
E B E G♯ C♯ D
1 5 1 3 13 ♭7
E7
E B E G♯ B D
1 5 1 3 5 ♭7
E9(no 3rd)
E B E B D F♯
1 5 1 5 ♭7 9
E13(no 3rd)
E B E A C♯ E
1 5 1 11 13 1
Em7
E B E G B D
1 5 1 ♭3 5 ♭7
Em7
7
E E B G B D
1 1 5 ♭3 5 ♭7
F13♯11
F C F A B D
1 5 1 3 ♯11 13
F6
F A C D
1 3 5 6
G
G D G G B D
1 5 1 1 3 5
G
G B D G B D
1 3 5 1 3 5

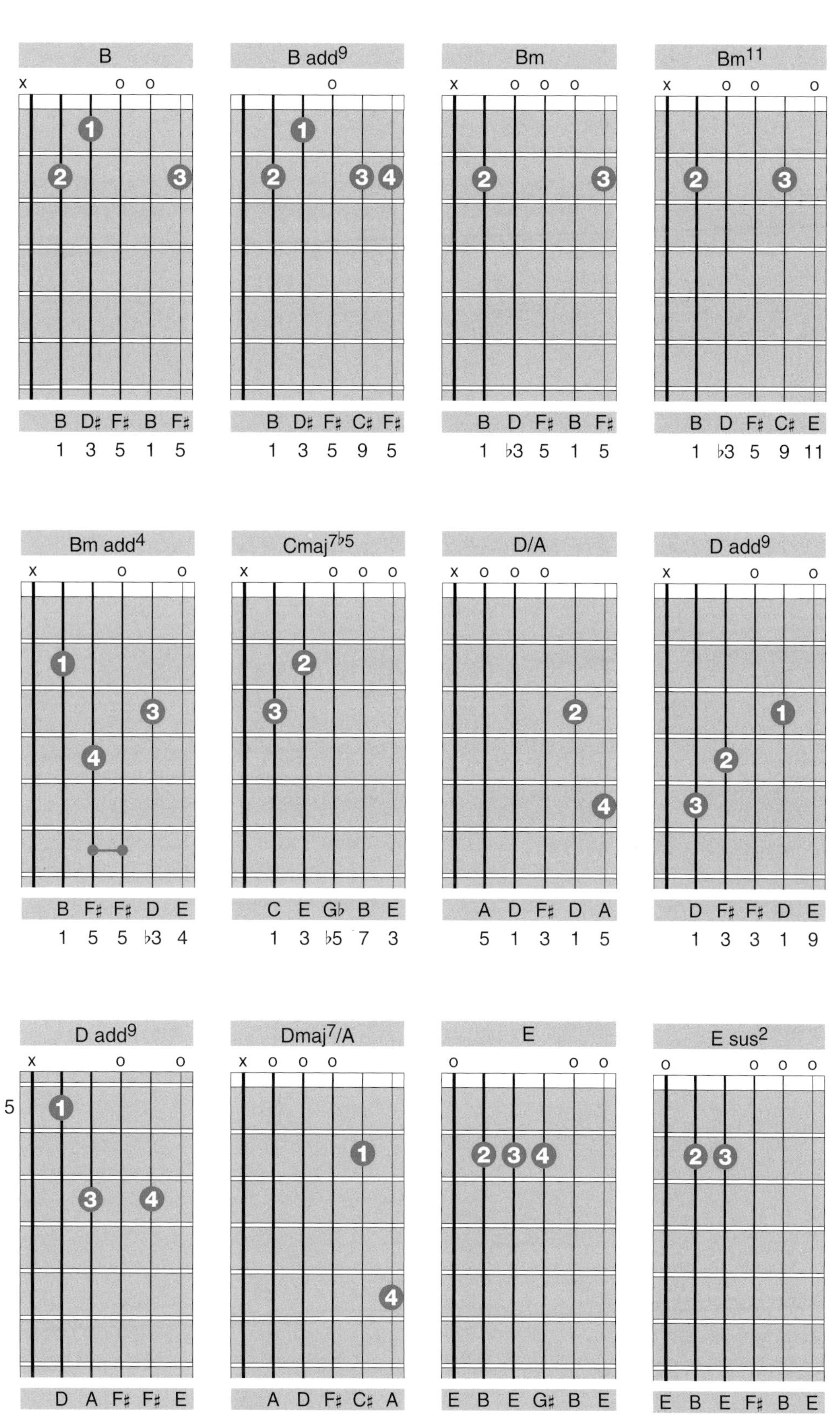

B
x o o
B D♯ F♯ B F♯
1 3 5 1 5
B add9
o
B D♯ F♯ C♯ F♯
1 3 5 9 5
Bm
x o o o
B D F♯ B F♯
1 ♭3 5 1 5
Bm11
x o o o
B D F♯ C♯ E
1 ♭3 5 9 11
Bm add4
x o o
B F♯ F♯ D E
1 5 5 ♭3 4
Cmaj7♭5
x o o o
C E G♭ B E
1 3 ♭5 7 3
D/A
x o o o
A D F♯ D A
5 1 3 1 5
D add9
x o o
D F♯ F♯ D E
1 3 3 1 9
D add9
x o o
5
D A F♯ F♯ E
1 5 3 3 9
Dmaj7/A
x o o o
A D F♯ C♯ A
5 1 3 7 5
E
o o o
E B E G♯ B E
1 5 1 3 5 1
E sus2
o o o o
E B E F♯ B E
1 5 1 2 5 1

EADF♯BE

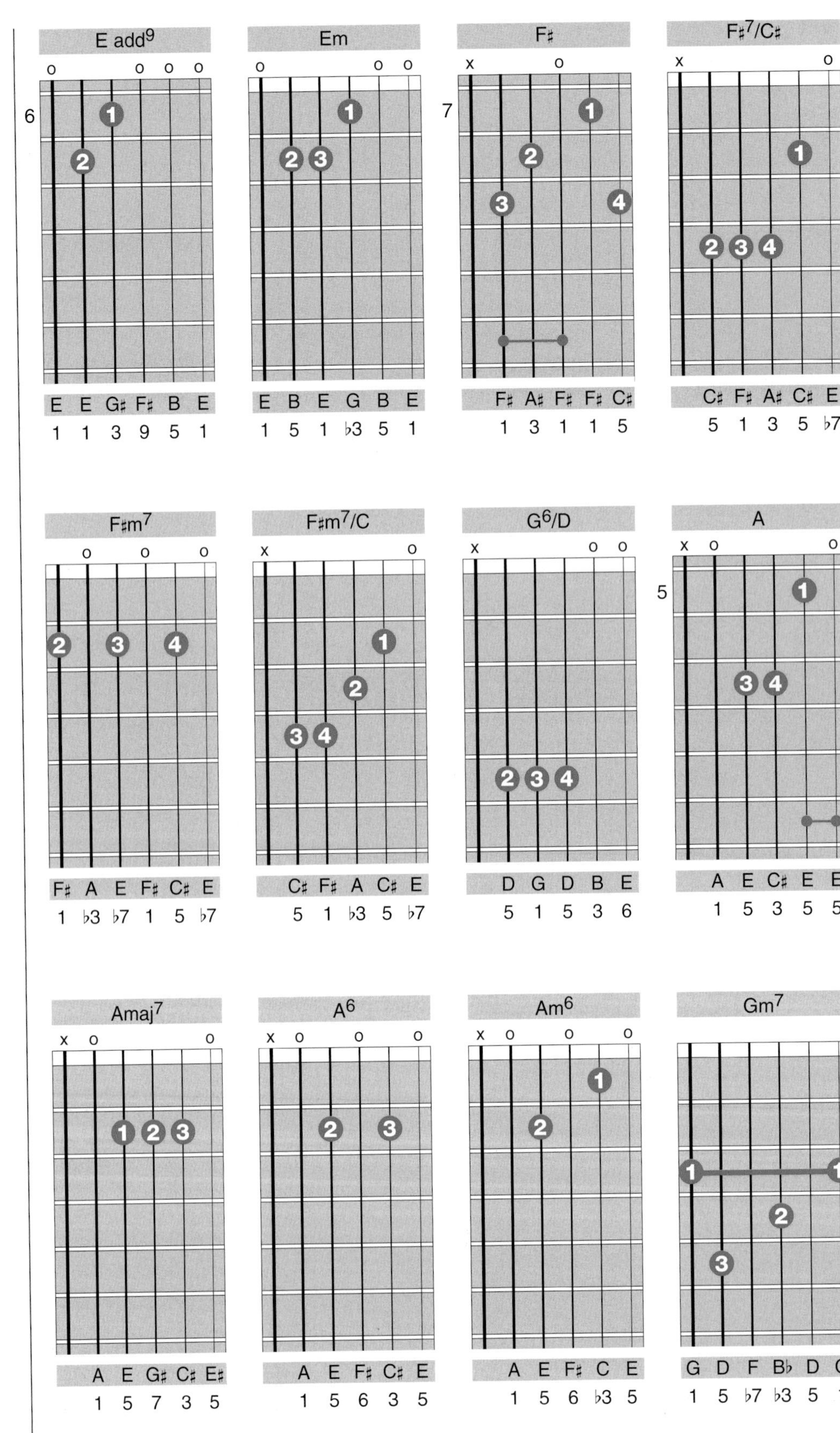
E add9
6
E E G♯ F♯ B E
1 1 3 9 5 1
Em
E B E G B E
1 5 1 ♭3 5 1
F♯
7
F♯ A♯ F♯ F♯ C♯
1 3 1 1 5
F♯7/C♯
C♯ F♯ A♯ C♯ E
5 1 3 5 ♭7
F♯m7
F♯ A E F♯ C♯ E
1 ♭3 ♭7 1 5 ♭7
F♯m7/C
C♯ F♯ A C♯ E
5 1 ♭3 5 ♭7
G6/D
D G D B E
5 1 5 3 6
A
5
A E C♯ E E
1 5 3 5 5
Amaj7
A E G♯ C♯ E♯
1 5 7 3 5
A6
A E F♯ C♯ E
1 5 6 3 5
Am6
A E F♯ C E
1 5 6 ♭3 5
Gm7
G D F B♭ D G
1 5 ♭7 ♭3 5 1

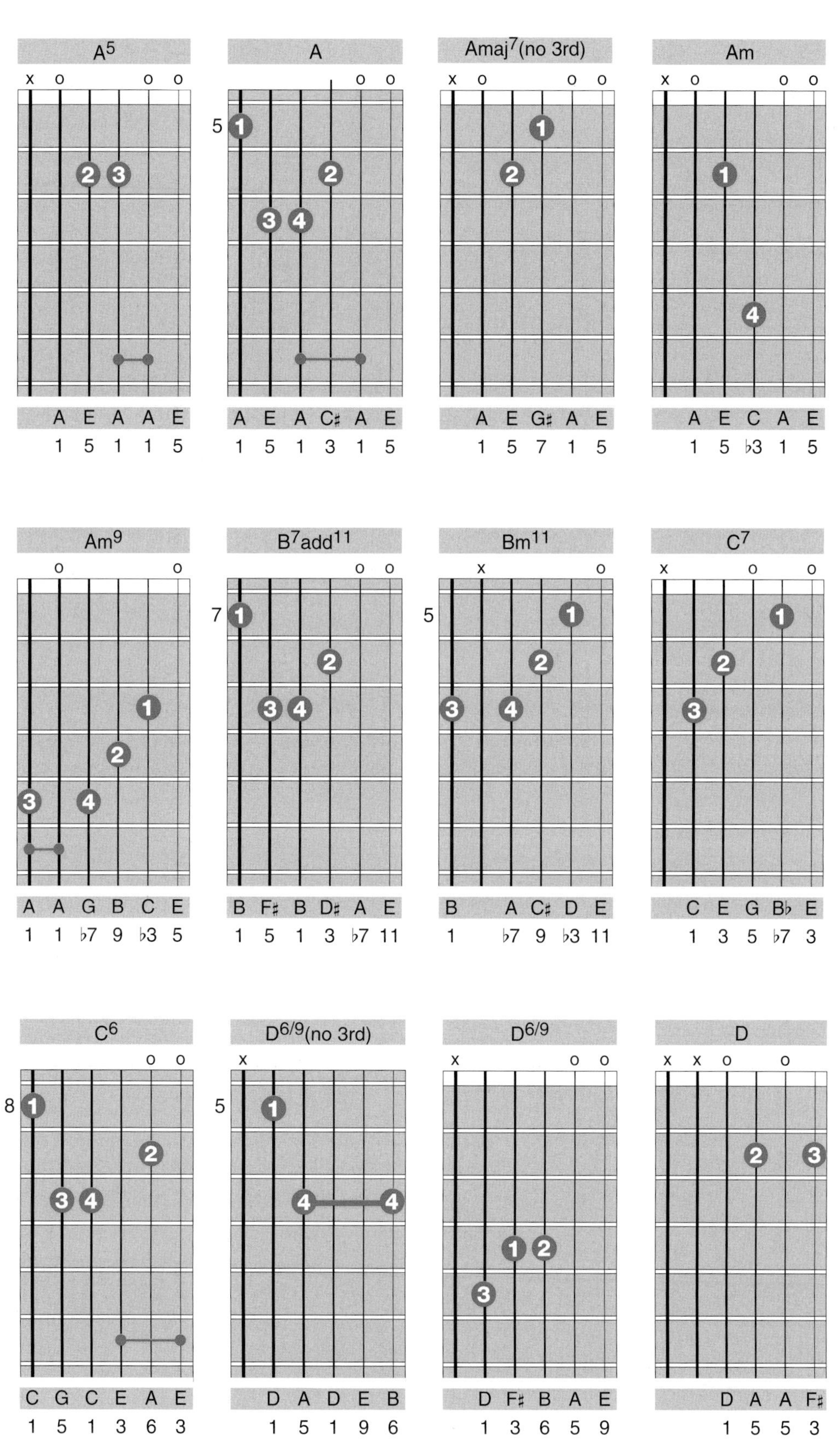

A5
x o o o
A E A A E
1 5 1 1 5
A
o o
5
A E A C♯ A E
1 5 1 3 1 5
Amaj7(no 3rd)
x o o o
A E G♯ A E
1 5 7 1 5
Am
x o o o
A E C A E
1 5 ♭3 1 5
Am9
o o
A A G B C E
1 1 ♭7 9 ♭3 5
B7add11
o o
7
B F♯ B D♯ A E
1 5 1 3 ♭7 11
Bm11
x o
5
B A C♯ D E
1 ♭7 9 ♭3 11
C7
x o o
C E G B♭ E
1 3 5 ♭7 3
C6
o o
8
C G C E A E
1 5 1 3 6 3
D6/9(no 3rd)
x
5
D A D E B
1 5 1 9 6
D6/9
x o o
D F♯ B A E
1 3 6 5 9
D
x x o o
D A A F♯
1 5 5 3

EADGAE

EADGAE

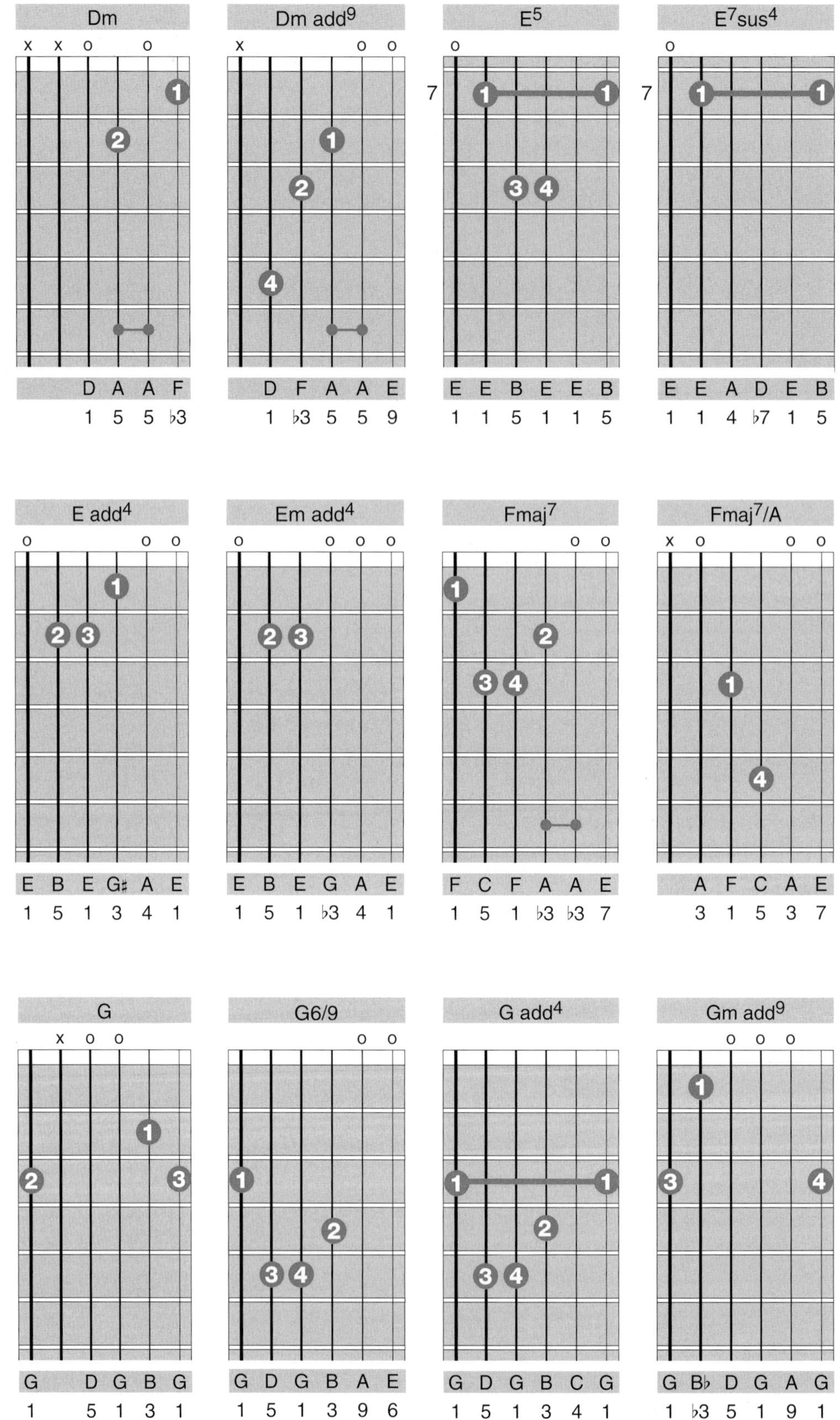
Dm
x x o o
D A A F
1 5 5 ♭3
Dm add9
x o o
D F A A E
1 ♭3 5 5 9
E5
o
7
E E B E E B
1 1 5 1 1 5
E7sus4
o
7
E E A D E B
1 1 4 ♭7 1 5
E add4
o o o
E B E G♯ A E
1 5 1 3 4 1
Em add4
o o o o
E B E G A E
1 5 1 ♭3 4 1
Fmaj7
o o
F C F A A E
1 5 1 ♭3 ♭3 7
Fmaj7/A
x o o o
A F C A E
3 1 5 3 7
G
x o o
G D G B G
1 5 1 3 1
G6/9
o o
G D G B A E
1 5 1 3 9 6
G add4
G D G B C G
1 5 1 3 4 1
Gm add9
o o o
G B♭ D G A G
1 ♭3 5 1 9 1

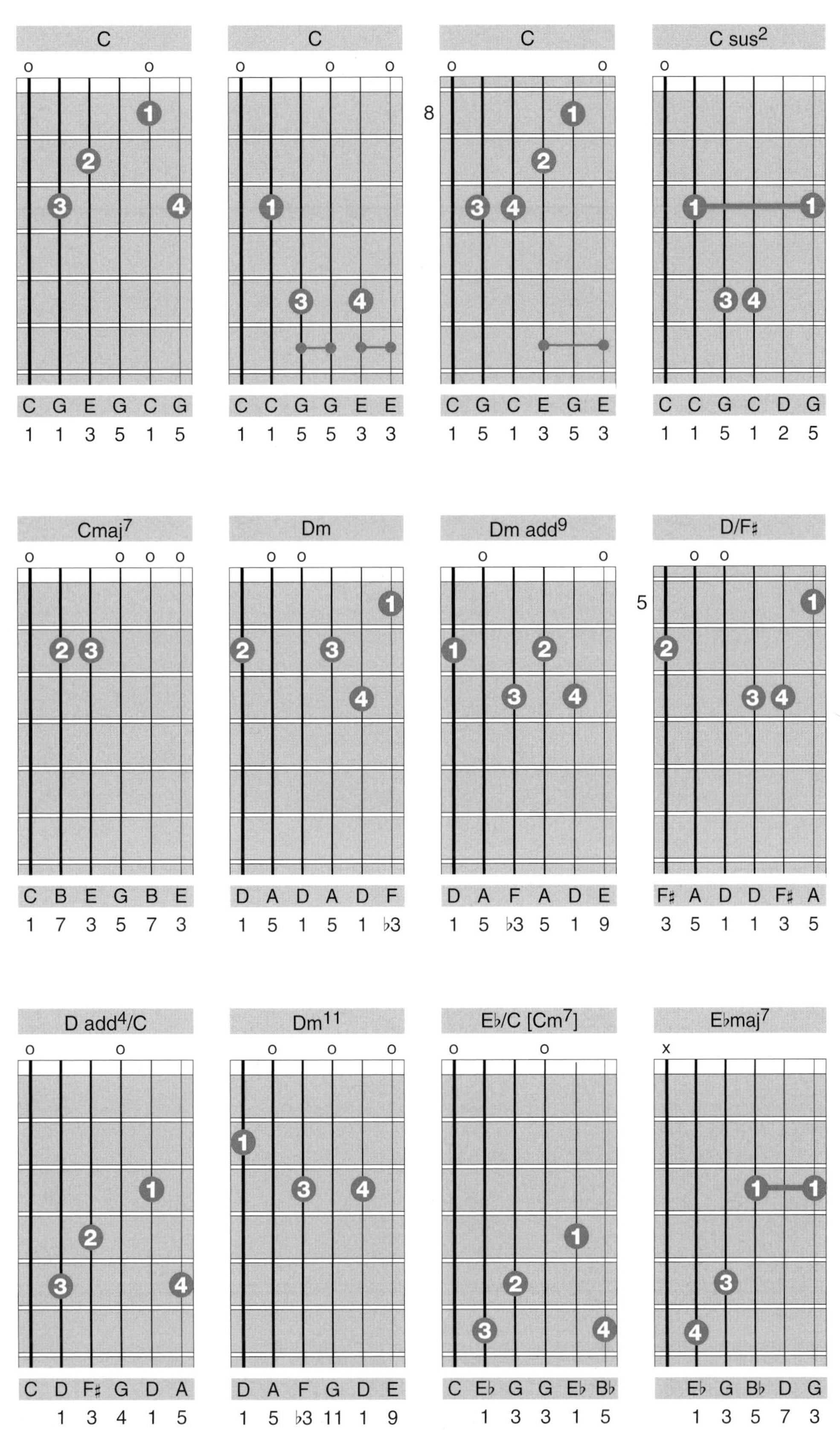
C
o o
C G E G C G
1 1 3 5 1 5
C
o o o
C C G G E E
1 1 5 5 3 3
C
o o
8
C G C E G E
1 5 1 3 5 3
C sus2
o
C C G C D G
1 1 5 1 2 5
Cmaj7
o o o o
C B E G B E
1 7 3 5 7 3
Dm
o o
D A D A D F
1 5 1 5 1 ♭3
Dm add9
o o
D A F A D E
1 5 ♭3 5 1 9
D/F♯
o o
5
F♯ A D D F♯ A
3 5 1 1 3 5
D add4/C
o o
C D F♯ G D A
1 3 4 1 5
Dm11
o o o
D A F G D E
1 5 ♭3 11 1 9
E♭/C [Cm7]
o o
C E♭ G G E♭ B♭
1 3 3 1 5
E♭maj7
x
E♭ G B♭ D G
1 3 5 7 3

CADGBE

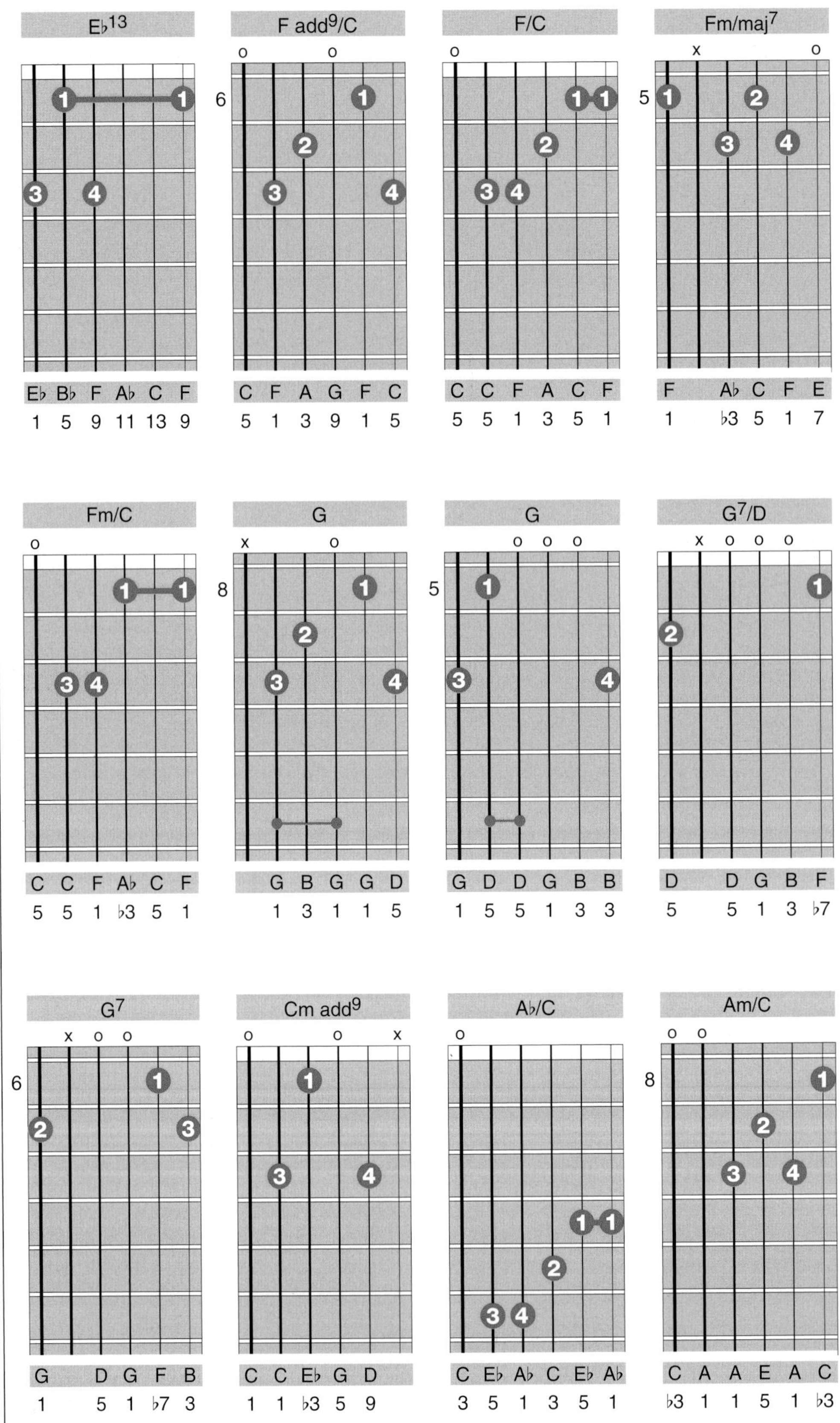
E♭13
E♭ B♭ F A♭ C F
1 5 9 11 13 9
F add9/C
6
C F A G F C
5 1 3 9 1 5
F/C
C C F A C F
5 5 1 3 5 1
Fm/maj7
5
F A♭ C F E
1 ♭3 5 1 7
Fm/C
C C F A♭ C F
5 5 1 ♭3 5 1
G
8
G B G G D
1 3 1 1 5
G
5
G D D G B B
1 5 5 1 3 3
G7/D
D D G B F
5 5 1 3 ♭7
G7
6
G D G F B
1 5 1 ♭7 3
Cm add9
C C E♭ G D
1 1 ♭3 5 9
A♭/C
C E♭ A♭ C E♭ A♭
3 5 1 3 5 1
Am/C
8
C A A E A C
♭3 1 1 5 1 ♭3

DADGBD

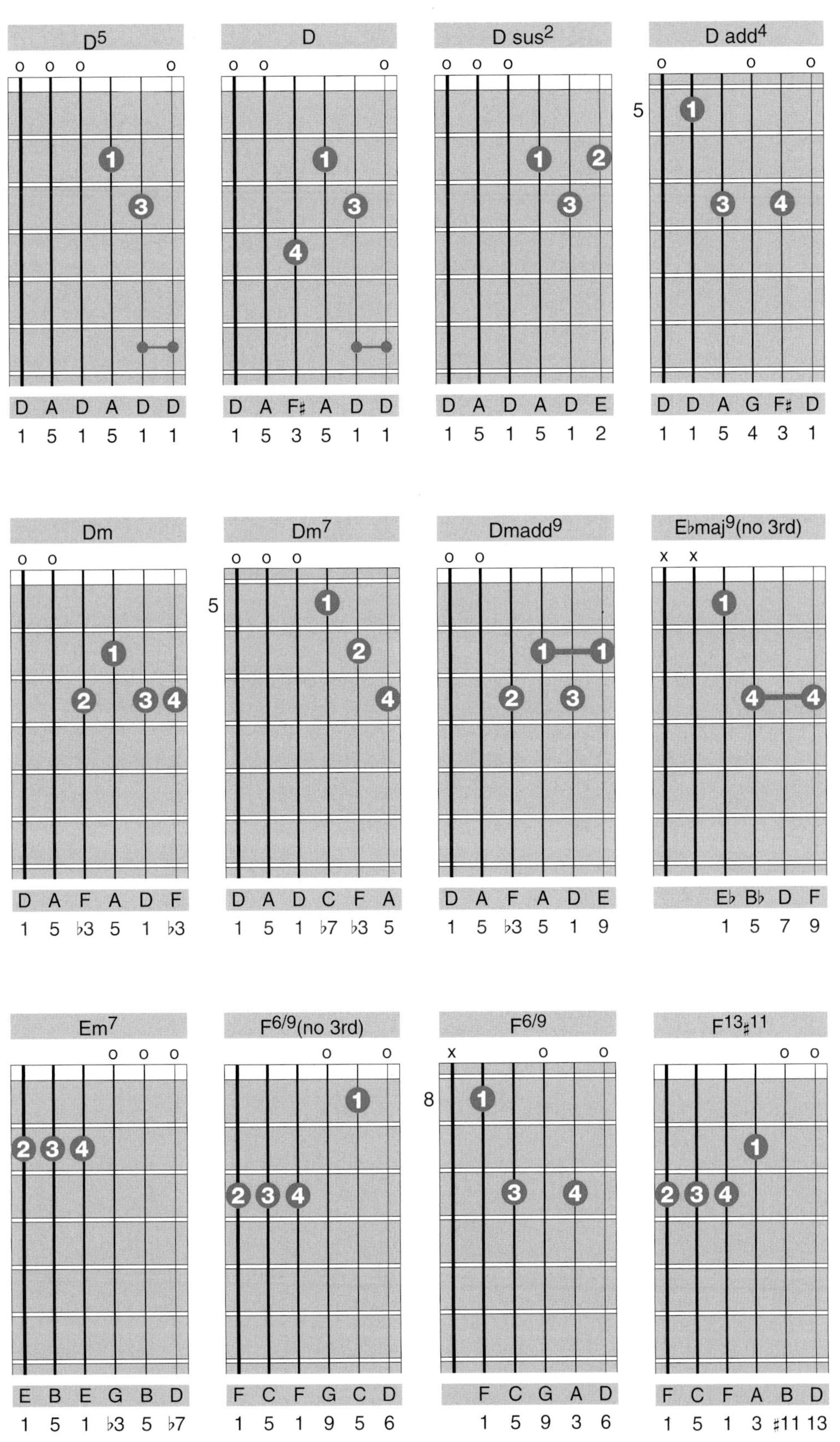
D5
D A D A D D
1 5 1 5 1 1
D
D A F♯ A D D
1 5 3 5 1 1
D sus2
D A D A D E
1 5 1 5 1 2
D add4
5
D D A G F♯ D
1 1 5 4 3 1
Dm
D A F A D F
1 5 ♭3 5 1 ♭3
Dm7
5
D A D C F A
1 5 1 ♭7 ♭3 5
Dmadd9
D A F A D E
1 5 ♭3 5 1 9
E♭maj9(no 3rd)
E♭ B♭ D F
1 5 7 9
Em7
E B E G B D
1 5 1 ♭3 5 ♭7
F6/9(no 3rd)
F C F G C D
1 5 1 9 5 6
F6/9
8
F C G A D
1 5 9 3 6
F13♯11
F C F A B D
1 5 1 3 ♯11 13

DADGBD

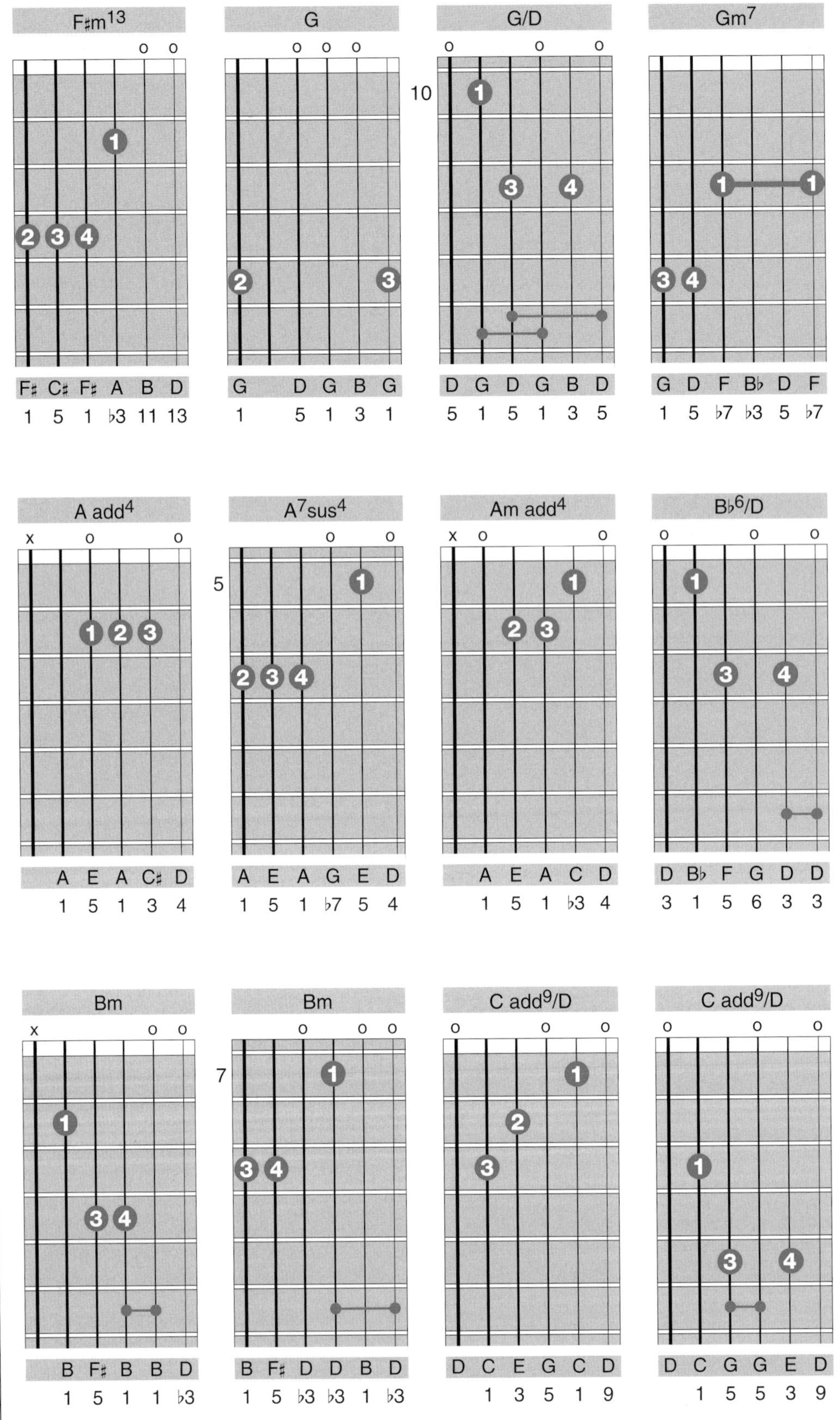
F♯m13
F♯ C♯ F♯ A B D
1 5 1 ♭3 11 13
G
G D G B G
1 5 1 3 1
G/D
10
D G D G B D
5 1 5 1 3 5
Gm7
G D F B♭ D F
1 5 ♭7 ♭3 5 ♭7
A add4
A E A C♯ D
1 5 1 3 4
A7sus4
5
A E A G E D
1 5 1 ♭7 5 4
Am add4
A E A C D
1 5 1 ♭3 4
B♭6/D
D B♭ F G D D
3 1 5 6 3 3
Bm
B F♯ B B D
1 5 1 1 ♭3
Bm
7
B F♯ D D B D
1 5 ♭3 ♭3 1 ♭3
C add9/D
D C E G C D
1 3 5 1 9
C add9/D
D C G G E D
1 5 5 3 9

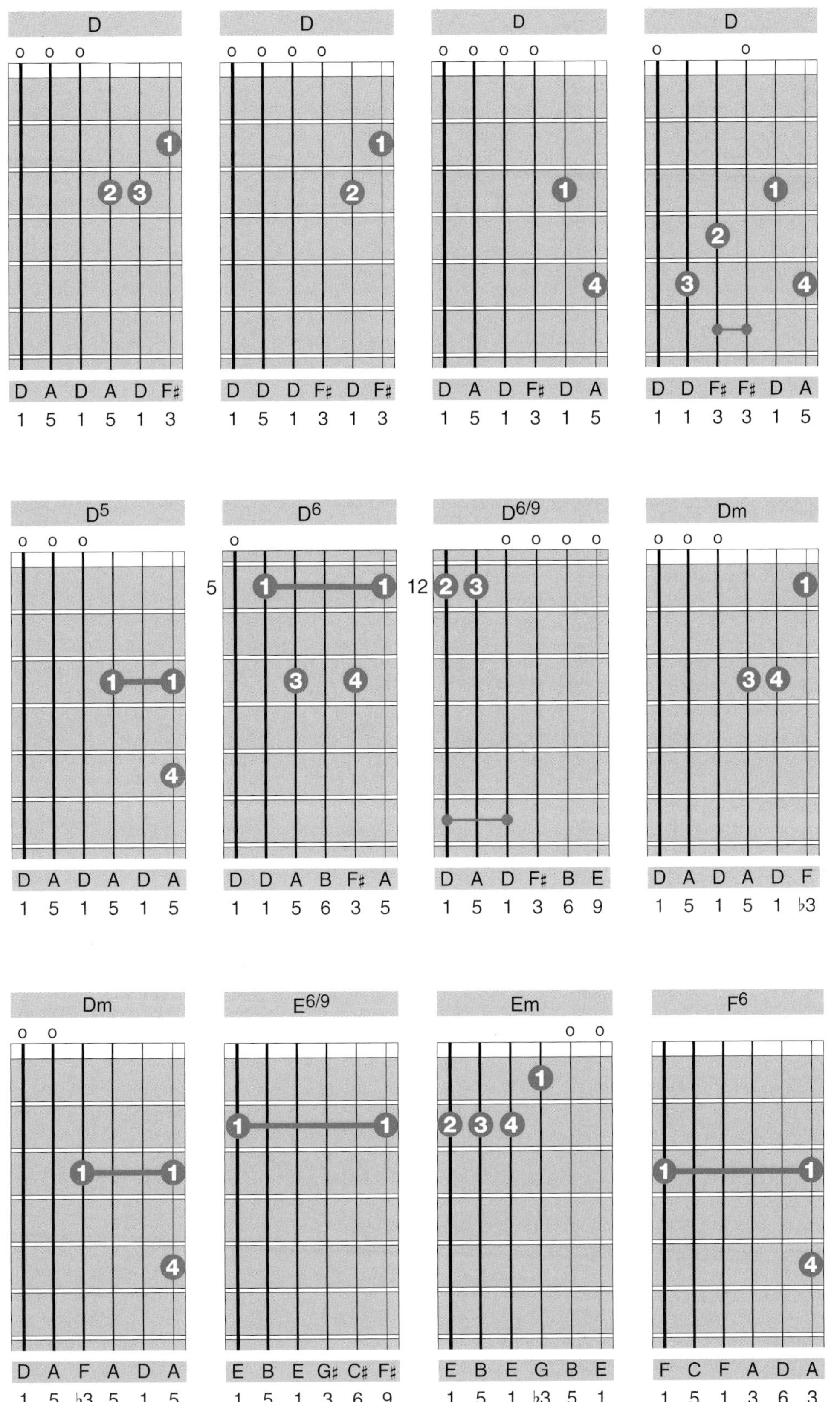
D
D A D A D F♯
1 5 1 5 1 3
D
D D D F♯ D F♯
1 5 1 3 1 3
D
D A D F♯ D A
1 5 1 3 1 5
D
D D F♯ F♯ D A
1 1 3 3 1 5
D5
D A D A D A
1 5 1 5 1 5
D6
5
D D A B F♯ A
1 1 5 6 3 5
D6/9
12
D A D F♯ B E
1 5 1 3 6 9
Dm
D A D A D F
1 5 1 5 1 ♭3
Dm
D A F A D A
1 5 ♭3 5 1 5
E6/9
E B E G♯ C♯ F♯
1 5 1 3 6 9
Em
E B E G B E
1 5 1 ♭3 5 1
F6
F C F A D A
1 5 1 3 6 3

DADF♯BE

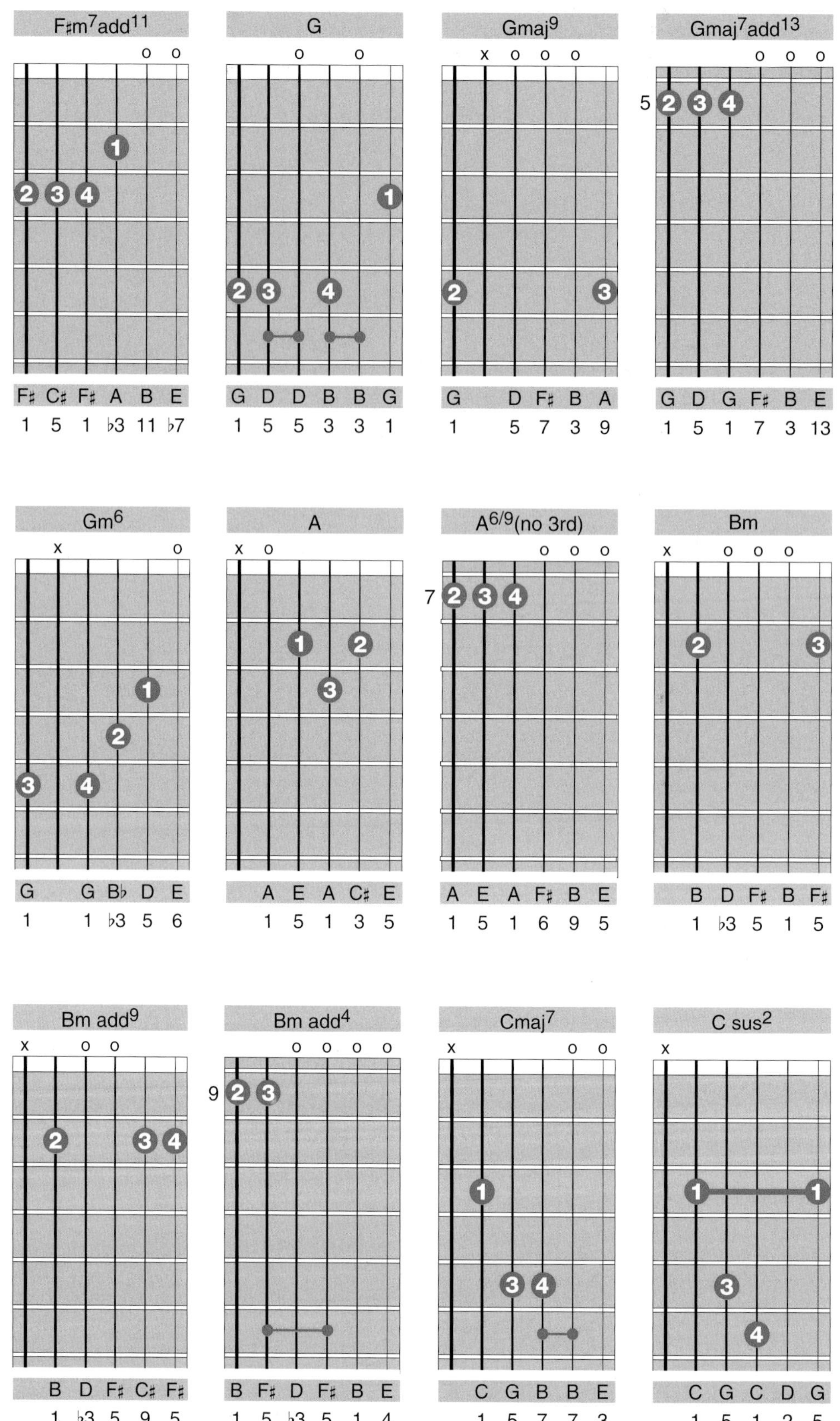
F♯m7add11
o o
1
2 3 4
F♯ C♯ F♯ A B E
1 5 1 ♭3 11 ♭7
G
o o
1
2 3 4
G D D B B G
1 5 5 3 3 1
Gmaj9
x o o o
2 3
G D F♯ B A
1 5 7 3 9
Gmaj7add13
o o o
5 2 3 4
G D G F♯ B E
1 5 1 7 3 13
Gm6
x o
1
2
3 4
G G B♭ D E
1 1 ♭3 5 6
A
x o
1 2
3
A E A C♯ E
1 5 1 3 5
A6/9(no 3rd)
o o o
7 2 3 4
A E A F♯ B E
1 5 1 6 9 5
Bm
x o o o
2 3
B D F♯ B F♯
1 ♭3 5 1 5
Bm add9
x o o
2 3 4
B D F♯ C♯ F♯
1 ♭3 5 9 5
Bm add4
o o o o
9 2 3
B F♯ D F♯ B E
1 5 ♭3 5 1 4
Cmaj7
x o o
1
3 4
C G B B E
1 5 7 7 3
C sus2
x
1 1
3
4
C G C D G
1 5 1 2 5

EADF♯BD

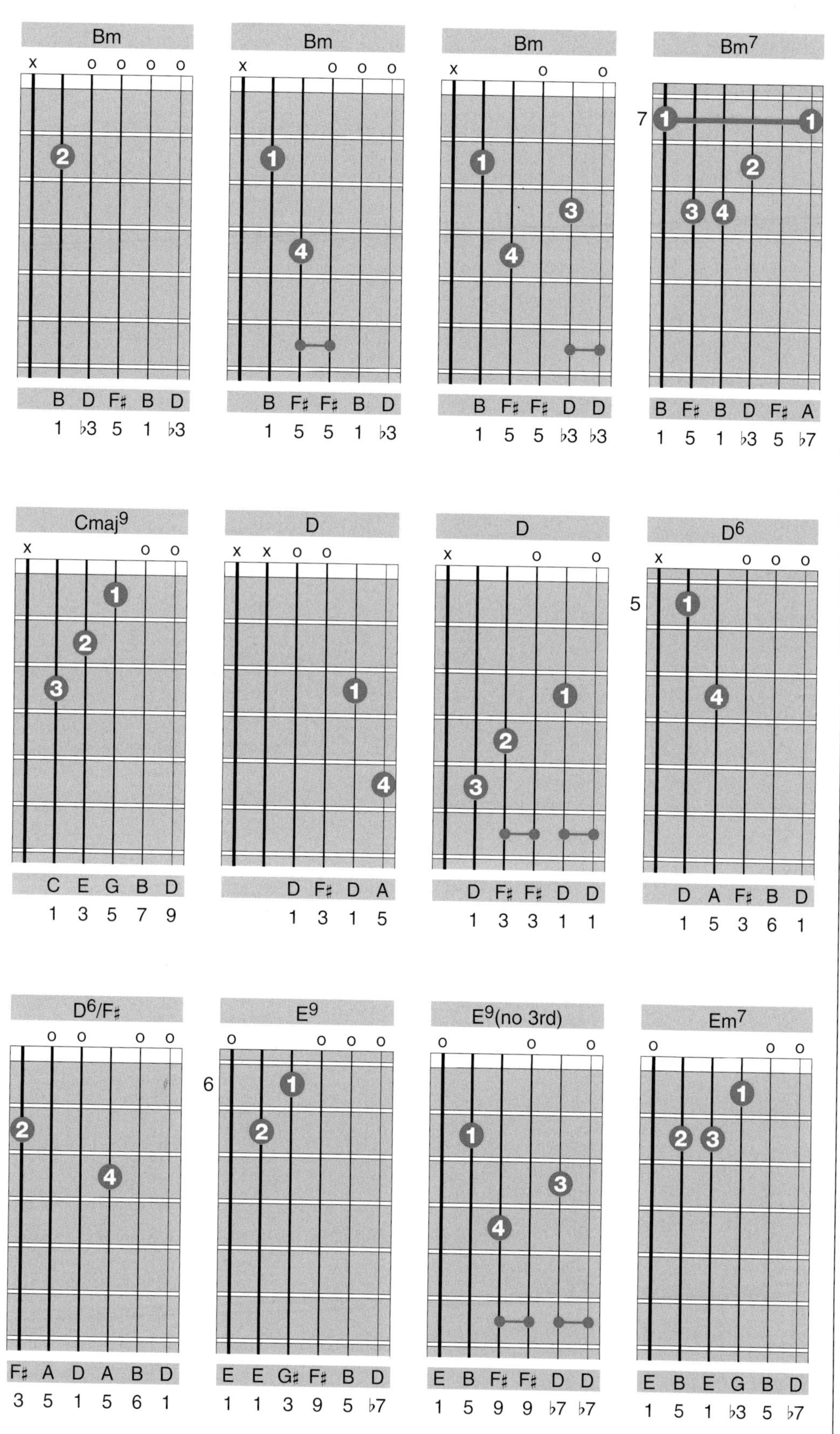
Bm
B D F♯ B D
1 ♭3 5 1 ♭3
Bm
B F♯ F♯ B D
1 5 5 1 ♭3
Bm
B F♯ F♯ D D
1 5 5 ♭3 ♭3
Bm7
7
B F♯ B D F♯ A
1 5 1 ♭3 5 ♭7
Cmaj9
C E G B D
1 3 5 7 9
D
D F♯ D A
1 3 1 5
D
D F♯ F♯ D D
1 3 3 1 1
D6
5
D A F♯ B D
1 5 3 6 1
D6/F♯
F♯ A D A B D
3 5 1 5 6 1
E9
6
E E G♯ F♯ B D
1 1 3 9 5 ♭7
E9(no 3rd)
E B F♯ F♯ D D
1 5 9 9 ♭7 ♭7
Em7
E B E G B D
1 5 1 ♭3 5 ♭7

EADF♯BD

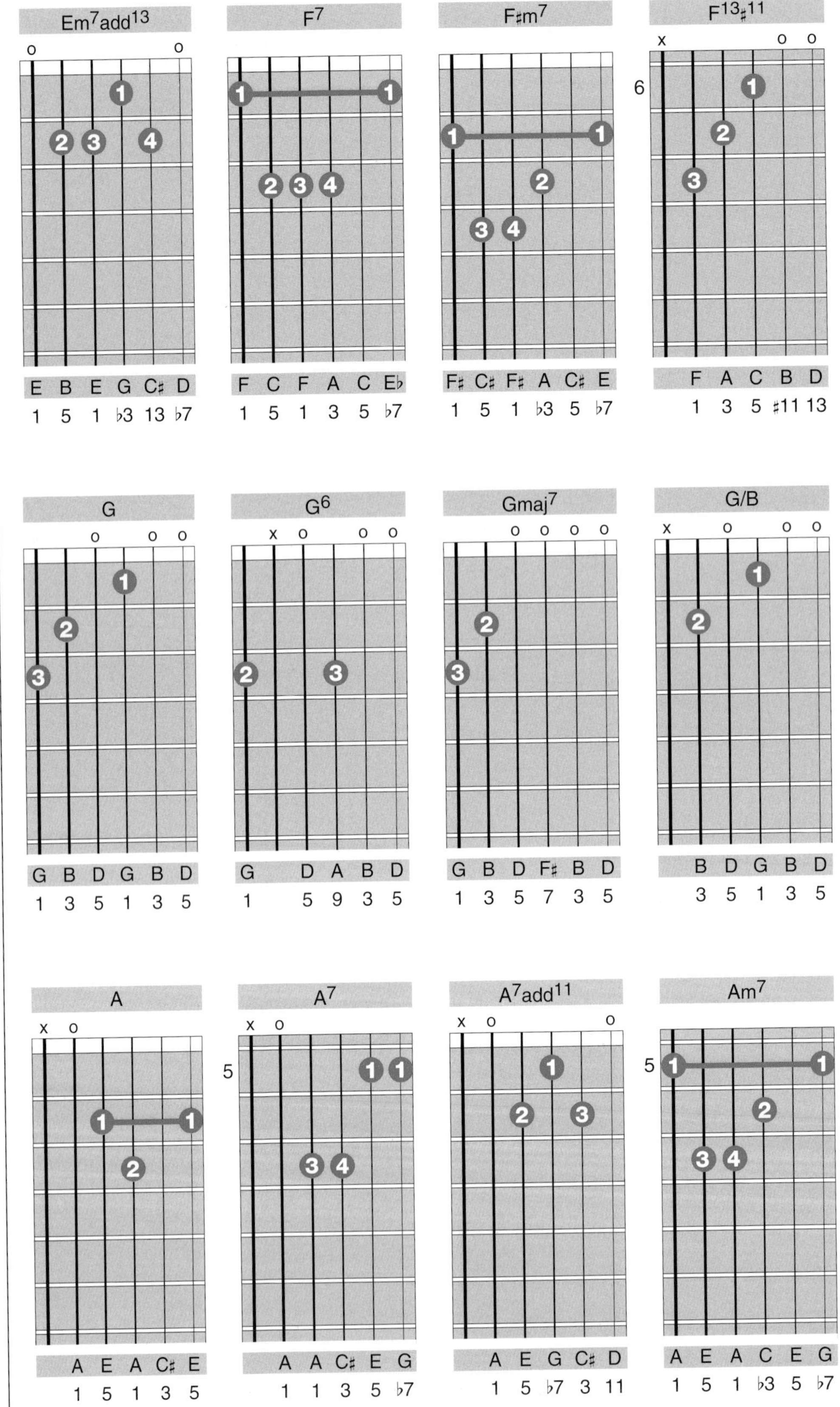
Em7add13
E B E G C♯ D
1 5 1 ♭3 13 ♭7
F7
F C F A C E♭
1 5 1 3 5 ♭7
F♯m7
F♯ C♯ F♯ A C♯ E
1 5 1 ♭3 5 ♭7
F13♯11
6
F A C B D
1 3 5 ♯11 13
G
G B D G B D
1 3 5 1 3 5
G6
G D A B D
1 5 9 3 5
Gmaj7
G B D F♯ B D
1 3 5 7 3 5
G/B
B D G B D
3 5 1 3 5
A
A E A C♯ E
1 5 1 3 5
A7
5
A A C♯ E G
1 1 3 5 ♭7
A7add11
A E G C♯ D
1 5 ♭7 3 11
Am7
5
A E A C E G
1 5 1 ♭3 5 ♭7

EADGAD

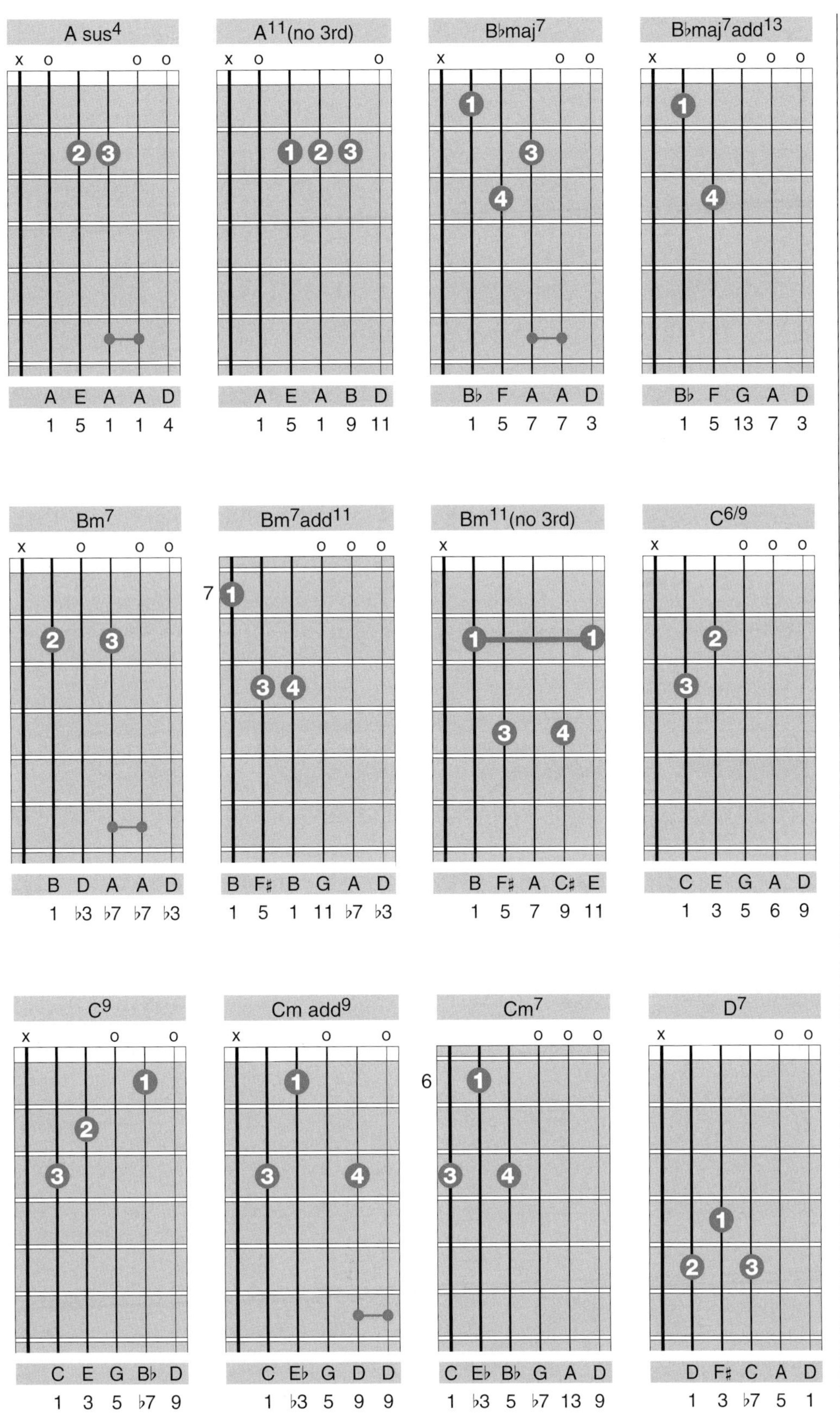

A sus4
A E A A D
1 5 1 1 4
A11(no 3rd)
A E A B D
1 5 1 9 11
B♭maj7
B♭ F A A D
1 5 7 7 3
B♭maj7add13
B♭ F G A D
1 5 13 7 3
Bm7
B D A A D
1 ♭3 ♭7 ♭7 ♭3
Bm7add11
7
B F♯ B G A D
1 5 1 11 ♭7 ♭3
Bm11(no 3rd)
B F♯ A C♯ E
1 5 7 9 11
C6/9
C E G A D
1 3 5 6 9
C9
C E G B♭ D
1 3 5 ♭7 9
Cm add9
C E♭ G D D
1 ♭3 5 9 9
Cm7
6
C E♭ B♭ G A D
1 ♭3 5 ♭7 13 9
D7
D F♯ C A D
1 3 ♭7 5 1

EADGAD

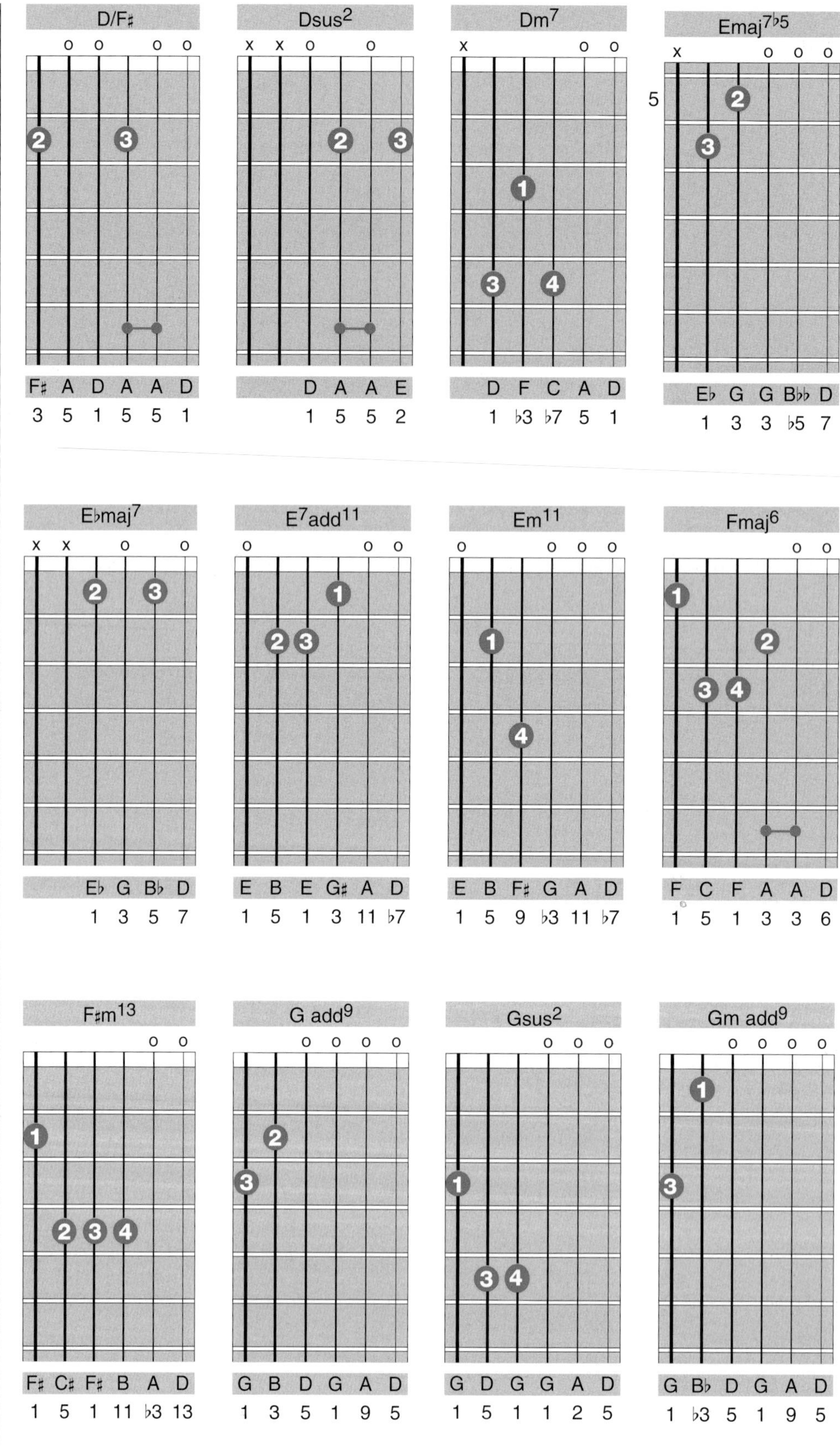
D/F♯
F♯ A D A A D
3 5 1 5 5 1
Dsus2
D A A E
1 5 5 2
Dm7
D F C A D
1 ♭3 ♭7 5 1
Emaj7♭5
5
E♭ G G B♭♭ D
1 3 3 ♭5 7
E♭maj7
E♭ G B♭ D
1 3 5 7
E7add11
E B E G♯ A D
1 5 1 3 11 ♭7
Em11
E B F♯ G A D
1 5 9 ♭3 11 ♭7
Fmaj6
F C F A A D
1 5 1 3 3 6
F♯m13
F♯ C♯ F♯ B A D
1 5 1 11 ♭3 13
G add9
G B D G A D
1 3 5 1 9 5
Gsus2
G D G G A D
1 5 1 1 2 5
Gm add9
G B♭ D G A D
1 ♭3 5 1 9 5

DGDGBD

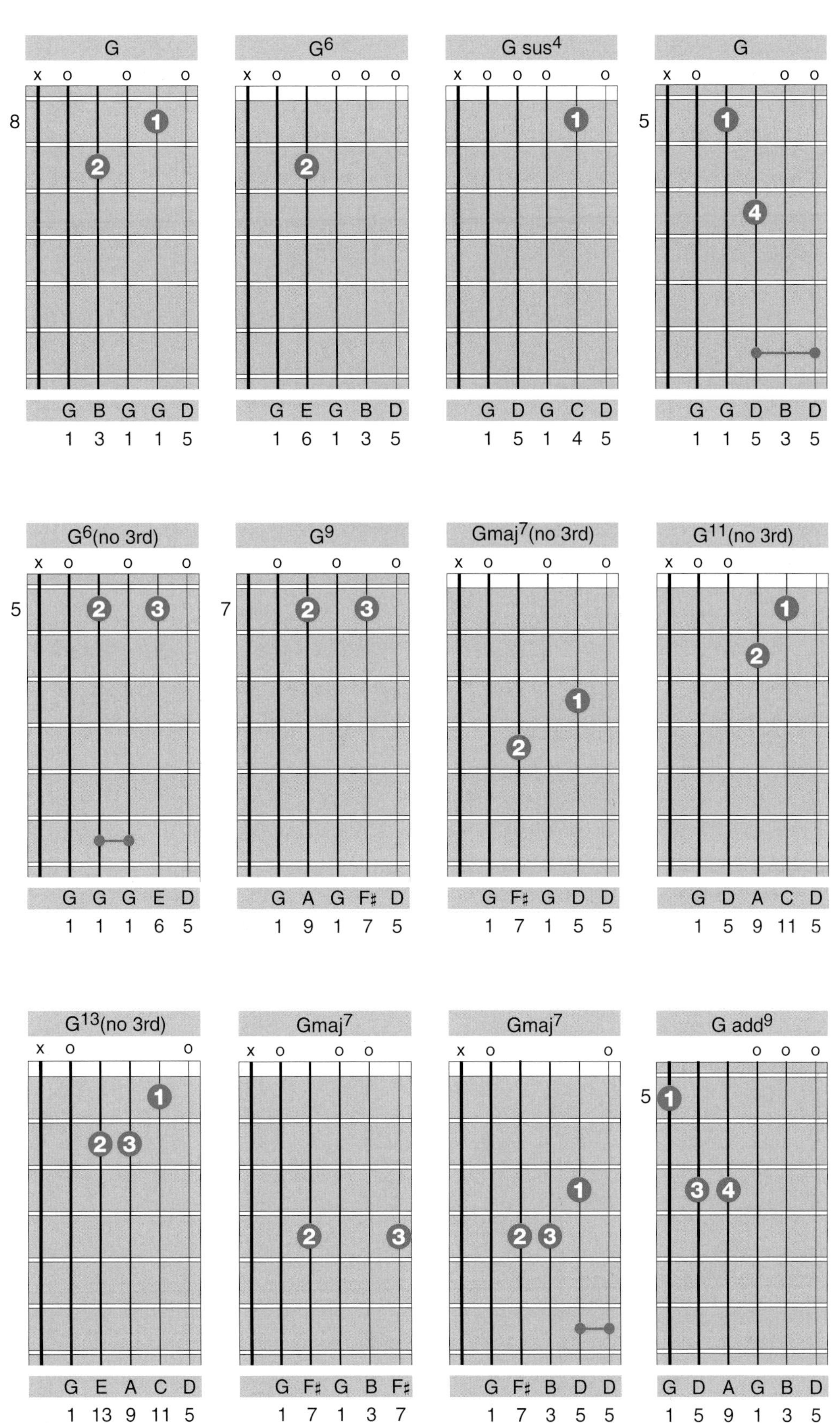
G
x o o o
8
G B G G D
1 3 1 1 5
G6
x o o o o
G E G B D
1 6 1 3 5
G sus4
x o o o o
G D G C D
1 5 1 4 5
G
x o o o
5
G G D B D
1 1 5 3 5
G6(no 3rd)
x o o o
5
G G G E D
1 1 1 6 5
G9
o o o
7
G A G F♯ D
1 9 1 7 5
Gmaj7(no 3rd)
x o o o
G F♯ G D D
1 7 1 5 5
G11(no 3rd)
x o o
G D A C D
1 5 9 11 5
G13(no 3rd)
x o o
G E A C D
1 13 9 11 5
Gmaj7
x o o o
G F♯ G B F♯
1 7 1 3 7
Gmaj7
x o o
G F♯ B D D
1 7 3 5 5
G add9
o o o
5
G D A G B D
1 5 9 1 3 5

DGDGBD

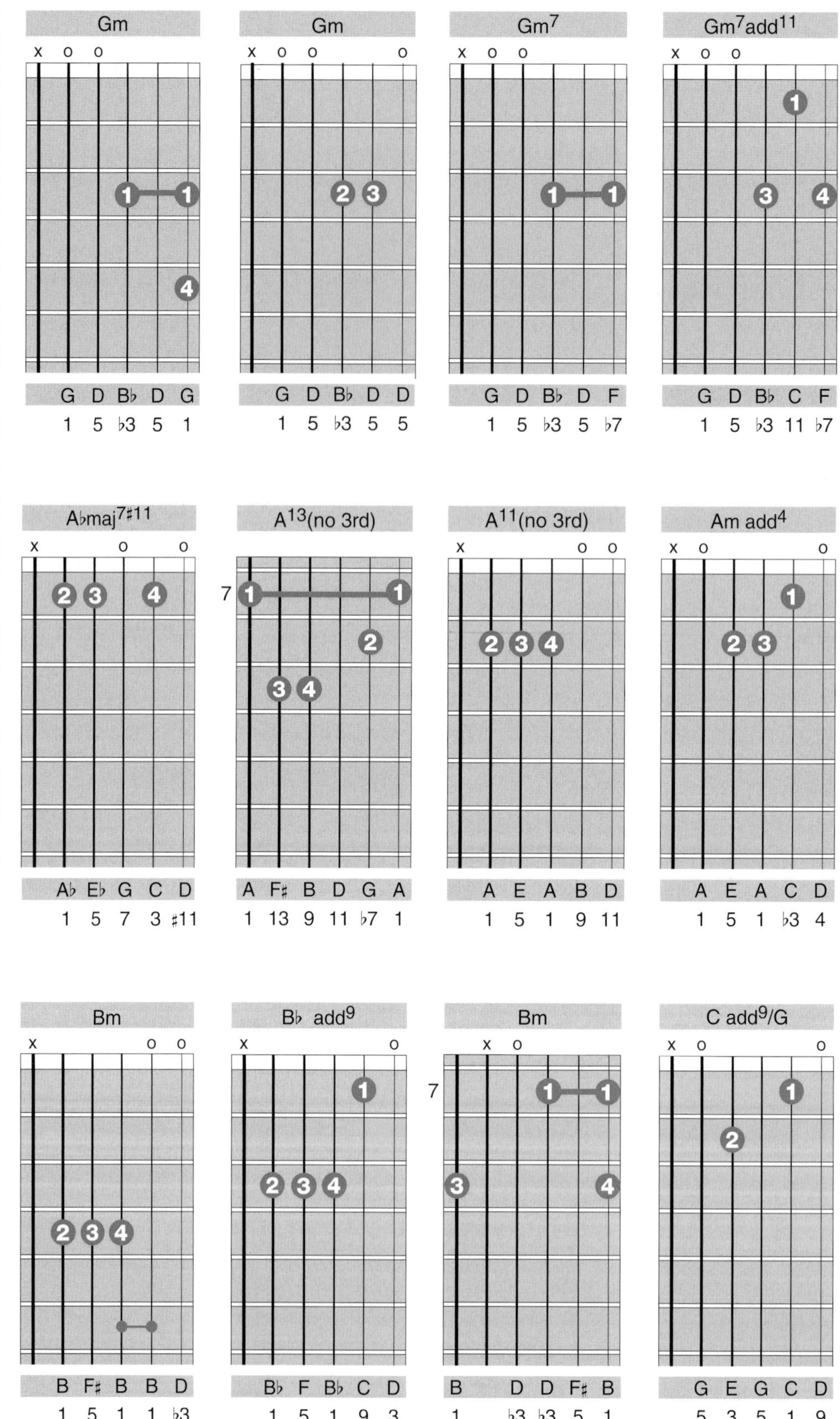
Gm
G D B♭ D G
1 5 ♭3 5 1
Gm
G D B♭ D D
1 5 ♭3 5 5
Gm7
G D B♭ D F
1 5 ♭3 5 ♭7
Gm7add11
G D B♭ C F
1 5 ♭3 11 ♭7
A♭maj7♯11
A♭ E♭ G C D
1 5 7 3 ♯11
A13(no 3rd)
7
A F♯ B D G A
1 13 9 11 ♭7 1
A11(no 3rd)
A E A B D
1 5 1 9 11
Am add4
A E A C D
1 5 1 ♭3 4
Bm
B F♯ B B D
1 5 1 1 ♭3
B♭ add9
B♭ F B♭ C D
1 5 1 9 3
Bm
7
B D D F♯ B
1 ♭3 ♭3 5 1
C add9/G
G E G C D
5 3 5 1 9

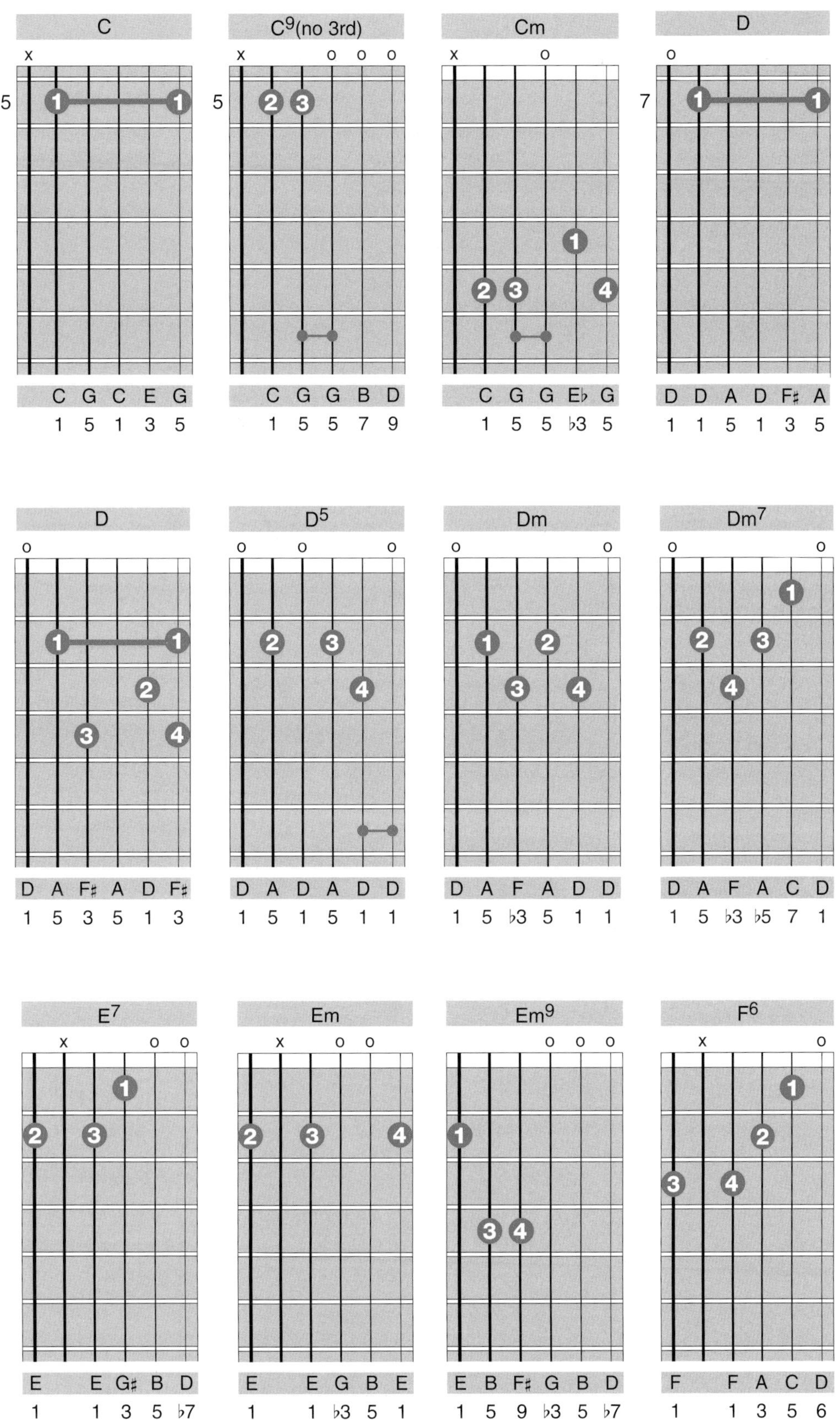
C
x
5
C G C E G
1 5 1 3 5
C9(no 3rd)
x o o o
5
C G G B D
1 5 5 7 9
Cm
x o
C G G E♭ G
1 5 5 ♭3 5
D
o
7
D D A D F♯ A
1 1 5 1 3 5
D
o
D A F♯ A D F♯
1 5 3 5 1 3
D5
o o o
D A D A D D
1 5 1 5 1 1
Dm
o o
D A F A D D
1 5 ♭3 5 1 1
Dm7
o o
D A F A C D
1 5 ♭3 ♭5 7 1
E7
x o o
E E G♯ B D
1 1 3 5 ♭7
Em
x o o
E E G B E
1 1 ♭3 5 1
Em9
o o o
E B F♯ G B D
1 5 9 ♭3 5 ♭7
F6
x o
F F A C D
1 1 3 5 6

DADF♯AD

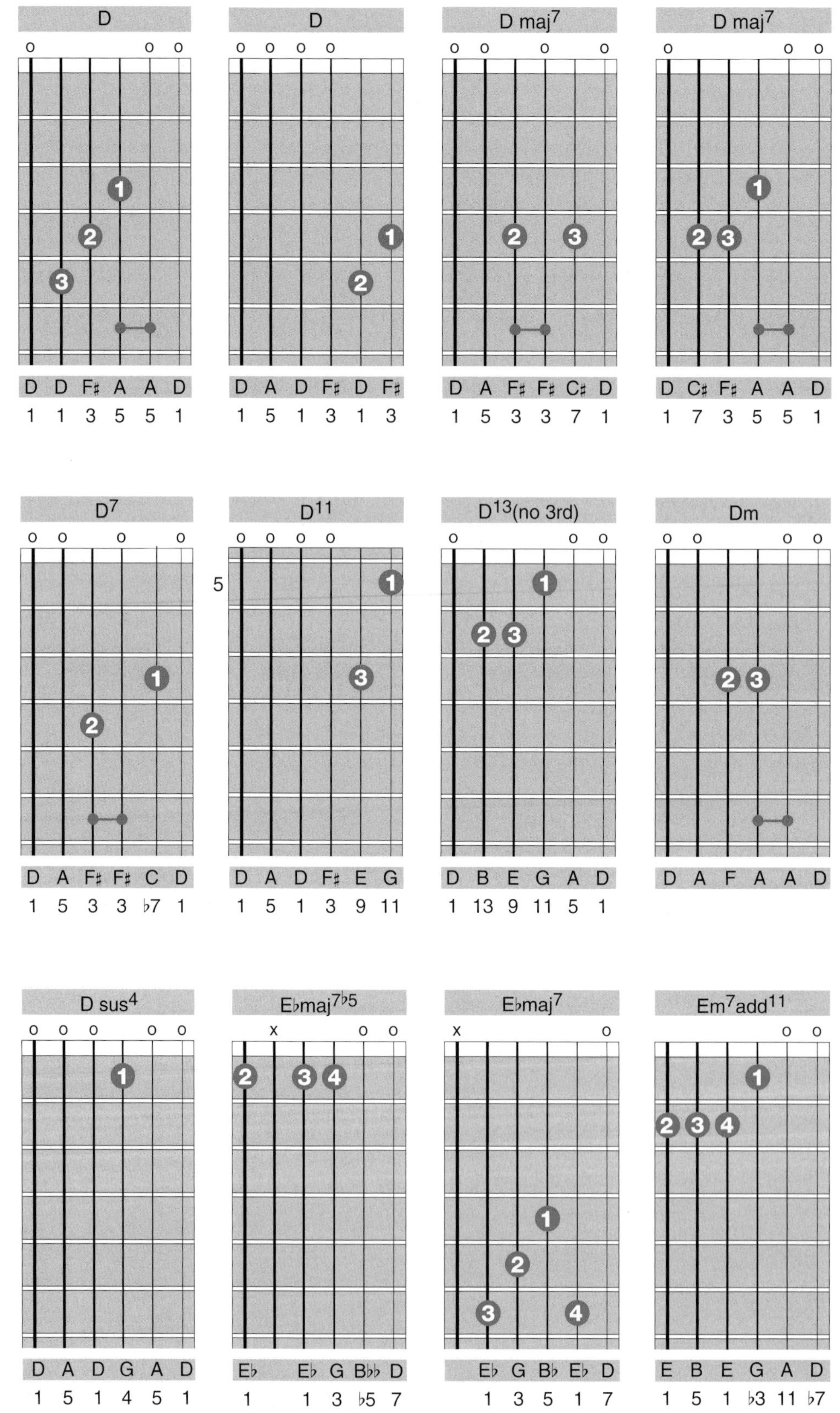
D
D D F♯ A A D
1 1 3 5 5 1
D
D A D F♯ D F♯
1 5 1 3 1 3
D maj7
D A F♯ F♯ C♯ D
1 5 3 3 7 1
D maj7
D C♯ F♯ A A D
1 7 3 5 5 1
D7
D A F♯ F♯ C D
1 5 3 3 ♭7 1
D11
5
D A D F♯ E G
1 5 1 3 9 11
D13(no 3rd)
D B E G A D
1 13 9 11 5 1
Dm
D A F A A D
D sus4
D A D G A D
1 5 1 4 5 1
E♭maj7♭5
E♭ E♭ G B♭♭ D
1 1 3 ♭5 7
E♭maj7
E♭ G B♭ E♭ D
1 3 5 1 7
Em7add11
E B E G A D
1 5 1 ♭3 11 ♭7

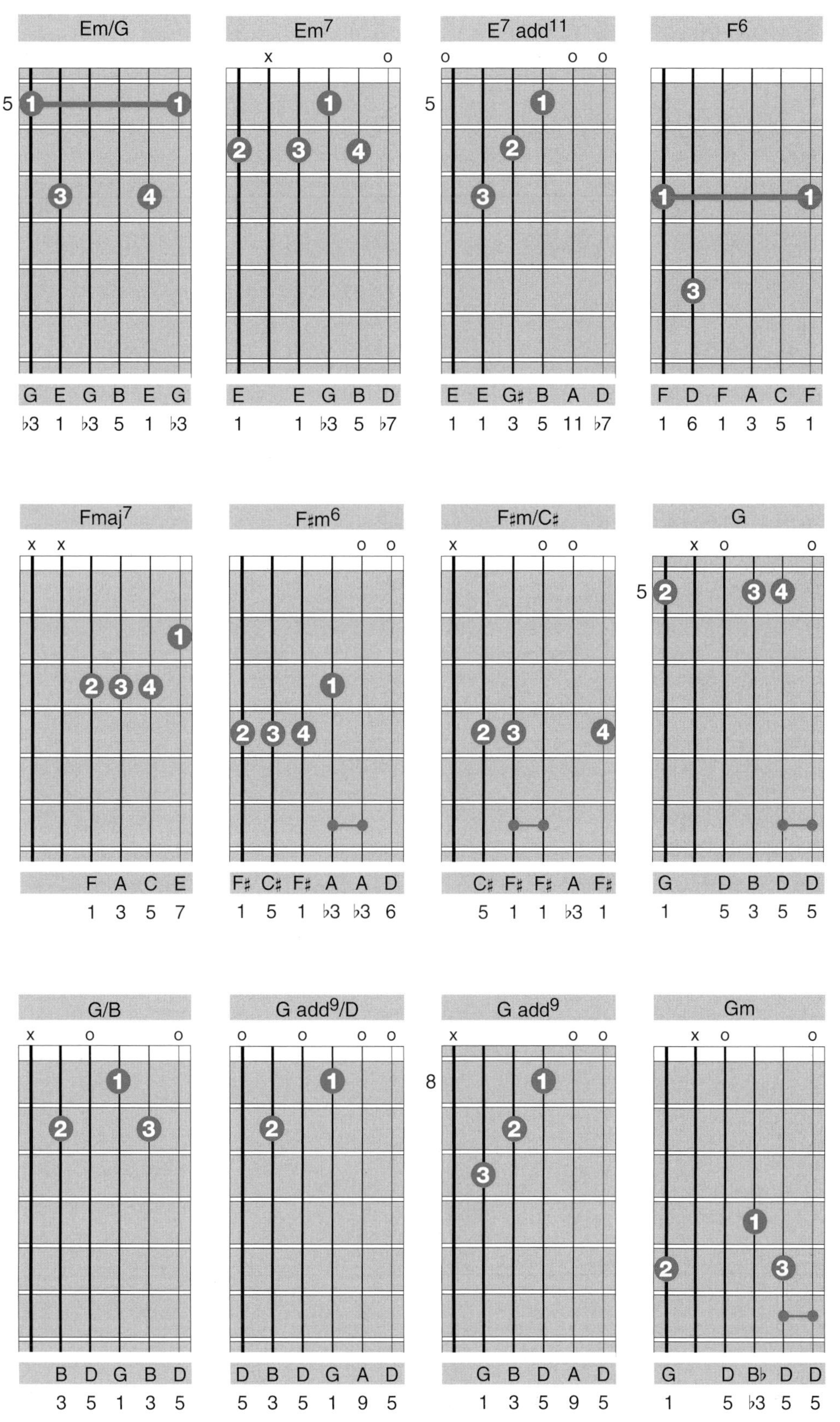

Em/G
5
G E G B E G
♭3 1 ♭3 5 1 ♭3
Em7
x o
E E G B D
1 1 ♭3 5 ♭7
E7 add11
o o o
5
E E G♯ B A D
1 1 3 5 11 ♭7
F6
F D F A C F
1 6 1 3 5 1
Fmaj7
x x
F A C E
1 3 5 7
F♯m6
o o
F♯ C♯ F♯ A A D
1 5 1 ♭3 ♭3 6
F♯m/C♯
x o o
C♯ F♯ F♯ A F♯
5 1 1 ♭3 1
G
x o o
5
G D B D D
1 5 3 5 5
G/B
x o o
B D G B D
3 5 1 3 5
G add9/D
o o o o
D B D G A D
5 3 5 1 9 5
G add9
x o o
8
G B D A D
1 3 5 9 5
Gm
x o o
G D B♭ D D
1 5 ♭3 5 5

Gm add⁹
o o
G D G B♭ A D
1 5 1 ♭3 9 5

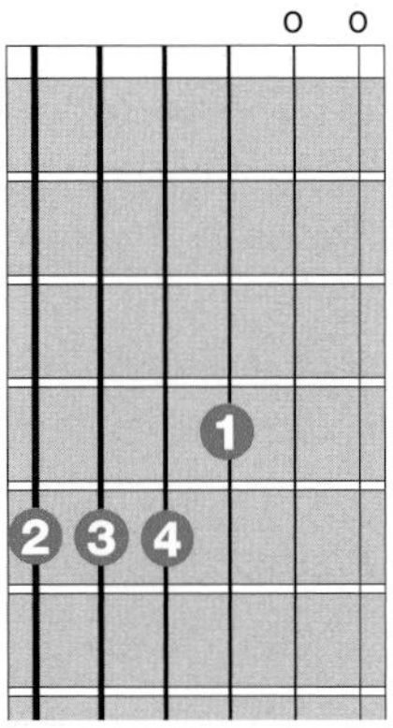

Gm add⁹/B♭
x o o o
B♭ D G A D
♭3 5 1 9 5

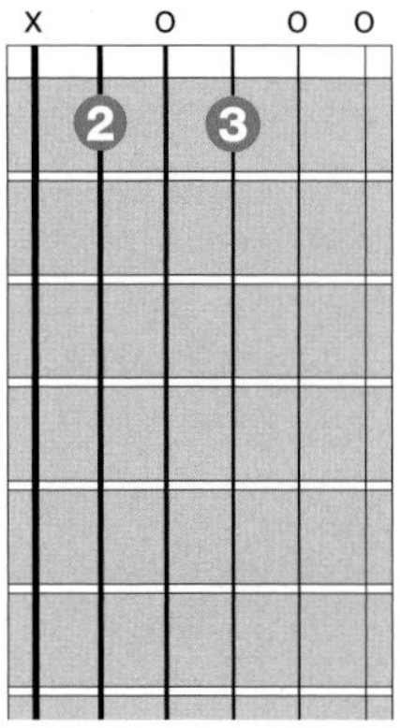

A 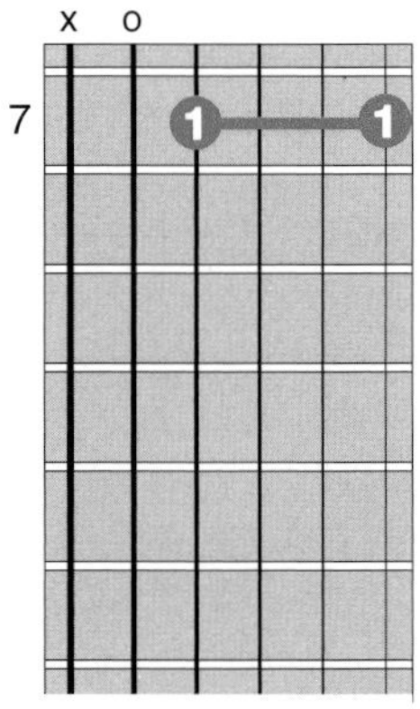
x o
7
A A C♯ E A
1 1 3 5 1

A⁷
x o
5
A G C♯ E A
1 ♭7 3 5 1

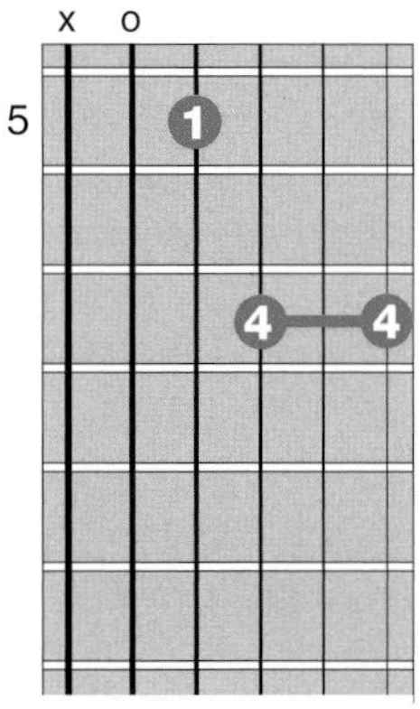

A sus⁴
x o o o
A E A A D
1 5 1 1 4

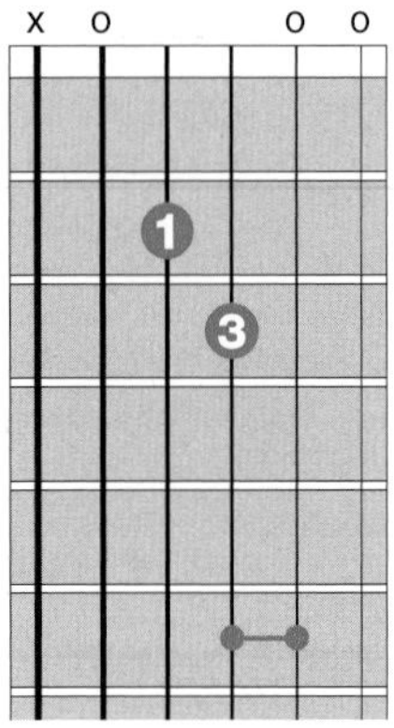

A⁵
x o o
A E A A E
1 5 1 1 5

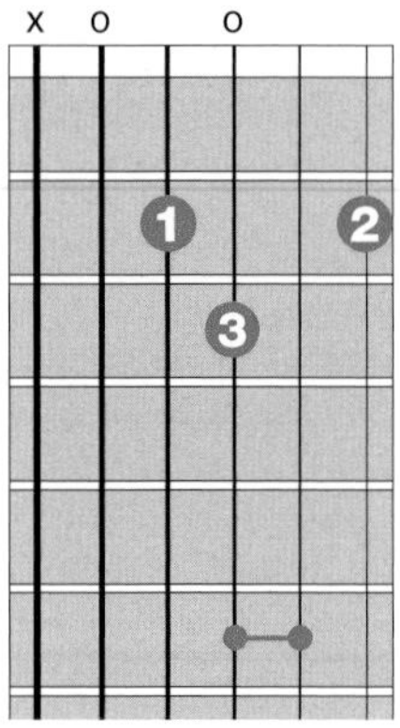

Am 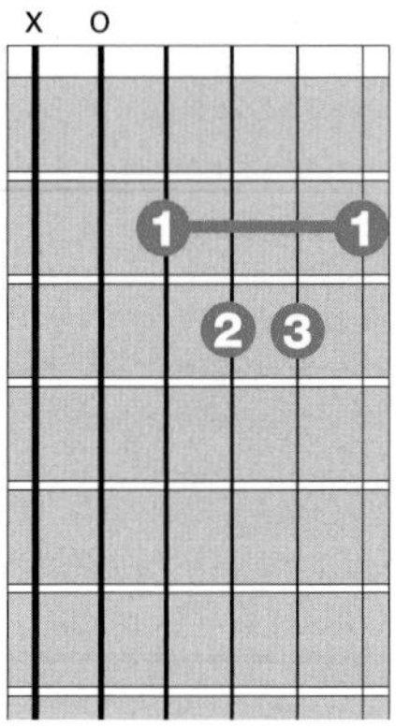
x o
A E A C E
1 5 1 ♭3 5

Bm add⁹
x o o
B F♯ F♯ C♯ D
1 5 5 9 ♭3

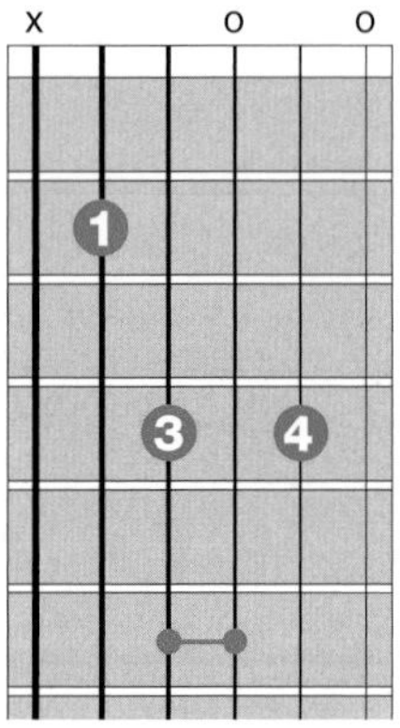

Bm⁷
o o
8
B F♯ B D A D
1 5 1 ♭3 ♭7 ♭3

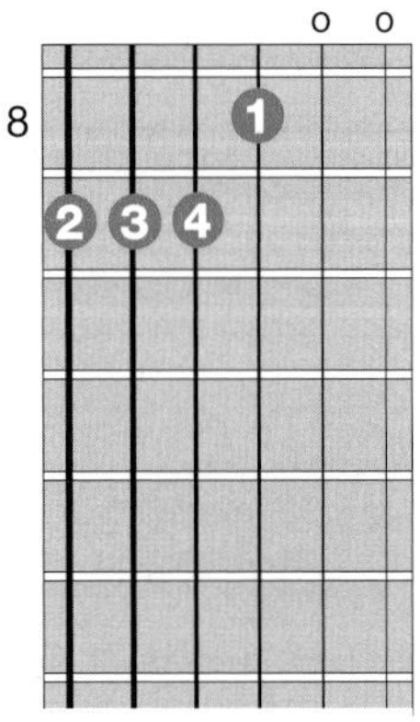

Bm 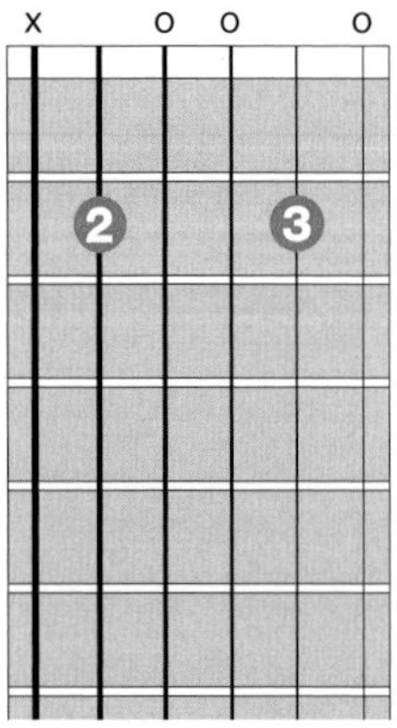
x o o o
B D F♯ B D
1 ♭3 5 1 ♭3

Bm 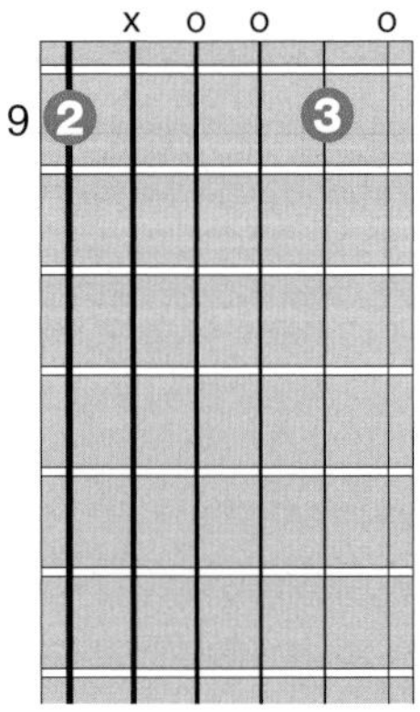
x o o o
9
B D F♯ F♯ D
1 ♭3 5 5 ♭3

C⁶ᐟ⁹
x o o
C E G A D
1 3 5 6 9

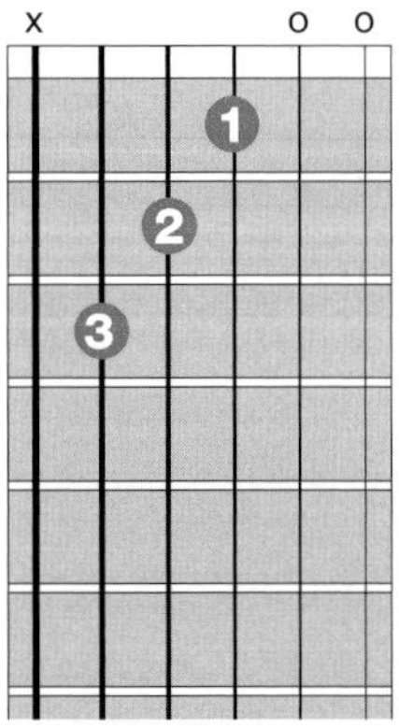

CGCGCE

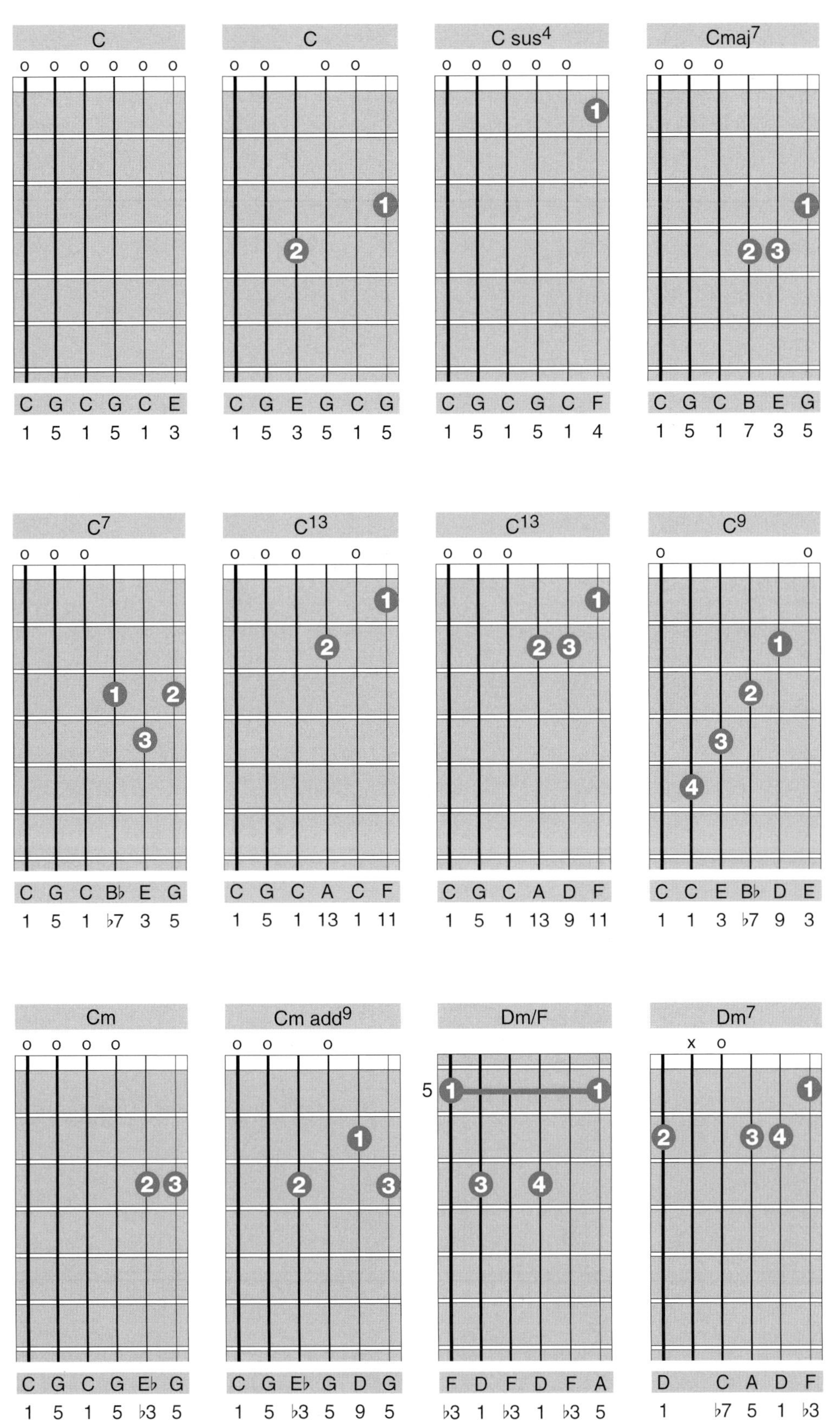
C
C G C G C E
1 5 1 5 1 3
C
C G E G C G
1 5 3 5 1 5
C sus4
C G C G C F
1 5 1 5 1 4
Cmaj7
C G C B E G
1 5 1 7 3 5
C7
C G C B♭ E G
1 5 1 ♭7 3 5
C13
C G C A C F
1 5 1 13 1 11
C13
C G C A D F
1 5 1 13 9 11
C9
C C E B♭ D E
1 1 3 ♭7 9 3
Cm
C G C G E♭ G
1 5 1 5 ♭3 5
Cm add9
C G E♭ G D G
1 5 ♭3 5 9 5
Dm/F
5
F D F D F A
♭3 1 ♭3 1 ♭3 5
Dm7
D C A D F
1 ♭7 5 1 ♭3

CGCGCE

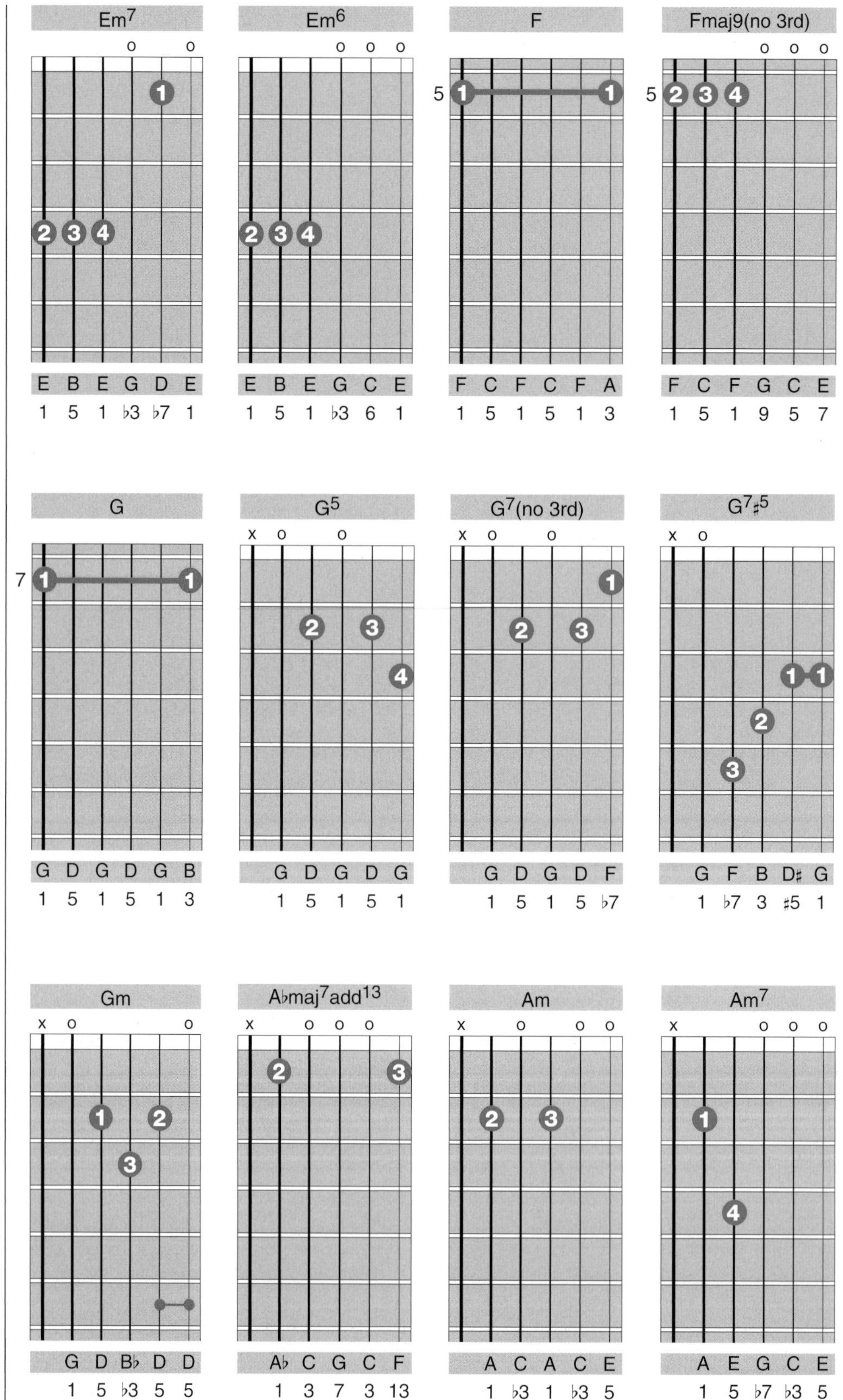

Em7
E B E G D E
1 5 1 ♭3 ♭7 1
Em6
E B E G C E
1 5 1 ♭3 6 1
F
F C F C F A
1 5 1 5 1 3
Fmaj9(no 3rd)
F C F G C E
1 5 1 9 5 7
G
G D G D G B
1 5 1 5 1 3
G5
G D G D G
1 5 1 5 1
G7(no 3rd)
G D G D F
1 5 1 5 ♭7
G7♯5
G F B D♯ G
1 ♭7 3 ♯5 1
Gm
G D B♭ D D
1 5 ♭3 5 5
A♭maj7add13
A♭ C G C F
1 3 7 3 13
Am
A C A C E
1 ♭3 1 ♭3 5
Am7
A E G C E
1 5 ♭7 ♭3 5

EAC♯EAE

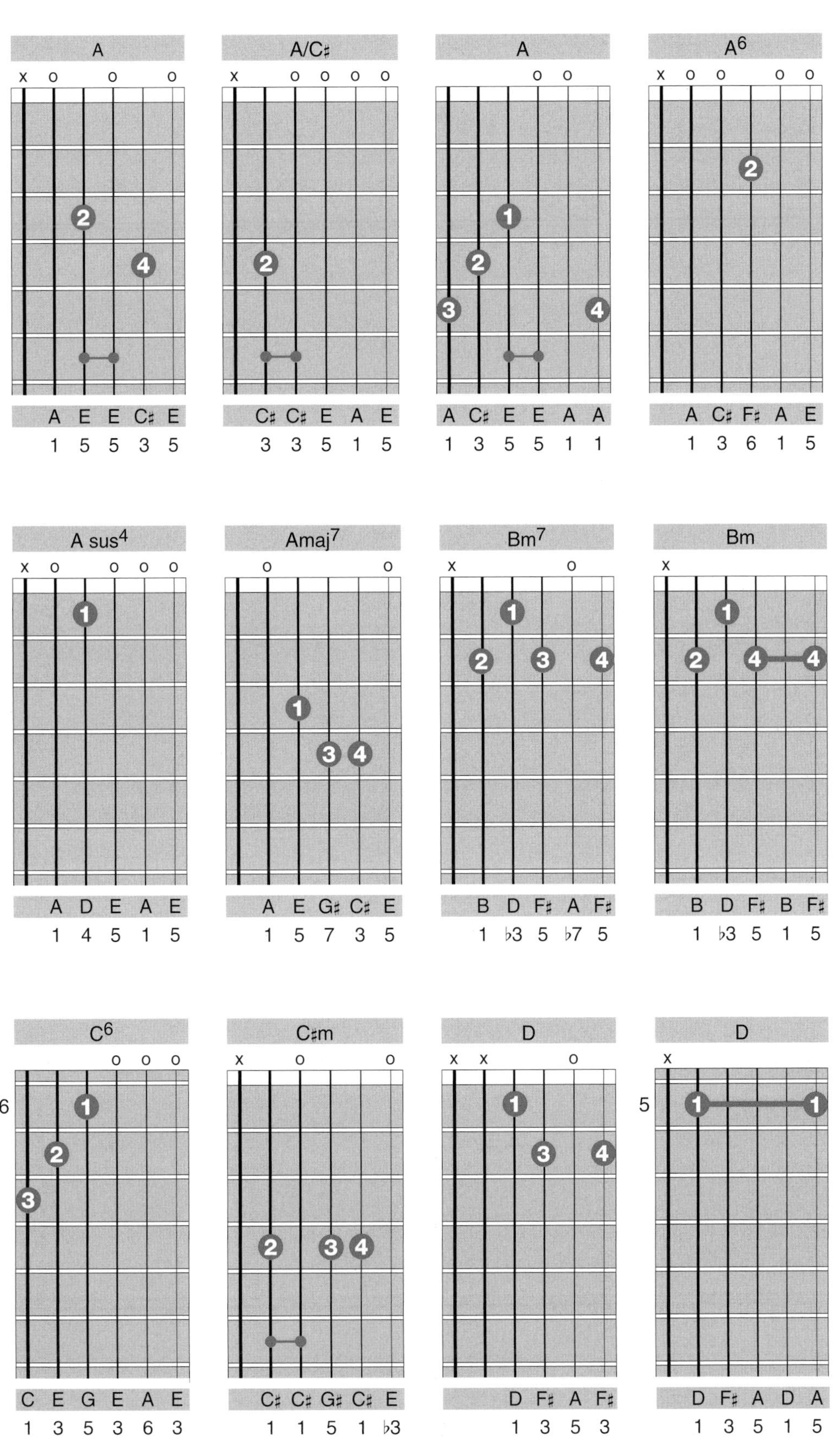
A
x o o o
A E E C♯ E
1 5 5 3 5
A/C♯
x o o o o
C♯ C♯ E A E
3 3 5 1 5
A
o o
A C♯ E E A A
1 3 5 5 1 1
A6
x o o o o
A C♯ F♯ A E
1 3 6 1 5
A sus4
x o o o o
A D E A E
1 4 5 1 5
Amaj7
o o
A E G♯ C♯ E
1 5 7 3 5
Bm7
x o
B D F♯ A F♯
1 ♭3 5 ♭7 5
Bm
x
B D F♯ B F♯
1 ♭3 5 1 5
C6
o o o
6
C E G E A E
1 3 5 3 6 3
C♯m
x o o
C♯ C♯ G♯ C♯ E
1 1 5 1 ♭3
D
x x o
D F♯ A F♯
1 3 5 3
D
x
5
D F♯ A D A
1 3 5 1 5

D add^{9}/F♯					
F♯	A	D	F♯	A	E
3	5	1	3	5	9

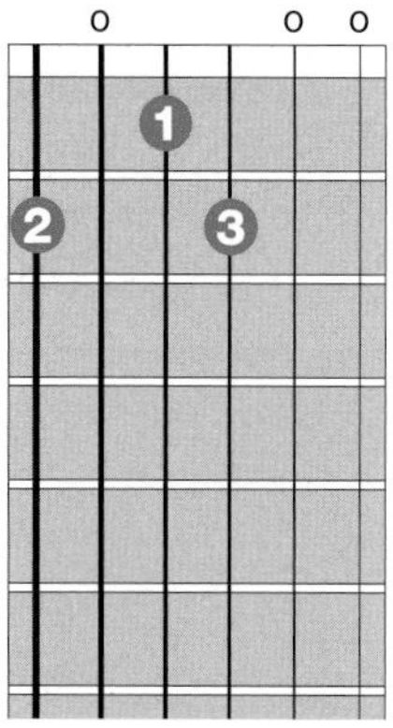

5

D/E					
E	D	F♯	A	D	A
	1	3	5	1	5

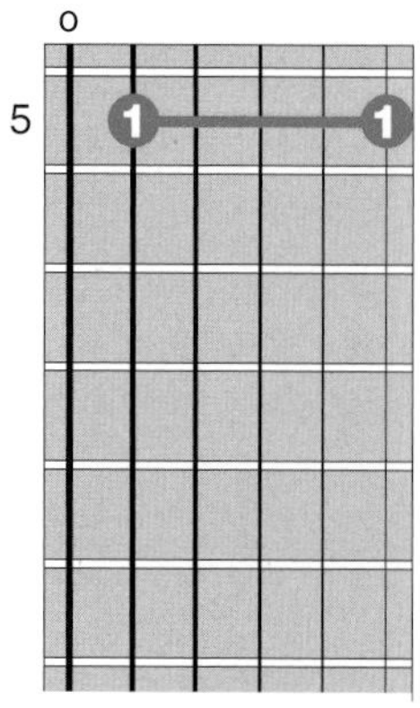

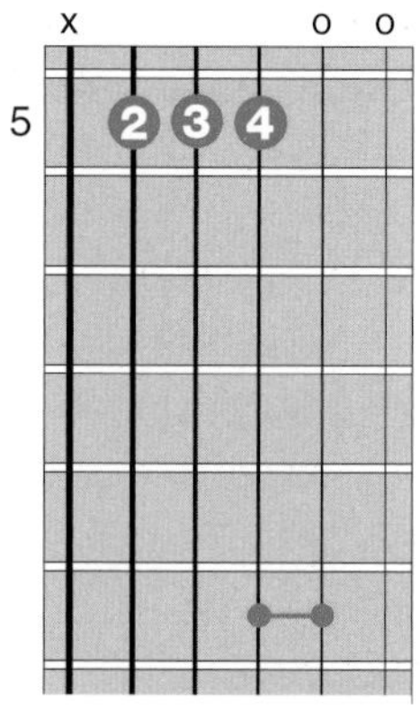

5

D add^{9}					
	D	F♯	A	A	E
	1	3	5	5	9

Dm add^{9}					
	D	F	A	A	E
	1	♭3	5	5	9

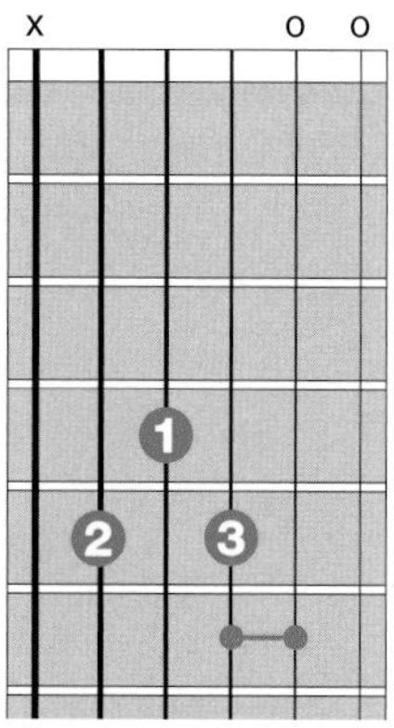

Fmaj^{7}♯^{5}					
F	A	C♯	F	A	E
1	3	♯5	1	3	7

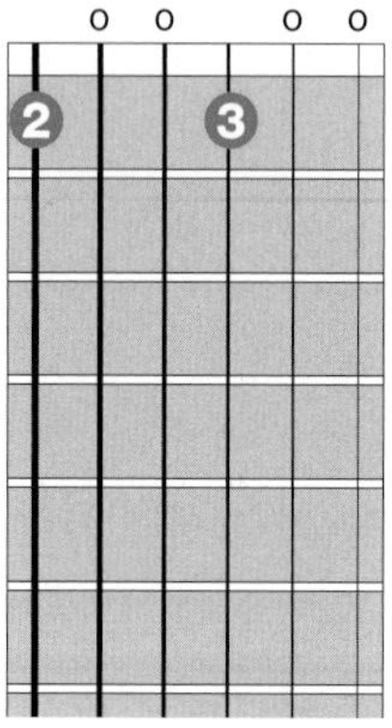

F♯m^{7}					
F♯	A	C♯	F♯	A	E
1	♭3	5	1	♭3	♭7

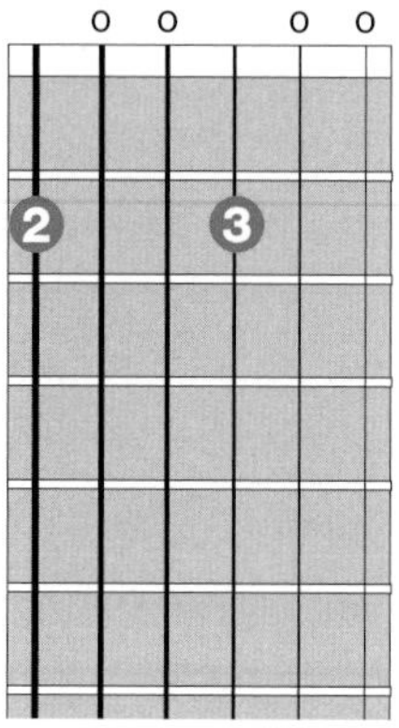

F♯m					
F♯	A	C♯	F♯	A	F♯
1	♭3	5	1	♭3	1

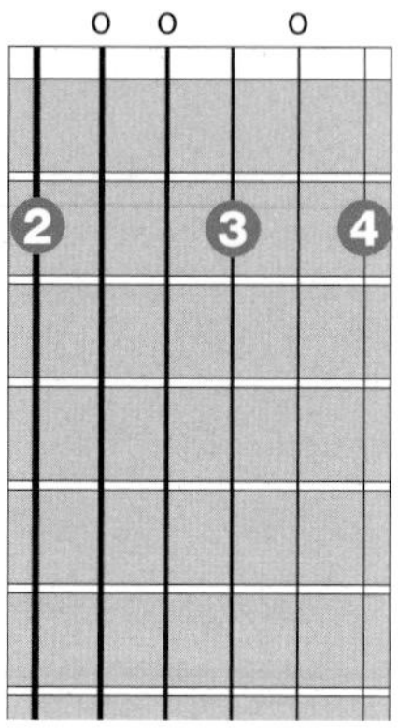

7

E(no 5th)					
E	E	G♯	E	E	E
1	1	3	1	1	1

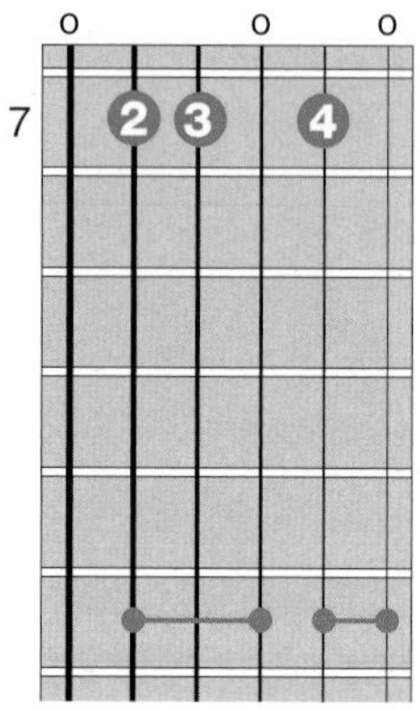

E^{11}					
E	B	D	F♯	A	E
1	5	♭7	9	11	1

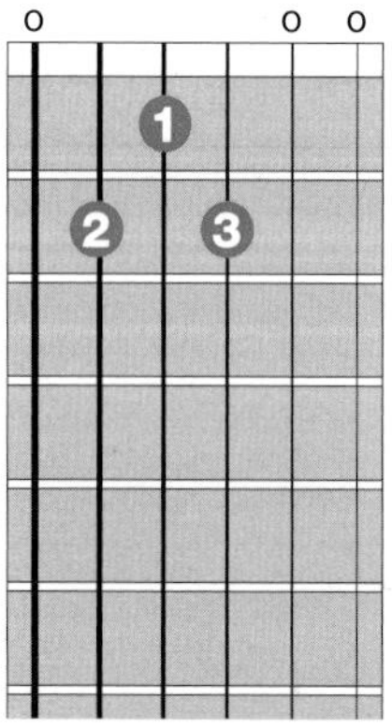

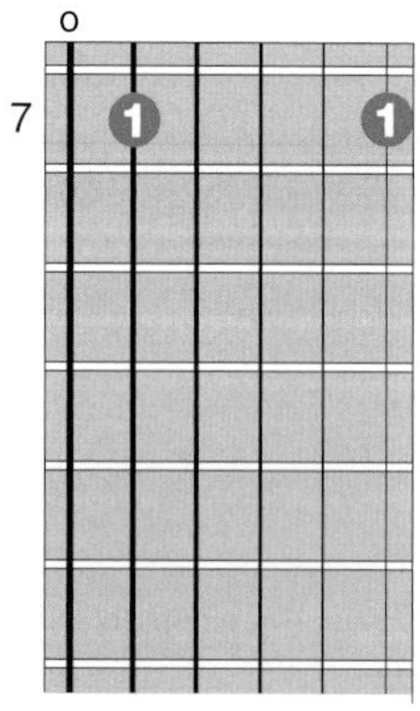

7

E					
E	E	G♯	B	E	B
1	1	3	5	1	5

10

G/E					
	G	B	D	G	D
	1	3	5	1	5

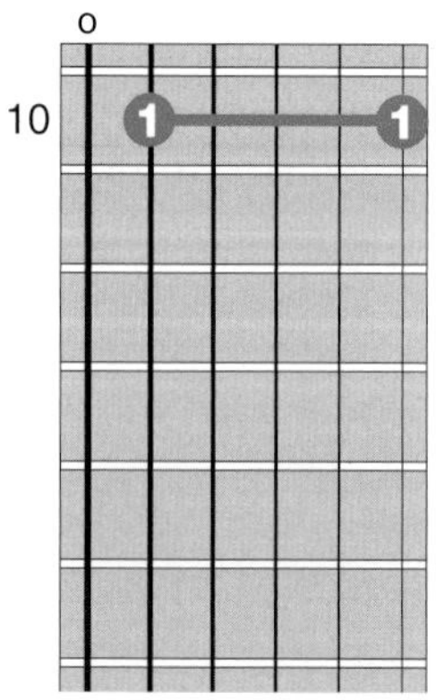

G$^{6/9}$					
G	B	D	E	A	G
1	3	5	6	9	1

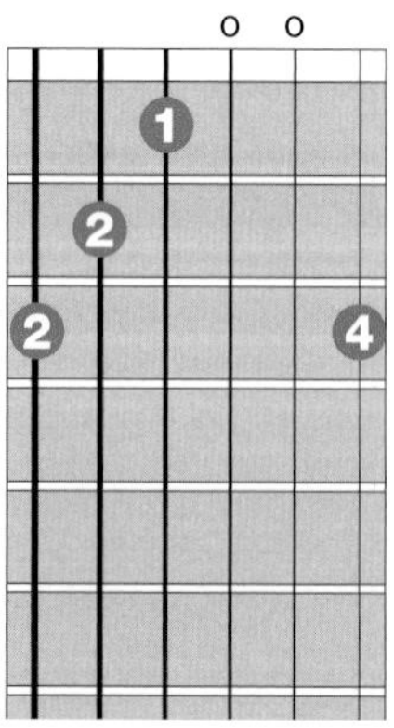

EG♯BEBE

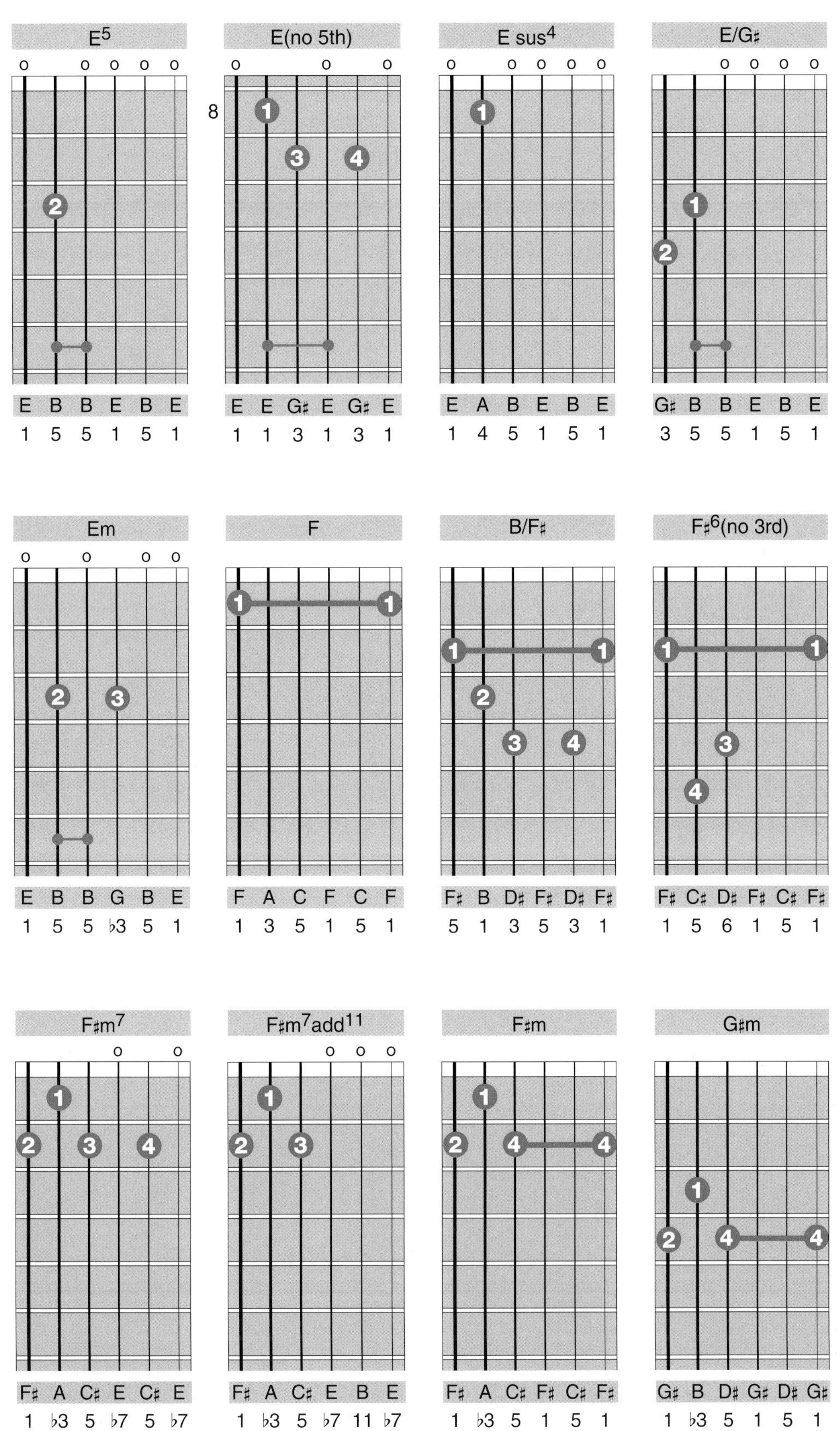
E5
E B B E B E
1 5 5 1 5 1
E(no 5th)
8
E E G♯ E G♯ E
1 1 3 1 3 1
E sus4
E A B E B E
1 4 5 1 5 1
E/G♯
G♯ B B E B E
3 5 5 1 5 1
Em
E B B G B E
1 5 5 ♭3 5 1
F
F A C F C F
1 3 5 1 5 1
B/F♯
F♯ B D♯ F♯ D♯ F♯
5 1 3 5 3 1
F♯6(no 3rd)
F♯ C♯ D♯ F♯ C♯ F♯
1 5 6 1 5 1
F♯m7
F♯ A C♯ E C♯ E
1 ♭3 5 ♭7 5 ♭7
F♯m7add11
F♯ A C♯ E B E
1 ♭3 5 ♭7 11 ♭7
F♯m
F♯ A C♯ F♯ C♯ F♯
1 ♭3 5 1 5 1
G♯m
G♯ B D♯ G♯ D♯ G♯
1 ♭3 5 1 5 1

EG♯BEBE

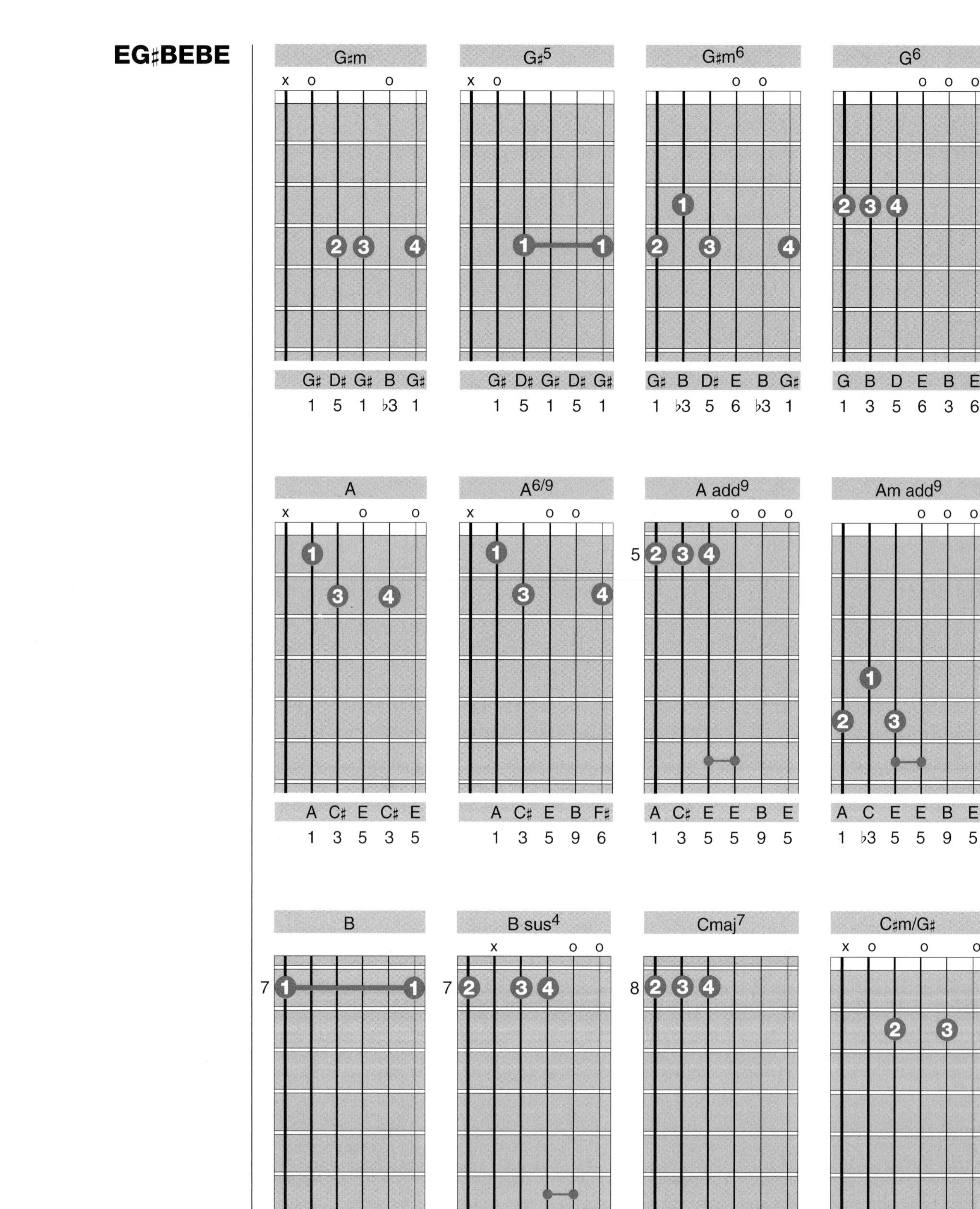
G♯m
x o o
G♯ D♯ G♯ B G♯
1 5 1 ♭3 1
G♯5
x o
G♯ D♯ G♯ D♯ G♯
1 5 1 5 1
G♯m6
o o
G♯ B D♯ E B G♯
1 ♭3 5 6 ♭3 1
G6
o o o
G B D E B E
1 3 5 6 3 6
A
x o o
A C♯ E C♯ E
1 3 5 3 5
A6/9
x o o
A C♯ E B F♯
1 3 5 9 6
A add9
o o o
5
A C♯ E E B E
1 3 5 5 9 5
Am add9
o o o
A C E E B E
1 ♭3 5 5 9 5
B
7
B D♯ F♯ B F♯ B
1 3 5 1 5 1
B sus4
x o o
7
B F♯ B B E
Cmaj7
8
C E G E B E
1 3 5 3 7 3
C♯m/G♯
x o o o
G♯ C♯ E C♯ E
5 1 ♭3 1 ♭3

DB♭DFB♭D

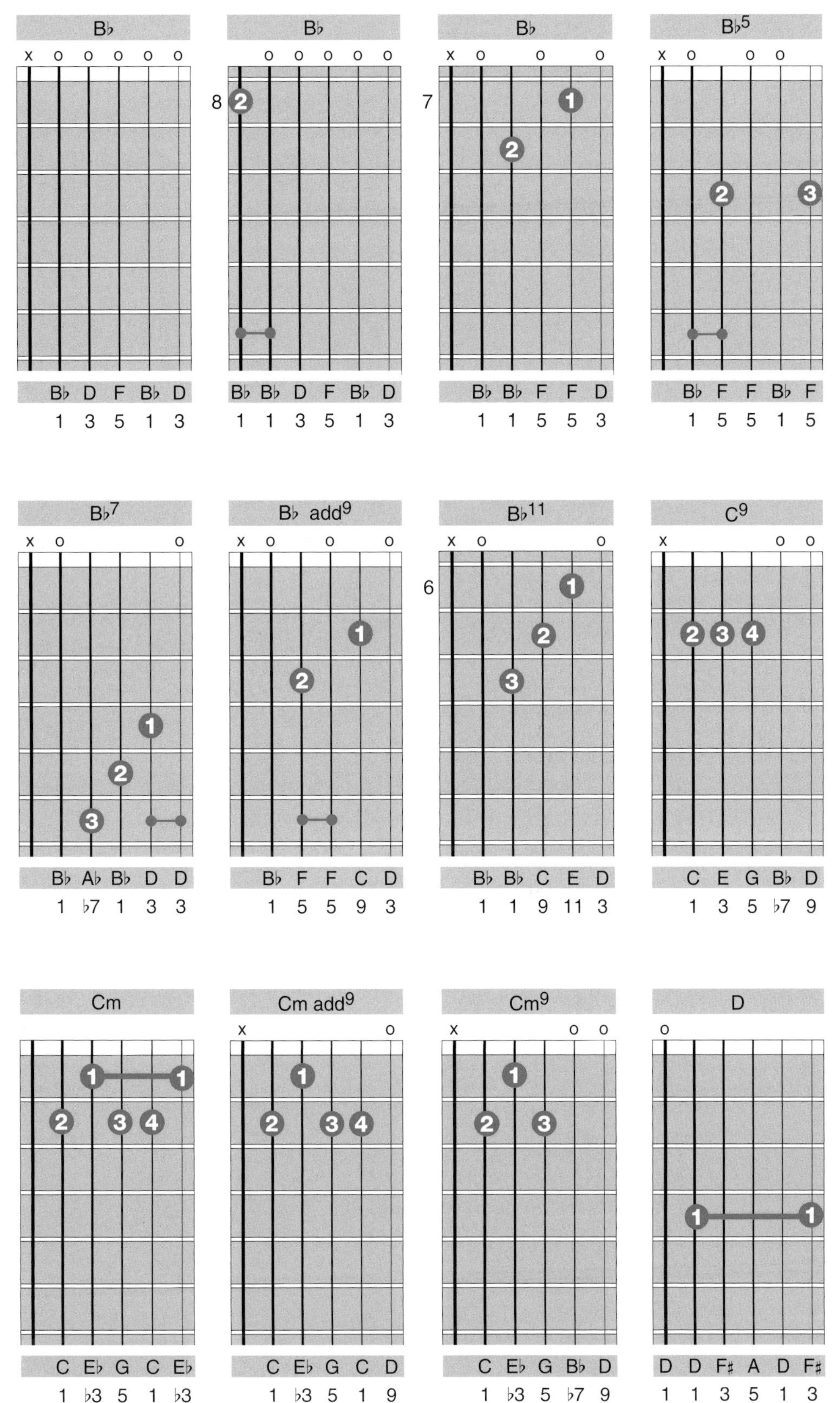

THE ALTERNATIVE CHORD MASTER

DB♭DFB♭D

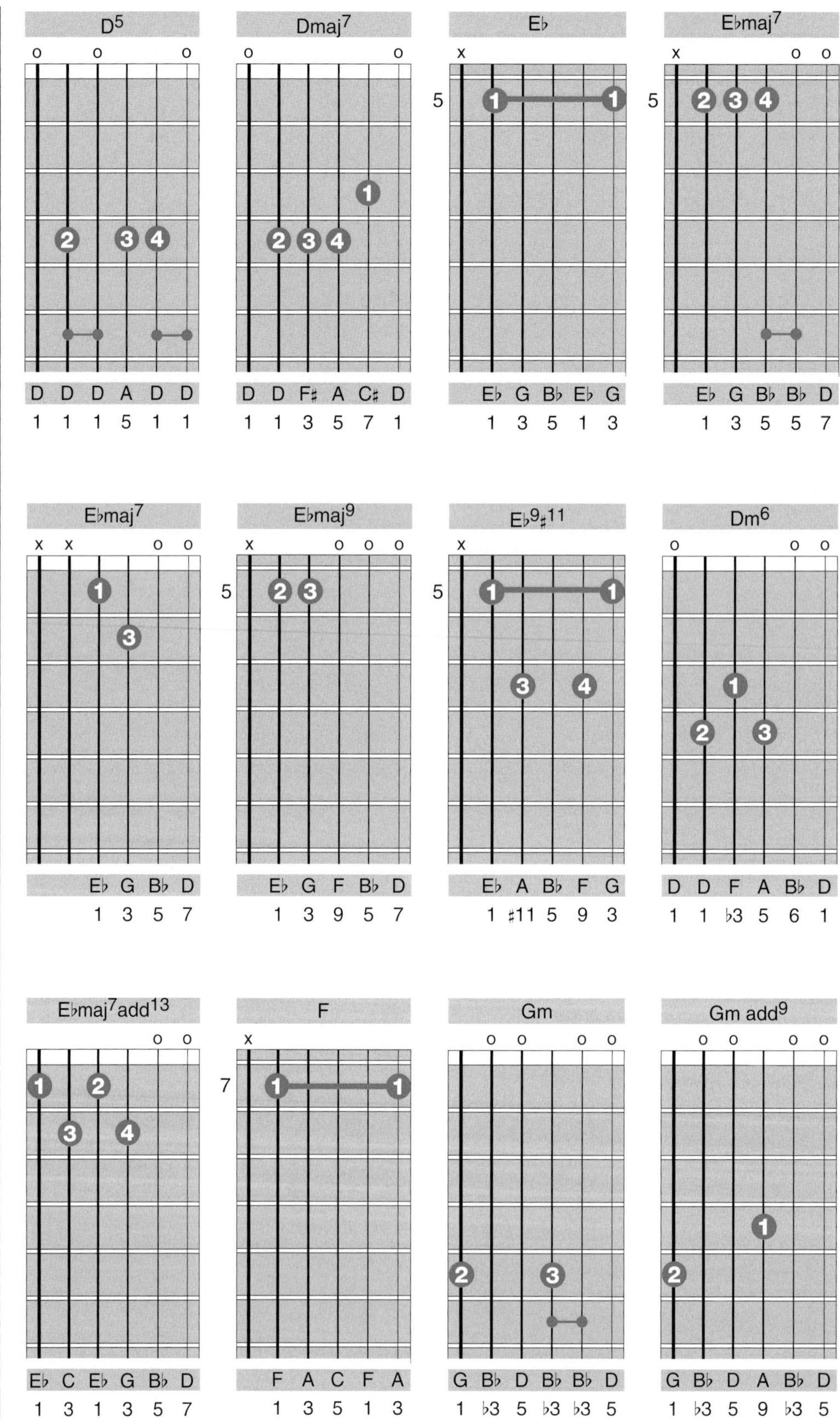
D5
D D D A D D
1 1 1 5 1 1
Dmaj7
D D F♯ A C♯ D
1 1 3 5 7 1
E♭
E♭ G B♭ E♭ G
1 3 5 1 3
E♭maj7
E♭ G B♭ B♭ D
1 3 5 5 7
E♭maj7
E♭ G B♭ D
1 3 5 7
E♭maj9
E♭ G F B♭ D
1 3 9 5 7
E♭9♯11
E♭ A B♭ F G
1 ♯11 5 9 3
Dm6
D D F A B♭ D
1 1 ♭3 5 6 1
E♭maj7add13
E♭ C E♭ G B♭ D
1 3 1 3 5 7
F
F A C F A
1 3 5 1 3
Gm
G B♭ D B♭ B♭ D
1 ♭3 5 ♭3 ♭3 5
Gm add9
G B♭ D A B♭ D
1 ♭3 5 9 ♭3 5

EAC♯F♯AE

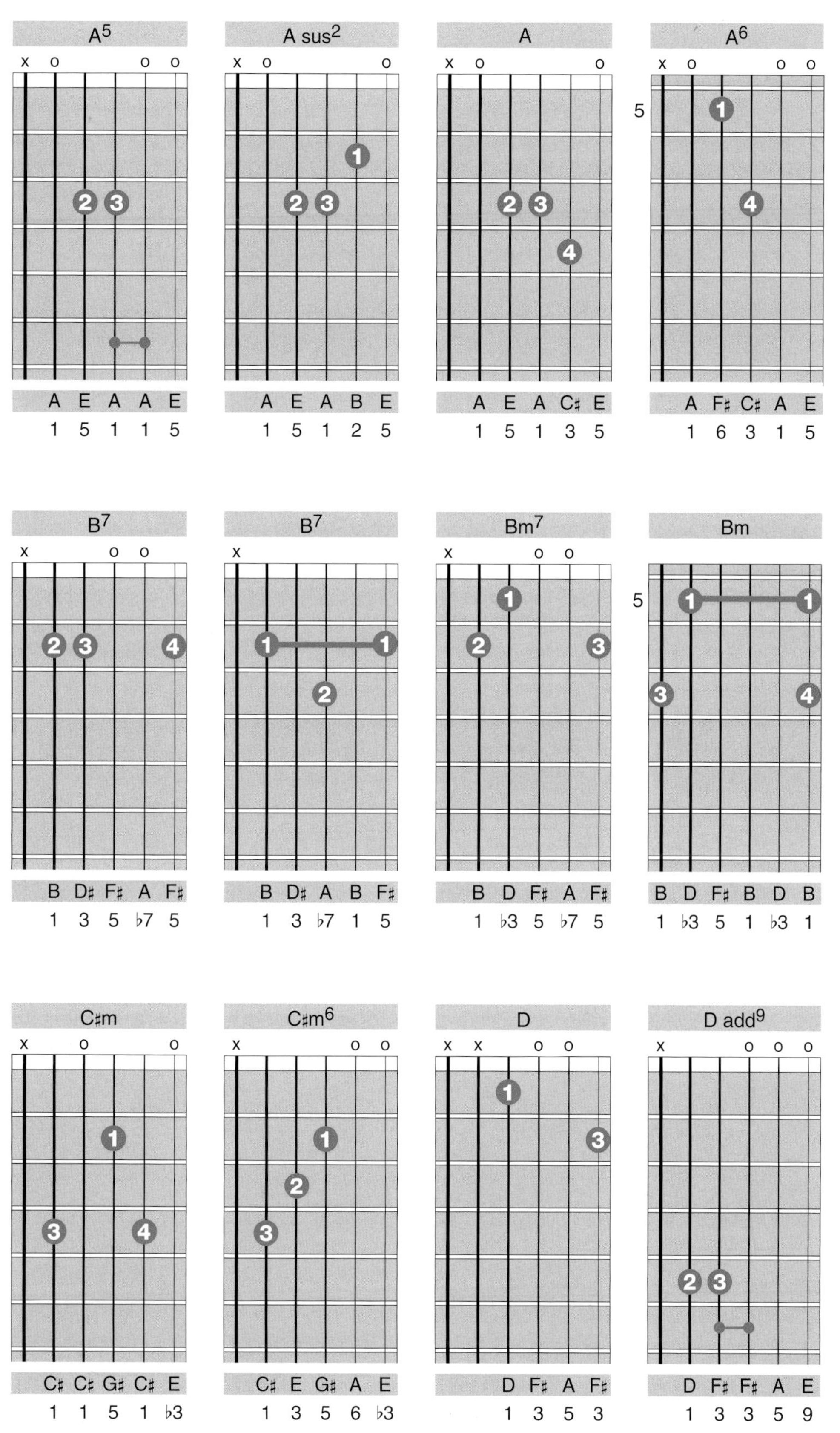
A5
A E A A E
1 5 1 1 5
A sus2
A E A B E
1 5 1 2 5
A
A E A C♯ E
1 5 1 3 5
A6
A F♯ C♯ A E
1 6 3 1 5
B7
B D♯ F♯ A F♯
1 3 5 ♭7 5
B7
B D♯ A B F♯
1 3 ♭7 1 5
Bm7
B D F♯ A F♯
1 ♭3 5 ♭7 5
Bm
B D F♯ B D B
1 ♭3 5 1 ♭3 1
C♯m
C♯ C♯ G♯ C♯ E
1 1 5 1 ♭3
C♯m6
C♯ E G♯ A E
1 3 5 6 ♭3
D
D F♯ A F♯
1 3 5 3
D add9
D F♯ F♯ A E
1 3 3 5 9

EAC♯F♯AE

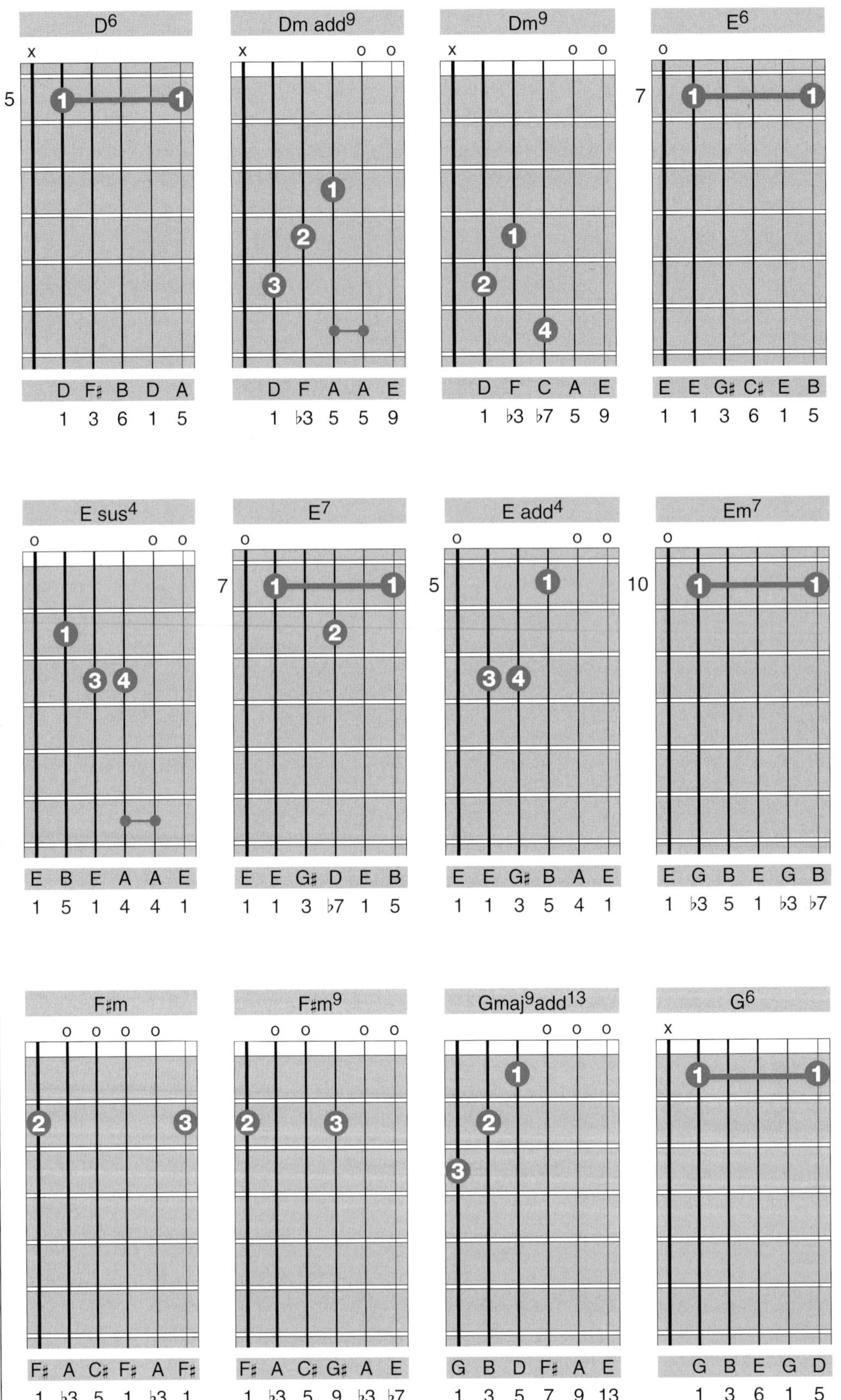
D6
D F♯ B D A
1 3 6 1 5
Dm add9
D F A A E
1 ♭3 5 5 9
Dm9
D F C A E
1 ♭3 ♭7 5 9
E6
E E G♯ C♯ E B
1 1 3 6 1 5
E sus4
E B E A A E
1 5 1 4 4 1
E7
E E G♯ D E B
1 1 3 ♭7 1 5
E add4
E E G♯ B A E
1 1 3 5 4 1
Em7
E G B E G B
1 ♭3 5 1 ♭3 ♭7
F♯m
F♯ A C♯ F♯ A F♯
1 ♭3 5 1 ♭3 1
F♯m9
F♯ A C♯ G♯ A E
1 ♭3 5 9 ♭3 ♭7
Gmaj9add13
G B D F♯ A E
1 3 5 7 9 13
G6
G B E G D
1 3 6 1 5

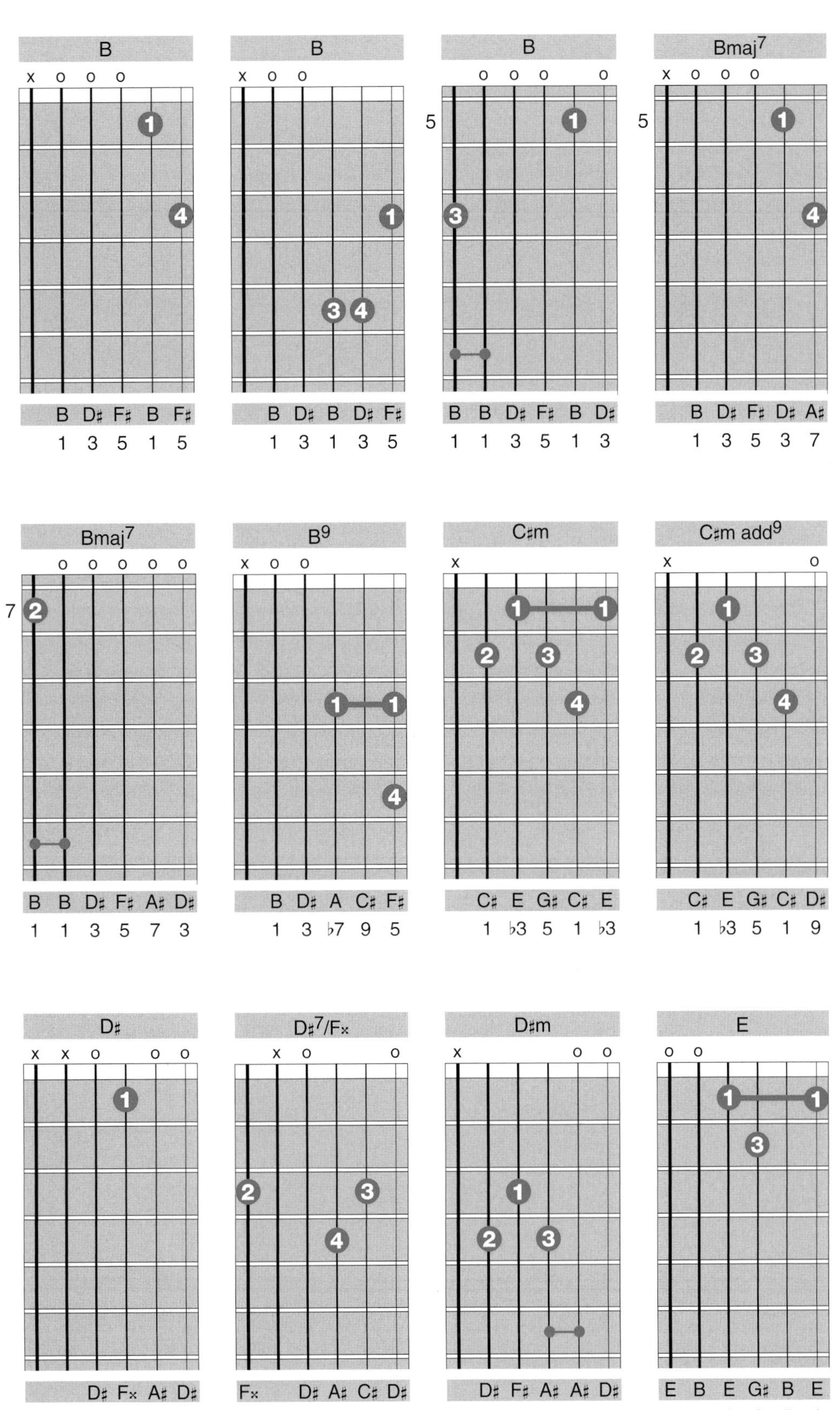
B
x o o o
B D♯ F♯ B F♯
1 3 5 1 5
B
x o o
B D♯ B D♯ F♯
1 3 1 3 5
B
o o o o
5
B B D♯ F♯ B D♯
1 1 3 5 1 3
Bmaj7
x o o o
5
B D♯ F♯ D♯ A♯
1 3 5 3 7
Bmaj7
o o o o o
7
B B D♯ F♯ A♯ D♯
1 1 3 5 7 3
B9
x o o
B D♯ A C♯ F♯
1 3 ♭7 9 5
C♯m
x
C♯ E G♯ C♯ E
1 ♭3 5 1 ♭3
C♯m add9
x o
C♯ E G♯ C♯ D♯
1 ♭3 5 1 9
D♯
x x o o o
D♯ F× A♯ D♯
1 3 5 1
D♯7/F×
x o o
F× D♯ A♯ C♯ D♯
3 1 5 ♭7 1
D♯m
x o o
D♯ F♯ A♯ A♯ D♯
1 ♭3 5 5 1
E
o o
E B E G♯ B E
1 5 1 3 5 1

EBD♯F♯A♯D♯

E

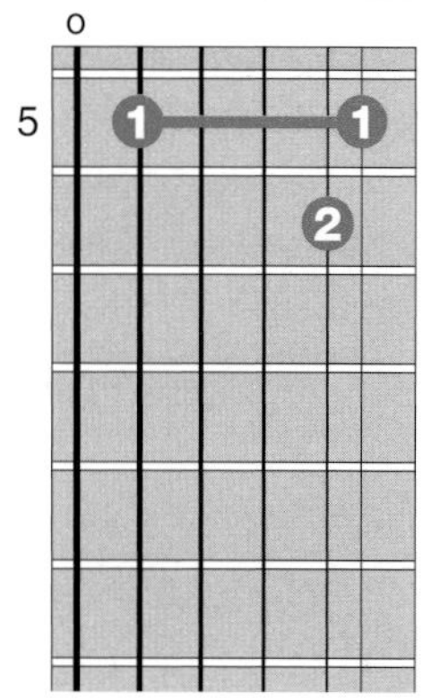

E E G♯ B E G♯
1 1 3 5 1 3

Emaj^7

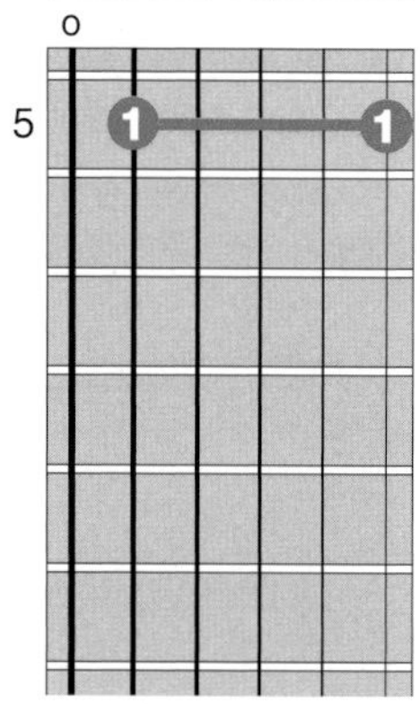

E E G♯ B D♯ G♯
1 1 3 5 7 3

Emaj^7

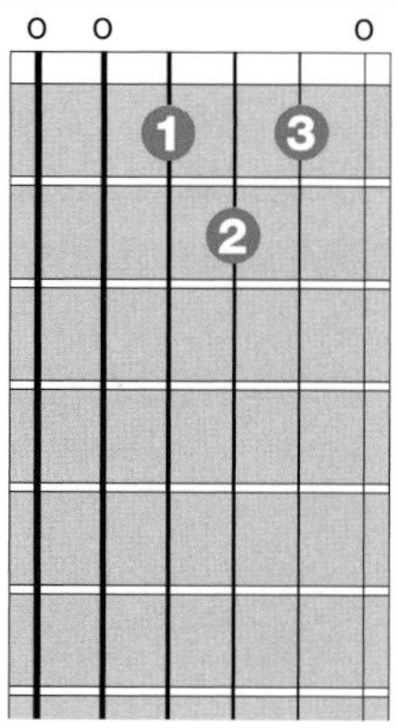

E B E G♯ B D♯
1 5 1 3 5 7

Emaj^9

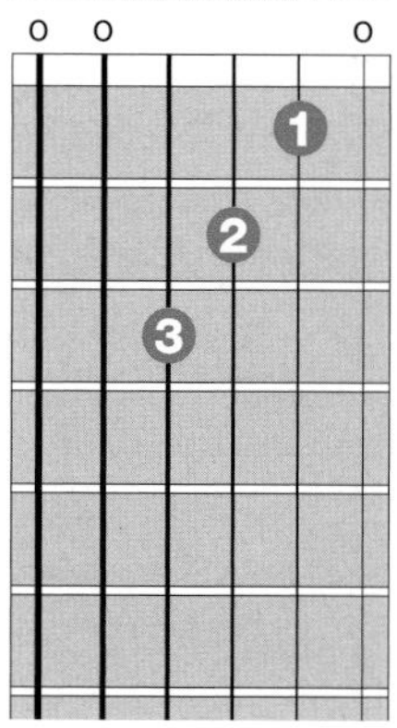

E B F♯ G♯ B D♯
1 5 9 3 5 7

Emaj^{7}add^{13}

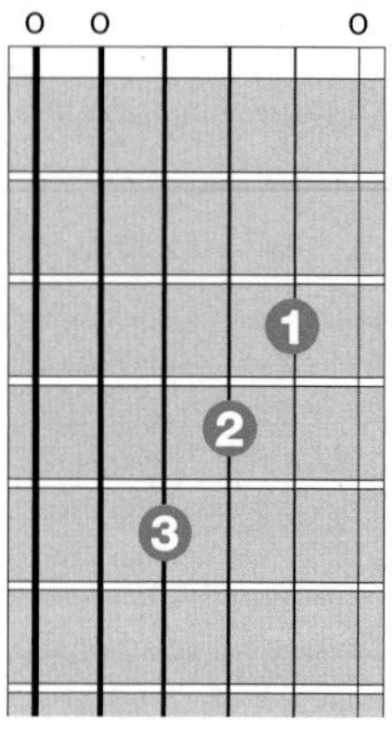

E B G♯ B C♯ D♯
1 5 3 5 13 7

Em

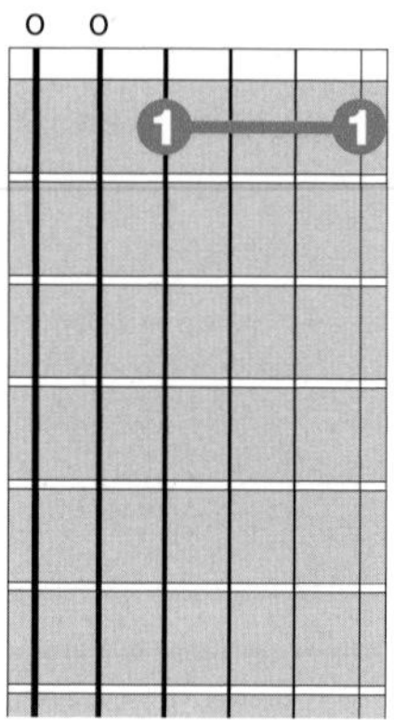

E B E G B E
1 5 1 ♭3 5 1

F♯

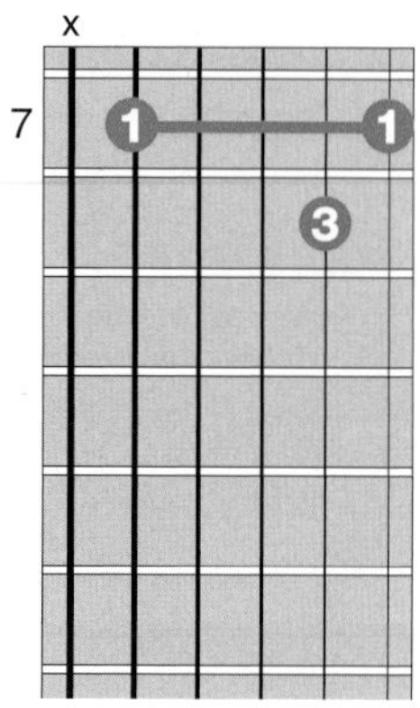

F♯ A♯ C♯ F♯ A♯
1 3 5 1 3

F♯^{6}

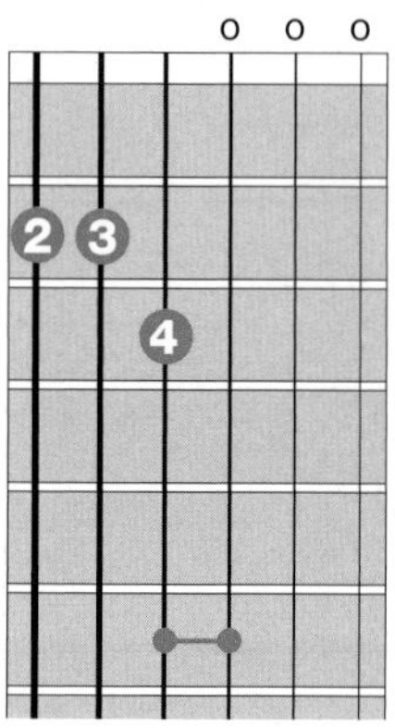

F♯ C♯ F♯ F♯ A♯ D♯
1 5 1 1 3 6

F♯^{7}add^{13}

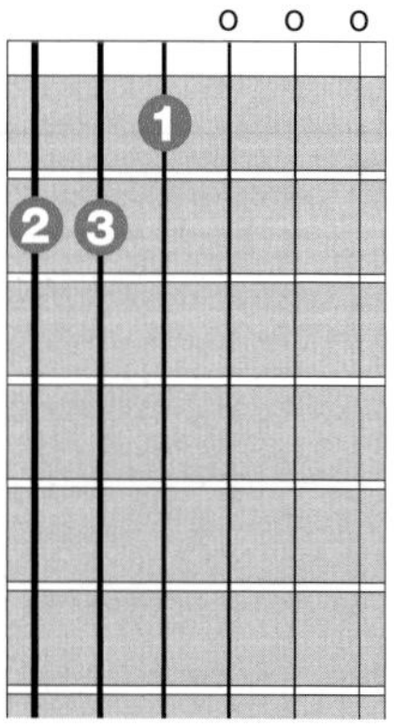

F♯ C♯ E F♯ A♯ D♯
1 5 ♭7 1 3 13

F♯m^9(no 3rd)

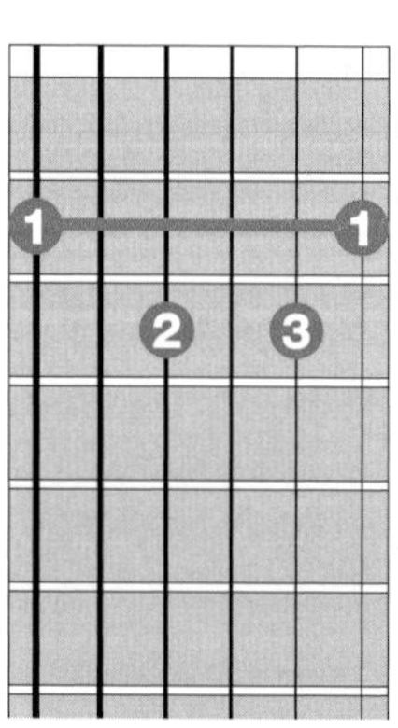

F♯ C♯ F♯ G♯ C♯ E♯
1 5 1 9 5 7

G♯m

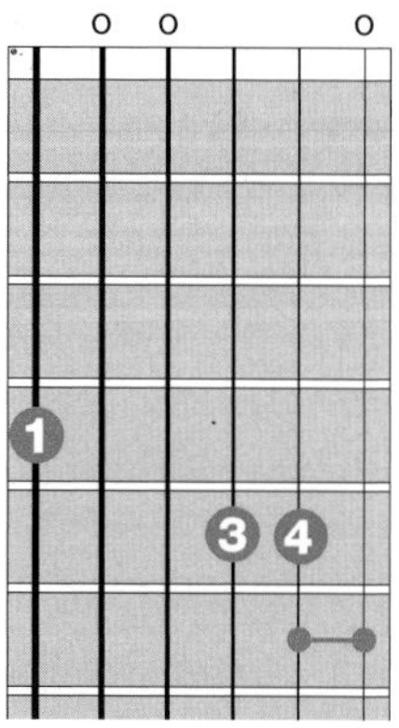

G♯ B D♯ B D♯ D♯
1 ♭3 5 ♭3 5 5

G♯m add^9

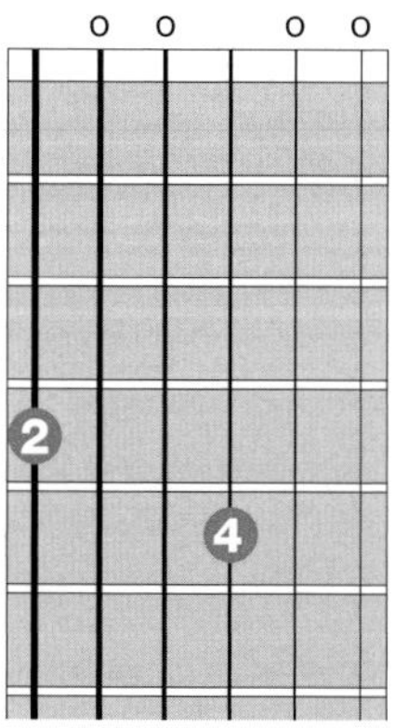

G♯ B D♯ B A♯ D♯
1 ♭3 5 ♭3 9 5

DGDGB♭D

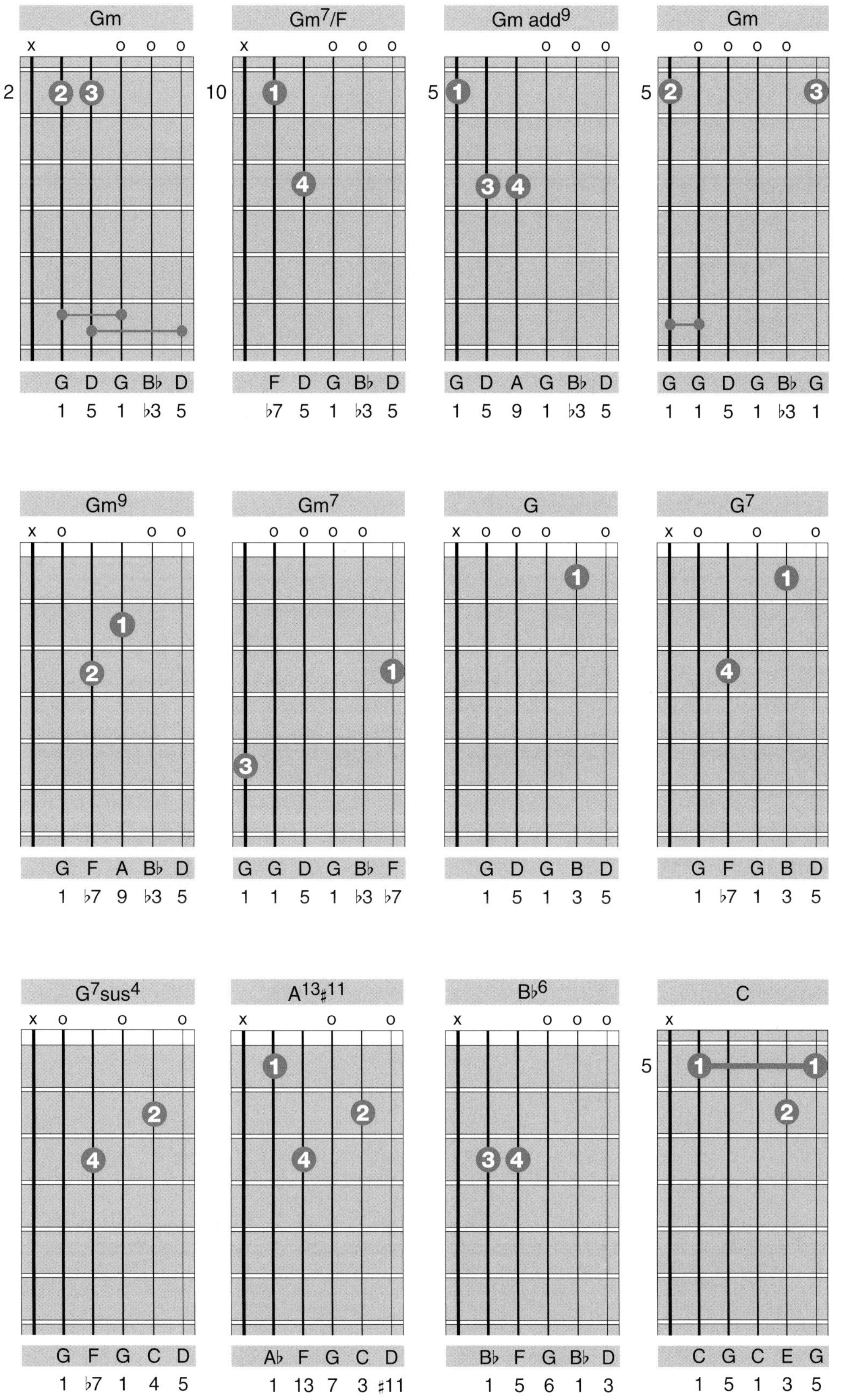

Gm
x o o o
12
G D G B♭ D
1 5 1 ♭3 5
Gm7/F
x o o o
10
F D G B♭ D
♭7 5 1 ♭3 5
Gm add9
o o o
5
G D A G B♭ D
1 5 9 1 ♭3 5
Gm
o o o o
5
G G D G B♭ G
1 1 5 1 ♭3 1
Gm9
x o o o
G F A B♭ D
1 ♭7 9 ♭3 5
Gm7
o o o o
G G D G B♭ F
1 1 5 1 ♭3 ♭7
G
x o o o o
G D G B D
1 5 1 3 5
G7
x o o o
G F G B D
1 ♭7 1 3 5
G7sus4
x o o o
G F G C D
1 ♭7 1 4 5
A13♯11
x o o
A♭ F G C D
1 13 7 3 ♯11
B♭6
x o o o
B♭ F G B♭ D
1 5 6 1 3
C
x
5
C G C E G
1 5 1 3 5

Cm^{9} (8)
C E♭ C G B♭ D
1 ♭3 1 5 ♭7 9

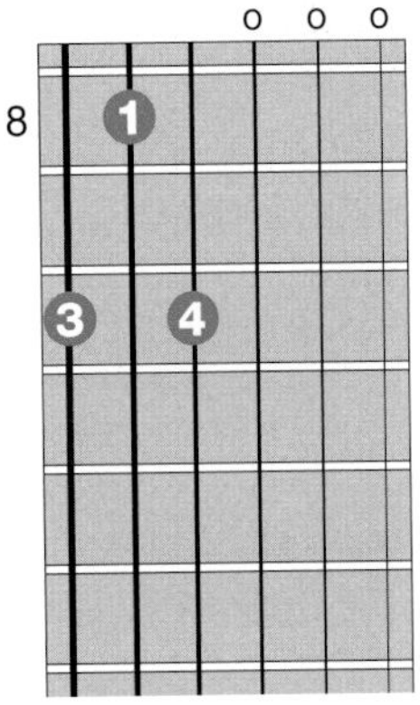

Cm$^{7♭5}$ (8)
C E♭ C E♭ G♭ B♭
1 ♭3 1 ♭3 ♭5 ♭7

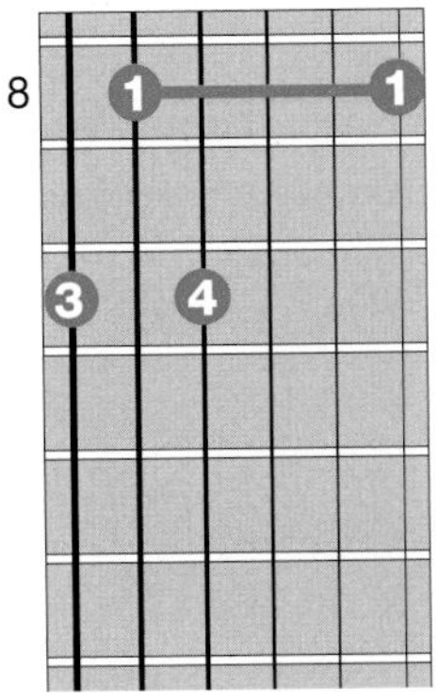

Cm$^{11♭5}$ (8)
C E♭ B♭ F G♭ B♭
1 ♭3 ♭7 11 ♭5 ♭7

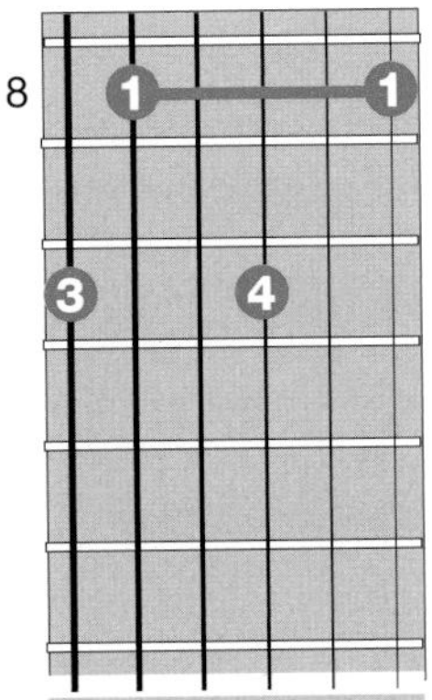

Cm (5)
C G C E♭ G
1 5 1 ♭3 5

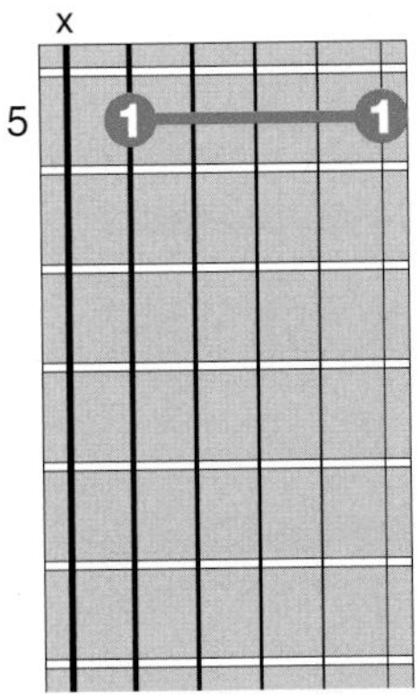

Dm (7)
D D A D F A
1 1 5 1 ♭3 5

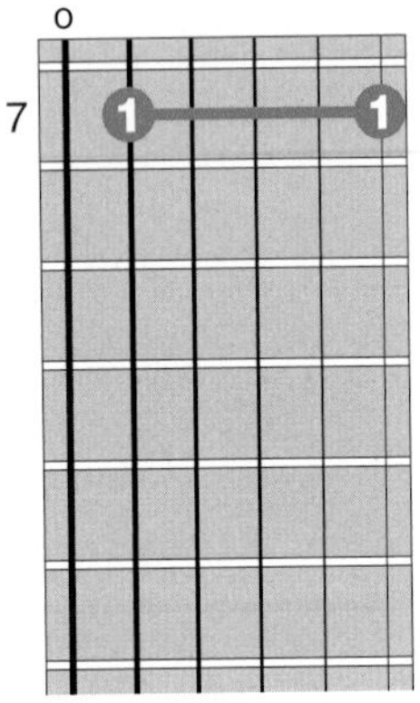

D^{7}(no 3rd) 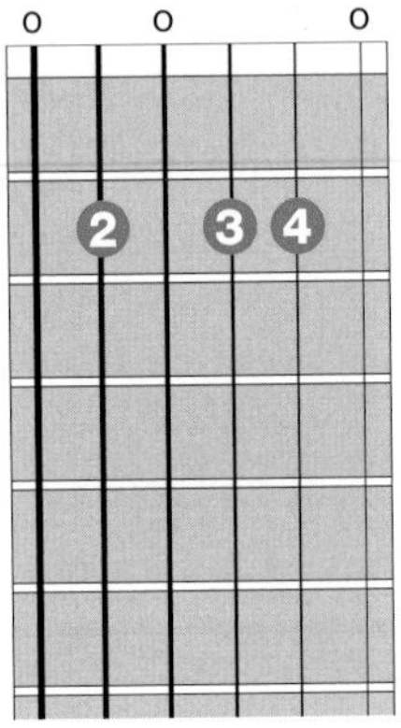
D A D A C D
1 5 1 5 ♭7 1

D add^{9}
D A F♯ A D E
1 5 3 5 1 9

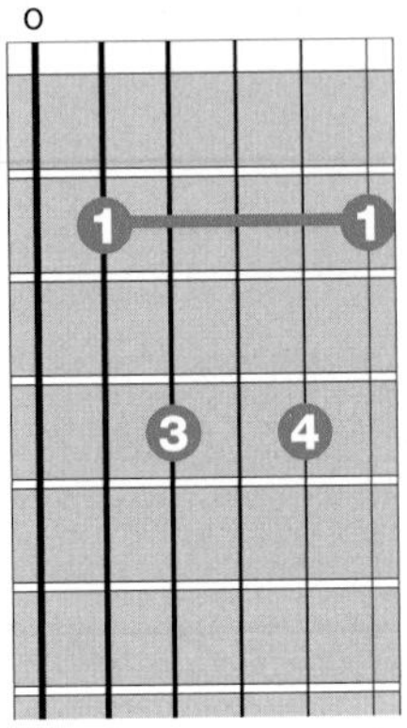

Dm add^{9}
D A F A C E
1 5 ♭3 5 ♭7 9

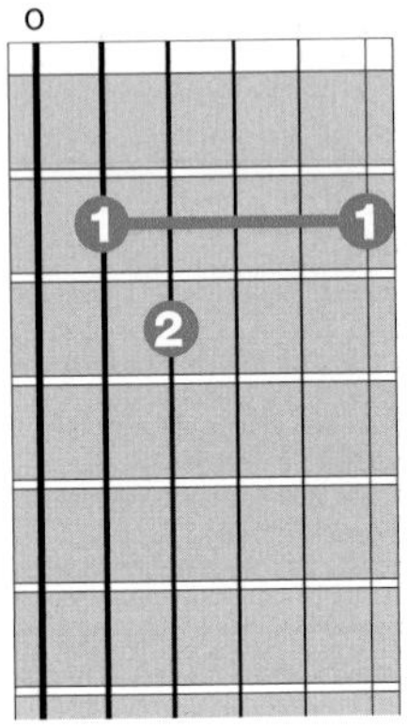

E♭maj^{9}
E♭ B♭ F G B♭ D
1 5 9 3 5 7

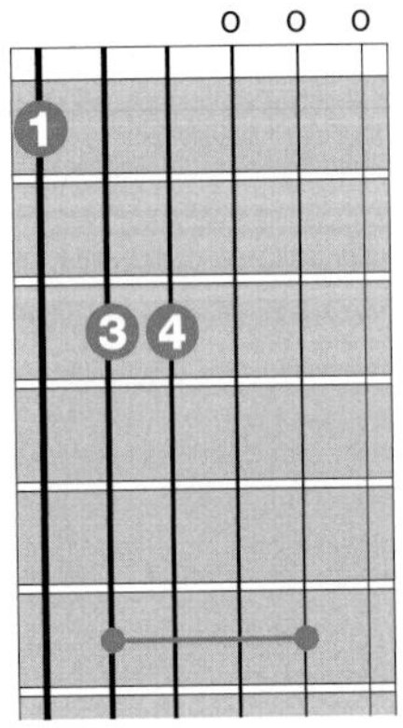

E♭maj^{7}add^{13} (8)
E♭ C G B♭ D
1 13 3 5 7

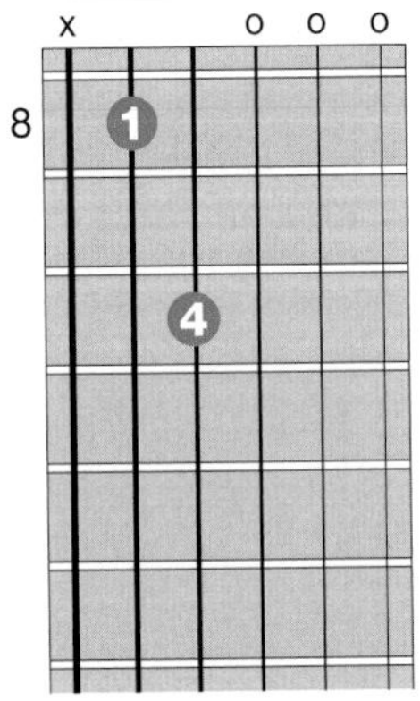

E^{13}(no 3rd) 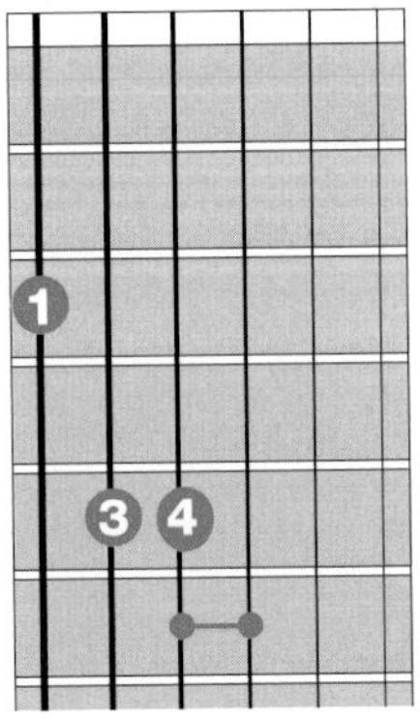
F C G G B♭ D
1 5 9 9 11 13

F 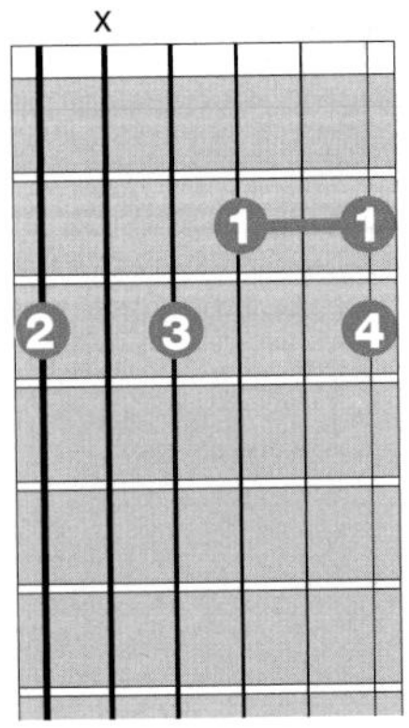
F F A C F
1 1 3 5 1

DADFAD

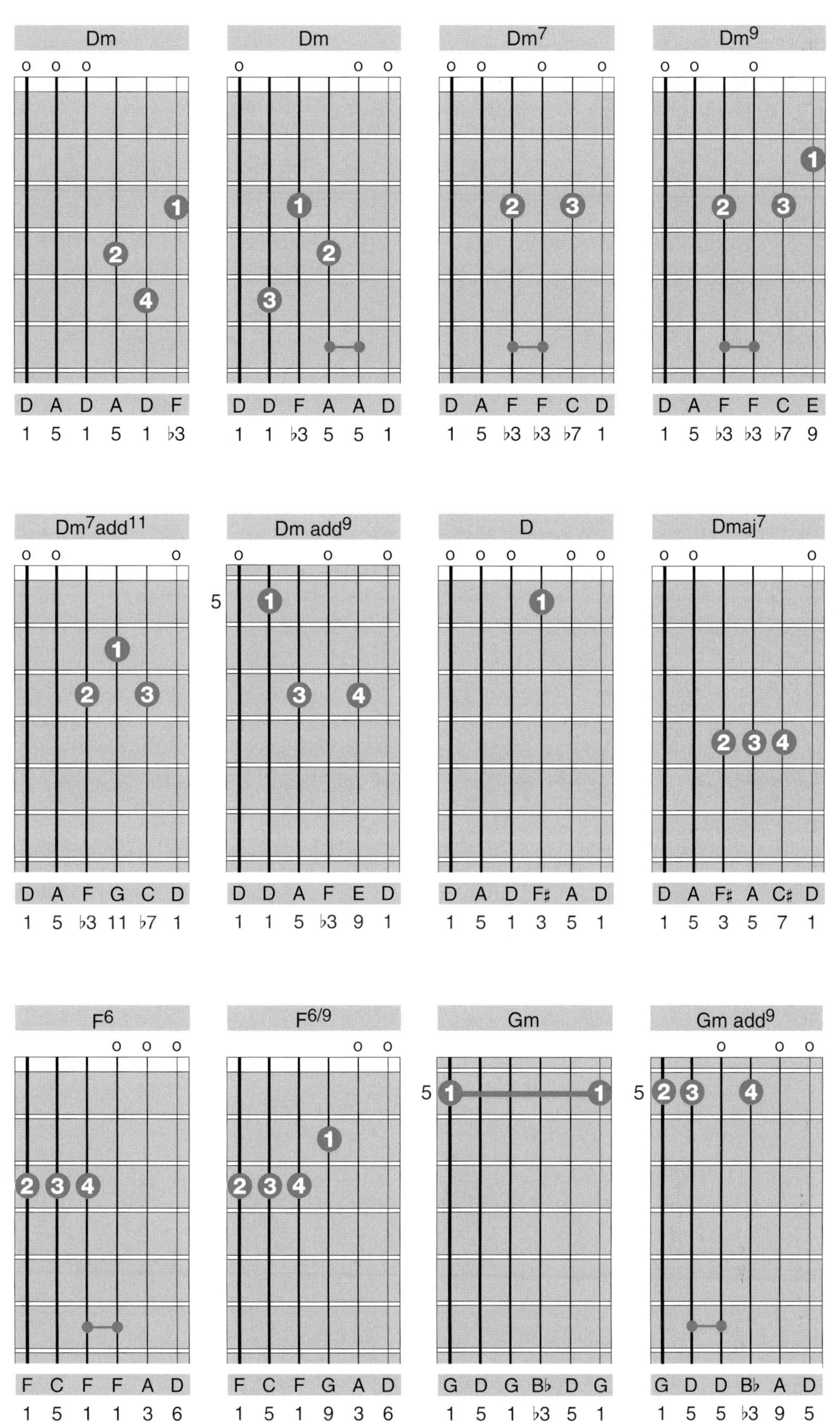
Dm
D A D A D F
1 5 1 5 1 ♭3
Dm
D D F A A D
1 1 ♭3 5 5 1
Dm7
D A F F C D
1 5 ♭3 ♭3 ♭7 1
Dm9
D A F F C E
1 5 ♭3 ♭3 ♭7 9
Dm7add11
D A F G C D
1 5 ♭3 11 ♭7 1
Dm add9
5
D D A F E D
1 1 5 ♭3 9 1
D
D A D F♯ A D
1 5 1 3 5 1
Dmaj7
D A F♯ A C♯ D
1 5 3 5 7 1
F6
F C F F A D
1 5 1 1 3 6
F6/9
F C F G A D
1 5 1 9 3 6
Gm
5
G D G B♭ D G
1 5 1 ♭3 5 1
Gm add9
5
G D D B♭ A D
1 5 5 ♭3 9 5

DADFAD

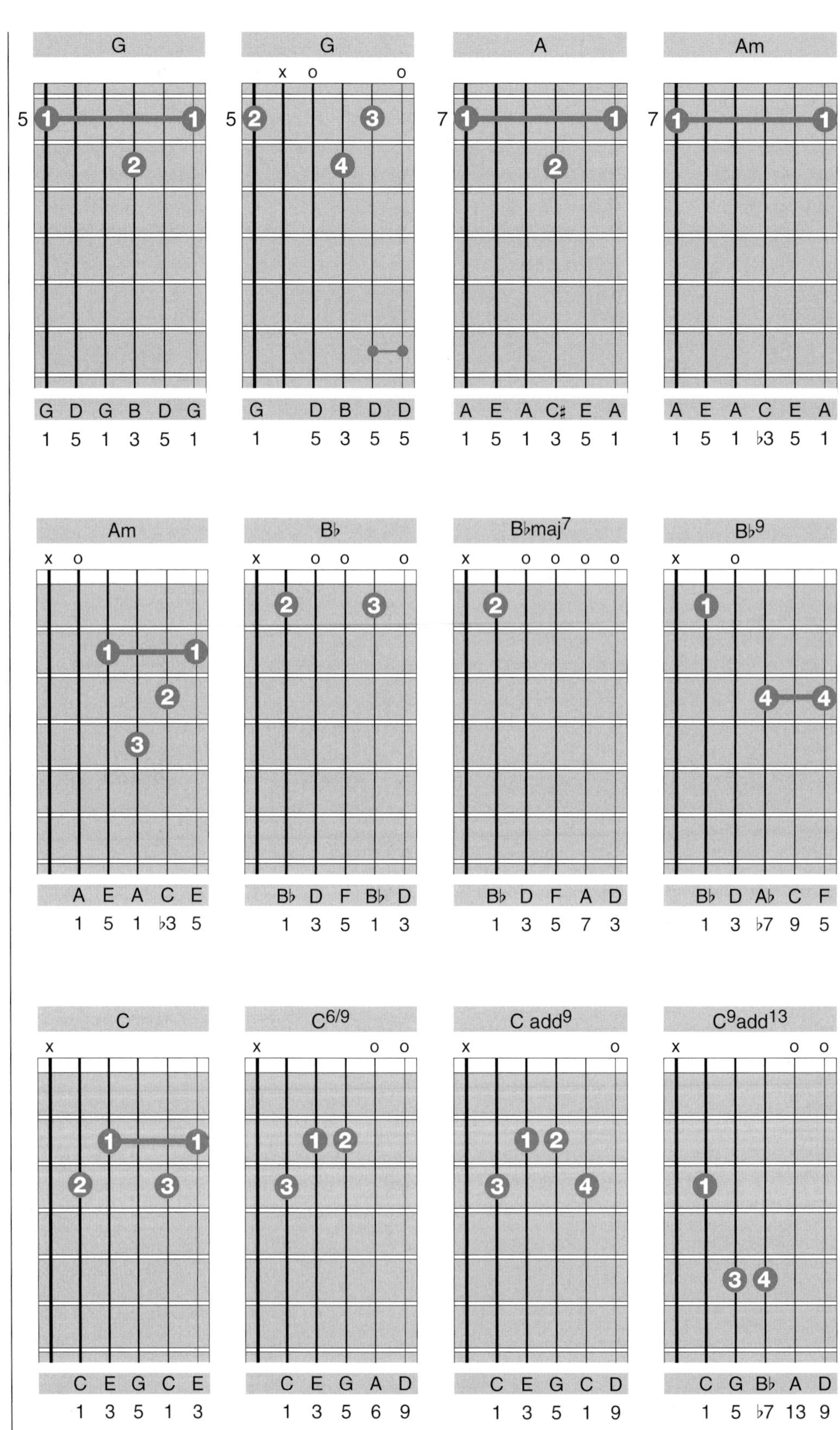
G
5
G D G B D G
1 5 1 3 5 1
G
x o o
5
G D B D D
1 5 3 5 5
A
7
A E A C♯ E A
1 5 1 3 5 1
Am
7
A E A C E A
1 5 1 ♭3 5 1
Am
x o
A E A C E
1 5 1 ♭3 5
B♭
x o o o
B♭ D F B♭ D
1 3 5 1 3
B♭maj7
x o o o o
B♭ D F A D
1 3 5 7 3
B♭9
x o
B♭ D A♭ C F
1 3 ♭7 9 5
C
x
C E G C E
1 3 5 1 3
C6/9
x o o
C E G A D
1 3 5 6 9
C add9
x o
C E G C D
1 3 5 1 9
C9add13
x o o
C G B♭ A D
1 5 ♭7 13 9

EACEAE

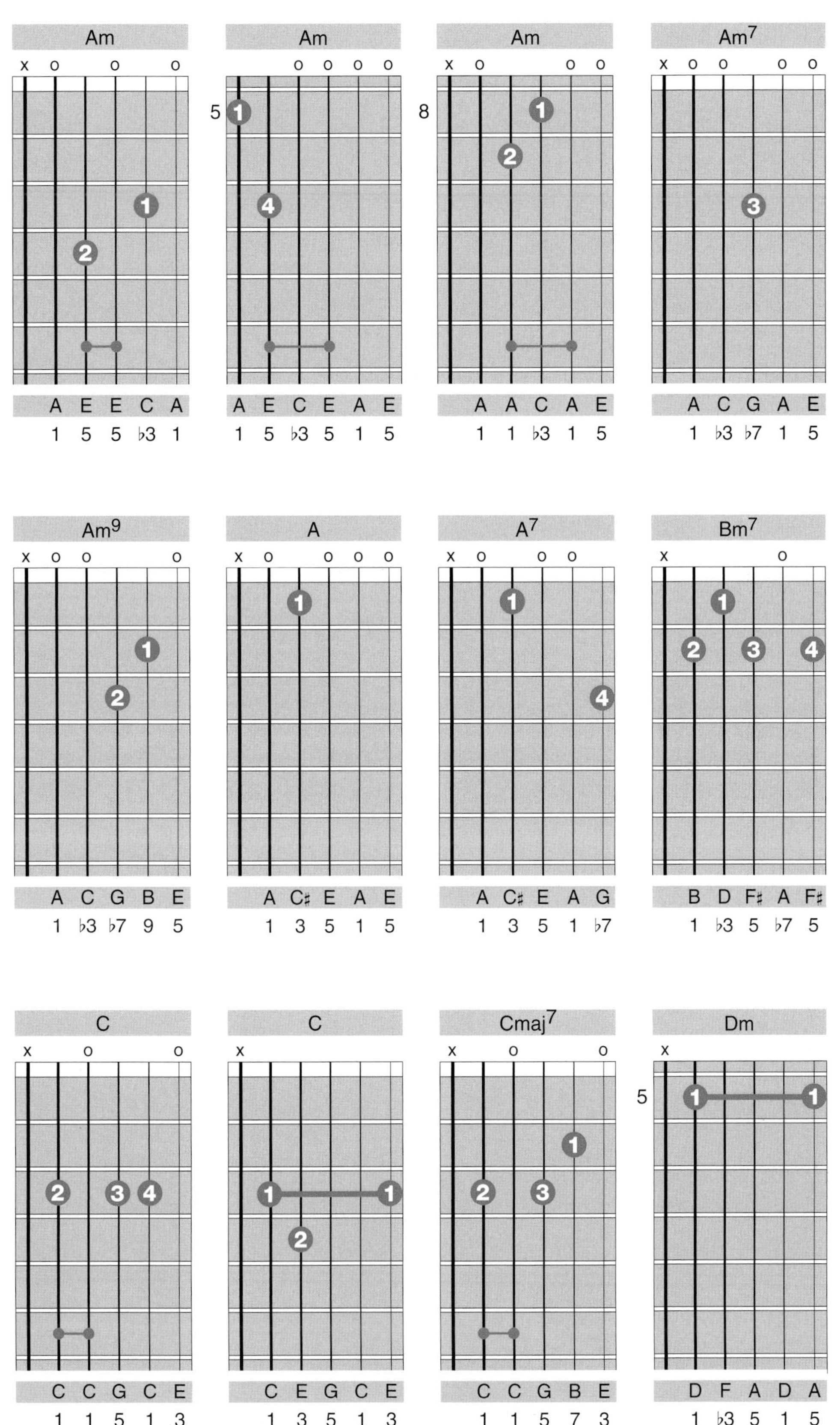
Am
A E E C A
1 5 5 ♭3 1
Am
5
A E C E A E
1 5 ♭3 5 1 5
Am
8
A A C A E
1 1 ♭3 1 5
Am7
A C G A E
1 ♭3 ♭7 1 5
Am9
A C G B E
1 ♭3 ♭7 9 5
A
A C♯ E A E
1 3 5 1 5
A7
A C♯ E A G
1 3 5 1 ♭7
Bm7
B D F♯ A F♯
1 ♭3 5 ♭7 5
C
C C G C E
1 1 5 1 3
C
C E G C E
1 3 5 1 3
Cmaj7
C C G B E
1 1 5 7 3
Dm
5
D F A D A
1 ♭3 5 1 5

EACEAE

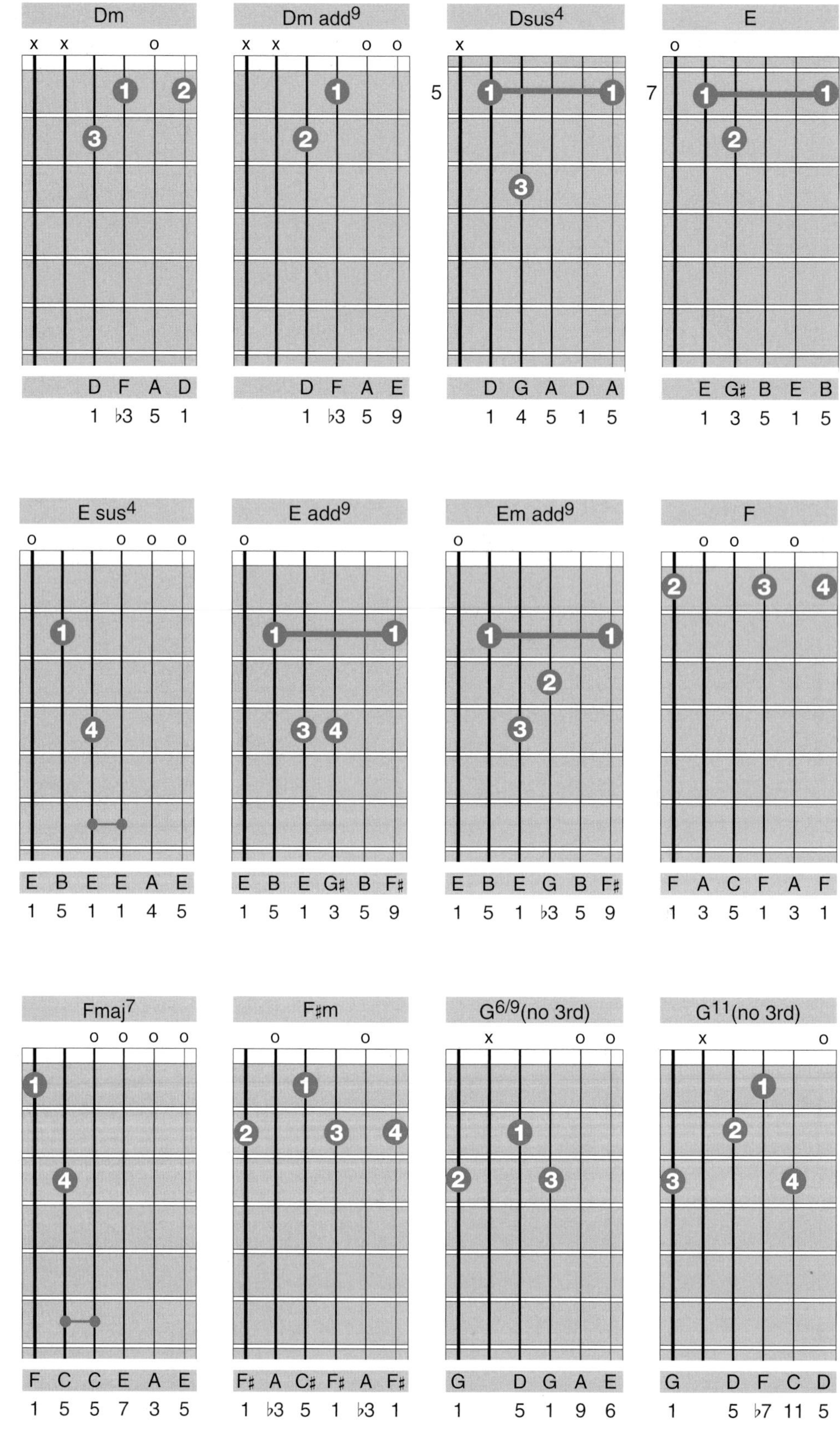
Dm
x x o
D F A D
1 ♭3 5 1
Dm add9
x x o o
D F A E
1 ♭3 5 9
Dsus4
x
5
D G A D A
1 4 5 1 5
E
o
7
E G♯ B E B
1 3 5 1 5
E sus4
o o o o
E B E E A E
1 5 1 1 4 5
E add9
o
E B E G♯ B F♯
1 5 1 3 5 9
Em add9
o
E B E G B F♯
1 5 1 ♭3 5 9
F
o o o
F A C F A F
1 3 5 1 3 1
Fmaj7
o o o o
F C C E A E
1 5 5 7 3 5
F♯m
o o
F♯ A C♯ F♯ A F♯
1 ♭3 5 1 ♭3 1
G6/9(no 3rd)
x o o
G D G A E
1 5 1 9 6
G11(no 3rd)
x o
G D F C D
1 5 ♭7 11 5

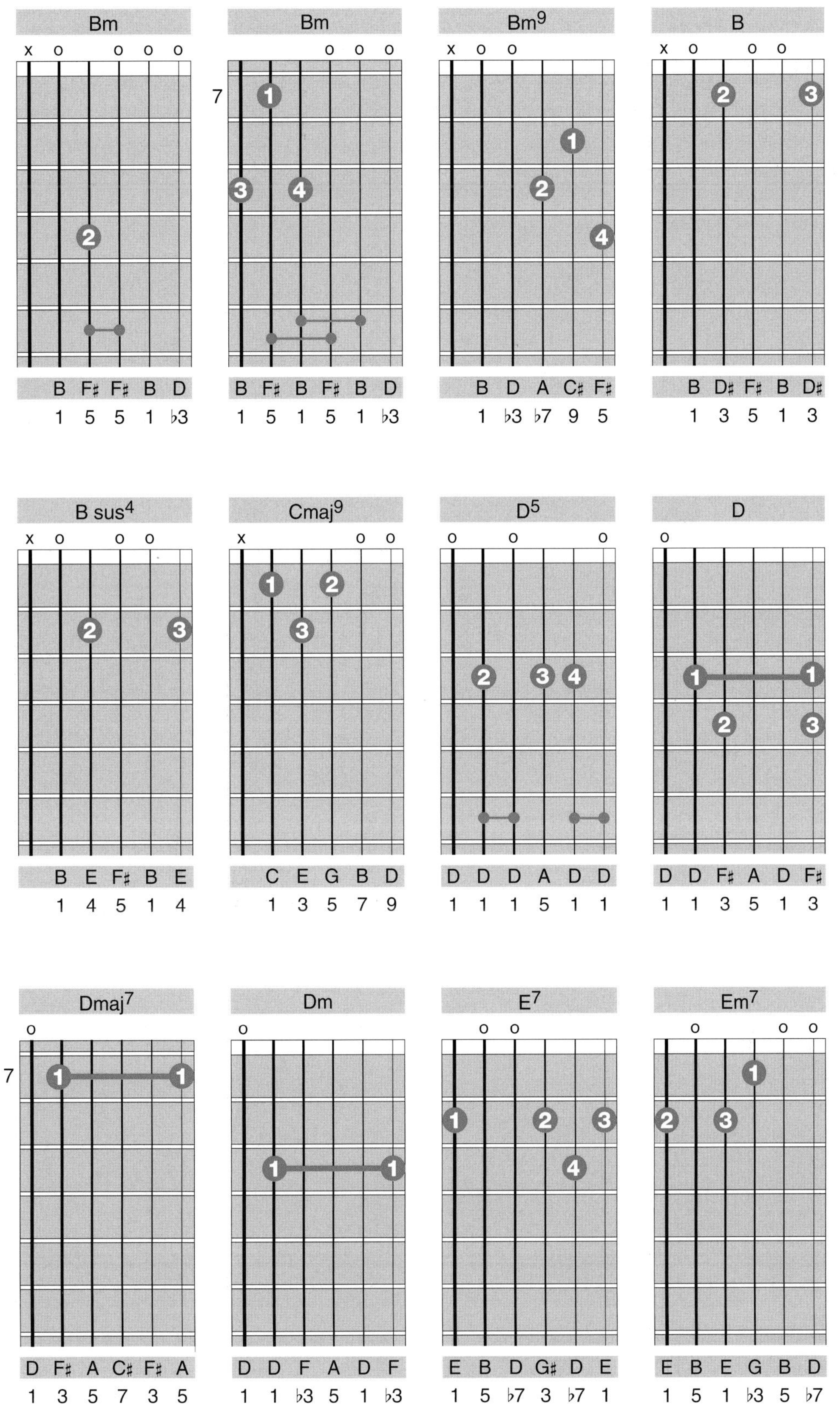

Bm
x o o o o
B F♯ F♯ B D
1 5 5 1 ♭3
Bm
o o o
7
B F♯ B F♯ B D
1 5 1 5 1 ♭3
Bm9
x o o
B D A C♯ F♯
1 ♭3 ♭7 9 5
B
x o o o
B D♯ F♯ B D♯
1 3 5 1 3
B sus4
x o o o
B E F♯ B E
1 4 5 1 4
Cmaj9
x o o
C E G B D
1 3 5 7 9
D5
o o o
D D D A D D
1 1 1 5 1 1
D
o
D D F♯ A D F♯
1 1 3 5 1 3
Dmaj7
o
7
D F♯ A C♯ F♯ A
1 3 5 7 3 5
Dm
o
D D F A D F
1 1 ♭3 5 1 ♭3
E7
o o
E B D G♯ D E
1 5 ♭7 3 ♭7 1
Em7
o o o
E B E G B D
1 5 1 ♭3 5 ♭7

DBDF♯BD

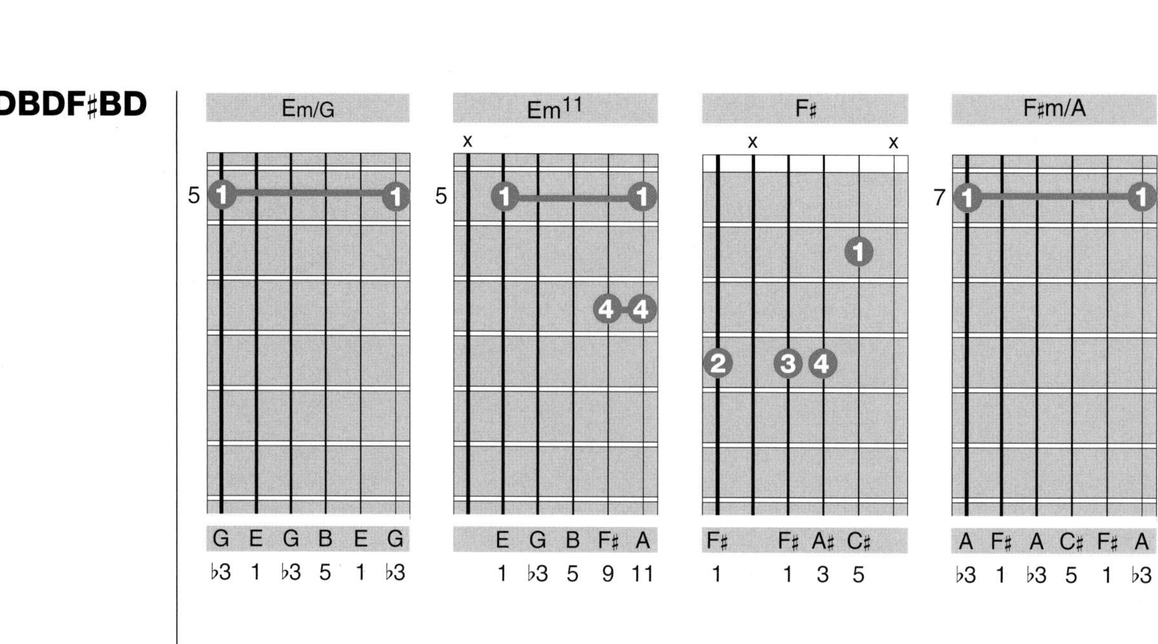
Em/G
5
G E G B E G
♭3 1 ♭3 5 1 ♭3
Em11
x
5
E G B F♯ A
1 ♭3 5 9 11
F♯
x x
F♯ F♯ A♯ C♯
1 1 3 5
F♯m/A
7
A F♯ A C♯ F♯ A
♭3 1 ♭3 5 1 ♭3

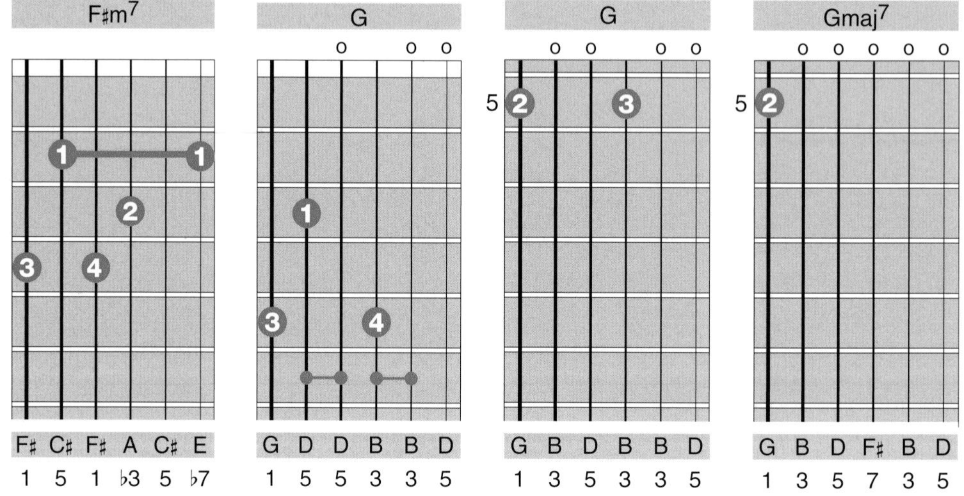
F♯m7
F♯ C♯ F♯ A C♯ E
1 5 1 ♭3 5 ♭7
G
o o o
G D D B B D
1 5 5 3 3 5
G
o o o o
5
G B D B B D
1 3 5 3 3 5
Gmaj7
o o o o o
5
G B D F♯ B D
1 3 5 7 3 5

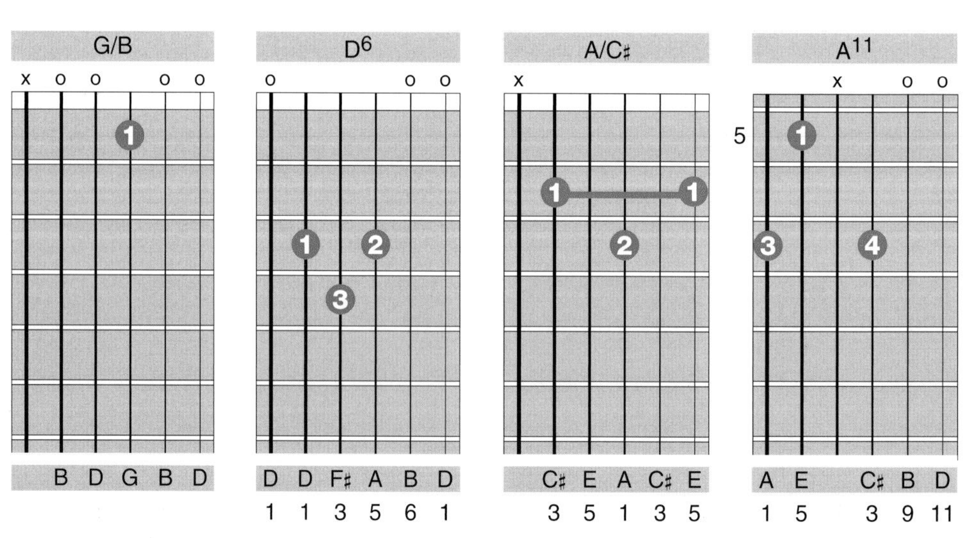
G/B
x o o o o
B D G B D
D6
o o o
D D F♯ A B D
1 1 3 5 6 1
A/C♯
x
C♯ E A C♯ E
3 5 1 3 5
A11
x o o
5
A E C♯ B D
1 5 3 9 11

EGBEBE

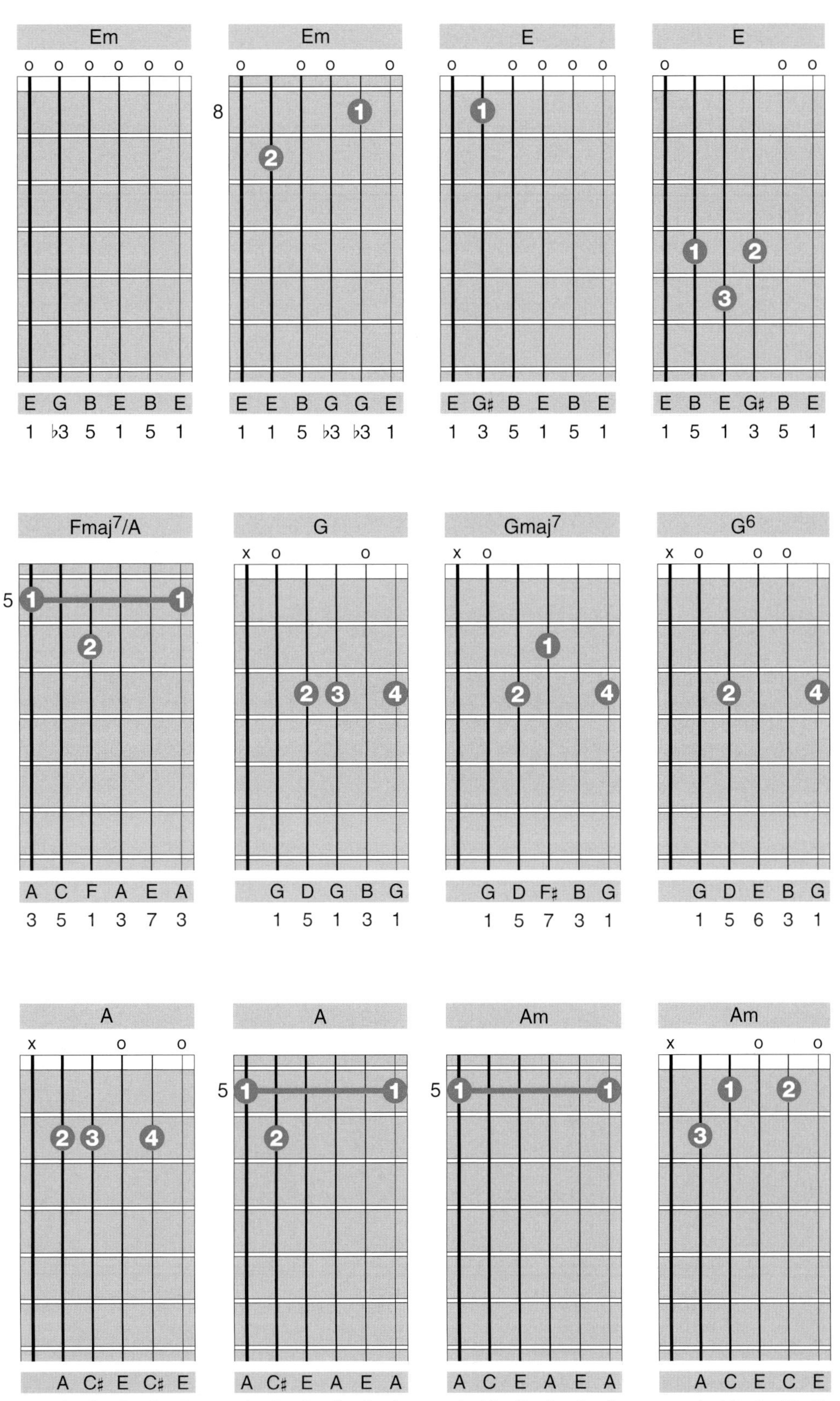
Em
o o o o o o
E G B E B E
1 ♭3 5 1 5 1
Em
8
o o o o
E E B G G E
1 1 5 ♭3 ♭3 1
E
o o o o o
E G♯ B E B E
1 3 5 1 5 1
E
o o o
E B E G♯ B E
1 5 1 3 5 1
Fmaj7/A
5
A C F A E A
3 5 1 3 7 3
G
x o o
G D G B G
1 5 1 3 1
Gmaj7
x o
G D F♯ B G
1 5 7 3 1
G6
x o o o
G D E B G
1 5 6 3 1
A
x o o
A C♯ E C♯ E
1 3 5 3 5
A
5
A C♯ E A E A
1 3 5 1 5 1
Am
5
A C E A E A
1 ♭3 5 1 5 1
Am
x o o
A C E C E
1 ♭3 5 ♭3 5

EGBEBE

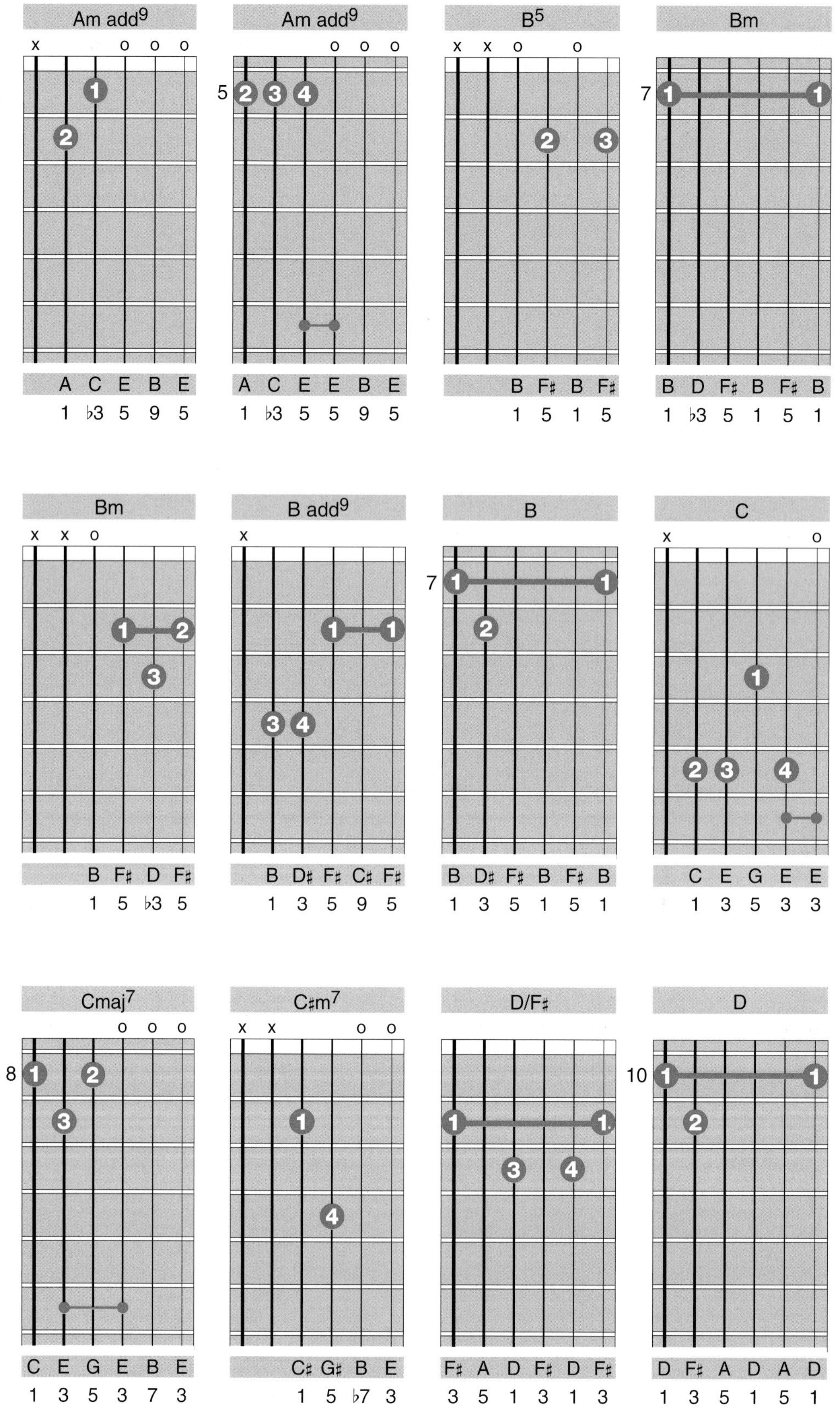
Am add9
A C E B E
1 ♭3 5 9 5
Am add9
5
A C E E B E
1 ♭3 5 5 9 5
B5
B F♯ B F♯
1 5 1 5
Bm
7
B D F♯ B F♯ B
1 ♭3 5 1 5 1
Bm
B F♯ D F♯
1 5 ♭3 5
B add9
B D♯ F♯ C♯ F♯
1 3 5 9 5
B
7
B D♯ F♯ B F♯ B
1 3 5 1 5 1
C
C E G E E
1 3 5 3 3
Cmaj7
8
C E G E B E
1 3 5 3 7 3
C♯m7
C♯ G♯ B E
1 5 ♭7 3
D/F♯
F♯ A D F♯ D F♯
3 5 1 3 1 3
D
10
D F♯ A D A D
1 3 5 1 5 1

Chord	Strings	Intervals
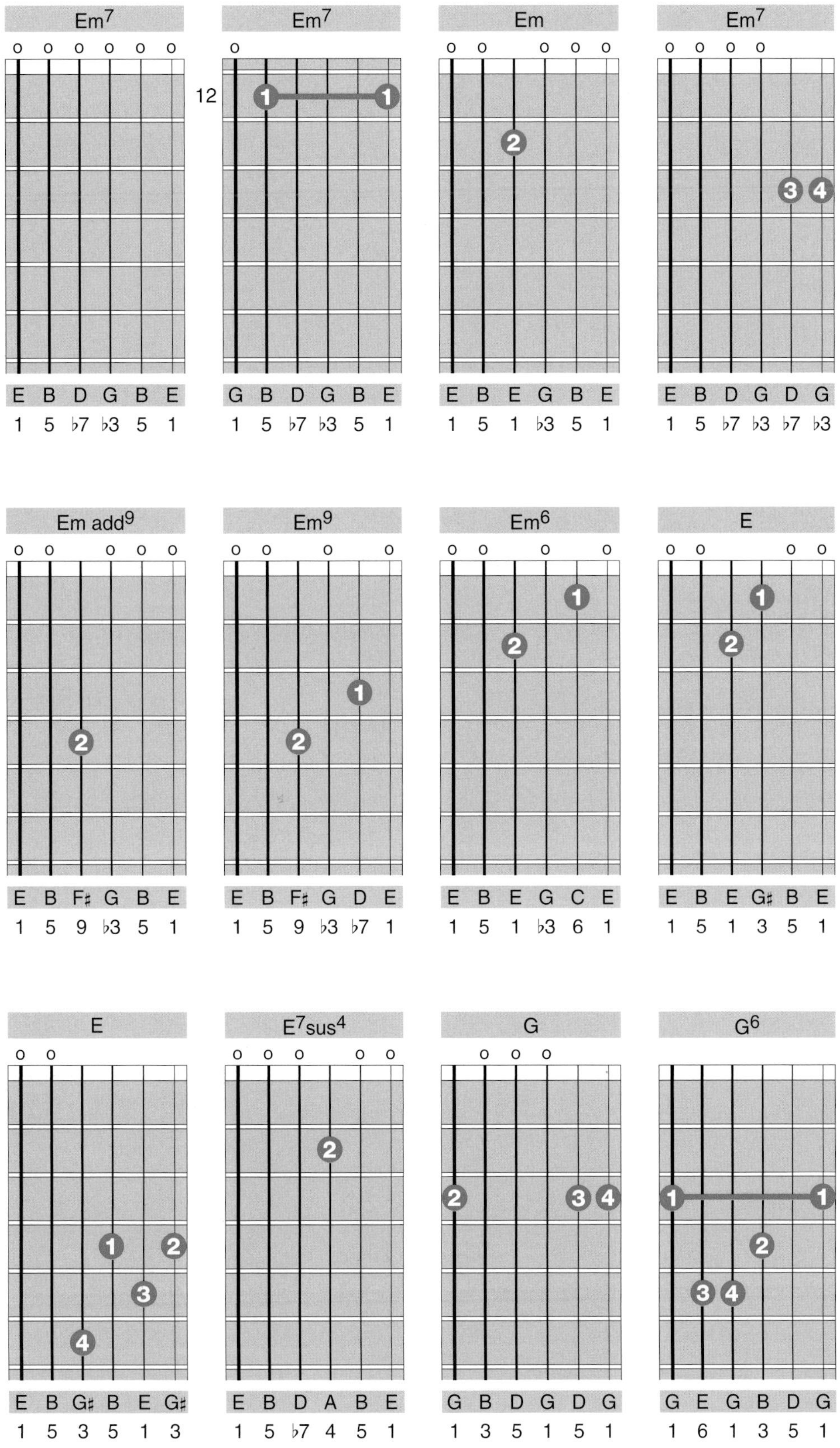 Em7	E B D G B E	1 5 ♭7 ♭3 5 1
Em7 (12)	G B D G B E	1 5 ♭7 ♭3 5 1
Em	E B E G B E	1 5 1 ♭3 5 1
Em7	E B D G D G	1 5 ♭7 ♭3 ♭7 ♭3
Em add9	E B F♯ G B E	1 5 9 ♭3 5 1
Em9	E B F♯ G D E	1 5 9 ♭3 ♭7 1
Em6	E B E G C E	1 5 1 ♭3 6 1
E	E B E G♯ B E	1 5 1 3 5 1
E	E B G♯ B E G♯	1 5 3 5 1 3
E7sus4	E B D A B E	1 5 ♭7 4 5 1
G	G B D G D G	1 3 5 1 5 1
G6	G E G B D G	1 6 1 3 5 1

EBDGBE

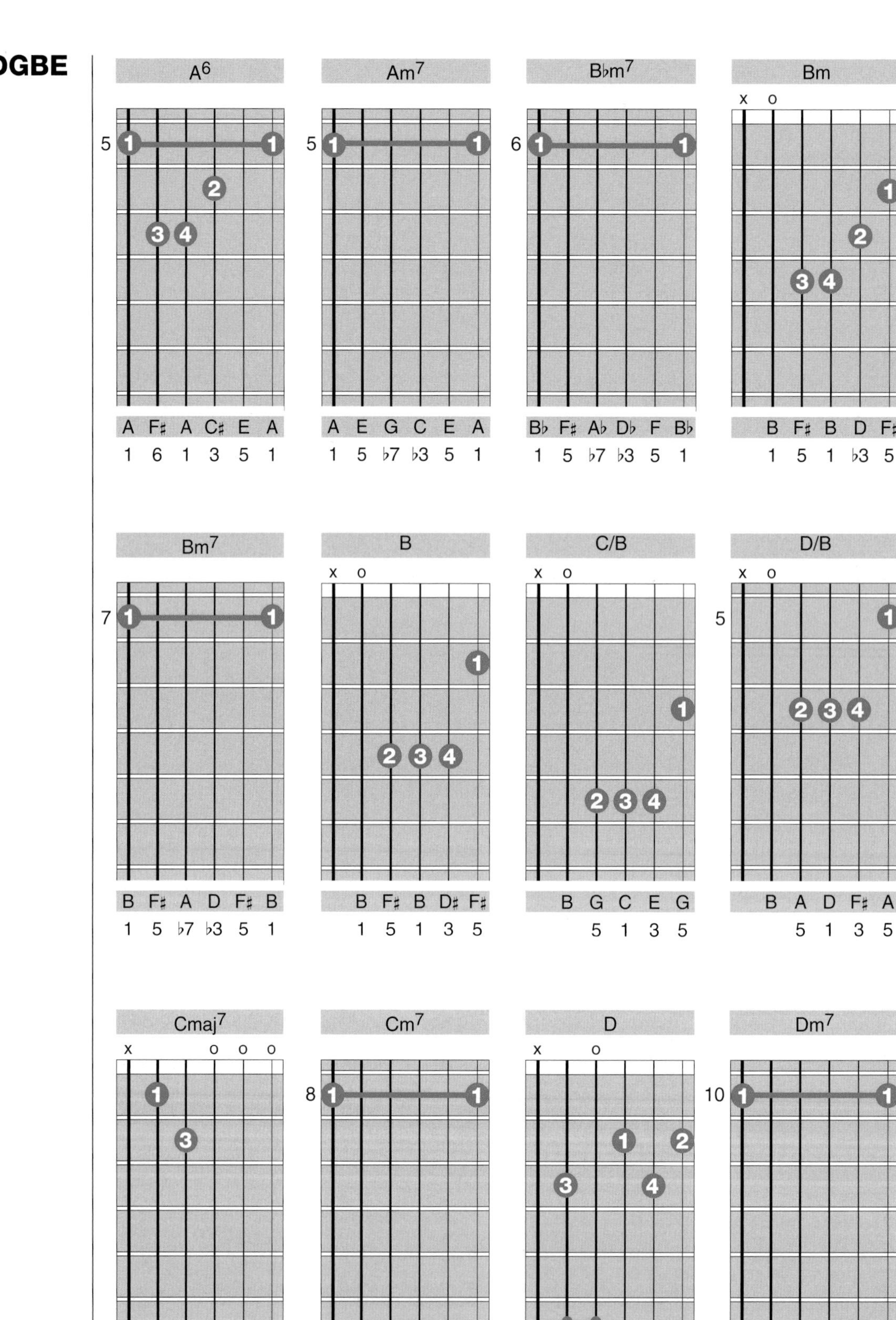
A6
5
A F♯ A C♯ E A
1 6 1 3 5 1
Am7
5
A E G C E A
1 5 ♭7 ♭3 5 1
B♭m7
6
B♭ F♯ A♭ D♭ F B♭
1 5 ♭7 ♭3 5 1
Bm
x o
B F♯ B D F♯
1 5 1 ♭3 5
Bm7
7
B F♯ A D F♯ B
1 5 ♭7 ♭3 5 1
B
x o
B F♯ B D♯ F♯
1 5 1 3 5
C/B
x o
B G C E G
5 1 3 5
D/B
x o
5
B A D F♯ A
5 1 3 5
Cmaj7
x o o o
C E G B E
1 3 5 7 3
Cm7
8
C G B♭ E♭ G C
1 5 ♭7 ♭3 5 1
D
x o
D D A D F♯
1 1 5 1 3
Dm7
10
D A C F A D
1 5 ♭7 ♭3 5 1

F♯F♯C♯F♯AE

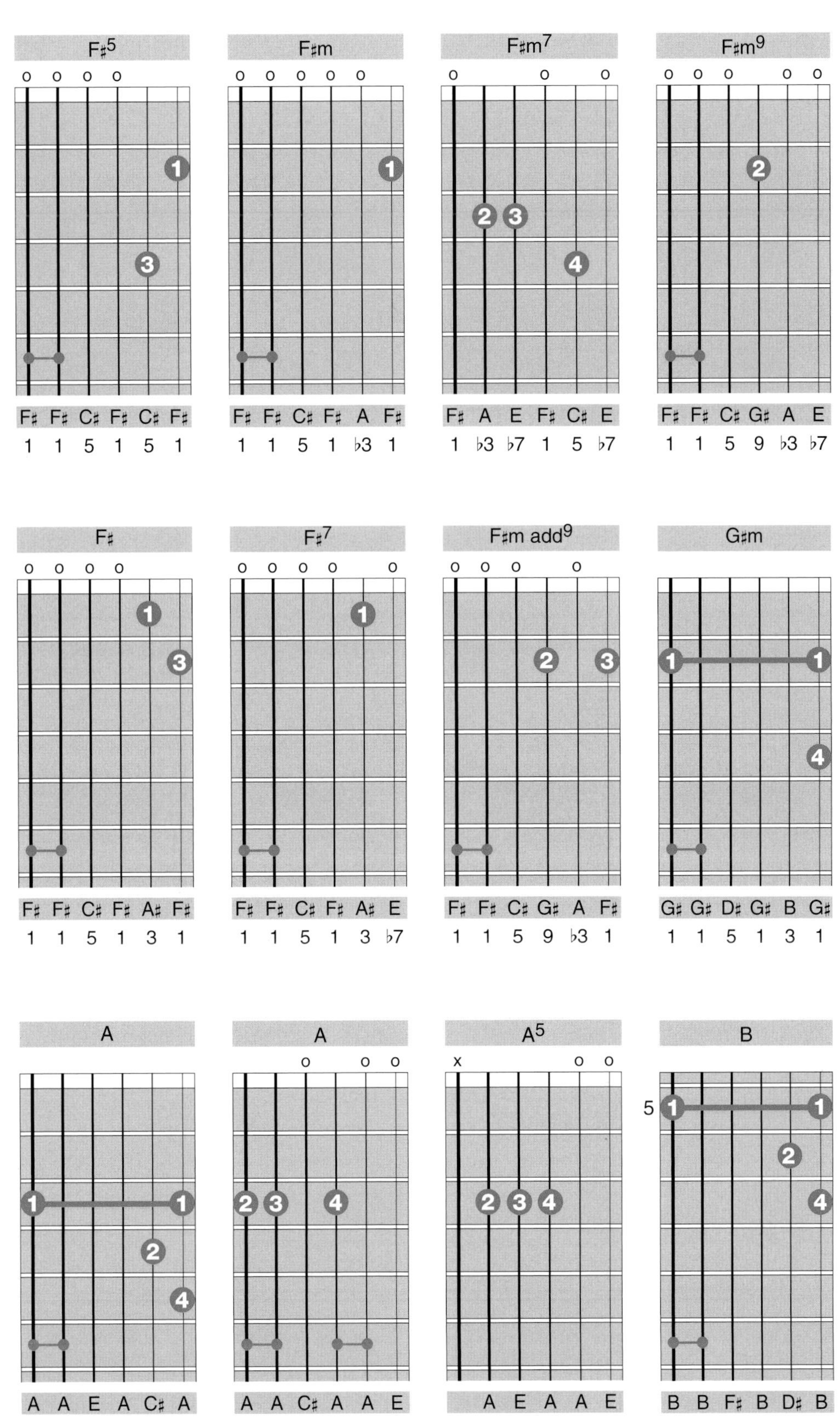
F♯5
F♯ F♯ C♯ F♯ C♯ F♯
1 1 5 1 5 1
F♯m
F♯ F♯ C♯ F♯ A F♯
1 1 5 1 ♭3 1
F♯m7
F♯ A E F♯ C♯ E
1 ♭3 ♭7 1 5 ♭7
F♯m9
F♯ F♯ C♯ G♯ A E
1 1 5 9 ♭3 ♭7
F♯
F♯ F♯ C♯ F♯ A♯ F♯
1 1 5 1 3 1
F♯7
F♯ F♯ C♯ F♯ A♯ E
1 1 5 1 3 ♭7
F♯m add9
F♯ F♯ C♯ G♯ A F♯
1 1 5 9 ♭3 1
G♯m
G♯ G♯ D♯ G♯ B G♯
1 1 5 1 3 1
A
A A E A C♯ A
1 1 5 1 3 1
A
A A C♯ A A E
1 1 3 1 1 5
A5
x
A E A A E
1 5 1 1 5
B
5
B B F♯ B D♯ B
1 1 5 1 3 1

F♯F♯C♯F♯AE

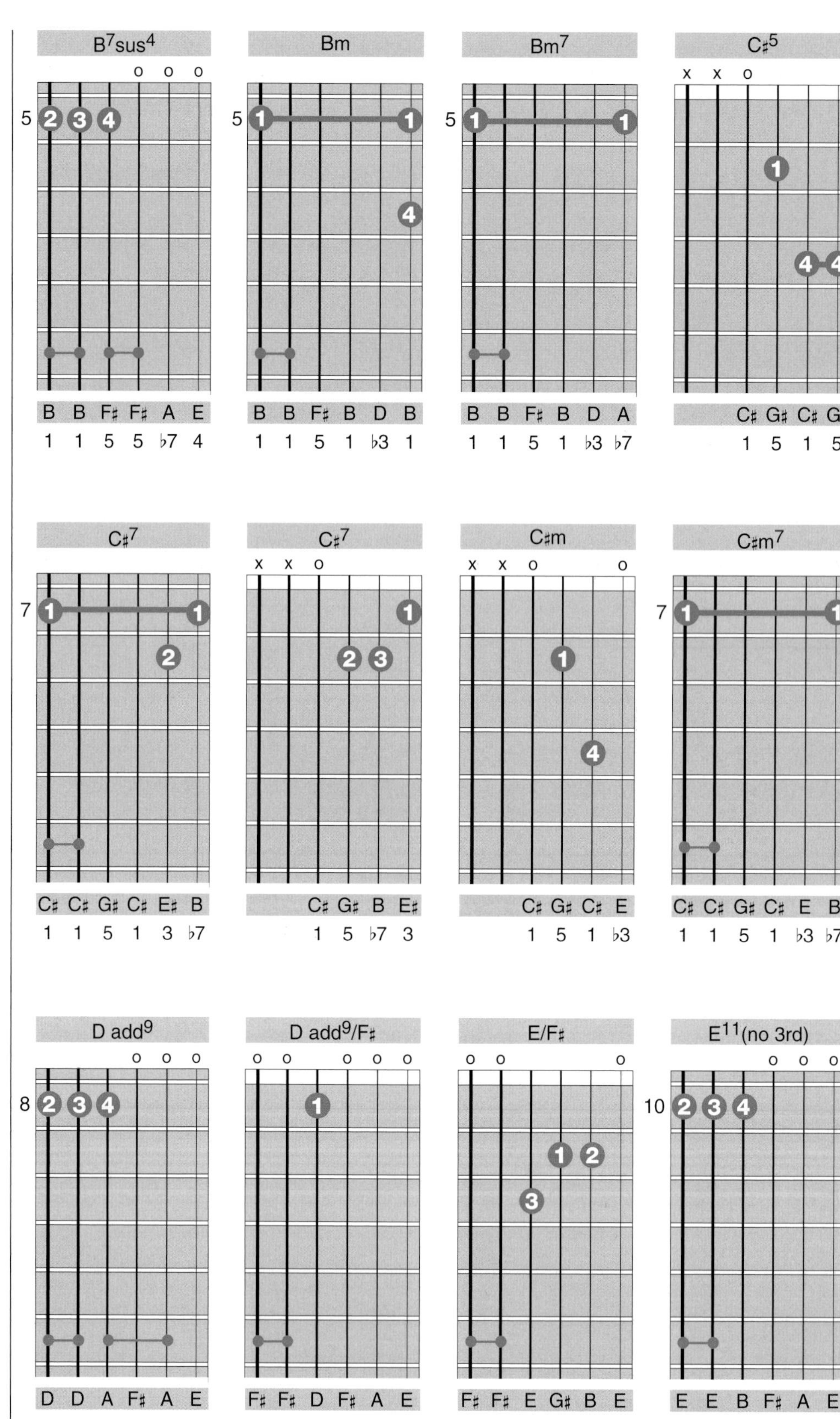
B7sus4
B B F♯ F♯ A E
1 1 5 5 ♭7 4
Bm
B B F♯ B D B
1 1 5 1 ♭3 1
Bm7
B B F♯ B D A
1 1 5 1 ♭3 ♭7
C♯5
C♯ G♯ C♯ G♯
1 5 1 5
C♯7
C♯ C♯ G♯ C♯ E♯ B
1 1 5 1 3 ♭7
C♯7
C♯ G♯ B E♯
1 5 ♭7 3
C♯m
C♯ G♯ C♯ E
1 5 1 ♭3
C♯m7
C♯ C♯ G♯ C♯ E B
1 1 5 1 ♭3 ♭7
D add9
D D A F♯ A E
1 1 5 3 5 9
D add9/F♯
F♯ F♯ D F♯ A E
3 3 1 3 5 9
E/F♯
F♯ F♯ E G♯ B E
1 3 5 1
E11(no 3rd)
E E B F♯ A E
1 1 5 9 11 1

DGDFB♭D

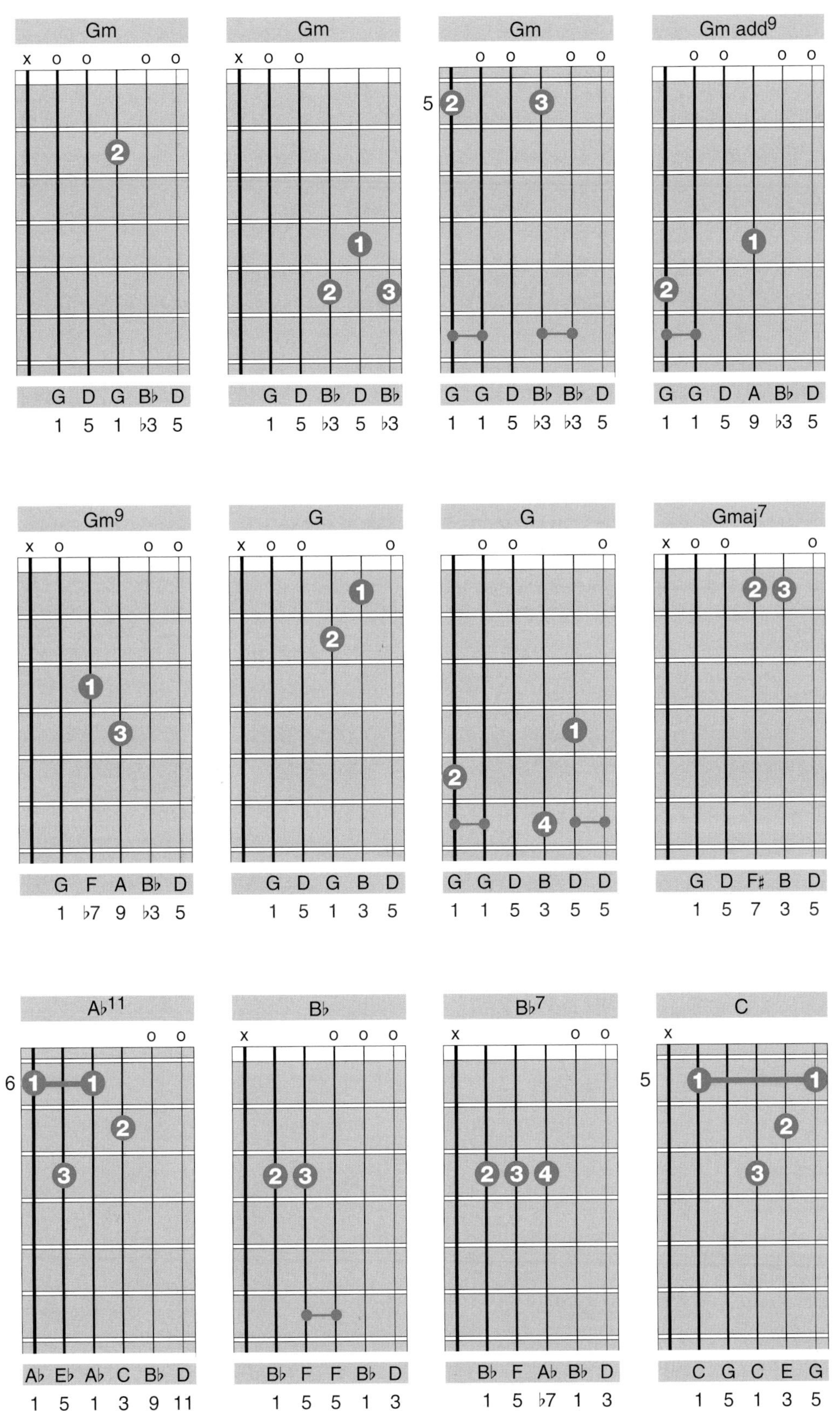

Gm
x o o o o
G D G B♭ D
1 5 1 ♭3 5
Gm
x o o
G D B♭ D B♭
1 5 ♭3 5 ♭3
Gm
o o o o
5
G G D B♭ B♭ D
1 1 5 ♭3 ♭3 5
Gm add9
o o o o
G G D A B♭ D
1 1 5 9 ♭3 5
Gm9
x o o o
G F A B♭ D
1 ♭7 9 ♭3 5
G
x o o o
G D G B D
1 5 1 3 5
G
o o o
G G D B D D
1 1 5 3 5 5
Gmaj7
x o o o
G D F♯ B D
1 5 7 3 5
A♭11
o o
6
A♭ E♭ A♭ C B♭ D
1 5 1 3 9 11
B♭
x o o o
B♭ F F B♭ D
1 5 5 1 3
B♭7
x o o
B♭ F A♭ B♭ D
1 5 ♭7 1 3
C
x
5
C G C E G
1 5 1 3 5

DGDFB♭D

Cmaj7
x, 5

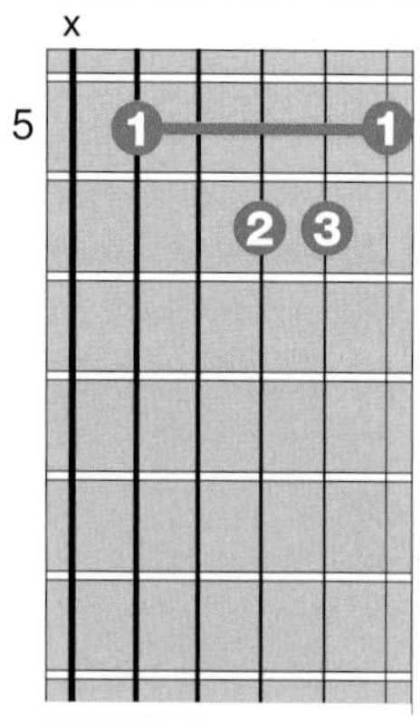

C	G	B	E	G
1	5	7	3	5

C7
x, 5

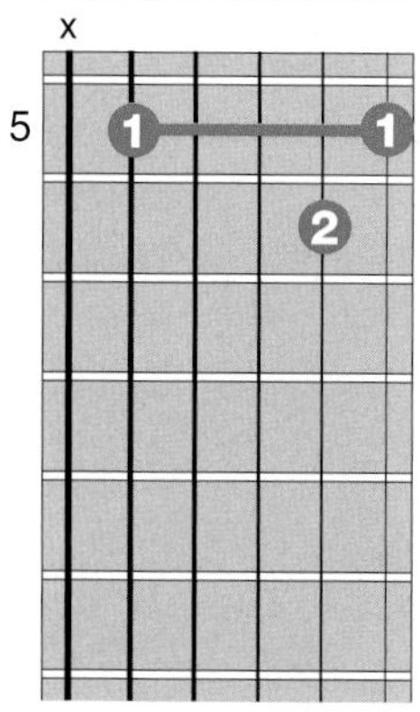

C	G	B♭	E	G
1	5	♭7	3	5

C7sus4
x, 5

C	G	B♭	F	G
1	5	♭7	4	5

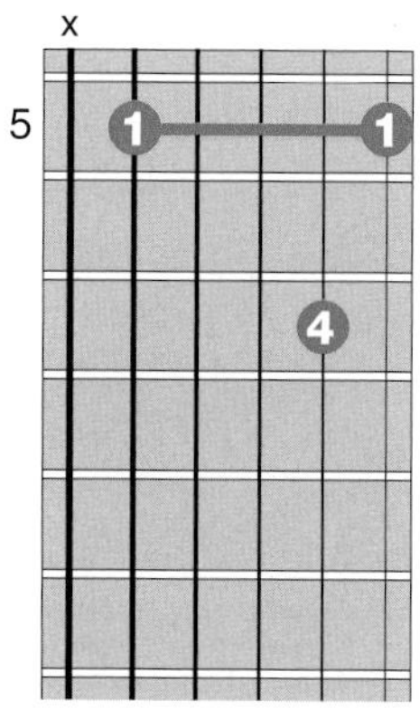

Cm
x, 5

C	G	C	E♭	G
1	5	1	♭3	5

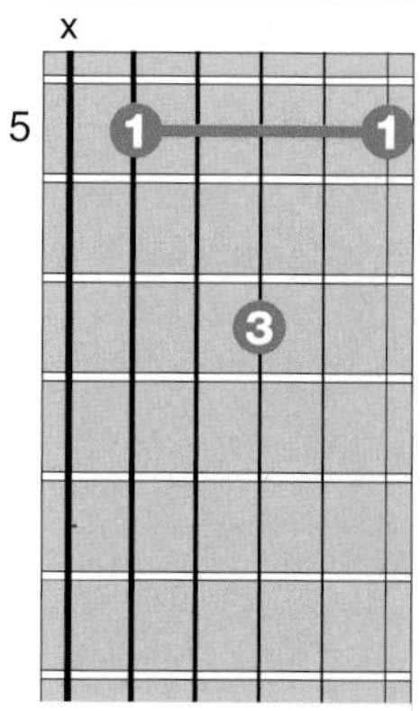

Cm7
x, 5

C	G	B♭	E♭	G
1	5	♭7	♭3	5

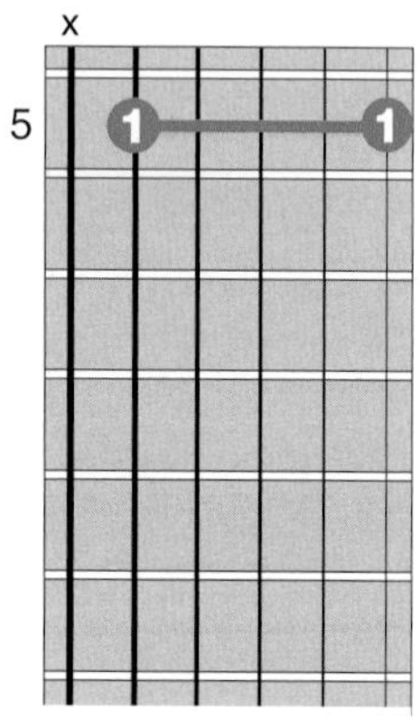

D
o, 7

D	D	A	D	F♯	A
1	1	5	1	3	5

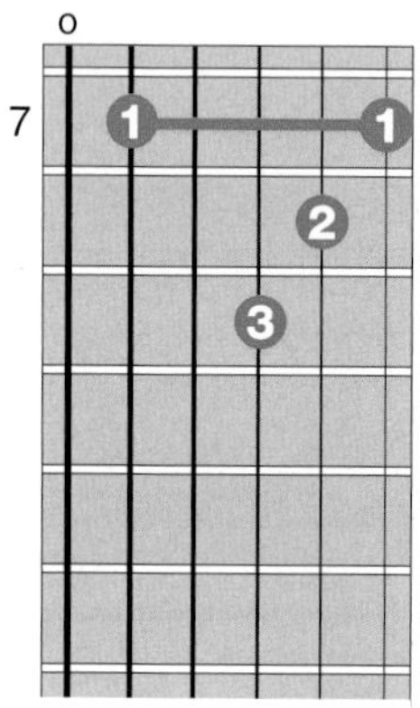

Dm
o, 7

D	D	A	D	F	A
1	1	5	1	♭3	5

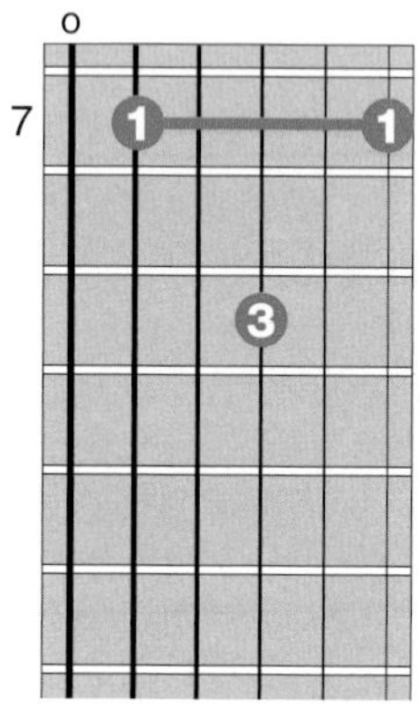

Dm7
o, 7

D	D	A	C	F	A
1	1	5	♭7	♭3	5

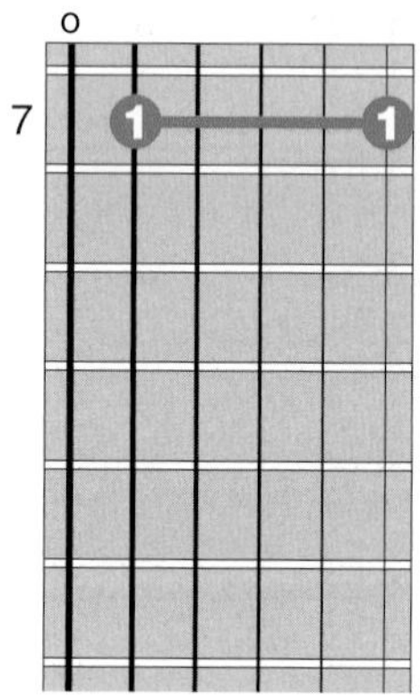

D7
o o o

D	A	D	F♯	C	D
1	5	1	3	♭7	1

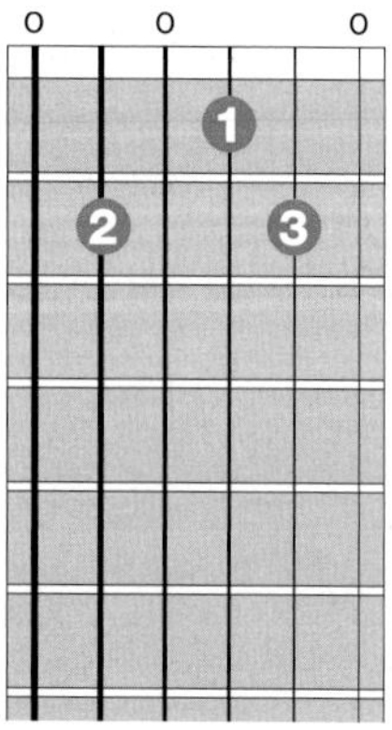

Dm7
o o o o

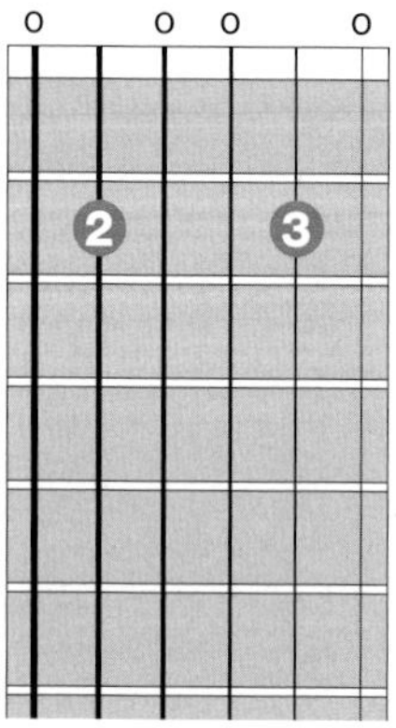

D	A	D	F	C	D
1	5	1	♭3	♭7	1

E♭maj7
o o o

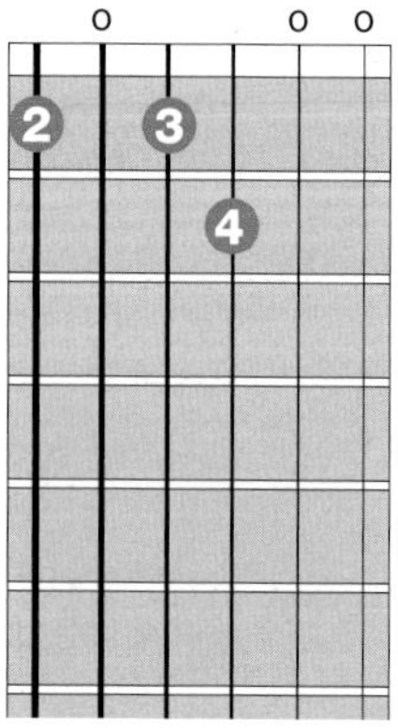

E♭	G	E♭	G	B♭	D
1	3	1	3	5	7

F
x x

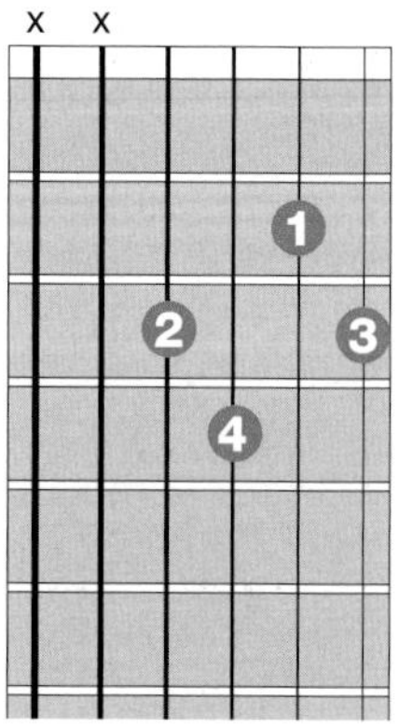

F	A	C	F
1	3	5	1

DADGAD

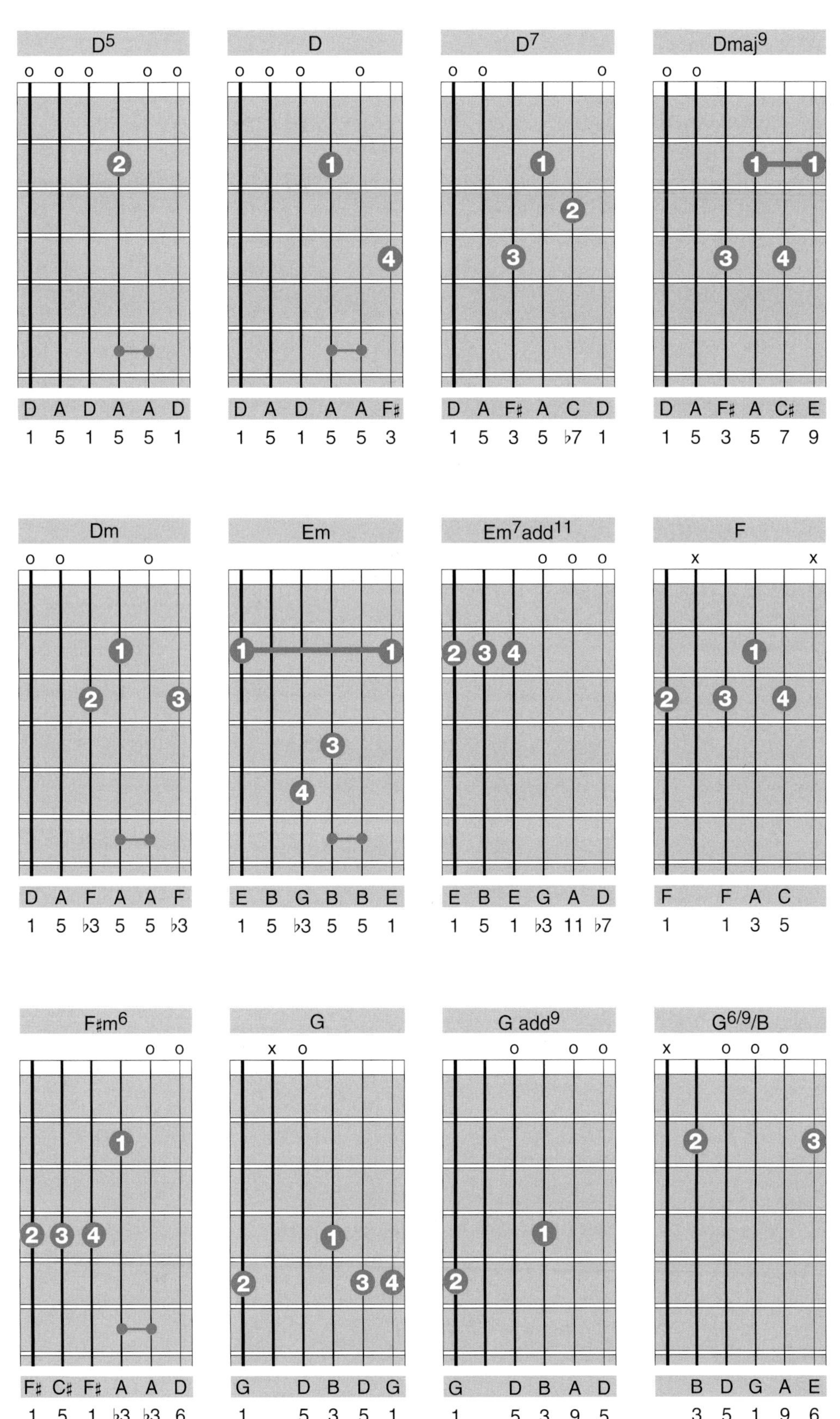

D5
o o o o o
D A D A A D
1 5 1 5 5 1
D
o o o o
D A D A A F♯
1 5 1 5 5 3
D7
o o o
D A F♯ A C D
1 5 3 5 ♭7 1
Dmaj9
o o
D A F♯ A C♯ E
1 5 3 5 7 9
Dm
o o o
D A F A A F
1 5 ♭3 5 5 ♭3
Em
E B G B B E
1 5 ♭3 5 5 1
Em7add11
o o o
E B E G A D
1 5 1 ♭3 11 ♭7
F
x x
F F A C
1 1 3 5
F♯m6
o o
F♯ C♯ F♯ A A D
1 5 1 ♭3 ♭3 6
G
x o
G D B D G
1 5 3 5 1
G add9
o o o
G D B A D
1 5 3 9 5
G6/9/B
x o o o
B D G A E
3 5 1 9 6

DADGAD

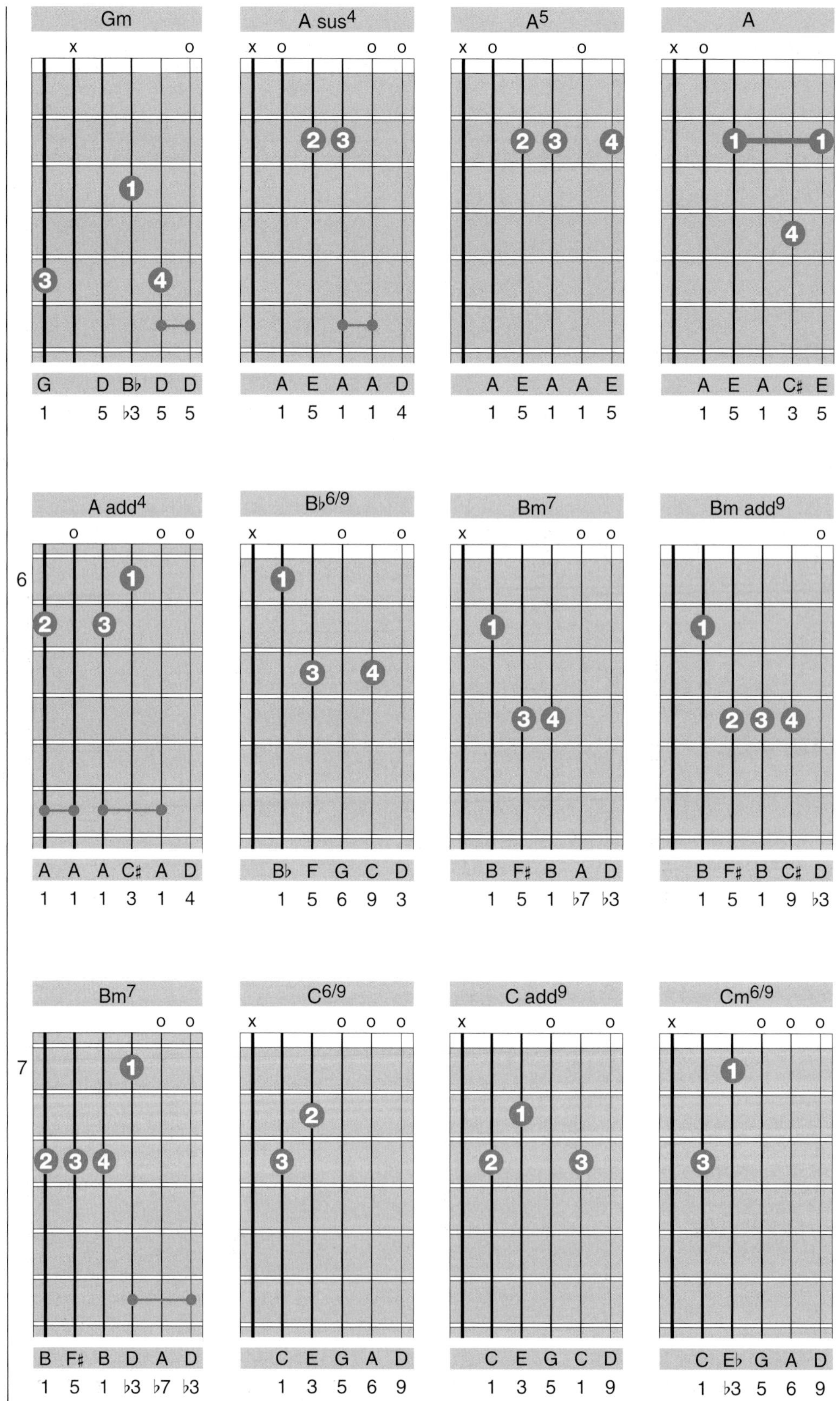
Gm
x o
G D B♭ D D
1 5 ♭3 5 5
A sus4
x o o o
A E A A D
1 5 1 1 4
A5
x o o
A E A A E
1 5 1 1 5
A
x o
A E A C♯ E
1 5 1 3 5
A add4
o o o
6
A A A C♯ A D
1 1 1 3 1 4
B♭6/9
x o o
B♭ F G C D
1 5 6 9 3
Bm7
x o o
B F♯ B A D
1 5 1 ♭7 ♭3
Bm add9
o
B F♯ B C♯ D
1 5 1 9 ♭3
Bm7
o o
7
B F♯ B D A D
1 5 1 ♭3 ♭7 ♭3
C6/9
x o o o
C E G A D
1 3 5 6 9
C add9
x o o
C E G C D
1 3 5 1 9
Cm6/9
x o o o
C E♭ G A D
1 ♭3 5 6 9

DADEAE

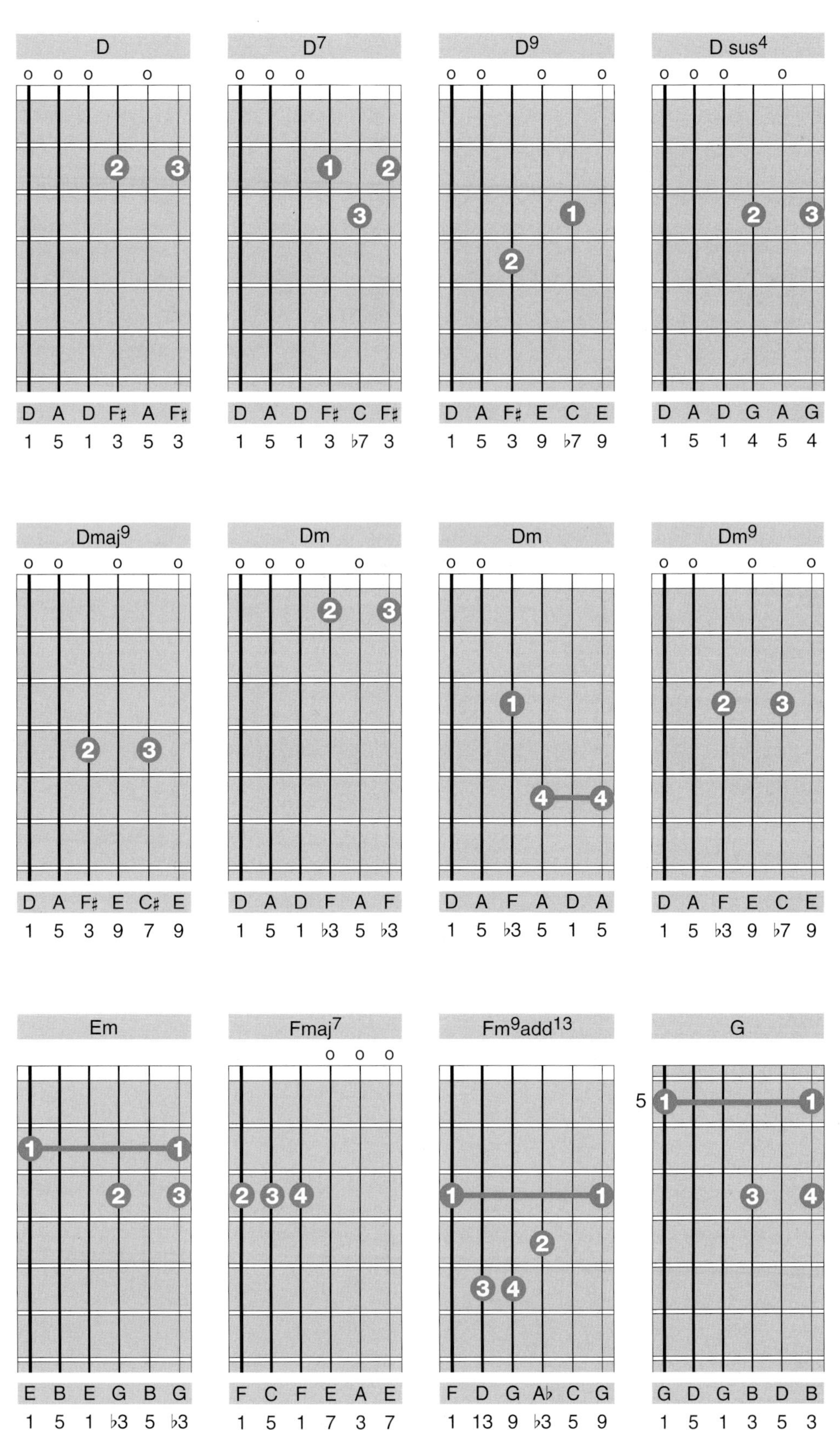
D
D A D F♯ A F♯
1 5 1 3 5 3
D7
D A D F♯ C F♯
1 5 1 3 ♭7 3
D9
D A F♯ E C E
1 5 3 9 ♭7 9
D sus4
D A D G A G
1 5 1 4 5 4
Dmaj9
D A F♯ E C♯ E
1 5 3 9 7 9
Dm
D A D F A F
1 5 1 ♭3 5 ♭3
Dm
D A F A D A
1 5 ♭3 5 1 5
Dm9
D A F E C E
1 5 ♭3 9 ♭7 9
Em
E B E G B G
1 5 1 ♭3 5 ♭3
Fmaj7
F C F E A E
1 5 1 7 3 7
Fm9add13
F D G A♭ C G
1 13 9 ♭3 5 9
G
5
G D G B D B
1 5 1 3 5 3

G sus^2

5

G	D	G	A	D	A
1	5	1	2	5	2

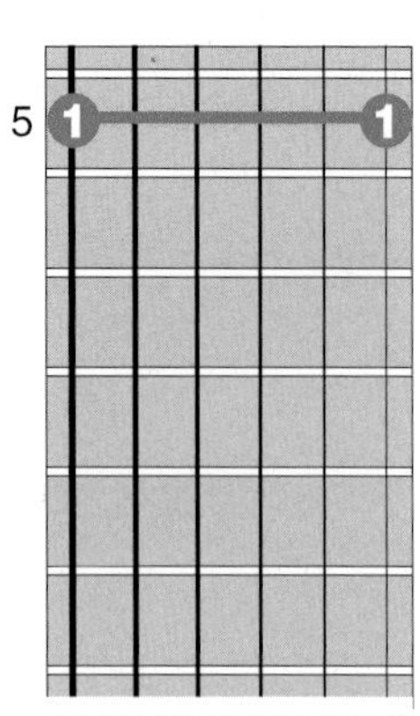

G$^{6/9}$

o o o

5

G	D	G	E	A	E
1	5	1	6	9	6

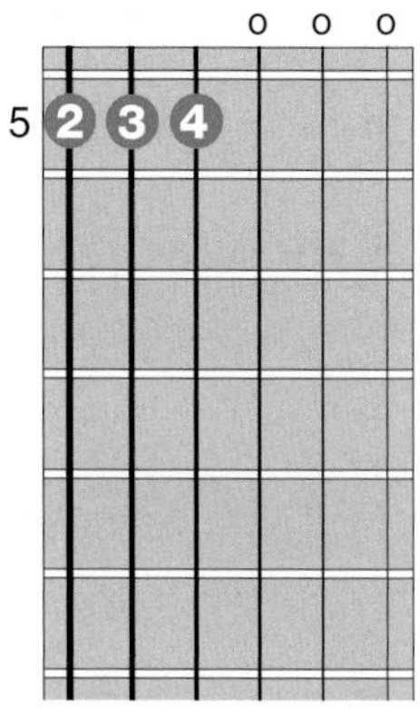

Gm

5

G	D	G	B♭	D	B♭
1	5	1	♭3	5	♭3

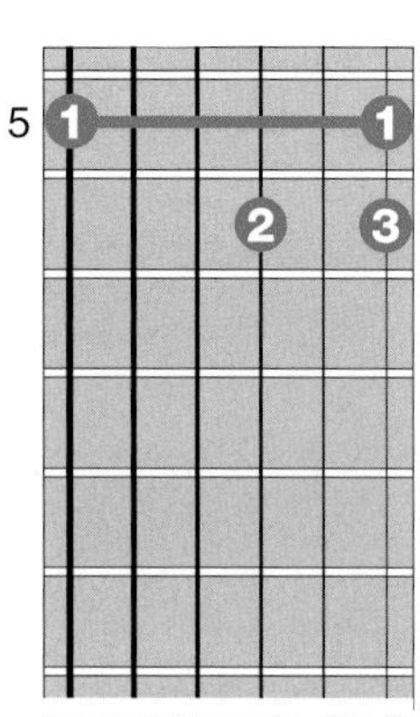

A

x o o o

	A	E	E	C♯	E
	1	5	5	3	5

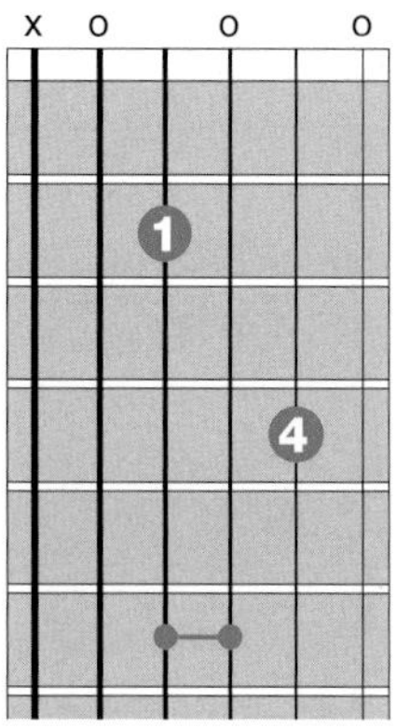

A sus^2

x o o o

	A	E	E	B	E
	1	5	5	2	5

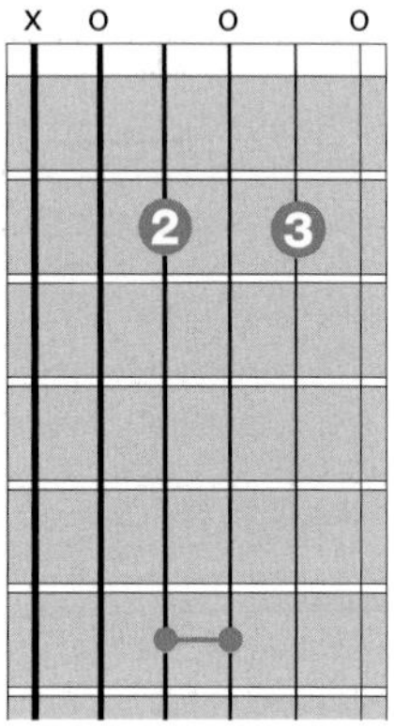

A sus^2

7

A	E	A	B	E	B
1	5	1	2	5	2

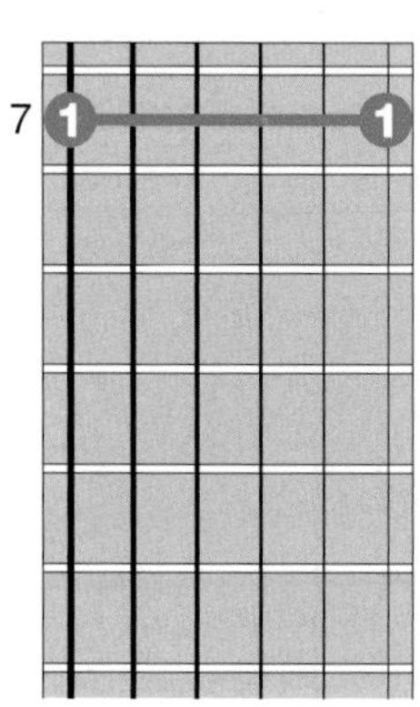

Am

x o o o

	A	E	E	C	E
	1	5	5	♭3	5

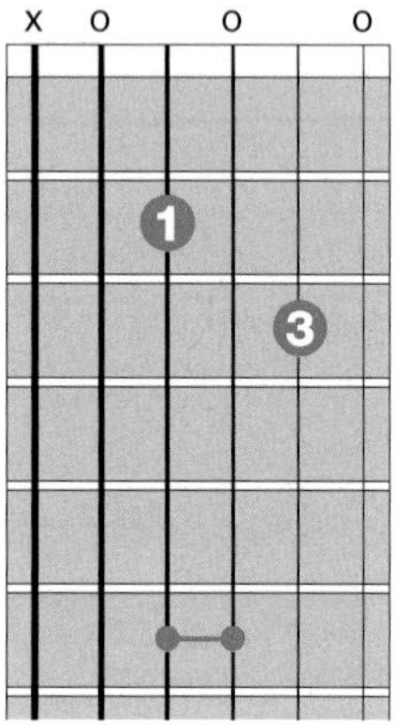

Am^7

x o o o

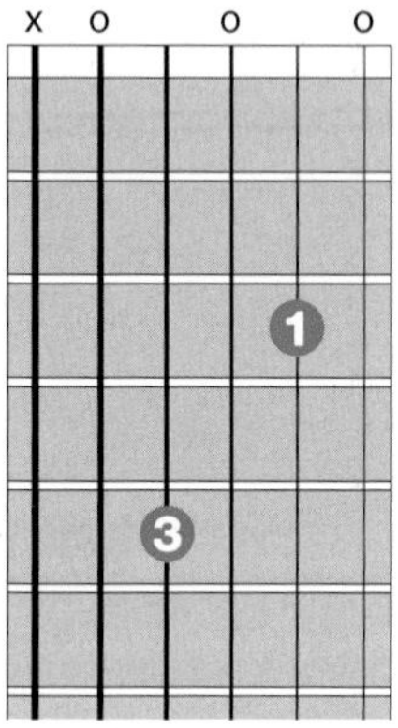

	A	G	E	C	E
	1	♭7	5	♭3	5

Bm

x o

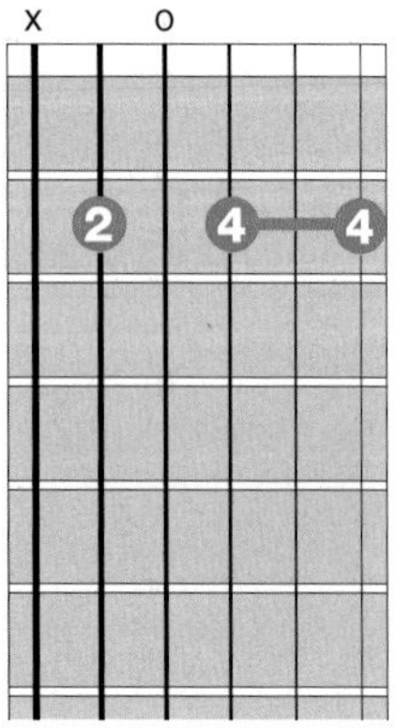

	B	D	F♯	B	F♯
	1	3	5	1	5

Bm^{7}add^1

o o o

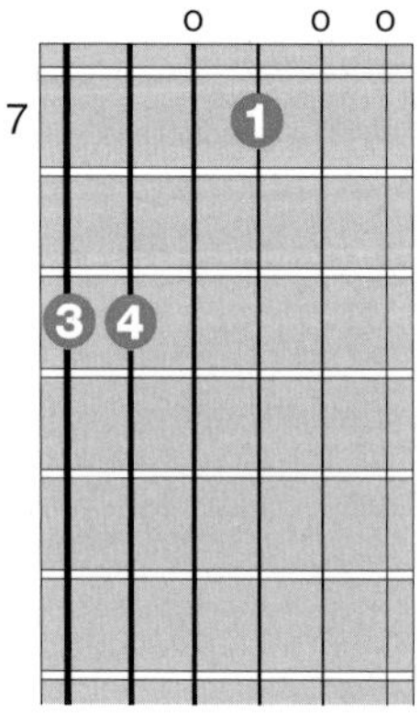

7

B	F♯	D	B	A	E
1	5	♭3	1	♭7	11

B^7

x o

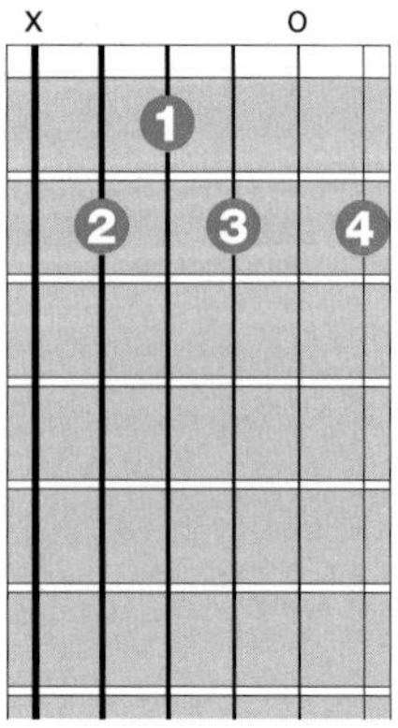

	B	D♯	F♯	A	F♯
	1	3	5	♭7	5

C

x o

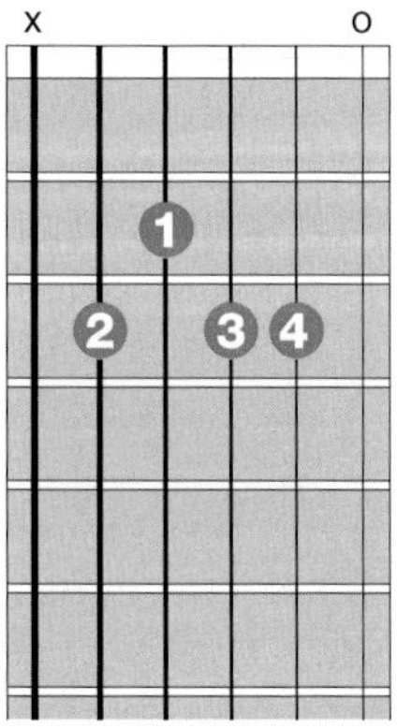

	C	E	G	C	E
	1	3	5	1	3

EADEAD

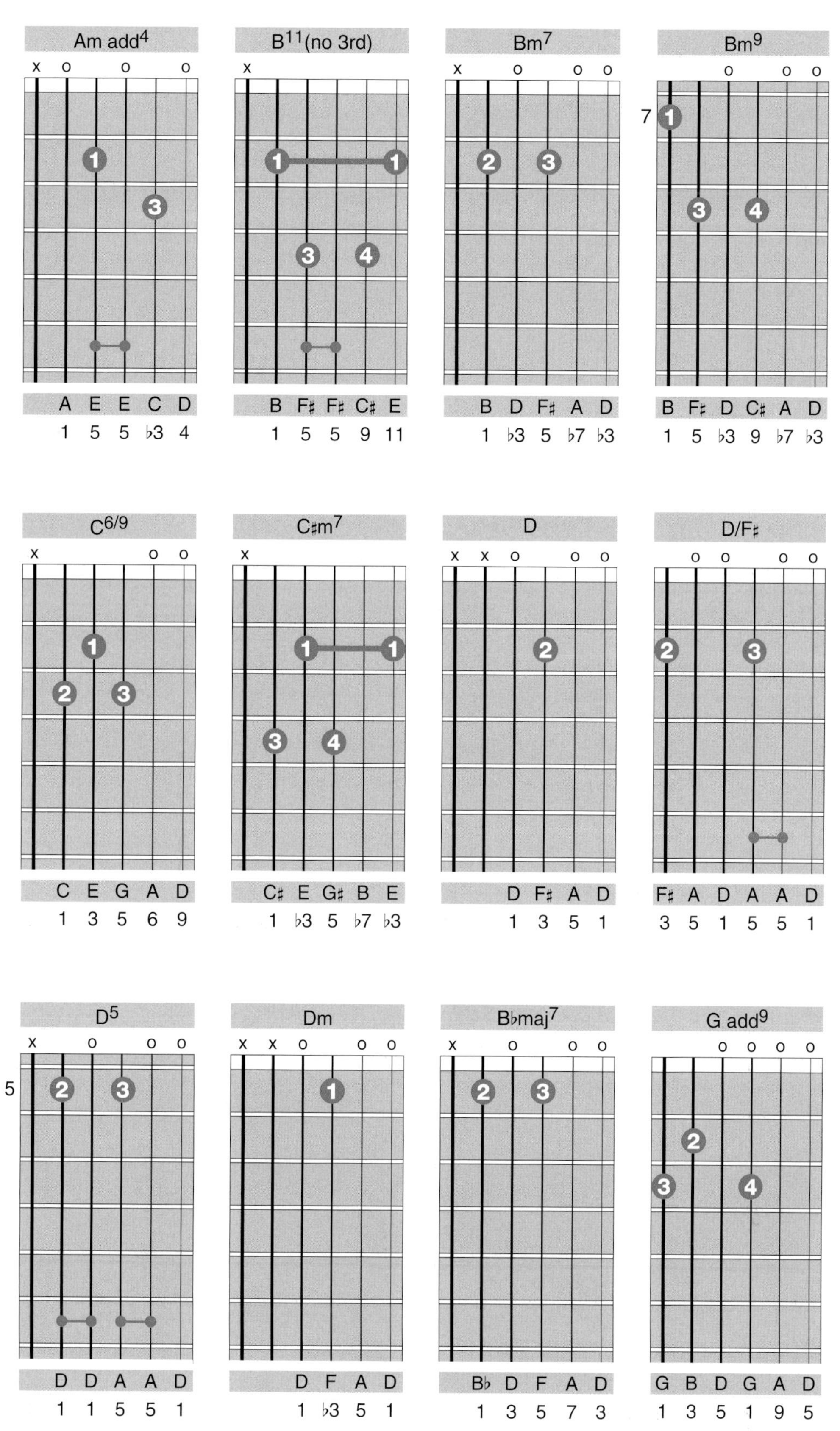
Am add4
x o o o
A E E C D
1 5 5 ♭3 4
B11(no 3rd)
x
B F♯ F♯ C♯ E
1 5 5 9 11
Bm7
x o o o
B D F♯ A D
1 ♭3 5 ♭7 ♭3
Bm9
o o o
7
B F♯ D C♯ A D
1 5 ♭3 9 ♭7 ♭3
C6/9
x o o
C E G A D
1 3 5 6 9
C♯m7
x
C♯ E G♯ B E
1 ♭3 5 ♭7 ♭3
D
x x o o o
D F♯ A D
1 3 5 1
D/F♯
o o o o
F♯ A D A A D
3 5 1 5 5 1
D5
x o o o
5
D D A A D
1 1 5 5 1
Dm
x x o o o
D F A D
1 ♭3 5 1
B♭maj7
x o o o
B♭ D F A D
1 3 5 7 3
G add9
o o o o
G B D G A D
1 3 5 1 9 5

EADEAD

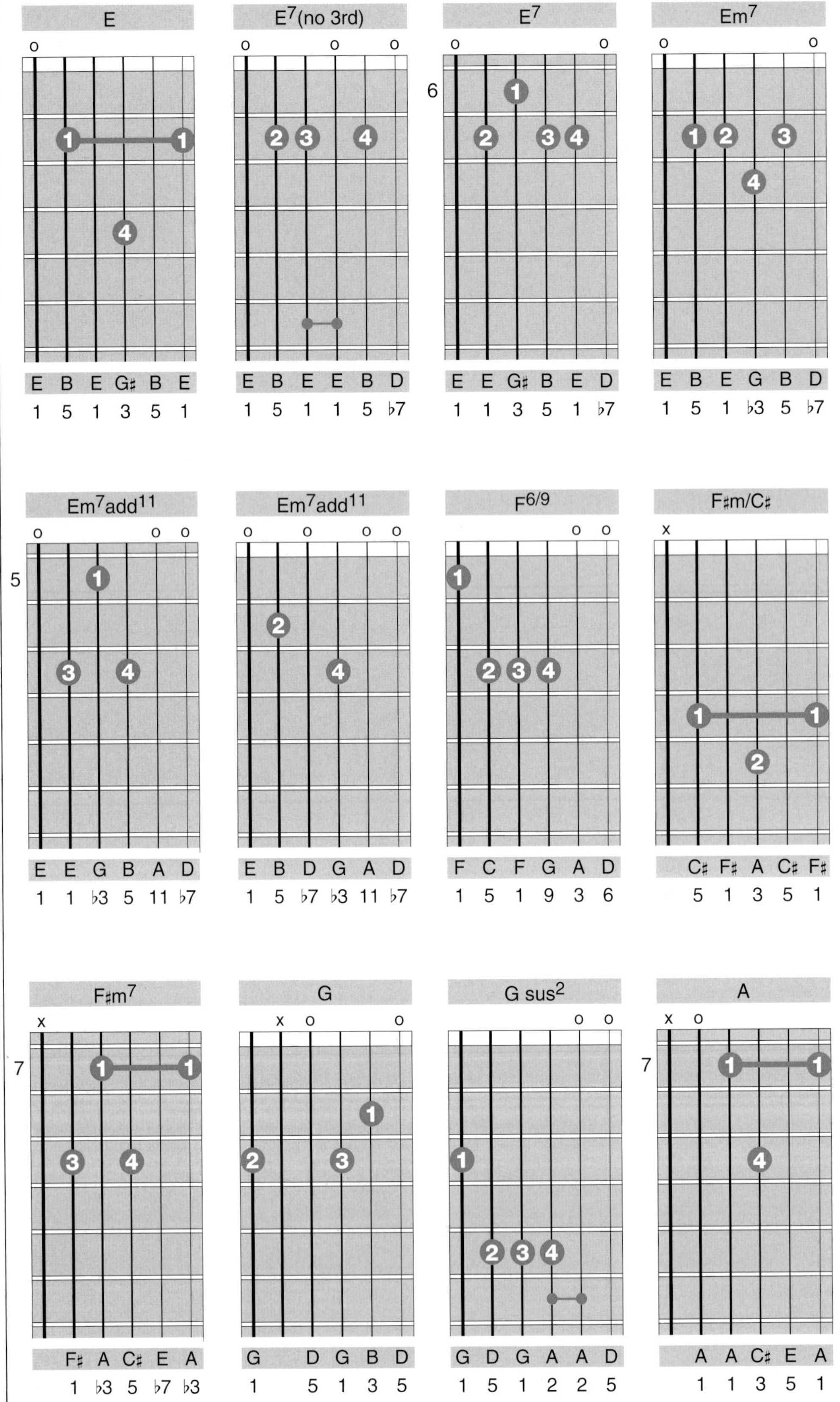
E
E B E G♯ B E
1 5 1 3 5 1
E7(no 3rd)
E B E E B D
1 5 1 1 5 ♭7
E7
6
E E G♯ B E D
1 1 3 5 1 ♭7
Em7
E B E G B D
1 5 1 ♭3 5 ♭7
Em7add11
5
E E G B A D
1 1 ♭3 5 11 ♭7
Em7add11
E B D G A D
1 5 ♭7 ♭3 11 ♭7
F6/9
F C F G A D
1 5 1 9 3 6
F♯m/C♯
C♯ F♯ A C♯ F♯
5 1 3 5 1
F♯m7
7
F♯ A C♯ E A
1 ♭3 5 ♭7 ♭3
G
G D G B D
1 5 1 3 5
G sus2
G D G A A D
1 5 1 2 2 5
A
7
A A C♯ E A
1 1 3 5 1

CGDGCD

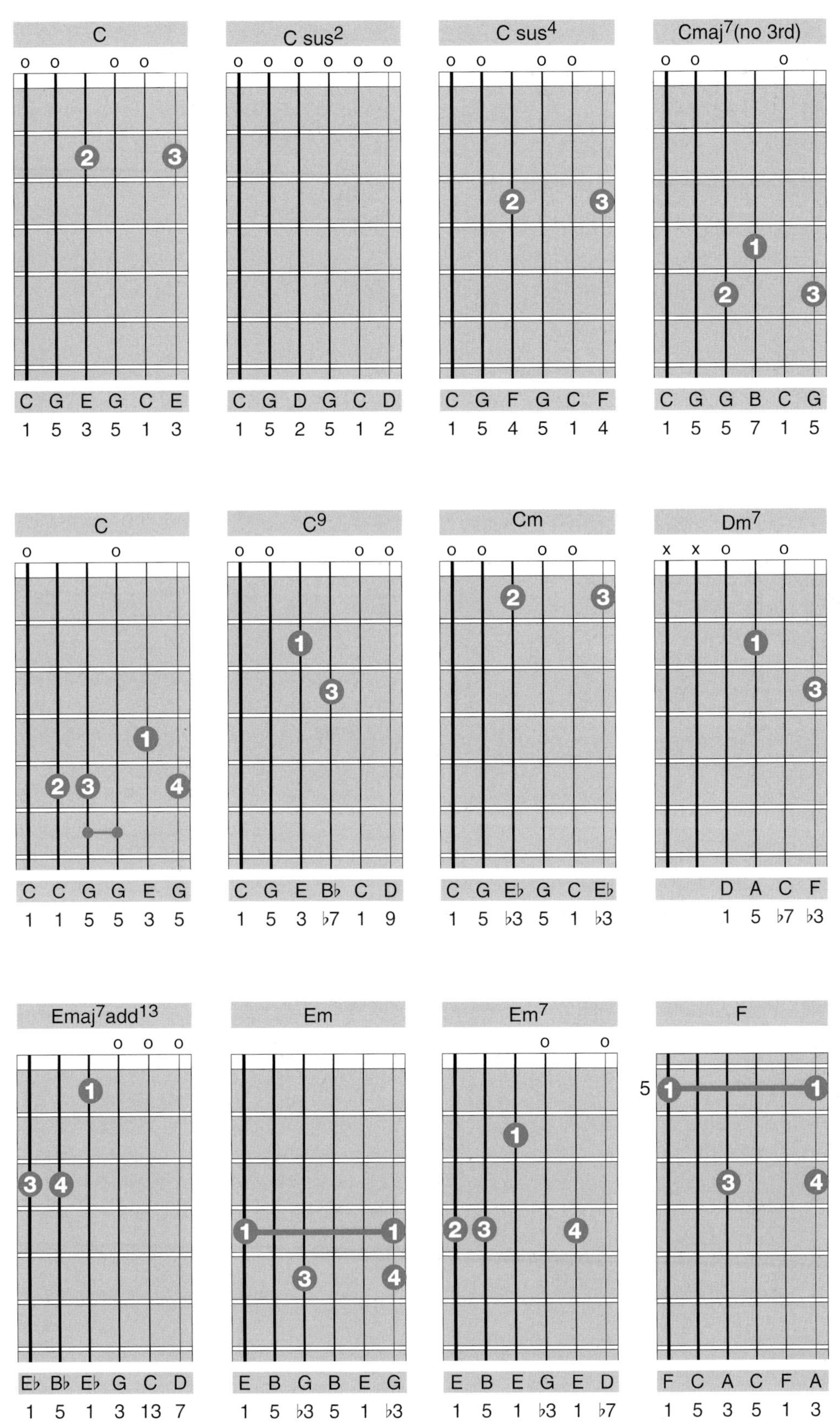

C
C G E G C E
1 5 3 5 1 3
C sus2
C G D G C D
1 5 2 5 1 2
C sus4
C G F G C F
1 5 4 5 1 4
Cmaj7(no 3rd)
C G G B C G
1 5 5 7 1 5
C
C C G G E G
1 1 5 5 3 5
C9
C G E B♭ C D
1 5 3 ♭7 1 9
Cm
C G E♭ G C E♭
1 5 ♭3 5 1 ♭3
Dm7
D A C F
1 5 ♭7 ♭3
Emaj7add13
E♭ B♭ E♭ G C D
1 5 1 3 13 7
Em
E B G B E G
1 5 ♭3 5 1 ♭3
Em7
E B E G E D
1 5 1 ♭3 1 ♭7
F
5
F C A C F A
1 5 3 5 1 3

CGDGCD

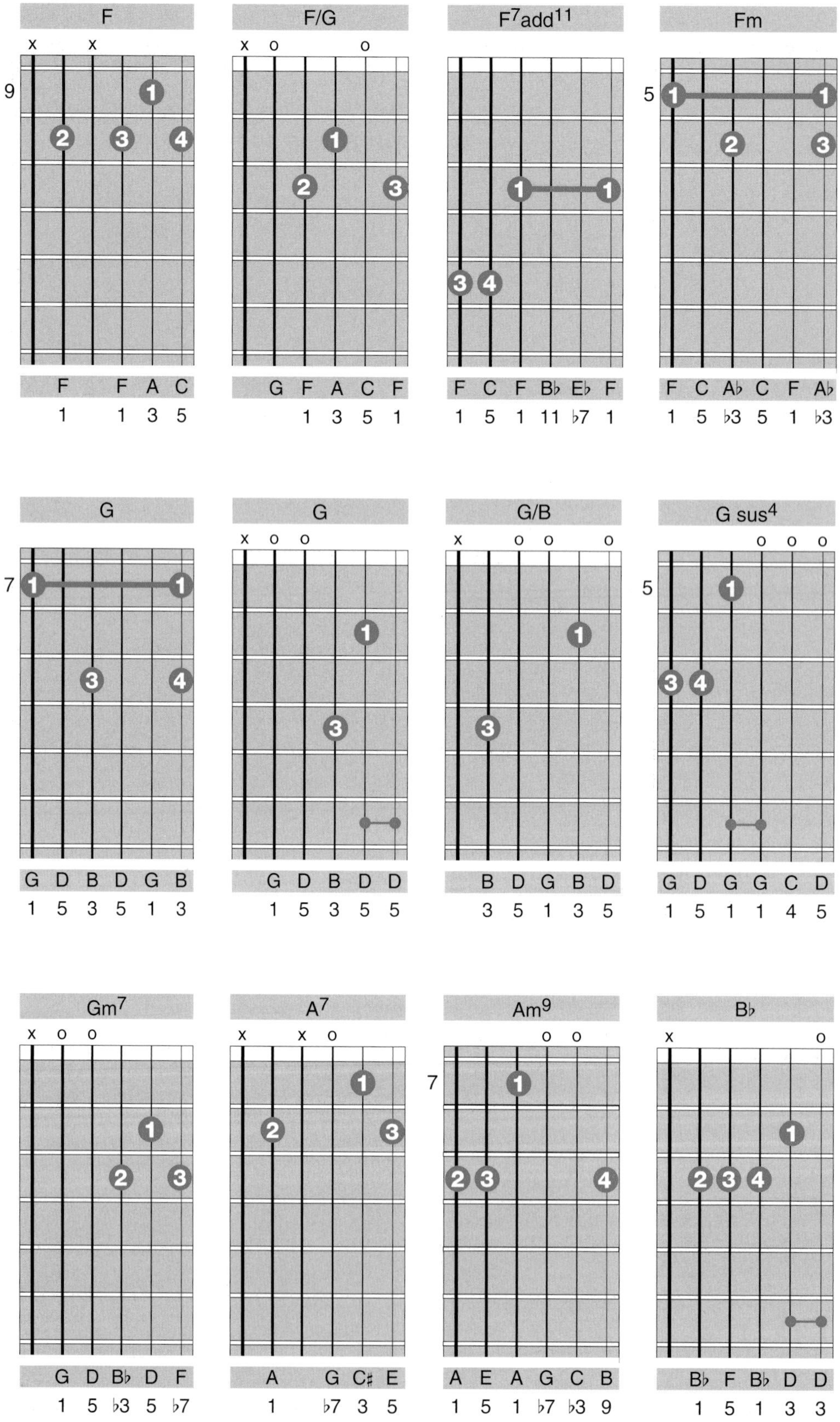

F
x x
9
F F A C
1 1 3 5

F/G
x o o
G F A C F
1 3 5 1

F⁷add¹¹
F C F B♭ E♭ F
1 5 1 11 ♭7 1

Fm
5
F C A♭ C F A♭
1 5 ♭3 5 1 ♭3

G
7
G D B D G B
1 5 3 5 1 3

G
x o o
G D B D D
1 5 3 5 5

G/B
x o o o
B D G B D
3 5 1 3 5

G sus⁴
o o o
5
G D G G C D
1 5 1 1 4 5

Gm⁷
x o o
G D B♭ D F
1 5 ♭3 5 ♭7

A⁷
x x o
A G C♯ E
1 ♭7 3 5

Am⁹
o o
7
A E A G C B
1 5 1 ♭7 ♭3 9

B♭
x o
B♭ F B♭ D D
1 5 1 3 3

EBEEBE

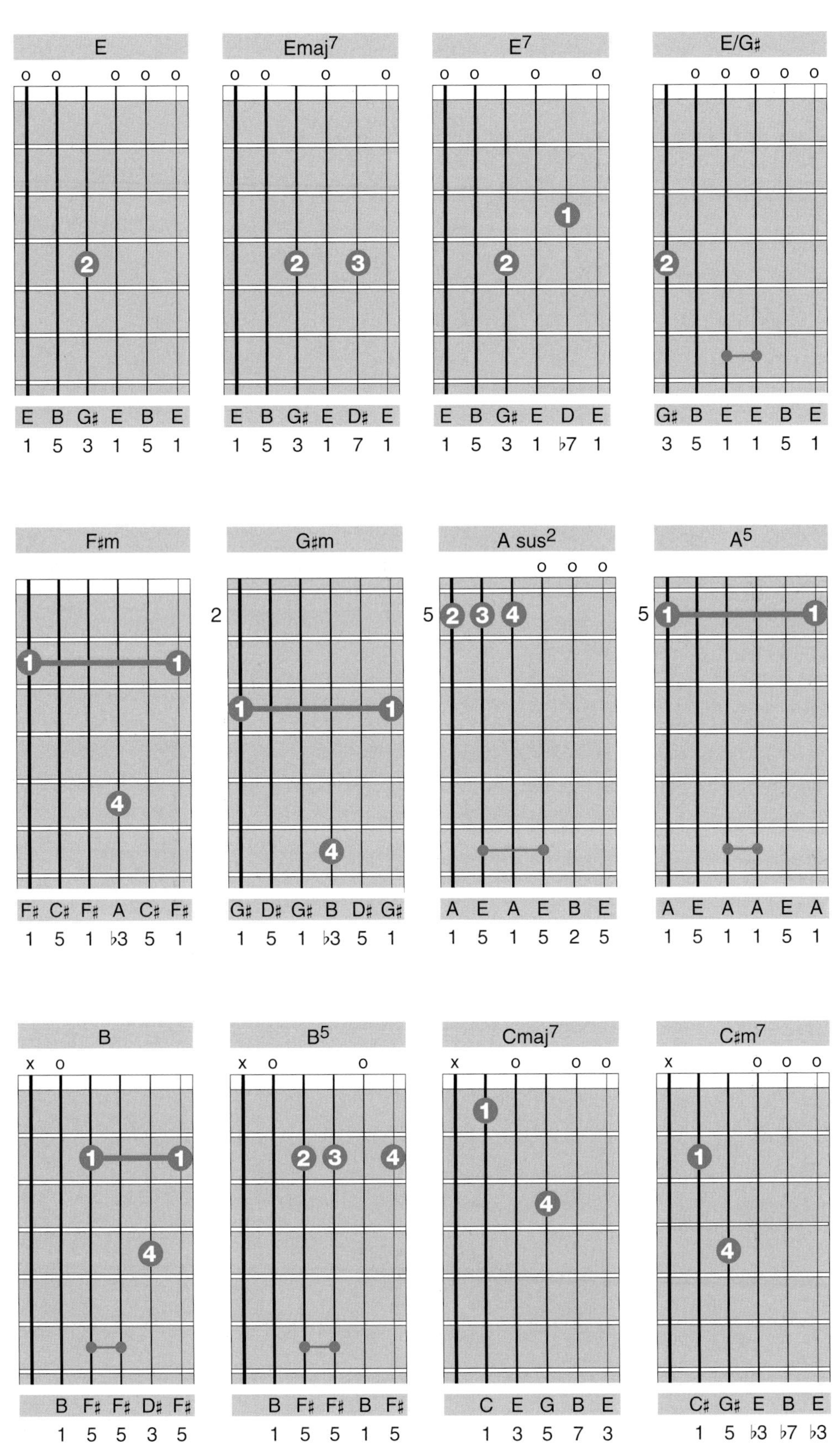
E
o o o o o
E B G♯ E B E
1 5 3 1 5 1
Emaj7
o o o o
E B G♯ E D♯ E
1 5 3 1 7 1
E7
o o o o
E B G♯ E D E
1 5 3 1 ♭7 1
E/G♯
o o o o o
G♯ B E E B E
3 5 1 1 5 1
F♯m
F♯ C♯ F♯ A C♯ F♯
1 5 1 ♭3 5 1
G♯m
2
G♯ D♯ G♯ B D♯ G♯
1 5 1 ♭3 5 1
A sus2
o o o
5
A E A E B E
1 5 1 5 2 5
A5
5
A E A A E A
1 5 1 1 5 1
B
x o
B F♯ F♯ D♯ F♯
1 5 5 3 5
B5
x o o
B F♯ F♯ B F♯
1 5 5 1 5
Cmaj7
x o o o
C E G B E
1 3 5 7 3
C♯m7
x o o o
C♯ G♯ E B E
1 5 ♭3 ♭7 ♭3

EACFAE

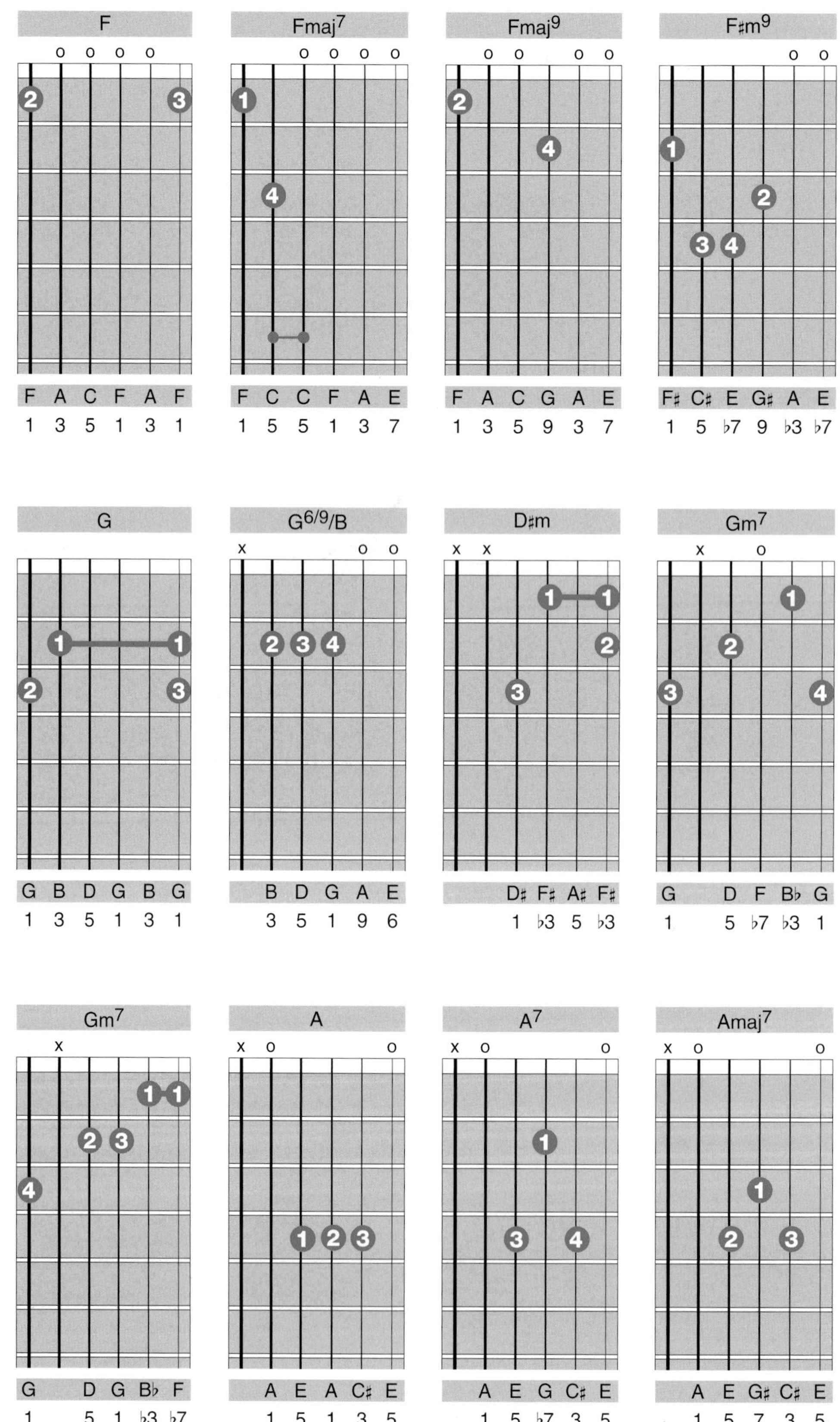
F
o o o o
F A C F A F
1 3 5 1 3 1
Fmaj7
o o o o
F C C F A E
1 5 5 1 3 7
Fmaj9
o o o o
F A C G A E
1 3 5 9 3 7
F♯m9
o o
F♯ C♯ E G♯ A E
1 5 ♭7 9 ♭3 ♭7
G
G B D G B G
1 3 5 1 3 1
G6/9/B
x o o
B D G A E
3 5 1 9 6
D♯m
x x
D♯ F♯ A♯ F♯
1 ♭3 5 ♭3
Gm7
x o
G D F B♭ G
1 5 ♭7 ♭3 1
Gm7
x
G D G B♭ F
1 5 1 ♭3 ♭7
A
x o o
A E A C♯ E
1 5 1 3 5
A7
x o o
A E G C♯ E
1 5 ♭7 3 5
Amaj7
x o o
A E G♯ C♯ E
1 5 7 3 5

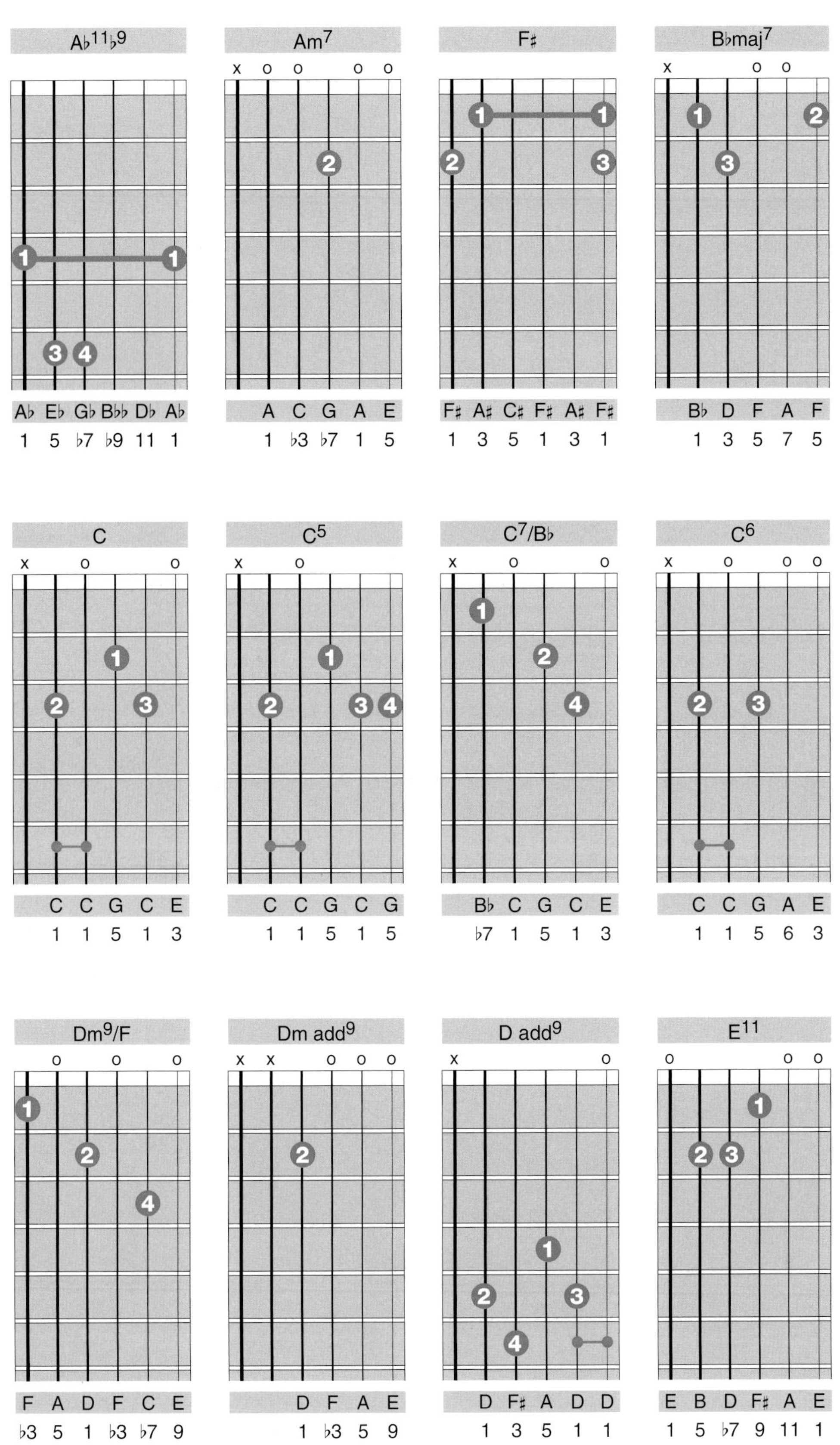
A♭11♭9
A♭ E♭ G♭ B♭♭ D♭ A♭
1 5 ♭7 ♭9 11 1
Am7
A C G A E
1 ♭3 ♭7 1 5
F♯
F♯ A♯ C♯ F♯ A♯ F♯
1 3 5 1 3 1
B♭maj7
B♭ D F A F
1 3 5 7 5
C
C C G C E
1 1 5 1 3
C5
C C G C G
1 1 5 1 5
C7/B♭
B♭ C G C E
♭7 1 5 1 3
C6
C C G A E
1 1 5 6 3
Dm9/F
F A D F C E
♭3 5 1 ♭3 ♭7 9
Dm add9
D F A E
1 ♭3 5 9
D add9
D F♯ A D D
1 3 5 1 1
E11
E B D F♯ A E
1 5 ♭7 9 11 1

APPENDICES

TUNING TRANSFORMATIONS

These tables show how to move from standard tuning to an open major or minor tuning on any note. As they move one re-tuned string at a time they pass through a number of intermediate tunings before reaching the desired target. These in-between tunings, though not open, offer other opportunities to explore. The total amount of detuning is shown by an = and a + or – figure in semitones.

Target pitch: open A

	pitch mvt	name
E A D G B E		
E A C♯ G B E	-1	A9
E A C♯ E B E	-3	Aadd9
E A C♯ E A E	-2 = -6	open A

No. of strings altered: 3
Interval signature: 5 4 3 5 7
Harmonic signature: 5 1 3 5 1 5

Target pitch: open A (II)

	pitch mvt	name
E A D G B E		
E A E G B E	+2	A9 (no 3rd)
E A E A B E	+2	Aadd9
E A E A C♯ E	+2 = +6	open A

No. of strings altered: 3
Interval signature: 5 7 5 4 3
Harmonic signature: 5 1 5 1 3 5

Target pitch: open Am

	pitch mvt	name
E A D G B E		
E A C G B E	-2	Am9
E A C E B E	-3	Amadd9
E A C E A E	-2 = -7	open Am

No. of strings altered: 3
Interval signature: 5 3 4 5 7
Harmonic signature: 5 1 ♭3 5 1 5

Target pitch: open Am (II)

	pitch mvt	name
E A D G B E		
E A E G B E	+2	A9 (no 3rd)
E A E A B E	+2	Aadd9
E A E A C E	+1 = +5	open Am

No. of strings altered: 3
Interval signature: 5 7 5 3 4
Harmonic signature: 5 1 5 1 3 5

Target pitch: open B♭

	pitch mvt	name
E A D G B E		
E A D G B D	-2	
E A D G B♭ D	-1	
E B♭ D G B♭ D	+1	(from string 5) open Gm/ B♭6
F B♭ D G B♭ D	+1	B♭6
F B♭ D F B♭ D	-2 = -3	open B♭

No. of strings altered: 5
Interval signature: 5 4 3 5 4
Harmonic signature: 5 1 3 5 1 3

Target pitch: open B♭m

	pitch mvt	name
E A D G B E		
E A D G B D♭	-3	
E A D G B♭ D♭	-1	
E A D♭ G B♭ D♭	-1	
E B♭ D♭ G B♭ D♭	+1	(from string 5) open Gm/ B♭6
F B♭ D♭ G B♭ D♭	+1	B♭6
F B♭ D♭ F B♭ D♭	-2 = -5	open B♭

No. of strings altered: 6
Interval signature: 5 3 4 5 3
Harmonic signature: 5 1 ♭3 5 1 ♭3

Target pitch: open B

	pitch mvt	name
E A D G B E		
E A D G B D♯	-1	
E A D F♯ B D♯	-1	
E A D♯ F♯ B D♯	+1	
E B D♯ F♯ B D♯	+2 = +1	(from string 5) open B

No. of strings altered: 4
Interval signature: x 4 3 5 4
Harmonic signature: x 1 3 5 1 3

Target pitch: open Bm

	pitch mvt	name
E A D G B E		
E A D G B D	-2	Em7add11
E A D F♯ B D	-1	E11
E B D F♯ B D	+2 = -1	(from string 5) open Bm

No. of strings altered: 3
Interval signature: x 3 4 5 3
Harmonic signature: x 1 ♭3 5 1 ♭3

Target pitch: open C

	pitch mvt	name
E A D G B E		
E A D G C E	+1	
E A C G C E	-2	(from string 5) Am7
E G C G C E	-2	open C first inversion
C G C G C E	-4 = -7	open C

No. of strings altered: 4
Interval signature: 7 5 7 5 4
Harmonic signature: 1 5 1 5 1 3

Target pitch: open Cm

	pitch mvt	name
E A D G B E		
E A D G B E♭	-1	
E A D G C E♭	+1	
E A C G C E♭	-2	
E G C G C E♭	-2	
C G C G C E♭	-4 = -8	open Cm

No. of strings altered: 5
Interval signature: 7 5 7 5 3
Harmonic signature: 1 5 1 5 1 ♭3

Target pitch: open D

	pitch mvt	name
E A D G B E		
E A D G B D	-2	
E A D G A D	-2	
E A D F♯ A D	-1	
D A D F♯ A D	-2 = -7	

No. of strings altered: 4
Interval signature: 7 5 4 3 5
Harmonic signature: 1 5 1 3 5 1

Target pitch: open Dm

	pitch mvt	name
E A D G B E		
E A D G B D	-2	
E A D G A D	-2	
E A D F A D	-2	
D A D F A D	-2 = -8	open D minor

No. of strings altered: 4
Interval signature: 7 5 3 4 5
Harmonic signature: 1 5 1 ♭3 5 1

Target pitch: open E♭

	pitch mvt	name
E A D G B E		
E A D G B Eb	-1	
E A D G B♭ E♭	-1	
E B♭ D G B♭ E♭	+1	
E♭ B♭ D G B♭ E♭	-1 = -2	open E♭maj7

No. of strings altered: 4
Interval signature: 7 4 5 3 5
Harmonic signature: 1 5 1 3 5 1

This is an example of where it can be better not to go for the full open tuning but stop at a major seventh, which only involves fretting one finger to cancel it out and produce a major chord from a single-finger barre. Also a string 6 E might be good for F and G root notes and A♭ on the bottom string even in an E♭ key.

Target pitch: open E

	pitch mvt	name
E A D G B E		
E A D G♯ B E	+1	
E A E G♯ B E	+2	
E B E G♯ B E	+2 = +5	open E

No. of strings altered: 3
Interval signature: 7 5 4 3 5 [same as open D]
Harmonic signature: 1 5 1 3 5 1

Target pitch: open E (II)

	pitch mvt	name
E A D G B E		
E A D E B E	-3	
E A B E B E	-3	
E G♯ B E B E	-1= -7	

No. of strings altered: 3
Interval signature: 4 3 5 7 5
Harmonic signature: 1 3 5 1 5 1

Target pitch: open Em

	pitch mvt	name
E A D G B E		
E B D G B E	+2	Em7
E B E G B E	+2 = +4	open E

No. of strings altered: 2
Interval signature: 7 5 3 4 5
Harmonic signature: 1 5 1 ♭3 5 1

Target pitch: open F

	pitch mvt	name
E A D G B E		
E A D G B C	-4	
E A D G A C	-2	
E A D F A C	-2	
E A C F A C	-2	
F A C F A C	+1 = -9	open F

No. of strings altered: 5
Interval signature: 4 3 5 4 3
Harmonic signature: 1 3 5 1 3 5 [Fm would require all 6 strings changed]

Target pitch: open F♯m

	pitch mvt	name
E A D G B E		
E A D G B C♯	-3	
E A D G A C♯	-2	
E A D F♯ A C♯	-1	
E A C♯ F♯ A C♯	-1	
C♯ A C♯ F♯ A C♯	-3 = -10	open F#m

No. of strings altered: 5
Interval signature: 8 4 5 3 4
Harmonic signature: 5 ♭3 5 1 ♭3 5

This is an interesting test case which involves tuning too far down. It has a weak harmonic signature, with only one root (located too high on open string 3) and two thirds. Better in this case to leave string 6 as E and finger F♯ on the second fret, also string 1 could be left as E (E A C♯ F♯ A E) like an A6 tuning, as measured from string 5.

Target pitch: open G

	pitch mvt	name
E A D G B E		
E A D G B D	-2	top drop D
E G D G B D	-2	Em7
D G D G B D	-2 = -6	open G

No. of strings altered: 3
Interval signature: 5 7 5 4 3
Harmonic signature: 5 1 5 1 3 5

Target pitch: open Gm

	pitch mvt	name
E A D G B E		
E A D G B D	-2	top drop D
E G D G B D	-2	Em7
D G D G B D	-2	open G
D G D G B♭ D	-1 = -7	open Gm

No. of strings altered: 4
Interval signature: 5 7 5 3 4
Harmonic signature: 5 1 5 1 ♭3 5

Target pitch: open A♭

	pitch mvt	name
E A D G B E		
E A D G B E♭	-1	
E A D G C E♭	+1	
E A D A♭ C E♭	+1	
E A C A♭ C Eb	-2	
E A♭ C A♭ C E♭	-1	
E♭ A♭ C A♭ C E♭	-1 = -3	open A♭

No. of strings altered: 6
Interval signature: 5 4 8 4 3
Harmonic signature: 5 1 3 1 3 5

Target pitch: open G♯m

	pitch mvt	name
E A D G B E		
E A D G B D♯	-1	
E A D G♯ B D♯	+1	
E A D♯ G♯ B D♯	+1	
E G♯ D♯ G♯ B D♯	-1	
D♯ G♯ D♯ G♯ B D♯	-1 = -1	open G♯m

No. of strings altered: 5
Interval signature: 5 7 5 3 4
Harmonic signature: 5 1 5 1 ♭3 5

TRANSFORMATIONS TABLE

Tunings are ranked according to the total number of semitones it takes to reach the tuning. Plus values mean a net increase in pitch (and string tension); minus values mean a net loss in pitch (and string tension). Strings changed are in bold.

+6	open E	E **B** **E** **G♯** B E
+6	open A	E A **E** **A** **C♯** E
+5	open Am	E A **E** **A** **C** E
+5	open Em	E **B** **E** G B E
+2	open Em7	E **B** D G B E
+1	open B	E **B** **D♯** **F♯** **B** **D♯** [from string 5]
0	standard	E A D G B E
0	Bmaj7	E **B** **D♯** **F♯** **A♯** **D♯**
-1	top semi	E A D G B **D♯**
-1	'lute'	E A D **F♯** B E
-1	open Bm	E **B** D **F♯** B **D** [from string 5]
-1	open G♯m	**D♯** **G♯** **D♯** **G♯** B **D♯**
-2	open Ebmaj7	**E♭** **B♭** D G **B♭** **E♭**
-2	drop D	**D** A D G B E
-2	top drop D	E A D G B **D**
-2	drop A	E A D G **A** E
-3	Em9	E A D **F♯** B **D**
-3	D6/9	**D** A D **F♯** B E
-3	open Bm	**D** **B** D **F♯** B **D**
-3	open B♭	**F** **B♭** D **F** **B♭** **D**
-3	open A♭	**E♭** **A♭** **C** **Ab** **C** **E♭**
-4	drop C	**C** A D G B E
-4	double drop D	**D** A D G B **D**
-4	E5	E **B** **B** **E** B E
-4	Em7add11	E A D G **A** **D**
-4	A6/F♯m7	E A **C♯** **F♯** **A** E [from string 5]
-5	D6	**D** A D **F♯** B **D**
-5	F♯m7	**F♯** **F♯** **C♯** **F♯** **A** E
-5	open B♭m	**F** **B♭** **D♭** **F** **B♭** **D♭**
-6	open G	**D** **G** D G B **D**
-6	Dsus4	**D** A D G **A** **D**
-6	'slack' open A	E A **C♯** **E** **A** E
-6	open B♭	**D** **B♭** **D** **F** **B♭** **D**
-6	Fmaj7	E A **C** **F** **A** E
-7	open Am	E A **C** **E** **A** E
-7	open Gm	**D** **G** D G **B♭** **D**
-7	open C	**C** **G** **C** G **C** E
-7	open D	**D** A D **F♯** **A** **D**
-7	'slack' open E	E **G♯** **B** **E** B E
-7	Dsus2	**D** A D **E** **A** E
-7	Asus4	E A D **E** **A** **D**
-8	open Dm	**D** A D **F** **A** **D**
-8	open Cm	**C** **G** **C** G **C** **E♭**
-8	'slack' open Em	E **G** **B** **E** B E
-9	Csus2	**C** **G** **C** G **C** **D**
-9	open Gm7	**D** **G** D **F** **B♭** **D**
-9	open F	**F** A **C** **F** **A** **C**
-10	open F♯m	**C♯** A **C♯** **F♯** **A** **Cv**

SONGWRITING TIPS

INDEX OF ARTISTS

Index of Tunings

CD Track Listing

TRACK		PAGE NO.	TRACK		PAGE NO.
1.	**DADGBE**	28	23.	**CGCGCE**	68
2.	**DADGBE**	29	24.	**EAC♯EAE**	70
3.	**EADGBD♯**	31	25.	**EG♯BEBE**	73
4.	**EADGBE♭**	33	26.	**DB♭DFB♭D**	74
5.	**EADGBD**	35	27.	**DB♭DFB♭D**	77
6.	**EADGBD**	36	28.	**EAC♯F♯AE**	80
7.	**EADF♯BE**	38	29.	**EBD♯F♯A♯D♯**	82
8.	**EADGAE**	40	30.	**DGDGB♭D**	86
9.	**EADGAE**	42	31.	**DGDGB♭D**	88
10.	**CADGBE**	44	32.	**DADFAD**	90
11.	**DADGBD**	47	33.	**EACEAE**	92
12.	**DADGBD**	49	34.	**DBDF♯BD**	93
13.	**DADF♯BD**	50	35.	**EGBEBE**	95
14.	**EADF♯BD**	52	36.	**EBDGBE**	98
15.	**EADF♯BD**	54	37.	**EBDGBE**	100
16.	**EADGAD**	55	38.	**F♯F♯C♯F♯AE**	102
17.	**EADGAD**	56	39.	**DADGAD**	106
18.	**DGDGBD**	61	40.	**DADEAE**	107
19.	**DGDGBD**	62	41.	**EADEAD**	110
20.	**DADF♯AD**	64	42.	**CGDGCD**	111
21.	**DADF♯AD**	65	43.	**EBBEBE**	114
22.	**CGCGCE**	67	44.	**EACFAE**	116

Acknowledgements

Quotations are taken from personal interviews and back issues of *Guitarist, Guitar Player, Guitar (UK), Guitar (USA), Mojo, Making Music, Guitar World, Frets, Folk Roots, Guild Gallery, Acoustic Guitar,* and *The Canadian Journal for Traditional Music*.

For their involvement in the preparation of this book I would like to thank Nigel Osborne, Tony Bacon, John Morrish, and Mark Brend. The CD was mastered by Tim Turan of Tim Turan Audio, Oxford. I would also like to thank readers who have posted online reviews of other books in this series.

The music on the CD remains copyright Rikky Rooksby. For commercial use in music libraries and similar please contact the author via the publisher.

Author Note

Rikky Rooksby is a guitar teacher, songwriter / composer, and writer on popular music. He is the author of the Backbeat titles *How To Write Songs On Guitar* (2000), *Inside Classic Rock Tracks* (2001), *Riffs* (2002), *The Songwriting Sourcebook* (2003), *Chord Master* (2004), *Melody* (2004), *Songwriting Secrets: Bruce Springsteen* (2005), *How To Write Songs on Keyboards* (2005), *Lyrics* (2006), and *Arranging Songs* (2008). He contributed to *Albums: 50 Years Of Great Recordings*, *Classic Guitars Of The Fifties*, *The Guitar: The Complete Guide For The Player*, and *Roadhouse Blues* (2003). He has also written *The Guitarist's Guide To The Capo* (Artemis 2003), *The Complete Guide To The Music Of Fleetwood Mac* (revised ed. 2004), 14 Fastforward guitar tutor books, four in the First Guitar series; transcribed and arranged more than 40 chord songbooks of music including Bob Dylan, Bob Marley, The Stone Roses, David Bowie, Eric Clapton, Travis, The Darkness, and *The Complete Beatles*; and co-authored *100 Years 100 Songs*. He has written articles on rock musicians for the new *Dictionary Of National Biography* (OUP), and published interviews, r[illegible] magazines such as *Guit*[illegible] *Bassist, Bass Guitar Mag*[illegible] *Playmusic, Sound On So*[illegible] wrote the monthly 'Pri[illegible] member of the Guild o[illegible] Composers, the Society [illegible] d the Vaughan Williams [illegible] www.rikkyrooksby.com